THE UNIDENTIFIED
&
CREATURES OF THE OUTER EDGE

The Early Works of

Jerome Clark
and
Loren Coleman

Anomalist Books
San Antonio • New York

**The Unidentified
& Creatures of the Outer Edge**
Copyright © 2006 by Jerome Clark
and Loren Coleman

ISBN: 19336655114

The Unidentified was originally published by
Warner Paperback Library in 1975.
Creatures of the Outer Edge was originally
published by Warner Books in 1978.

Cover design by Ansen Seale

All rights reserved, including the right to reproduce
this book or portions thereof in any form whatsoever.
For information, go to **anomalistbooks.com** or write
to:

Anomalist Books
5150 Broadway #108
San Antonio, TX 78209

Anomalist Books
PO Box 577
Jefferson Valley, NY 10535

CONTENTS

Introduction to this Double Edition 1

Book One: **The Unidentified**

An Introductory Note 8

UFOland:
  Other Worlds and the Otherworld 9
Fairyland:
  The Magical Impulse 45
Voices from Heaven:
  The Religious Impulse 93
The Airships:
  The Technological Impulse 131
UFOs:
  The Mystery in the Machine 165
Paraufology:
  Understanding the Incomprehensible 225

Selected Bibliography 251

A Note on UFO and Fortean Publications 261

Index 263

Book Two: **Creatures of the Outer Edge**

Introduction   11

Chapter One:
  Mystery Animals   15
Chapter Two:
  The Bigfeet   28
Chapter Three:
  The Manimals   51
Chapter Four:
  Phantom Cats and Dogs   117
Chapter Five:
  Things with Wings   165
Chapter Six:
  Phantasms   195

Epilogue:
  A Year Filled with Monsters   208

Bibliography   228

INTRODUCTION

Written three decades ago, *The Unidentified* and *Creatures of the Outer Edge* long ago took on lives of their own and acquired a passionate, enduring following. As the two of us look at these works today, we see a record of our youthful interests and enthusiasms. We see an original, creative approach that would prove influential – though we could not have known it at the time – in the evolving debates about anomalous and paranormal phenomena. We see lots of interesting cases and stories, many of which still intrigue and enthrall us well into our adulthoods.

At the time we wrote these two books, we were a decade and a half into our careers as anomalists, both of us having started down this path in our young teens. In the late 1960s and 1970s we were under the added influence of counterculture currents then omnipresent, though they are barely felt in this very different era. It was, however, the counterculture that led us to the theories of the psychological philosopher Carl Gustav Jung (1875-1961), at least as understood by our youthful selves. To us Jung provided a framework in which ostensible anomalies and paranormal incidents could be reevaluated. We thought then that Jung's key unlocked all kinds of doors, exposing links that would connect such apparently disparate phenomena as fairylore, cryptozoological creatures, and flying-saucer contact tales.

Soon after these books were published, our ideas and perspectives began moving on to what we believe are more intellectually sustainable interpretations. These are documented in our later, separate books and in another collaboration, *Cryptozoology A to Z*, published in 1999.

Yet *The Unidentified* found an audience. The reviews at the time of publication were gratifyingly favorable, and even today we encounter readers who remember the book fondly. Though a pivotal book to some, we can't help judging it from the greater knowledge and experience maturity inevitably brings. Its shortcomings will be apparent to any sophisticated reader. Some of it is, let's face it, credulous by any definition. It embraces the preposterous Cottingley fairy photographs, then a manifest hoax, subsequently (in the 1980s) a confessed one. C.A.A. Dellschau, who figures in Chapter Four, was indeed a fascinating character, but it was his rich, fantasy-ridden imagination that makes him interesting, not his nonexistent connection with late 19th-Century reports of mystery airships.

Nonetheless, *The Unidentified* also boasts its share of lucid moments and a place in the history of the UFO discussion. It brought fresh air into a controversy long stalemated between literalists ("believers") and rejectionists ("debunkers"). It sought to by-pass the tedious all-or-nothing approach that had always characterized the anomalies controversy. It allowed for vivid, bizarre experiences with otherworldly entities without demanding that such things be hauled into event-level reality. If high-strangeness accounts are about things that *feel* real even if they are not, in fact, real, we may not be able to explain them within the context of current knowledge, but at least we have a useful frame of reference that does not call us to dismiss testimony – and an enormous amount of it – at all costs. Neither does it demand that we embrace the presence of things that, for all kinds of good reasons, cannot be. One doesn't have to grant, for example, the existence of fairies to take note of centuries of puzzling reports which need some sort of accounting. You can call them anomalies of consciousness, or anomalies of the imagination, and still, we are left with profound mysteries concerning how we experience the world.

In *Creatures of the Outer Edge* we extended our puerile planetary-poltergeist thoughts (mostly confined to Chapter Six, thankfully) largely because our publisher wanted the two books to be of a piece, bound by a common theme. Our youthful intellectual experimentation this time, however, stayed mostly out of the way of the stories – the data, if you want to call them that.

Creatures chronicles all sorts of now famous "monsters," including Mothman, the suspect Owlman, thunderbirds, phantom panthers, devil dogs, big birds, and – everyone's favorite – Bigfoot. Much of this was new and novel then, and numerous writers have ever after recycled our reporting and investigation in their own books and articles. In the 1977 appendix we introduced to the world the Dover Demon, which is now an iconic figure among anomalists and cryptozoologists. Whether you believe such things exist in reality (however defined) or you don't, *Creatures* is one entertaining and, at times, scary tour through a twilight zone of hidden life or unbridled imagination. In terms of sheer fun, it's one of our favorite self-penned books.

Unidentified and *Creatures* brought us into the world as authors and pushed us onward into further adventures. We hope you enjoy these early works of ours and take from them what you will, overlooking the occasional excesses of enthusiasm for their more substantive aspects. If this is your first experience of Clark and Coleman, we hope you will be encouraged to seek out our later work to see where we – both together and independently – took it all from here.

Jerome Clark, 10-10-05 Loren Coleman,
Minnesota Maine

Book One:
THE UNIDENTIFIED

CONTENTS

UFOland:
　Other Worlds and the Otherworld　　　9
Fairyland:
　The Magical Impulse　　　45
Voices from Heaven:
　The Religious Impulse　　　93
The Airships:
　The Technological Impulse　　　131
UFOs:
　The Mystery in the Machine　　　165
Paraufology:
　Understanding the Incomprehensible　　　225

To the memory of Charles Fort,
from whom we hope always to be learning.

Giants and fairies. We accept them, of course.
... Science of today, the superstition of tomorrow. Science of tomorrow — the superstition of today.
— Charles Fort, in *The Book of the Damned*

AN INTRODUCTORY NOTE

In preparing *The Unidentified: Notes Toward Solving the UFO Mystery* we have been fortunate enough to have had the assistance of the following persons, without whom we would have gotten nowhere:

Mary Margaret Fuller and Betty Lou White of *Fate*; Charles Bowen of England's *Flying Saucer Review*; Peter Rogerson of *Merseyside UFO Bulletin*; Brad Steiger, John A. Keel, Lucius Farish, Richard Crowe, P. G. Navarro, David Schroth, Clint Williams, Mark A. Hall, and Jay Garon; and two very special ladies. Needless to say, none of them should be held accountable for the conclusions we have drawn in this book.

Portions of chapters one, two, four, five, and six originally appeared in *Fate* and are reprinted by permission. A portion of chapter one originally appeared in *Flying Saucer Review* and is reprinted by permission.

Jerome Clark
Loren Coleman

Moorhead, Minnesota
San Francisco, California

UFOLAND:
OTHER WORLDS AND
THE OTHERWORLD

> It is clear from the accumulating body of evidence that the phenomenon of the UFO represents a far more profound challenge to our physical and psychological concepts of reality than has hitherto been assumed.
> —Peter Rogerson

1

"We will all be making great progress when the term *spacecraft* replaces UFO," a letter in a flying saucer magazine advised not long ago, "for that is what they are."

"Further extensive study of UFOs probably cannot be justified in the expectation that science will be advanced thereby," a U. S. Government-sponsored probe concluded in 1969.

So what are we supposed to think?

The believer points to the growing number of reports—in America alone, for example, a recent Gallup Poll reveals that fifteen million persons are sure they have seen UFOs—and speaks of "reliable witnesses," photographs, radar/visual sightings, an occasional impression on the ground where the spacecraft is alleged to have landed.

The skeptic counters by asking, Where is the proof? "I will believe," one of them said, "when shown wreckage, machinery, or bodies"—which the UFOs, for all their incalculably vast numbers, have spectacularly failed to produce. Yet when the skeptic goes on to "explain" the reports put forward by the proponents of the extraterrestrial hypothesis (ETH), he gets himself into some real difficulties, and his "explanations" usually end up as grotesque mental exercises positing notions at least as improbable as the reports themselves.

But if the skeptic has failed to make his case, so has the believer, who, for all his efforts to alert us to the presence of spaceships in our atmosphere, has managed to demonstrate only that *something* is going on, something very strange for which no satisfactory accounting has yet been made. Yet as strange as these UFO sightings undoubtedly are, there is at the same time an oddly mundane, undeniably terrestrial quality to them which makes them all the more mysterious. As John A. Rimmer writes in *Merseyside UFO Bulletin* (December 1970):

> The greatest objection to the ETH is the strongly humanistic aspect that the phenomenon appears to adopt. The UFOs and their occupants act, by and large, in ways that we would expect an alien race to behave. We are all familiar with countless landing reports in which the entities have seemed to gather rock and soil samples. It must be significant that these reports have come in the decade in which a great deal of the efforts of Western man have been devoted to obtaining just such samples from the moon. . . . Of course we have no right to assume that the denizens of any other planet would have the same scientific preoccupations as us. As ufologists we seem prepared to accept that such matters as UFO propulsion methods, alien physiology, and advanced technologies may be so far advanced beyond anything that we are able to comprehend that they will appear to us as "magic." Yet paradoxically we also seem prepared to assume that the beings behind such marvels are going to behave exactly like us when we meet them face to face.

Furthermore, a careful examination of UFO lore uncovers a considerable number of incidents whose relationship to the idea of extraterrestrial visitors is problematical at best. These stories contain motifs which seem to connect them with phenomena one would have thought far outside the province of ufology.

Some examples:

On December 4, 1970, Mrs. Wallace Bowers of Vader, Washington, heard her children calling for her to come outside. Stepping out the door, she was astounded to discover huge footprints in the inch-deep snow covering her yard. When she examined them closely she found that the tracks sank all the way through the snow; the gravel underneath was crushed down about an inch and a half. The prints measured fifteen inches in length and nearly six inches across. She called the sheriff's office immediately. Vader is in the middle of Bigfoot country, where sightings of the Pacific Northwest's legendary hairy giant are reported from time to time, and Mrs. Bowers uneasily recalled how strangely the family dog had behaved the night before.

At 7:15 A.M. three days later, on the seventh, Mrs. Bowers again heard her children calling, "Mommy, come look!" The children were at the window, staring out at something moving across the sky. At first, according to their mother, it "looked like a bright star," but then it got closer and for ten minutes the observers were able to view it carefully.

It appeared to be centered by a dome around which a larger circle seemed to be revolving. It was deeper orange in the center, with the light diffusing toward the outer edge, but with a definite bright rim.

Mrs. Bowers said it seemed tipped sideways slightly, rather like an airplane banking, and then it hovered briefly over the nearby Bonneville power lines. After it left the power lines it changed from orange to a bright, clear light, and at one time seemed to make one last sweep closer, again turning orange. The children thought they saw a "gray shape" drop away from the UFO just before it vanished in the distance.

During the sighting Mrs. Bowers switched on the intercom in the house, only to hear a peculiar "sharp" sound. "And the funny thing is," she told a reporter for the *Centralia-Chehalis Chronicle*, "we tried to use the intercom the night before and we got that same sharp sound."

But that was not to be all. Later in the week (the UFO sighting occurred on a Monday) Mrs. Bowers was putting a log in the living room fireplace when she saw the curtains moving in the boys' bedroom, which was visible from where she stood.

"All the children were in the living room with me," she

said. "And all I could think of was getting them safely out of there. So I loaded them into the car and we left, but I definitely saw a shape in the bedroom as we drove away." They returned only after Mr. Bowers had come home from work.

"I feel sure that was probably a prowler," Mrs. Bowers said. "We've had trouble in our neighborhood and I don't think it's related to the others. But the footprints and the saucer—I don't know. . . ."

Nonetheless, the "prowler" was a strange one: he took nothing. He rummaged through the bedrooms but afterward the Bowerses could find nothing missing. While it is of course impossible to prove anything, we cannot help thinking of the mysterious "gray shape" the children thought they saw, and then of a long tradition of bedroom apparitions which no one has ever mistaken for invaders from other planets.

The Vader incident anticipates a much more complex series of events in Louisiana, Missouri, and Roachdale, Indiana, during the summer of 1972.

Louisiana's "Momo" (for "Missouri monster") scare began on July 11 at 3:30 P.M., when Terry Harrison, age eight, and his brother Wally, five, were playing in their yard on the outskirts of the city (pop. 4,600). Their yard sat at the foot of Marzolf Hill, which would play a central role in what was about to occur. The boys had gone off by some old rabbit pens in the weeds next to the Harrison property when suddenly an older sister, Doris, who was inside, heard them scream. She looked out the bathroom window and saw something standing by a tree—"six or seven feet tall, black and hairy. It stood like a man but it didn't look like one to me."

The thing was flecked with blood, apparently from the dead dog it carried under its arm. Its face could not be seen under the mass of hair covering it, and it seemed to be without a neck.

The Harrisons' dog got very sick shortly after the incident. Its eyes grew red and it vomited for hours afterward, finally recovering after a meal of bread and milk.

That same afternoon Mrs. Clarence Lee, who lived half a block away, heard animal sounds, growling, and "carrying on something terrible." Not long afterward she talked with a farmer whose dog, a recent gift, had disappeared. He wondered if the "monster" had taken it.

Three days later, on July 14, Edgar Harrison, Terry and Doris's father and a deacon in the Pentecostal church, conducted the regular Friday evening prayer meeting at his house. Around eight-thirty it had started to break up, and as Harrison and a dozen or so of his congregation lingered, talking, they sighted two "fireballs" soaring from over Marzolf Hill and descending into the trees behind an abandoned school across the street. The first object was white, and the second one, which appeared five minutes later, was green.

About nine-fifteen Harrison heard ringing noises such as might be caused by throwing stones against the metal water reservoir which stands at the top of the hill. The reservoir, which holds a million and a half gallons of water, is in an area where neighborhood children often play. After one especially loud ring, Harrison said, "I heard something that sounded like a loud growl. It got louder and louder and kept coming closer." Harrison wanted to stay and see what was making the noise but his terrified family forced him to drive off with them.

We do not have the space here to recount the entire Momo scare. We will skip over the other monster sightings several Louisiana residents reported, noting only that a foul odor, which investigator Richard T. Crowe, who smelled it, described as resembling "rotten flesh or stagnant water," came to be associated with the mysterious beast, an almost inevitable feature of these hominoid reports. Area residents found several sets of tracks, some of which seem to have proved fraudulent, others of which remain unexplained.

Though he himself never saw the monster, Harrison did succeed in making two startling discoveries which add a whole new dimension to the riddle. First, he noted that the notorious odor always appeared just when searchers appeared to be on to something, leading him to believe that the odor was really a stink gas used to distract the searchers' attention. On several occasions witnesses reported seeing a small glowing light which exploded, leaving the stench in its wake.

On the night of July 29 Harrison and a group of college

students, standing on top of the hill, heard what sounded like a shot near the road. They rushed down the hill until they got close to the road, where they all distinctly heard an old man's voice saying, "You boys stay out of these woods."

The voice seemed to have come from a nearby clump of trees no more than twenty feet by fifty feet, but an immediate and thorough search failed to turn up anything.

A week later, on August 5, another evidently disembodied voice spoke to Pat Howard and a friend, who were camped out in Harrison's backyard. The two were drinking coffee when someone or something said, "I'll take a cup of your coffee." Again a search produced no results.

Crowe's investigation uncovered a number of Louisiana UFO sightings which did not make the papers, presumably because reporters were already busy enough running down monster stories and rumors. Nonetheless, on the night of August 26 a "fireball" alighted on top of a large cottonwood tree at the first railroad crossing on River Road. It shot out two spurts of red light and then zoomed out of sight. On the following three nights colored lights were observed along the top of the limestone bluff at the northern end of River Road. The witnesses, the Harrison and Shade families (Mrs. Shade is Mrs. Harrison's sister), thought that the lights were signaling back and forth to each other. Sunday night, the thirtieth, at nine o'clock, an orange, glowing UFO with lighted "windows" landed in the thicket at the top of the bluff and sat there for five hours before it "went straight up into the air and disappeared," in Mrs. Lois Shade's words.

Just four days before this the Shades had had another strange experience. On the evening of the partial eclipse (July 26) the entire family had seen "a perfect gold cross on the moon," Mrs. Shade said. "The road was lit up as bright as day from the cross." They interpreted the sight as an omen from heaven.

As Momo disappeared from Missouri an equally weird intruder appeared at Roachdale, Indiana (pop. 900). Mrs. Lou Rogers and her infant son, Keith, were the first to sense the presence of a mysterious "something." At the time—early August—she and her husband, Randy, were renting a farm outside the town (located forty miles west of Indianapolis in the west-central part of the state). Late one evening she stepped outside with Keith to roll up the windows of the family car. The sky had clouded up and it had started to sprinkle. As she stood there in the dark she heard a noise rather like a growl; it sounded like "boo" or "oo." Mrs. Rogers, a young woman who is not easily frightened ("You hear all kinds of strange noises in the country," she told us), thought nothing of it and went on with what she was doing.

But then she heard it again. Her little boy was terrified, and she began to take notice. The growl was "real deep" but it emanated from a human voice, not an animal's. She suddenly felt as though someone or something was breathing down her neck. Turning quickly, she peered around in the darkness. She could see nothing but she knew that something was out there, so she and little Keith beat a retreat into the house.

Though she was unaware of it then, just an hour and a half earlier a luminous object had alighted over a cornfield separating their house from a neighbor's, hovered briefly, and then "just sort of blew up." One of her younger brothers, who happened to be looking out a Ladoga farmhouse window at the time, was among those who saw it. Later he mentioned it to his sister and her husband. He thought a plane had exploded. None had. Whatever it was that had, it left no traces—except for, possibly, the creature that seemed to take up residence for the next weeks in that very cornfield.

During the next few nights the Rogerses began to hear strange noises around the house. "It sounded as if someone was going around the place pounding on the siding and windows," Rogers said. "Whatever it was, it must have gotten braver each night because the noise got louder and louder with each night." As it got braver, Rogers got uneasier. He borrowed his father's shotgun and kept it handy for occasions when the marauder came around. When he heard it, he would rush outside into the night to catch glimpses of an enormously broad-shouldered, shadowy figure fleeing into the cornfields. It stood about six feet tall and was bipedal.

"At a certain hour," Lou Rogers said, "it would always come around—between ten and eleven-thirty at night. You could feel it coming, somehow. It's hard to explain. The feeling would just keep getting stronger and stronger, and then when it got strongest you knew something had to happen; the knocking would start. This happened every night for two or three weeks.

"Another thing about it—it smelled *rotten*. Like dead animals or garbage."

Randy and Lou Rogers never saw the creature completely clearly because of its habit of appearing only in the dark, but they were able to observe that it was hairy and black. Once, when Mrs. Rogers was washing dishes, she saw it ducking up and down on the other side of the window above the sink.

The couple tried to think of rational explanations but none seemed to fit.

"We sort of thought it might be a gorilla," Mrs. Rogers explained. "It would stand like a man but it would run on all fours. Even on all fours it was as tall as my husband, who's five-feet-nine. It was real broad."

But it could hardly have been a gorilla, even aside from the unlikelihood of one's running loose in rural Indiana. This thing was quite something else.

"What was weird," said Mrs. Rogers, "was that we could never find tracks, even when it ran over mud. It would run and jump but it was like somehow it wasn't touching anything. When it ran through weeds you couldn't hear anything. And sometimes when you looked at it, it looked like you could see *through* it."

If the Rogerses were taking it all in fairly calmly—in fact, until the community-wide furor started, during the third week of August, they kept word of their experiences mostly to themselves and a handful of friends—the rest of Roachdale wasn't. The story hit the papers on August 22, but the day before, when conservation officer William Woodall came down from Crawfordsville to investigate, he found residents in near panic. Woodall listened sympathetically to their stories, even the wildest ones, and on the first day alone interviewed five persons from four different families who said they had seen the thing. Among those he talked with were the Rogerses, who reported that the creature had left their farm after Randy and several friends had set out one night to try to capture it. One of the group encountered the creature when it stepped out of a roadside ditch. The man yelled, "Stop or I'll shoot!" It didn't and he did but it got away.

Among the fifty or so persons who claimed they had seen the thing, the Burdine family had by far the most dramatic experience.

On August 22, around nine o'clock in the evening, Carter Burdine and his uncle, Bill ("Junior") Burdine, arrived at Carter's farm to discover the remains of over sixty chickens which something had literally ripped apart and scattered along a path leading two hundred feet from the coop to the front yard of the house. Whatever had killed them had done no more than that—it had not eaten them.

They called town marshal Leroy Cloncs, who came within a few minutes. As they stood there discussing the situation the three heard a noise between the chicken coop and the road. Cloncs got into his car and drove slowly up the road while Junior Burdine walked behind. The car was starting to get ahead of him, and Burdine, his thoughts on something else, was not expecting to see anything. Then suddenly something rose out of the ditch and dashed across the road within six feet of him, but moving so fast that Burdine did not get a good look at it or have time to shoot.

The two men did find the spot where it crossed the fence on the opposite side of the road. "That fence was just mashed to the ground," Burdine said later. "That thing was *heavy*." It left a trail of trampled weeds and grass. Carter Burdine, who heard it, said it had to have been running on two feet. (Readers will recall that the Rogerses said they could *not* hear it running, and that, moreover, it ran on all fours.)

Within a matter of hours the thing was back. Carter and Junior were returning to the farm in the early-morning hours, after dropping Carter's wife off in town with some relatives. In the headlights of their car they caught sight of the creature, standing in the chicken-house door.

"This thing completely blocked out the lights inside the chicken house," Junior told us. "The door is six feet by eight. Its shoulders came up to the top of the door, up to where the neck should have been. But this thing didn't have a neck. To me it looked like an orangutan or a gorilla. It had long hair, with kind of a brownish cast to it. Sort of a rust-lookin' color. I never saw its eyes or its face. It was making a groaning racket."

The creature dashed for the barn and leaped into the hay mow. Carter and his father, Herman Burdine, approached the barn, guns ready. Junior went around the building. A moment later Herman and Carter heard him yell, "Bring me a light!"

Herman said, "By the time Carter and I got out of the barn and around the corner, my brother was firing at something across the field. I didn't see a thing but I pulled up and started firing in the same direction."

"I shot four times with a pump shotgun," Junior said. "The thing was only about a hundred feet away when I started shooting. I must have hit it. I've killed a lot of rabbits at that distance."

But even though Junior could not understand how he could have missed, the creature gave no indication that it had been touched. Its hair did not fly up and it left no blood. Weirdly, it made no sound as it ran, nor did it leave any tracks.

The Burdines trudged back to the chicken house to count their losses. About a hundred ten chickens had been destroyed—ripped open and then drained of blood. Of an original flock of two hundred chickens, Carter had lost all but thirty.

Later, when Woodall investigated, he searched carefully through the strewn remains, looking for hair or other physical traces of the killer. He could find nothing.

"I never could find any concrete physical evidence, ever," Woodall recalled in an interview with Jerome Clark several months afterward. "All I ever had to go on were a lot of people's stories of what they saw."

One supposed clue—several strands of animal hair—turned out to be from a horse, a Purdue University laboratory analysis revealed. Theories about the creature's true identity, such as that it was an escaped kangaroo or a mentally ill man garbed in a buffalo robe, similarly proved groundless.

By the end of the week reports had subsided. The creature that came to Roachdale had gone back to wherever it had come from.

2

If these incidents are mysterious enough, others raise still more questions about the nature of ufoland, a shadowy otherworld which seems to house a wide assortment of enigmatic residents whose forms, while varied, still retain a curious consistency.

For instance, if the following incident had occurred anytime since World War II, UFO literature would recount it as a sighting of an alien spaceship and its occupants. Instead, the narrator, an Oxford student who told the story to his instructor, folklorist W. Y. Evans-Wentz, saw it as proof of the reality of the "spiritual world":

Some few weeks before Christmas, 1910, at midnight on a very dark night, I and another young man (who, like myself, was then about twenty-three years of age) were on horseback on our way home from Limerick. When near Listowel we noticed a light about half a mile ahead. At first it seemed to be no more than a light in some house; but as we came nearer to it and it was passing out of our direct line of vision we saw that it was moving up and down, to and fro, diminishing to a spark, then expanding into a yellow luminous flame. Before we came to Listowel we noticed two lights, about one hundred yards to our right, resembling the light seen first. Suddenly each of these lights expanded into the same sort of yellow luminous flame, about six feet high by four feet broad. In the midst of each flame we saw a radiant being having human form. Presently the lights moved toward one another and made contact, whereupon the two beings in them were seen to be walking side by side. The beings' bodies were formed of a pure dazzling radiance, white like the radiance of the sun, and much brighter than the yellow light or aura surrounding them. So dazzling was the radiance, like a halo, round their heads that we could not distinguish the countenances of the beings; we could only distinguish the general shape of their bodies; though their heads were very clearly outlined because this halolike radiance, which was the brightest light about them, seemed to radiate from or rest upon the head of each being. As we traveled on, a house intervened between us and the lights and we saw no more of them. It was the first time we had ever seen such phenomena, and in our hurry to get home we were not wise enough to stop and make further examination. But ever since that night I have frequently seen, both in Ireland and in England, similar lights with spiritual beings in them.

In October 1817 Edmund Lenthal Swifte, Keeper of the Crown Jewels, had a very strange experience which is equally difficult to classify. At the time he and his family were residing in the Tower of London. One Saturday night the four of them—Swifte, wife, seven-year-old son, and sister-in-law—had sat down to eat supper. All the doors were shut; heavy curtains covered the windows, and two table candles provided the only light in the room. The son and the sister-in-law faced each other from opposite ends of the table. Swifte himself sat at the foot and his wife sat opposite the chimneypiece which projected far into the room. As Swifte recalled in an 1860 *Notes and Queries*, according to Janet Bord's article "UFOs in Folklore":

I had offered a glass of wine and water to my wife, when, on putting it to her lips, she paused and exclaimed: "Good God! What is that?" I looked up and saw a cylindrical figure, like a glass tube, seemingly about the thickness of my arm, and hovering between the ceiling and the table; its contents appeared to be a dense fluid, white and pale azure, like the gathering of a summer cloud, and incessantly mingling within the cylinder. This lasted about two minutes, when it began slowly to move before my sister-in-law; then, following the oblong shape of the table, *before* my son and myself; pausing *behind* my wife, it paused for a moment over her right shoulder (observe, there was not a mirror opposite to her in which she could there behold it). Instantly she crouched down, and with both hands covering her shoulder, she shrieked out, "O Christ! It has seized me!" Even now, while writing, I feel the fresh horror of that moment. I caught up my chair, struck at the wainscot behind her, rushed upstairs to the children's room, and told the terrified nurse what I had seen. Meanwhile the other domestic had hurried into the parlor, where their mistress recounted to them the scene, even as I was detailing it above stairs.

Oddly, neither the boy nor the sister-in-law saw the mysterious phenomenon even though it should have been clearly visible to them.

Another, more recent story of a miniature UFO seems almost to parody the whole idea of ETH. According to ufologist John A. Keel, in late August 1965 (during a nationwide UFO flap) a young Seattle woman awoke at two o'clock in the morning and found herself paralyzed. As she lay there, helpless, a football-sized, dull gray object sailed in through an open window and landed on tripod legs on her floor. A tiny ramp descended from the "craft" and five or six little people dressed in tight-fitting clothes climbed down it to work on repairs. Their job finished, they stepped back into the craft and flew away. Only then was the witness, who was certain that she was wide awake, able to move.

An even tinier "UFO" figures in an account sent to one of the authors by a personal acquaintance, Sean Blackburn, a talented young musician from Minneapolis:

It was not a dark or stormy nite, no shots rang out, and nobody screamed. Just an ordinary fall afternoon, Steve Swensen and I in an upstairs bedroom of Clover farm. Clover was a rock band then (September '69) and their farm was near Motley, Minnesota, on Swan Creek, with a big five-bedroom house with a wood furnace. Steve was laid back on the bed, pluckin' a guitar, and I remember we were paying particular attention to every subtle nuance of tone. I jumped up and said, "Hey, a Martian spaceship," when I saw the floating black thing hovering near the ceiling in a corner. The idea just popped into my head that the item was actually a craft, full of life, and we were being *visited*. So I told Steve he should "play some 'friendly Martian' music" and maybe they'd come closer. He did, and they did. They came down toward the guitar, went around the neck, between the neck and Steve's arm (without touching anything), up past his face, paused over the sound hole a few seconds, and floated back up to a different corner of the small (ten by twelve?) room. Just then Tom Lamberson burst into the room to tell us something; the door opened inward and the air currents blew the craft about and we lost it. Tom was a classical-guitar player and he broke his thumbnail as he pushed open the door. (Cruel bummer; doesn't heal for at least a month.)

What the craft reminded me of in appearance and size was a piece of soot like those that filled the room once when I burned a plastic birthday-candle holder. Or kinda like a black sperm-shaped thing . . . The walls of the room were bare of posters, book shelves, etc., and were painted a light color, so we were able to see it easily most of the time. The event left me with a good feeling, except for when Tom broke his thumbnail, but I don't know if they're related (those two events).

Then there is this report, given to *Flying Saucer Review* and reprinted by Gorden Creighton, "A Weird Case From the Past": by Mrs. I. J. Goodwin of Stranden, Bournemouth, England:

I was born in 1924 at 57 North Road, Hertford, Herts. One day in 1929, at about the age of five, I was playing in the garden. With me was my eight-year-old brother (Mr. Priest, now living at Moordown, Bournemouth). He was suffering from an infected knee, due to a fall, and was consequently confined at that time to a chair.

At that date the road was a lane, with just two pairs of houses, one of which was ours, and behind the houses there was an orchard.

So far as I can truthfully recall, what happened was that we heard the sound of an engine—what I would today liken to a quieted version of a trainer plane. My brother and I looked up and saw, coming over the garden fence from the orchard, this small airplane (of biplane type) which swooped down and landed briefly, almost striking the dustbin [garbage pail]. It remained there for possibly just a few seconds and then took off and was gone, but in that short time I had a perfect view not only of the tiny biplane but also of a perfectly proportioned tiny pilot wearing a leather flying helmet, who waved to us as he took off.

Neither my brother nor I ever spoke of the strange sight, so far as I can recall, until about ten years ago when, in the presence of our mother and of other members of the family, I asked him whether he recalled the episode. He replied that he too had wondered many times, over the years, about that tiny plane and its tiny occupant.

May I be permitted to add here that my brother is so honest that he would certainly not claim anything beyond what he could truthfully recall of an experience.

I am very sorry that I cannot swear to the **exact** measurements but I would estimate the wing span of the tiny aircraft at no more than twelve to fifteen inches, with the tiny pilot in perfect proportion thereto.

Although I do not recall his having said it, my brother apparently went into the house and told mother: "That airplane nearly hit the dustbin."

This is a true and honest account as I remember it. The house and garden still exist, but the orchard has long ceased to be there.

So where do all of these increasingly improbable events lead us? Perhaps to this, taken from a letter written by a Mrs. Hardy, a settler in the Maori districts of New Zealand, to Sir Arthur Conan Doyle:

After reading about what others have seen I am encouraged to give you an experience of my own, which happened about five years ago [1915?]. Will you please excuse my mentioning a few domestic details connected with the story? Our home is built on the top of a ridge. The ground was leveled for some distance to allow for sites for the house, buildings, lawns, etc. The ground on either side slopes steeply down to an orchard on the left, and shrubbery and paddock on the right, bounded by the main road. One evening when it was getting dusk I went into the yard to hang the tea towels on the clothesline. As I stepped off the veranda I heard a sound of soft galloping coming from the direction of the orchard. I thought I must be mistaken, and that the sound came from the road, where the Maoris often gallop their horses. I crossed the yard to get the pegs, and heard the galloping coming nearer. I walked to the clothesline, and stood under it with my arms uplifted to peg the towel on the line, when I was aware of the galloping close behind me, and suddenly a little figure, riding a tiny pony, rode right under my uplifted arms. I looked round, to see that I was surrounded by eight or ten tiny figures on tiny ponies like dwarf Shetlands. The little figure who came so close to me stood out quite clearly in the light that came from the window, and I could not see his face. The faces of the others were quite brown, also the ponies were brown. If they wore clothes they were close-fitting, like a child's jersey suit. They were like tiny dwarfs, or children of about two years of age. I was very startled, and called out, "Goodness! what is this?" I think I must have frightened them, for at the sound of my voice they all rode through the rose trellis across the drive, and down the shrubbery. I heard the soft galloping dying away into the distance, and listened until the sound was gone, then went into the house. My daughter, who has had several psychic experiences, said to me: "Mother, how white and startled you look! What have you seen? And who were you speaking to just now in the yard?" I said, "I have seen the fairies ride!"

A modern report from England links fairies and UFOs by more than implication.

The affair seems to have begun at 11:35 P.M. on May 31, 1964, when the Bell family of Leam Lane, Gateshead, Durham, saw three egg-shaped luminous flashes passing across the sky from east to west. The flashes were visible for about three seconds each. Thirteen-year-old Keith Bell wondered if these were connected in any way with the silvery disc he had seen above the farm around noon on the twenty-eighth. At any rate, the same night the Bells saw the flashes many of the neighbors were kept awake by a strange humming noise which began at 12:30 A.M. and ended half an hour later. One of them described it as being "like a swarm of bees, but about twenty times louder."

The really incredible events did not occur until June 2, however, when fourteen-year-old David Wilson, passing Leam Lane Farm at 5:30 P.M., noticed a group of approximately ten "children" standing about twenty yards from a haystack. When David got closer, to within a hundred feet or so of the scene, he was startled to see six or eight small human beings on top of the stack. They stood from two to two and a half feet tall and were dressed in green suits, with hands that seemed to be like "lighted electric bulbs." (It is possible, perhaps, that the beings were carrying something like flashlights, but apparently this idea did not occur to the witness.) They were digging through the haystack as if looking for something.

Other children in the area also reported seeing the humanoids. One, a little girl, said their leader was "dressed in black and carried a baton with pink stripes." Another girl supposedly saw one of the dwarfs sitting on the roof of a barn. In still another case, children claimed that they had watched a dwarf riding on the back of a cow. One girl observed a circular silvery object the size of a car take off from the ground in a spinning motion and give off an orange glow.

Folklore tells us that fairies, who usually dress in green, often engage in the kind of playful behavior the humanoids are credited with here. Those who continue to insist that fairies are purely the creations of fancy, and UFOs of a rational extraterrestrial civilization, will find no comfort in the fact that several weeks later another group of children, this time in Liverpool, reported "little green men in white hats throwing stones and tiny clods of earth at one another on the bowling green." A woman said she had seen "strange objects glistening in the sky whizzing over the river toward Liverpool from the Irish Sea."

3

We have just examined a handful of reports which alone, by themselves, cast serious doubts on the ETH. In the pages ahead we shall review many more. By the time we have finished we hope to have demonstrated why our mysterious, uninvited visitors cannot be spacemen. We will discover, as we study data from a wide range of subjects which on the surface appear to have nothing to do with UFOs, that the truth about flying saucers is much, much stranger than anyone has yet suspected. We will find that ufoland is a shadowy twilight land, unimaginably distant and yet unimaginably close, whose weird and wonderful inhabitants have faces that are oddly familiar.

But how did they get linked with hypothetical civilizations on other worlds? A very important question whose answer is fundamental to our understanding of the way the UFO enigma—and all the other enigmas to which it is related—work.

The idea of interplanetary visitors is not, of course, exactly new, though it has been only in the post-World War II era that the notion has lost its novelty for the majority of people.

Actually, as endless numbers of potboilers on "ancient astronauts" keep reminding us, it is quite an old idea which seems to have arisen spontaneously among widely separated peoples in prehistoric and early historic times. It does not necessarily follow, however, that extraterrestrial visits sparked all of these myths, since our primeval ancestors just as often located gods in trees, caves, mountains, bodies of water, and other places. Nonetheless, as civilization advanced and man grew to understand his environment better, he forced the gods to relinquish more and more of their terrestrial domain. Finally, driven off the face of the earth, the gods fled to the sky, a safely inaccessible region which human beings could freely populate with the creatures of imagination.

During the seventeenth century, for instance, the Jesuit scholar Athanasius Kircher remarked on the "wonderful beauty" of the young men of Venus. That, as we shall see in time, qualifies him as a true prophet. A hundred years later the redoubtable Emanuel Swedenborg claimed astral visits with residents of Jupiter as well as with angels and such departed worthies as Plato and Aristotle. Through him the assorted celestial spirits dictated volumes of material fully as tedious as the pronouncements of "Venusians" in our own day. In the late nineteenth century Thomas Blot's *The Man from Mars* detailed an interplanetary gab session in the mountains of California. UFO historian Lucius Farish, who has seen one of the rare remaining volumes, explains, "The Martian had not arrived by spaceship, but through a process which seems to have been a mixture of astral projection and teleportation. . . . Long discourses by the Martian, largely of a philosophical/sociological nature, are contained in the book."

Observers first connected extraterrestrials with strange flying objects during the great "airship" scare of 1896–97 (see chapter four). The considerable majority of Americans assumed that the ships, if they existed at all, were of terrestrial construction, a belief which may have had some foundation in fact, but a tiny handful thought otherwise. The *Van Buren* [Arkansas] *Daily Argus* for May 12, 1897, said, not quite accurately, that "Captain Bostick stands alone in his theory, he asserting that it is an invention of some inhabitant of Mars who is down on a prospecting tour and is studying our system of government." The *Colony* [Kansas] *Free Press* mostly concurred, but suggested that the Martians actually were scientists on "a tour of inspection of the solar system." The *St. Louis Post-Dispatch* fretted that the Martians might be hostile.

The most spectacular piece of "evidence," however, came from Aurora, Texas, where one day in April 1897 an airship reputedly crashed, disgorging a humanoid pilot and papers printed in an unknown language. The creature, described as a "Martian," was supposedly buried in the local cemetery. Until recently modern ufologists discounted the story. But in 1973 the matter was revived, this time with national publicity, as some of the older residents told an inquiring reporter that they remembered the incident. Investigators even thought that they had located the unmarked grave where the creature lay. Unfortunately, at this juncture things got bungled somehow, apparently through the clumsy antics of some flying saucer fans. The authorities refused to cooperate further, ordered everyone out of town, and left the whole tantalizing question unresolved.

(Our guess, by the way, is that there is nothing in the alleged grave, regardless of whether the original story is true. UFOs simply do not leave behind that kind of unambiguous physical evidence.)

In 1864 Jules Verne published the first modern science fiction novel, *From the Earth to the Moon,* helping to implant the idea of space travel in the public mind. By the turn of the century the more literate H. G. Wells imaginatively recounted an invasion from Mars and other wonders. Subsequent novels and stories by such writers as Edgar Rice Burroughs and William Hope Hodgson enjoyed a wide reading, and a whole body of popular literature about space and spacemen started filling library shelves. In 1926 Hugo Gernsback founded *Amazing Stories,* the first magazine devoted exclusively to fantastic fiction. Science fiction's audience grew steadily, and after World War II interest reached epidemic proportions.

A parallel development further served to generate speculation about the possibilities of travel in outer space. Before the war a group of scientists, science fiction buffs, and rocketry enthusiasts organized the British Interplanetary Society in an effort to encourage rational discussion of spaceflight. In Germany and in the Soviet Union a handful of visionary scientists began to dream of the day when man would take his place among the stars.

Adolf Hitler, whose dreams were of another order entirely, early saw the potential value of rockets as weapons of war and backed their development. Some of the scientists, most notably the famous Hermann Oberth (who one day, fittingly enough, would become a vocal supporter of the ETH), did not share Hitler's particular political hallucinations, and opted to leave the country. Others, like Wernher von Braun and Walter Doernberger, made their peace with Naziism but continued to dream as their V-1 and V-2 rockets rained terror and destruction on Western Europe.

When the great post-war UFO wave broke, northern Europeans, still traumatized by memories of the horrors of rocket warfare (between September 6, 1944, and March 27, 1945, the Germans had launched 3,745 V-2 missiles against targets in Europe), naturally assumed that the "ghost rockets" were foreign weapons. The UFOs for their part did little to allay such fears: most of them appeared out of the southeast, from the direction of Peenemunde, now in Soviet hands. With Cold War paranoia already in full swing, Europe was rife with rumors about Stalin's intentions, and the Soviet refusal to allow the Allies to investigate persistent reports of war-material construction in the Russian zone contributed measurably to the growing uneasiness. The Swedish newspaper *Aftonbladet* speculated that "Sweden is systematically being dotted in on a Russian artillery map . . . and is being used as an object of demonstration directed not to us but to the big world."

In May 1946 a wealthy Swedish industrialist named Gosta Carlsson made the first known ufonaut sighting of the modern era. It did not come to light until 1971, when Carlsson gave the story to the magazine *Allers* (No. 44). Carlsson said he had seen a "disc-shaped object with a cupola" resting in a glade next to a lakeshore outside the town of Angelholm in the southern part of the country. Investigating further, he walked toward the device, only to be stopped about forty feet away by "a man in white, closely fitting overalls [who] seemed to be some sort of guard." With a gesture the "guard" ordered the intruder to halt, which he did. Carlsson stood quietly and observed eleven persons, four of them women, moving about the craft. Some were using tools to repair a window.

"They wore short black boots and gloves, a black belt around the waist, and a transparent helmet," Carlsson said. "The women had ashen-colored hair but I could not see the hair of the men, as they wore black caps. They were all brown-colored, as if sunburned."

He stepped closer. Again the guard made a warning gesture. Then he pointed a "black box" in Carlsson's direction. The industrialist thought that the man was going to take his picture; but the only sound he heard was a click from his forehead lamp, which suddenly ceased working. Later, when Carlsson returned home and examined the lamp, he found that the battery, though a new one, had run out.

"One of the women came out of the cabin with an object in her hand," he related. "She went to the edge of the wall of light [a purple light which emanated from a "lampshade" above the UFO] and threw the object beyond the area of light. At the same time I heard her laugh." This was the only vocal sound Carlsson heard anyone utter. Otherwise the strangers spoke not a word.

(According to Sven-Olof Fredrickson, "Mr. Carlsson later retrieved the object. An investigation in 1971 showed nothing exceptional. It was composed, among other things, of silicon. Its shape had been altered by the witness, and it looked like a staff.")

The witness decided to vacate the scene for a while. Half an hour later, returning by a different route, he saw the object rise slowly above the trees with a whining sound. At two thousand feet it slowed its ascent, wobbled a little, changed from red to purple, and accelerated away at tremendous speed.

Not very surprisingly, Carlsson took the object to be "some sort of military device" from a foreign country. (Twenty-five years later, though, he was speculating that the light surrounding the UFO "was created to isolate them from our world and atmosphere.") While clearly the witness had a UFO experience, still there is some slight ambiguity suggested here, in the fact that the incident lacks many of the weird, otherworldly overtones we have come to expect in such encounters. In Carlsson's account the UFO beings sound almost like southern Europeans. (Oddly enough, late in the 1940s an American Army general commented mysteriously that there was no truth to the "rumor"—which no one else had ever heard—that Spaniards were piloting the flying saucers. One wonders if this remark was not inspired by reports like Carlsson's.)

Our next early ufonaut sighting took place in Oklahoma City in late August 1946. Margaret Sprankle, an employee at Tinker Air Force Base, was on her way home from work. At 5:15 P.M., as she approached her house, she happened to look up at her evergreen tree to see if it needed trimming. Much to her astonishment, she saw a disc-shaped object of "weathered aluminum finish" hovering at a slight angle three hundred feet above the tree. A minute and a half later the UFO silently accelerated and shot into the northwest sky, vanishing in five seconds.

The bottom quarter of the saucer (that is, as seen from the side, not from below) was dotted with twelve to fourteen "portholes." Through them she could see the same number of occupants, men of apparently normal human size, with bald or light-colored heads that were slightly more round than ours.

As one who was well acquainted with military aircraft (she possessed a special pass which entitled her to board classified government planes), she recognized that the disc was nothing conventional and she thought that *it might be a craft from another planet.*

4

So as 1946 passed into 1947 interplanetary visitors became an idea whose time had come. The time had passed for fairies, angels, and other manifestations of the supernatural otherworld. Magic had gone, Christianity's long era was nearing an end, and so was the happy, nineteenth century Industrial Age illusion that man's technology would make a heaven of earth. That notion had been a casualty of two years, in which this same technology generated slaughter of mind-numbing magnitude and whose legacy, when peace finally came, was the atomic bomb and the prospect of a nuclear Armageddon. If ever there was a time when men needed gods, this was it; but the machines had created a world that closed itself to the possibility of belief in gods, though not to the need to believe in them.

In *Flying Saucers: A Modern Myth of Things in the Skies* the late C. G. Jung reflected:

The present world situation is calculated as never before to arouse expectations of a redeeming, supernatural event. If these expectations have not dared to show themselves very clearly, this is simply because no one is deeply rooted enough in the traditions of earlier centuries to consider an intervention from heaven as a matter of course . . . rationalistic enlightenment predominates, and this abhors all leanings toward the "occult." . . .

This attitude on the part of the overwhelming majority provides the most favorable basis for a projection, that is, for a manifestation of the unconscious background. Undeterred by rationalistic criticism, it thrusts itself to the forefront in the form of a symbolic rumor, accompanied and reinforced by the appropriate visions, and in so doing activates an archetype that has always expressed order, deliverance, salvation, and wholeness. It is characteristic of our time that, in contrast to its previous expressions, the archetype should now take the shape of an object, a technological construction, in order to avoid the odiousness of a mythological personification. Anything that looks technological goes down without difficulty with modern man. The possibility of space travel makes the unpopular idea of a metaphysical intervention much more acceptable.

The legendary Kenneth Arnold sighting brought on the mammoth 1947 wave and secured a permanent place for the UFO in the lore of our age. Curiously, though, of the 853 North American reports from the period which Ted Bloecher logged in his exhaustive *Report on the UFO Wave of 1947*, not one involves occupants.

But in Bauru, Brazil, on July 23, only twenty-nine days after the Arnold encounter, surveyor Jose C. Higgins not only saw a 150-foot disc land but also reportedly communicated with its crew, three seven-foot-tall beings dressed in "transparent suits covering head and body and inflated like rubber bags," with "metal boxes" on their backs.

The sudden arrival of the UFO caused Higgins's fellow

workers to scatter, but Higgins himself stayed to watch the entities disembark. They were identical in appearance, with huge round eyes and no hair of any kind on their heads. Their legs were longer than those of normal human beings. The witness could not tell if they were men or women but he found them strangely beautiful.

They surrounded him and one leveled a metal tube at him. Higgins thought that they were trying to force him into the craft, but their fear of bright sunlight helped him elude them. He hid in a thicket for half an hour while the beings gamboled and leaped about with great agility, sometimes tossing large stones.

Early in the course of the encounter one of them poked eight holes into the ground with a stick, then pointed at the largest one in the middle and indicated to Higgins that this was (or represented?) "Alamo," while the seventh hole was "Orque." Finally the beings returned to their craft and departed.

On August 14, 1947, Professor R. L. Johannis was wandering through the mountains of northeastern Italy when he allegedly spotted a flying saucer resting on a rocky riverbank two hundred feet away. He walked up to the machine, and as he examined it he noticed two "boys" who had just emerged from a grove of trees to his right. He shouted to them about the disc and started running toward them, only to discover that, according to his account, "The two 'boys' were dwarfs, the likes of which I had never seen or imagined." He suddenly seemed to be paralyzed "or to be dreaming."

The creatures, less than three feet tall, wore blue overalls made of some unknown material, and red belts and collars. They had large heads. (Just how large is not clear. Johannis asserted that they "were bigger than the head of a normal man"; he does not explain if he means this absolutely or relatively.)

Charles Bowen's *The Humanoids* offers the following accounts:

They had no signs of hair [Johannis wrote in 1964] but in place of it they were wearing a sort of dark brown, tight-fitting cap, like an alpinist's bonnet. The "skin" of their faces was an earthy green. . . . The "nose" was straight, geometrically cut, and very long. Beneath it was a mere slit, shaped like a circumflex accent, which I saw opening and closing again at intervals, very much like the mouth of a fish. The "eyes" were enormous, protruding, and round. Their appearance and color were like the color of two well-ripened yellow-green plums.

In the center of the eyes I noticed a kind of vertical "pupil." I saw no traces of eyebrows or eyelashes, and what I would have called the eyelids consisted of a ring, midway between green and yellow, which surrounded the base of these hemispherical eyes just like the frame of a pair of spectacles.

After two or three minutes Johannis recovered from his astonishment sufficiently to raise his hand (apparently he had also recovered from his paralysis), wave it toward the dwarfs and then toward the UFO, and ask who they were and where they came from. Unfortunately his hand happened to be holding his rock pick, and the beings, startled, seemed to interpret Johannis's motion as a hostile gesture, to which one of them responded by shooting him with a "thin puff of smoke" or ray. The witness was knocked off his feet as if by a violent electric shock. Feeling "deprived of all strength," he discovered that he could barely move.

Meanwhile, the two midgets were coming towards me, and they halted at a spot two meters [about seven feet] from me, where my pick had fallen. I managed to roll over onto one side and I saw one of them bend down and pick up the tool, which was longer than he was. And this was how I was able to see his green "hand" quite distinctly. It had eight fingers, four of them opposable to the others! It wasn't a hand: it was a claw, and the fingers were without joints.

The entities, who appeared to be having trouble breathing, made their way back to the craft. Several minutes later it shot straight up into the air, leaving in its wake a hailstorm of stones and earth. It hovered overhead for a time. "Then," Johannis wrote, "it suddenly grew smaller and vanished." A sudden blast of wind hit him and rolled him down the riverbed until he ended up lying against some stones.

It took Johannis almost three hours to get moving once again:

My bones all felt as if they were broken and my legs were weak and trembling, as though after a fearful bout of drinking. I looked in my rucksack for my thermos flask of coffee and was not surprised to find it shattered to pieces, but what did surprise me was not being able to find any trace of its metal casing. Also gone were my aluminum fork and an aluminum can that had contained my cold lunch.

Johannis asserted that at the time of his supposed experience he had not heard of flying saucers, since the Italian papers had not reported the American sightings. He claimed that he considered several theories—from Soviet secret weapon to vehicle piloted by members of "some still-unknown civilization still hidden away in some unexplored regions of the world, like the Matto Grosso of Brazil" (!)—in an effort to comprehend what had happened to him.

Because Johannis did not come forward with his testimony until nearly seventeen years later, the story is necessarily suspect and so the recitation of familiar motifs like the "paralysis beam" and the "slitlike mouths"—found in any number of post-1947 accounts—is not so convincing as it would be under other circumstances. Moreover, we must note that by profession the man is a science fiction writer and a painter with a brilliant imagination.

Of course, it does not have to follow that therefore he is a liar. If his story is a hoax, his motives for concocting it are hard to understand—he is well known in his native country and respected as a writer and an artist. As thousands of people have learned over the past three decades, there is precious little to be gained from openly stating that one has undergone a fantastic UFO experience.

From one point of view, Johannis's status as an imaginative individual fascinated by the possibility of extraterrestrial life (a prime concern of science fiction, of course) might well have rendered him particularly susceptible to certain ideas just starting to well out of the collective unconscious and manifest themselves in the conscious life of world culture. Johannis, more than most people, was prepared for the notion of interplanetary visitors. Though then ignorant of the UFO phenomenon (which he says he first heard of two months later, while visiting the United

States), nonetheless he was among that small prophetic minority (then a rather bizarre assortment of physical scientists, SF fans, poets, and lunatics) who foresaw the coming of the Space Age. Already something of a visionary, a member of a kind of cultural vanguard, he would help midwife the birth of a myth in whose siring he had unknowingly played some small role.

But by nature visionaries must forever be ahead of their time, and even then Johannis was no exception. In America they were seeing saucer-shaped objects performing incredible maneuvers in the sky; in the popular mind, this was quite incredible enough. Several years would have to pass before anyone would tolerate talk of "little green men" whose existence, if it could be proved, presumably would settle once and for all the question of extraterrestrial visitors. Nonetheless, Johannis's alleged experience pointed ahead to the day, just a few years in the future, when people generally would accord a measure of serious consideration to reports of "spacemen." This would occur, of course, when ETH had been firmly established in the collective mind as the most likely (indeed the *only*) nonconventional explanation for UFO sightings.

So was Johannis's a "real" experience? A question like this is almost impossible to answer, as we shall have many occasions to observe in the pages ahead, because in the UFO myth "objective" and "subjective" elements are often indistinguishable. Perhaps significantly, however, Johannis relates that early in the experience he felt as if he were "dreaming." Anyone who remembers his dreams (and especially his nightmares) will recognize the element of paralysis or helpless immobility in the face of a terrifying situation, which our "witness" reports undergoing. Most significant, contacts with fairies, folklore indicates, take place when the percipient is *lying down*, suggesting strongly that, whether he knows it or not, the individual in question is in a dream or trance state. Possibly the motif of the "paralysis beam," which we will encounter time and again in ufonaut stories, is a sly hint from the unconscious, tipping off the percipient that he is not really a participant in these events, that (as in dreams) he can only observe them from a position of physical immobility; the unconscious and its contents have a life of their own, and as we watch them, puzzled and occasionally horrified, we find that we are really at their mercy.

The relationship of the Johannis tale to certain archetypal material in the collective unconscious* is suggested further in the fact that the event occurred *in the mountains,* where from time immemorial men have gone to commune, not always happily, with the gods. One of them was Elijah,

---

*Jung told the Society for Psychical Research in a 1919 lecture, "The other part of the unconscious is the *superpersonal* or *collective* unconscious. The contents of the collective unconscious are not personal but collective; i.e., they do not appertain to one individual only, but at least to a group of individuals and as a rule to a whole nation, and finally to the whole of mankind. The contents of the collective unconscious are not acquired during an individual's life, but are congenital instincts and primordial forms of apprehension, the so-called archetypes or ideas. Although the child possesses no congenital representations, it yet possesses a highly developed brain with possibilities of functioning in a definite way. The brain is an ancestral inheritance. It is the organic result of the psychic and nervous function of the whole ancestry of man. Thus the child brings into life with him an organ ready to function in the same way that it has functioned through all previous ages. There in the brain are the preformed instincts and also the primordial types or images, the foundations upon which mankind has always formed his thought and feeling, which includes the whole wealth of mythological motives. It is, of course, not easy to prove the existence in a normal man of the collective unconscious, but there are obvious traces of mythological images, at least in his dreams. The existence of a collective unconscious is more easily disclosed in certain cases of mental derangement, especially in dementia praecox. There one sometimes meets with an astonishing development of mythological imagery. Certain patients develop symbolic ideas which can never be accounted for by the experience of their individual life, but only by the history of the human mind. What is displayed is a sort of primitive mythological thinking producing its own primordial forms unlike normal thinking, which makes use of personal experience."

Elsewhere in his voluminous writings Jung calls these primordial types or images "archetypal images." The archetype itself, buried deep and inaccessibly in the collective unconscious, is invisible. "Consequently," Jungian psychologist Jolande Jacobi has explained (*Complex/Archetype/Symbol in the Psychology of C. G. Jung*), "one can *never* encounter the 'archetype as such' *directly*, but *only indirectly*, when it is manifested in the archetypal image, in a symbol, or in a complex or symptom." Since the archetype is by definition totally mysterious, so the resulting image or symbol will be mysterious, and its precise function will remain beyond our conscious understanding—even though it expresses metaphorically a fundamental psychic truth.

the Old Testament prophet/visionary who was scooped up by a "chariot of fire." Then, we are told, he "went up by a whirlwind into heaven." Johannis noted that as the UFO shot away he was "struck by a tremendous blast of wind ... which rolled me over and over on the ground and filled my eyes with dust." We are also reminded here of the "fairy wind," defined in *Funk & Wagnalls Standard Dictionary of Folklore, Mythology and Legend* as a "sudden blast or gust of wind, or whirlwind, believed to be caused by the fairies. Sometimes it is said to be caused by the passing of the fairy host; sometimes they are said to be *in* it; sometimes it is just the stir caused by fairies at work. ... The fairy wind is often greatly feared, for such winds sometimes cause harm to people or cattle, such as *injuries to the eye, making them fall* [our emphasis], etc." Fairies, in common with other supernatural beings, are frequently said to dwell in the mountains.

But before the skeptical reader smiles too complacently we must caution him that the hallucination theory does not quite account for everything Johannis says happened to him. To quote again from his account, published in Charles Bowen's *The Humanoids*:

As a result of my experience, I had made inquiries in the village the next day (August 15, 1947), as to whether anybody had noticed any sort of "airplane" the day before. Two people (an old man and a boy) told me, separately, that they had seen one, in the one case at 8:30 A.M. and in the other case at approximately 10:00 A.M. The old man had been sitting down in the village square enjoying the sunshine. He noticed a red globe being "carried aloft by the wind" behind the mountain on the slope of which the village lies. The boy was with his mother and other people, working in a field scarcely outside the village, and he noticed a red ball ("like the ones they have at fairs") which was rising at great speed and vanished in the clear sky.

Neither does the theory of hallucination—at least as hallucination is ordinarily understood—tell us why Johannis should have been missing his metal implements (including his pick, which he searched for, unsuccessfully, the following day).

5

Let us leave this problem for the moment and return to Jose Higgins's report. Of the witness himself we know only that he was a "surveyor" and that for all practical purposes he was the only percipient. (We can ignore the alleged "other workmen" who, if they existed at all, seem to have fled before the occupants emerged from their craft.) But we need not know anything about Higgins's private life in order to understand the story's psychological content— Higgins's vision was not a private aberration, but a preview of what was coming to all of us. And he saw, even if he did not understand, the message it had brought to modern man.

First, *the beings arrive in a round object*. The circle, as Jung explained in his *Flying Saucers*, traditionally is a symbol of psychic wholeness, the harmonious balancing of the conscious and the unconscious minds even though the two are fundamentally unalike. A man's unconscious, for example, is dominated by the *anima*, or feminine archetype. (Conversely, the *animus*, or masculine archetype, shapes a woman's unconscious.) In *The Development of Personality* Jung explained this strange phenomenon as "an hereditary factor of primordial origin engraved in the living organic system of man, an imprint or 'archetype' of all the ancestral experiences of the female, a deposit, as it were, of all the impressions ever made by woman." Traditionally men have associated light with the male principle (the conscious mind) and darkness with the female (the unconscious). However, brilliant light—as opposed to the ordinary light of the conscious world—traditionally represents wholeness and the overcoming of duality, especially when it is manifested in a circle or mandala. The psyche attempts to integrate these opposites so that it can attain *individuation*, "the process by which a person becomes a psychological 'in-dividual,' that is, a separate, indivisible unity or 'whole' " (Jung, *The Archetypes and the Collective Unconscious*).

The UFO carries three occupants. For many thousands of years the number three "has been regarded as a symbol of the 'pure abstract spirit' " (Jolande Jacobi, *The Psychology of C. G. Jung*). J. E. Cirlot explains that "it represents the solution of the conflict posed by dualism. . . . It is the harmonic product of the action of unity upon duality." Here the symbol implies that the three messengers from the sky (three can also represent heaven and the Trinity) have come to resolve a fundamental psychic conflict.

The beings are hermaphroditic, yet "strangely beautiful." The archetype of the hermaphrodite (a person possessing the physical traits of both sexes) symbolizes the spiritual bi-sexuality—or, perhaps more accurately, the biunity—of the psyche; it "reconciles one of the most important pairs of psychological opposites—male and female" (M.-L. von Franz, in the anthology *Man and His Symbols*). As such it represents individuation, which occurs when the masculine conscious and the feminine unconscious are in tune with each other. When this happens the individual is released from the psychic tension caused by conflict between opposites; he is "at one" with himself and the world. For example, in heaven, the state of perfect beauty and bliss where all opposites are united, angels (of whom Higgins's "spacemen" can be viewed as modern-day counterparts) are reputedly hermaphroditic. Significantly, Plato held that the gods first created man in the form of a *sphere* which incorporated elements of both sexes.

When the three surround Higgins, they make a quaternity. "Four," Jacobi writes, is "an archetypal expression of the highest significance for the psyche. With this fourth term the 'pure spirit' takes on 'corporeity' and a form adequate to physical creation. Along with the masculine spirit, the father principle which represents only one half of the world, the quaternity comprises the feminine and bodily aspect as its opposite pole—the two are needed to form a whole."

The beings try to lure him into the disc but Higgins evades them because they cannot step out into the light. The meaning here is obvious. As symbols of the unconscious (darkness), the three beings cannot enter the conscious mind (light) without the psychic equilibrium of the quaternity, which Higgins, who resists their entreaties, refuses to provide. Therefore the psychic victory the ternary implies cannot be realized in the external, conscious life. The circular disc's grayish white metal suggests symbolically the potential for unity but not its accomplishment. Higgins's refusal to enter it destroys the quaternity. (The four archetypal functions of the psyche are thinking and sensation [male] and intuition and feeling [female].) Individuation, the realization of the psyche's full potential, is no longer possible.

One of the beings pokes eight holes into the ground, apparently in a circle, and points to the seventh and then to the largest one, which is in the center. Ostensibly this action, which sounds exactly like something out of a pulp science fiction story, is intended to impart a message about the "spacemen's" home planet. From a psychological point of view, however, the circle suggests a mandala, a prime archetype of psychic unity in which all dualities are joined around a center: "the union of opposites through the middle path," Jung wrote in his introduction to *The Secret of the Golden Flower*, "that most fundamental item of inward experience which could respectably be set against the Chinese concept of Tao." In Western terms Jung called it a "revolving around oneself" with all sides participating in the movement, in one sense curiously like planets revolving around a sun. "Thus," he wrote, "the circular movement has also the moral significance of activating all the light and dark forces of human nature, and with them, all the psychological opposites of whatever kind they may be. . . . [One] primordial concept of an absolutely complete creature is that of Platonic man, round on all sides and uniting within himself two sexes."

The archetypal implications of the number seven in the context of a "celestial vision" are most revealing. Gertrude and James Jobes note, "Many believe that the existence of the universe depends on the harmony of the Seven, that they are related to the seven days of creation and control the cycle of the week, are the link between the Will of Heaven and events on earth, effect changes, determine the course or length of life, and they are consulted in human destiny" (*Outer Space: Myths, Name Meanings, Calendars*).

The "Seven" here referred to are the sun, moon, Mercury, Venus, Mars, Jupiter, and Saturn—the visible heavens. (Uranus, Neptune, and Pluto were not discovered until fairly recent times, and then only through powerful telescopes. Thus, of course, they do not figure in the ancient traditions which form the foundations of the archetypes.) In numerous legends "the Seven . . . are identified as aspects of the Seven Powers, sometimes called the Wandering Deities or Sentinels of Law and Order, watchmen of the heavens who wandered among the stars and prepared occurrences on earth" (Jobes). In Christianity, as but one example, the number of angels before God's throne is seven.

In Buddhism and in other Eastern religions and traditions, "The universe is conceived as having seven stages, one above another—that is, the seven planetary heavens," Mircea Eliade remarks in *Myths, Dreams, and Mysteries*. ". . . . Elevation into the supreme Heaven, that is, the act of transcending the world, takes place near to a 'Center' that the 'break" occurs from one place to another, and, therefore, the passing from Earth to Heaven."

In other words the UFO being, "the watchman of the heavens," is warning Higgins that he has rejected the possibility of transcendence (individuation, or union with the "center" of the psyche), and that he has far to go now before he can ever hope to get there. Further, the being's specification of the seventh planet symbolizes the masculine archetype (traditionally uneven numbers are viewed as masculine), or the conscious mind, out of touch with the anima of the (feminine) unconscious. The total number of "planets," eight, is suggestive of the quarternity. "Eight is a double quaternity," Jung remarked in *Flying Saucers*, "and, as an individuation symbol in the mandalas, plays almost as great a role as the quaternity itself."

Finally, *the beings run and jump about and throw stones*. This curious playfulness, so reminiscent of the reported behavior of fairies, opposes the "spacemen" to the humorless masculine "thinking" function which denies the instinctual, nonrational side of the psyche associated with the feminine. As a surveyor, Higgins by definition has accepted the primacy of science and mathematics, tools of pure reason, and for him the very earth is nothing more than an instrument to be measured; it certainly is not to be enjoyed on its own terms, as the beings clearly are doing.

What this incident tells us, then, takes us to the core of the UFO myth. As a warning to the human race from the collective unconscious, it speaks in the symbolic language of the psyche. It says that modern man is dangerously out of balance (we will be hearing that word *balance* again, by the way); he is out of touch with his soul, and by denying his capacity for mystery and wonder he has endangered his very existence. Ignoring the needs of the unconscious, he has busily constructed a machine-dominated world which values only the logical, thinking function. In his grotesquely sterile existence he has lost even the survival instinct—his machines, products of the brain, untouched by the heart, threaten to engulf him, and ultimately to reduce the planet to radioactive ash or total environmental decay.

The "spacemen," as "sentinels of [psychic] law and order," show a way back. Salvation is to be achieved through a balancing of the conscious and the unconscious minds, a bonding of male and female, science and magic. The story's moral is an old one: We have gained the world but lost our soul.

Recent events in history demonstrate clearly how the unconscious has acted to restore psychic equilibrium. In our time we have seen the phenomenal proliferation of cults centered on such decidedly nonrational pursuits as esoteric religion, meditation, and astrology. Just as significantly, social movements favoring world peace (rejecting the machinations of a soul-less political order) and ecology (advocating the containment of rampant technology) have attracted a massive following. Likewise, the feminist movement seeks to undo the evils of patriarchal dominance and all that it implies by arguing for the restoration of the masculine-feminine balance.

All this tends to confirm John Rimmer's contention that the UFO functions in part as an "antiscientific symbol." He writes in England's *Merseyside UFO Bulletin* (Vol. 2, No. 4):

Perhaps in its permanent inaccessibility [the UFO] is a symbol of purity. In a world violated and sullied by radiation, smoke, fumes, the excrement of a scientific society, the UFO is almost a virgin image of our time. Consider the so-called occupants of these craft. What are they but the dwarfs and elves, the pastoral inhabitants of unsullied hedgerow and field and the dark northern forests that we have left behind us? The hippie mystic sees the UFO as the Grail above Glastonbury; the French farmer sees the "occupants" as small, grotesque creatures of tree root and woodland glade. . . . Each perceives a phenomenon that is part of his past, a movement against the Establishment's glorification of scientific progress.

Like all effective magic the UFO is a perversion of the orthodoxy, rather than something totally different from it. It is the spacecraft of the scientist, but a spacecraft that does strange, irrational things: the occupants, although weird and unearthly, apparently wear spacesuits not so terribly different from the ones worn by those symbols of scientific progress, the astronauts. Magic in the past was twisted from religion—the Black Mass a horrific perversion of Christian ritual, not something totally different, but close enough to disturb even more. So the UFO parodies, one hopes in more pleasant form, the developments of science. The UFO's essentially unscientific nature can be seen in the strange, almost obsessive interest it holds for scientists who are most vehement in denying its existence. . . .

For every action there is an equal and opposite reaction. Perhaps for every scientific advance there is an equal and opposite mystical reaction. . . . It is clear that the UFO mystery now is one of Gothic strangeness and wonder. It has retreated so far from scientific method that it is doubtful if it will ever be capable of explanation in any rational manner. The world of the UFO is peopled with a Tolkien-like collection of entities with no rational pattern of behavior. If there is an overall plan it must be infinitely more convoluted than the most farcical Italian *opera buffo*. In this at least the victory of antiscience is almost complete. Nothing so incredibly irrational could be taken seriously by any scientist.

FAIRYLAND:
THE MAGICAL IMPULSE

> And see not ye that bonny road
> Which winds about the fernie brae?
> That is the road to fair Elfland
> Where you and I this night maun gae.
> —from "Thomas Rymer," a traditional ballad

1

On the afternoon of July 17, 1967, a group of French children set out on a walk through the bushy fields leading upward to the forest which surrounds the village of Arc-sous-Cicon. Five-year-old Patricia Bepoix, who had run ahead of her companions, was wandering through the thicket when suddenly she screamed, turned around, and fled all the way home. Sobbing, she explained to her mother that she had surprised some "little Chinamen" behind a bramble bush; one of them, she said, had stood up as if he was about to grab her.

A ten-year-old boy in the party did not observe the little men but he did see what he called "smoke" coming out of a bush. (In a subsequent interview, according to investigator Joel Mesnard, "it sounded more like a vertical, luminous, yellowish beam of light.")

The boy's sister, fifteen-year-old Joelle Ravier, and her friend Marie-Reine Mairot heard the story and hastened to the scene, where they spotted a weird humanoid creature running from bush to bush, his short legs moving faster than a human being's could. Three feet tall, black in color, he wore a short jacket which floated behind him as he ran. The children noticed that his belly protruded, but they could not see his arms or his face.

Joelle and Marie-Reine pursued the creature until he disappeared into a bush. From this bush they heard someone talking in a strange, singsong voice. Suddenly frightened, they made a rapid exit.

According to Joel Mesnard's account in *Flying Saucer Review* (January-February 1973):

On July 23 (six days later), it was still possible to see, around the bramble bush where the strange little creature had vanished, a dozen very pronounced marks where the grass—which was very green everywhere else—was of a yellow, straw color, and dry. One could actually feel that the grass on the stained areas was quite warm to the touch, whereas the surrounding grass felt cool. Moreover, the stained areas still gave off a certain odor.

The shortest route to the forest, from the spot where the creature was seen, is through a succession of clumps of shrubbery. And along the extent of 400 or 500 meters [approximately 150 to 175 feet] from the spot to the pine forest, six other marks, roughtly in a straight line, were found, which seemed as it were to blaze a trail. Nowhere else in the fields around about were such marks found.

According to Joelle Ravier's parents, who have known the district for a long time, these marks have an altogether unusual character owing to the way the grass is colored, and owing to the sharp outlines of the marks, and it is impossible to consider them to be due to the urine of the cattle, which merely produces a brownish coloring which is far less pronounced.

On the evening of the seventeenth, the same day as the alleged encounter at Arc-sous-Cicon, two astronomers at the observatory at Besancon saw a luminous spherical object which hovered briefly, then shot away toward the south. French newspapers, connecting this sighting with the earlier incident, chose to label the humanoids "Martians," an identification the children had not made. Taking her cue from the press accounts, however, even Joelle Ravier took to calling by that designation the entity she had seen, leading English ufologist Gordon Creighton to comment, "One of the sad myths of our time is that in some fashion or other we are 'better educated' than our forebears were.

Such, alas, is certainly not the case. Previous generations, in all cultures and in all parts of the world, would have recognized these creatures for what they are. There would have been less silly talk about 'Martians.' "

Earlier in the year two English schoolboys observed a similar apparition, but beyond a literal description, "a little blue man with a tall hat and a beard," they gave it no name. The incident occurred about 1:45 P.M. on January 28, 1967, on Studham Common, near Whipsnade Park Zoo, an isolated area in the Chiltern Hills. Alex Butler, one of seven boys on their way to school in the rain, happened to look south over the Dell (a shallow valley where the children often played hide-and-seek) and was startled to see the creature. He and a friend rushed toward the mysterious intruder, only to have him vanish in a "puff of smoke."

But the two kept looking for him. The being rewarded their persistence by reappearing, this time on the opposite side of the bushes from where he had first stood. Again they tried to approach him; again he vanished, to appear at the bottom of the Dell. The sound of "foreign-sounding babble" in nearby bushes, however, caused the boys to feel uneasy for the first time, and as the creature made its fourth appearance they were considerably relieved to hear the school whistle summoning them back to mundane reality.

Inside the Studham Village Primary School, their teacher, Miss Newcomb, commented on the boys' excited demeanor and finally got them to explain, albeit reluctantly ("You'll never believe us," they cautioned her), what had happened. She interviewed all seven separately and heard substantially the same story, which she had them write down. The reports were put in a booklet called *The Little Blue Man on Studham Common*.

Several of England's leading UFO researchers, including R. H. B. Winder, Gordon Creighton, and *Flying Saucer Review* editor Charles Bowen, conducted an investigation of the incident. They discovered that several local people had in recent months reported seeing UFOs; in fact, two supposedly had landed near where the "little blue man" had appeared. Interviewed in the presence of their teacher, the boys told the ufologists (in the words of Winder's summary):

They estimate the little man as three feet tall (by comparison with themselves) with an additional two feet accounted for by a hat or helmet best described as a tall brimless bowler, i.e. with a rounded top. The blue color turned out to be a dim grayish-blue glow tending to obscure outline and detail. They could, however, discern a line which was either a fringe of hair or the lower edge of the hat, two round eyes, a small, seemingly flat triangle in place of a nose, and a one-piece vestment extending down to a broad black belt carrying a black box at the front about six inches square. The arms appeared short and were held straight down, close to the side; at all times. The legs and feet were indistinct.

The "puff of smoke" seemed to have been a whirling cloud of yellowish-blue mist.

Visitors from other planets—or something else? "When they disappear," an Irish farmwoman told folklorist Walter Evans-Wentz around the turn of the century, "they go like fog." She was not referring to UFO beings. Rather, she was noting matter-of-factly the characteristic behavior of the humanoid inhabitants of isolated, wooded rural areas. She called them the "good people." We call them the fairies.

Myths, so the banal axion has it, die hard, but a growing body of scholarship, combining the techniques of anthropology and psychoanalysis, disputes this conventional wisdom and argues instead that myths don't die at all; they just put on new faces. The familiar world of conscious thought and experience goes its own way, blithely ignoring the needs of the unconscious mind and even disputing its very existence. But the unconscious remains. Its language, which it speaks in myth and symbol, may change, but its meaning remains the same. The old gods and demons and spirits continue to haunt us, ghosts in the machines which were supposed to have supplanted them.

For example, consider these two short paragraphs from two books which on the surface appear to have little in common. The first is from Lady Augusta Gregory's *Visions and Beliefs in the West of Ireland* (1920), a compilation of the popular superstitions of the peasantry. The second is from Ivan T. Sanderson's *Invisible Residents* (1970), an examination of the UFO mystery.

The *Sidhe* [the "hill people"—the fairies] cannot make themselves visible to all. They are shape changers; they can grow small or grow large, they can take any shape they may choose; they appear as men or women wearing clothes of many colors, of today or some old forgotten fashion, or they are seen as bird or beast, or a barrel or a flock of wool. They go by us in a cloud of dust; they are as many as the blades of grass.

The Irish see little green men; the northern Italians, tall blue men . . . ; the Latin Americans are attacked by horrible little hairy dwarfs, apparently made of metal against which machetes and knives shatter; peaceable and loving but disturbed North Americans meet gorgeous blondes sitting on rocks in the woods who admonish them to ban the bomb; and so on and on.

One is tempted to conclude, as does Jacques Vallee (whose excellent *Passport to Magonia* first documented the parallels between fairies and flying saucers), that "there exists a natural phenomenon whose manifestations border on both the physical and the mental. There is a medium in which human dreams can be implemented. . . ."

It is not clear, though, just what dreams Joelle Ravier and Alex Butler were dreaming: science fictional visions of little men from Mars, or whimsical reveries of the supernatural folk of the forest. Maybe, like the modern-day Irish farmers who tell of seeing "leprechauns" stepping out of flying saucers, they were dreaming of both.

2

William Blake, the nineteenth century English poet, artist, and mystic, once asked a woman with whom he happened to be engaged in conversation if she had ever seen a fairy's funeral.

"Never, sir," she replied.

"I have," Blake remarked, "but not before last night. I was walking alone in my garden. There was great stillness among the branches and flowers and more than common sweetness in the air. I heard a low and pleasant sound and

I knew not whence it came. At last I saw the broad leaf of a flower move and underneath I saw a procession of creatures of the size and color of green and gray grasshoppers, bearing a body laid out on a rose leaf, which they buried with songs, and then disappeared. It was a fairy funeral."

Blake's biographers do not record how the lady in question responded to this startling bit of information, but it is probably safe to assume that her reaction was not unlike the reader's own: incredulous and skeptical. For centuries before Blake's time, in fact as far back as Chaucer's generation, people of education and sophistication had ceased believing that fairies might exist, although literary artists like Spenser and Shakespeare had continued to find delight in the fairy mythology and evoked it imaginatively in such immortal poetic dramas as *The Faerie Queen* and *A Midsummer Night's Dream*. But for someone outside the peasantry to admit to anything more than literary or folkloristic interest in the fairy-faith was tantamount to a confession of lunacy. Even late in the nineteenth century, when some of the great pioneering folklorists (Andrew Lang most notably) became involved with the scientific study of psychic phenomena, practically none of them would concede the possibility that fairylore might have a genuinely paranormal foundation.

Clearly, from the point of view of his contemporaries, Blake had said nothing to upset orthodox thought on the matter, for was he not a visionary who talked of having seen angels in trees?

But the late folklorist John Cuthbert Lawson was not a mystic and certainly was not given to "seeing things." A brilliant scholar and field researcher, he spent two years in Greece (1898–1900) studying the popular traditions of the nation's peasantry. In the course of his investigations he was told repeatedly of a supernatural race of beautiful women called the Nereids, the Greek version of the fairies which in one form or another are known virtually all over the world. (We shall examine the Nereid tradition in more detail shortly.) As he wrote in his *Modern Greek Folklore and Ancient Greek Religion*:

As for the peasants, let them deny or avow their belief,

there is probably no nook or hamlet in all Greece where the womenfolk at least do not scrupulously take precautions against the thefts and the malice of the Nereids, while many a man may still be found ready to recount in all good faith stories of their beauty and passion and caprice. Nor is it a matter of faith only; more than once I have been in villages where certain Nereids were known by sight to several persons (so at least they averred); and there was a wonderful agreement among the witnesses in the description of their appearance and dress. I myself once had a Nereid pointed out to me by my guide, and there certainly was the semblance of a female figure draped in white and tall beyond human stature flitting in the dusk between the gnarled and twisted boles of an old olive yard. What the apparition was, I had no leisure to investigate; for my guide with many signs of the cross and muttered invocations of the Virgin ordered my mule to perilous haste along the rough mountain path.

Another folklorist, writing nearly a century earlier, from the Isle of Man, told Sir Walter Scott, "As to circles in grass ["Fairy rings," a ring of mushrooms where fairies are said to dance], and the impression of small feet among the snow, I cannot deny but that I have seen them frequently, and once thought I heard a whistle, as though in my ear, when nobody that could make it was near me." Scott, who recorded these words in his *Minstrelsy of the Scottish Border,* observed, perhaps not too surprisingly, "In this passage there is a curious picture of the contagious effects of a superstitious atmosphere. Waldron [the correspondent] had lived so long among the Manx that he was almost persuaded to believe their legends."

And so Scott neatly backed away from having to confront the disturbing implications of these remarks, offered by a man whom Scott elsewhere called "a scholar and a gentleman." For Scott, as well as for succeeding generations of folklore students, it might be permissible ("quaint") for the uneducated and unwashed to believe in fairies—after all, these unfortunates know no better—but it is clearly out of the question for persons of breeding to suggest, however obliquely, that there might be a core of unexplained truth to this belief.

Before we pursue the question any further, let us first explore some of the background out of which the fairy tradition has grown. We warn the reader, however, that the subject is one of such considerable complexity that a short summary like the one that follows can hardly do it full justice.

MacEdward Leach defines fairies as "a type of supernatural being, usually invisible, sometimes benevolent and helpful, sometimes evil and dangerous, sometimes just mischievous and whimsical, dwelling on the earth in close contact with man." The word itself comes indirectly from the Latin *fatum* (fate), as filtered through the late Latin *fata* into Middle English. Originally (and, as we shall see, significantly) *fairy* meant "enchantment" and referred to the world of illusion wherein supernatural beings allegedly dwelled. The beings themselves were called *fays*.

Eventually, of course, *fairy* came to denote the individual inhabitants of the otherworld. In the Celtic countries it was (and is, in those isolated places where the faith survives) considered dangerous to mention fairies by name, so a number of euphemisms, like "the good people" and "the gentry," came to be employed instead. A wise move, at least in the context of popular superstition, because fairies (Walt Disney movies notwithstanding) are possessed of an uncertain temperament and a considerable capacity for harming human beings.

In England the first written references to fairies appear in Anglo-Saxon chronicles but it is likely that the fairy faith was around long before then. Folklorists place the origin of the belief back to sometime in the dim mists of prehistory but disagree on exactly what it was that gave rise to such a stubborn, continuing tradition. The most likely theory is that the fairy myth is a debased memory of an ancient nature religion which populated the natural order with supernatural beings who directed the processes of fertility and growth. Folklorists once believed that fairies originally were a race of pygmies overcome by early conquerors of Europe; these aborigines supposedly were driven to the hills and caves and lived in comparative secrecy until historical times, when they presumably died out, surviving only in tales that grew in the telling until the pygmies had become a mysterious other-race with awesome powers. Some scholars have speculated that the fairy faith is a modern remnant of the old cult of the dead, a notion reinforced by persistent tales of dead persons reappearing in the company of fairies.

Unfortunately none of these hypotheses by itself accounts for the wide distribution and durability of the fairy faith, and even considered together they leave much to be desired. Twentieth-century students have all but abandoned the pygmy theory, citing a number of serious objections, chief among them the fact that there is no archaeological evidence that a pygmy race ever existed in prehistoric (or, for that matter, historic) Europe. But the most serious objection of all is that fairies exist not only in hoary tradition but in the testimony of many thousands of individuals, from peasants to Ph.D.'s, *who claim to have seen them themselves.*

The innumerable folklore studies of the subject are filled with such accounts, usually listed with no attempt by their presumably skeptical authors to explain them. The implication seems to be not that these stories are unexplainable but that, since fairies cannot exist, no explanation is necessary. Those with less clearly defined notions of what is possible and not possible, however, will find these alleged sightings extraordinarily fascinating and disturbing. Let us review some of them.

The first comes from a man who was a folklorist himself, and a well known and highly respected figure in the intellectual and cultural life of Victorian England: the Reverend S. Baring-Gould, who wrote in one of his books:

In the year 1838, when I was a small boy of four years old, we were driving to Montpelier on a hot summer day over the long straight road that traverses a pebble-and-rubble-strewn plain, on which grows nothing save a few aromatic herbs. I was sitting on the box with my father when, to my great surprise, I saw legions of dwarfs of about two feet high running along beside the horses; some sat laughing on the pole, some were scrambling up the harness to get on the backs of the horses. I remarked to my father what I saw, when he abruptly stopped the carriage and put me inside beside my mother, where, the conveyance being closed, I was out of the sun. The effect was that, little by little, the host of imps diminished in number till they disappeared altogether.

An incident like this reminds us very much of an item

from a recent article on children's UFO sightings which appeared in *FSR Case Histories #6*. In the words of author Eileen Buckle: "Recently a young man related . . . a remarkable low-level sighting he had at the age of fifteen when traveling by car with his family. An apparently solid object kept pace with the car for twenty minutes. All the family saw it clearly, except the father. Strangely, he was unable to see it at all."

Those inclined to accuse Reverend Baring-Gould of suffering from sunstroke-induced hallucination should consider his next accounts:

When my wife was a girl of fifteen, she was walking down a lane in Yorkshire, between green hedges, when she saw seated in one of the privet hedges a little green man, perfectly well made, who looked at her with his beady black eyes. She was so frightened that she ran home. She remembers that it was a summer day. . . .

One day a son of mine was sent into the garden to pick peapods for the cook to shell for dinner. Presently he rushed into the house as white as chalk to say that while he was thus engaged, and standing between the rows of peas, he saw a little man wearing a red cap, a green jacket, and brown knee-breeches, whose face was old and wan, and who had a grey beard and eyes as black and hard as sloes. He stared so intently at the boy that the latter took to his heels.

According to Edwin Hartland's *County Folklore*, Hollingworth recorded this incident, said to have occurred in 1842, in his *History of Stowmarket*:

S—— living for thirty years at the cottages in the hop ground on the Bury road, coming home one night twenty years since, in the meadow now a hop ground, not far from three ashen trees, in very bright moonlight, saw the fairies. "There might be a dozen of them, the biggest about three feet high, and small ones like dolls. Their dresses sparkled as if with spangles, like the girls at shows at Stow fair. They were moving round hand in hand in a ring, no noise came from them. They seemed light and shadowy, not like solid bodies. I passed on, saying, the Lord have mercy on me, but them must be the fairies, and being alone then on the path over the field could see them as plain as I do you. I looked after them when I got over the style, and they were there, just the same moving round and round. I ran home and called three women to come back with me and see them. But when we got to the place they were all gone. I could not make out any particular things about their faces. I might be forty yards from them and I did not like to stop and stare at them. I was quite sober at the time."

In *Ghostland* psychical researcher Elliott O'Donnell recounted an experience which supposedly occurred to a relative who one night was driving his buggy along a road from Hospital to Ballynanty in Limerick (Ireland), an area often claimed as *Sidhe* territory:

The horse had come to a dead stop, and was standing still, shivering, whilst the roadside was crowded with a number of tiny shadowy figures that were surging round the car trying to drag the unfortunate driver, who was quite frantic with terror, from his seat. Mr. B., however, concluding that what he saw could only be the fairies . . . of whose existence he had hitherto been very skeptical, seized the reins and urged the horse forward. Meanwhile his servant seemed to be still paralyzed with fright, and it was not until they were well out of sight that the man found himself once again in possession of his tongue and normal faculties. . . . Then he described what had befallen him. . . . He was driving along quite all right, till the horse suddenly stopped, and when he looked down to see what was the cause of it, he perceived a crowd of fairies, who rushed at him, and tried to drag him off the car. He said their touch was so cold it benumbed him. But by praying hard he held on. The cause of the attack was apparent.

"It was all because we came on them, sorr, when they were dancing. They won't be disturbed when they are at their revels and enjoying themselves, Had they got me down into the road, maybe I should have lost my sight or my hearing or the use of my limbs, and in any case my soul."

(UFO cases in which car engines suddenly cease operation and humanoid ufonauts attempt, successfully or unsuccessfully, to abduct the terrified occupants are so frequently found in the literature that virtually every book on the subject contains at least several examples. Ufologists who believe that UFOs are the product of a superior extraterrestrial technology explain these stoppages as "electromagnetic effects" from the spaceship propulsion system. So far as we know, they have not yet argued that these would render animals immobile as well.)

On September 20, 1909, Mrs. Biddy Grant of Upper Toughal, Ireland, gave this account to Evans-Wentz, who printed it in his monumental *The Fairy-Faith in Celtic Countries*. It illustrates the frequent association in the folk mind of fairies and the dead:

I saw *them* once as plain as can be—big, little, old, and young. I was in bed at the time, and a boy whom I had reared since he was born was lying ill beside me. Two of *them* came and looked at him; then came in three of *them*. One of *them* seemed to have something like a book, and he put his hand to the boy's mouth; then he went away, while others appeared, opening the back window to make an avenue through the house; and through this avenue came great crowds. At this I shook the boy, and said to him, "Do you see anything?" "No," he said, but as I made him look a second time he said, "I do." After that he got well.

These *good people* were the spirits of our dead friends, but I could not recognize them. I have often seen them that way while in my bed. Many women are among them. I once touched a boy of theirs, and he was just like feathers in my hand; there was no substance in him, and I knew he wasn't a living being. I don't know where they live; I've heard they live in the *Carrige* (rocks). Many a time I've heard of their *taking* people or leading them astray. They can't live far away when they come to me in such a rush. They are as big as we are. I think these fairy people are all through this country and in the mountains.

Two years earlier, a blind old man living with his wife in an Irish glen told Lady Archibald Campbell an incredible story. He said he had actually captured a fairy and kept it for two weeks before it got away. It supposedly was two feet tall, with dark but clear skin and red hair. He wore a red cap, green clothes, and boots.

I gripped him close in my arms and took him home. I called to the woman [his wife] to look at what I had got. "What doll is it you have there?" she cried. "A living one," I said, and put it on the dresser. We feared to lose it; we kept the door locked. It talked and muttered to itself queer words. . . . It might have been near on a fortnight since we had the fairy, when I said to the woman, "Sure, if we show it in the great city we will be made up [rich]. So we put it in a cage. At night we would leave the cage door open, and we would hear it stirring through the house. . . . We fed it on bread and rice and milk out of a cup at the end of a spoon.

Finally the "leprechaun" escaped, and after that the couple's fortunes, never much to begin with, declined even further. The man lost his sight and he and his wife lived on to die in the desperate poverty they always had known.

One of the most impressive cases of all appeared in 1938 in a Dublin newspaper. The *Irish Press* reported that "Watching for fairies has leaped into sudden popularity in West Limerick." Its reporter interviewed a number of men and boys who asserted that they had observed troops of fairies passing by and had even chased them—to no avail, since, the Irishmen said, "they jumped the ditches as fast as a grayhound."

The first witness, a schoolboy named John Keely, allegedly met a single fairy walking along a road in the afternoon. He ran off to tell some older friends, who with tongue in cheek urged him to go back and talk with the little fellow. Young Keely, taking them at their word, returned to the scene, approached the fairy, and asked him where he was from. The fairy answered curtly, "I'm from the mountains and it's all equal to you what my business is."

The next day two fairies appeared at the crossroads between Ballingarry and Kilfinney, six miles from Rathkeale, during the daylight hours. They were skipping rope, witnesses claimed, and "they could leap the height of a man." As others watched from the bushes, John Keely walked up to the fairies and one of them let him hold his hand. The two, in the company of the rest of the fairies, set off down the road. Just where the fairies intended to take the boy, we will never know, for suddenly they spotted the men hiding nearby and, taking fright, fled away "like the wind," with Keely and friends in hot pursuit.

Describing them to the reporter, witnesses said that the

fairies were about two feet tall and had 'hard, hairy faces like men, and no ears." They were dressed in red and one of them wore a white cape, and they wore knee breeches and 'vamps" instead of shoes. Several men who had chased the gnomes claimed that "though they passed through hedges, ditches, and marshes, they appeared neat and clean all the time."

Finally, to bring us closer to home, our friend Brad Steiger writes (in *Revelation: The Divine Fire*) of his own encounter in midwestern America:

> I can still recall the time in my childhood when I lay in my bed and watched out of the window in fascination as a rather smallish man with a conical hat stood on his tiptoes to another window and watched my parents as they moved about in the kitchen of our farmhouse. After several moments of seemingly enthralled observation on both of our parts, the little man must have felt an uncomfortable sensation of someone watching him. He turned to look at me over his shoulder, and I got a good look at his tiny, pinched features in the light from the kitchen window. He smiled, shook his head; and then I am not sure what happened, but it seemed that he simply disappeared. At the time, I was convinced that I had seen a brownie or an elf. In my later years I had regarded the episode as the single most vivid dream of my childhood.

Steiger's story recalls others we have heard. The sister of one of the authors claims to have had a similar experience in childhood. When word got out that we were writing a book that dealt in part with fairylore, several friends and acquaintances confided, "I'd almost forgotten this because my parents told me I was just seeing things, but once, when I was little, I saw . . ." Coincidentally, just the day before I (Jerome Clark) sat down to type these words, a letter came from a woman in New York State. "As a small child," she wrote, "I distinctly remember the little red elves that pestered me by darting at me in the darkened bedroom. They were dressed in red. I have never mentioned this to anyone before because, as I grew older, I thought it was all childish imagination."

We suspect that small children frequently have these visions (though, alas, neither of us did); but since they are so at variance with the conventional "wisdom" which encumbers us in maturity, most people dismiss them from memory somewhere on the way to adulthood. Readers will recall that the 1967 French and English witnesses were children, too. We wonder how long they will remember their observations as "real" events.

3

For reasons of space our concern here is primarily with the fairy traditions of Western Europe, and most especially the British Isles. But as we already have observed, the fairy faith is a global phenomenon, which is not to say that it is everywhere the same; only that in many different countries, in many different cultures, beliefs persist concerning the existence of a supernatural other-race which lives hidden in nature while at the same time exhibiting a curious interest in the affairs of men. What makes these divergent beliefs so fascinating is that even though they differ in some important respects, nonetheless the essential features remain amazingly and disturbingly consistent.

The Nereids (Greece). Earlier we quoted J. C. Lawson's account of his experience with what was supposed to have been a Nereid. Belief in these alleged beings was not, at least until recently, confined to the superstitious peasantry. Some of the leading citizens of Greece are said to have waxed uneasy at the mere mention of these beautiful, dangerous women who have played an integral part in the folk religion of Greece since centuries before Christ. The early Greeks knew them as nymphs (which means simply "young women") whose queen was the goddess Artemis, "Lady of the Wild Things."

(As late as the sixteenth century, according to an Italian document, both priests and laypeople of Crete testified they had seen "Diana and her fair nymphs" bathing and then disappearing in the waters of the Gulf of Mirabella. Lawson comments, "It would have been highly interesting to know the names of the goddess which the Italian writer translated as 'Diana.' . . . It is scarcely likely that the Italian name had been adopted in Crete. More probably the slovenly fashion of miscalling Greek deities by Latin names was as common then as now. . . . Yet the traditional connection of Artemis with this district in Crete warrants the assumption that the leader of the nymphs of whom the story tells was in personality, if not also in name, the ancient Greek goddess, and no Italian importation.")

These nymphs, like the fairies of other lands, reputedly were, and are, long-lived but not immortal. ("A crow lives twice as long as a man, a tortoise twice as long as a crow, and a Nereid twice as long as a tortoise," an Arcadian peasant told Lawson), and occupy an intermediate position between human beings and angels. Originally the Greeks knew them by four different names, each denoting the specific haunt of the nymphs: Nereids (sea nymphs), Oreads (mountain nymphs), Dryads (tree nymphs), and Naiads (water nymphs). But by 1900, and perhaps long before, only classicists were aware of the last three, and the Greeks were calling all the nymphs, wherever they found them, Nereids.

Nereids are almost always female; in fact, if we are willing to consider the possibility that Nereids might exist in some form outside the realm of pure fantasy, we might venture to declare male Nereids nothing more than a folkloristic embellishment growing out of something at once more real and considerably less easy to dismiss. Lawson's suggestion that male Nereids are the invention of old wives' tales born out of the necessity of finding husbands for these fairy women strikes us as a reasonable one, especially since Greek women must have looked upon the nymphs, whose beauty and passion, actual or imagined, surely entered into the erotic fantasies of their husbands, as something of a threat to the security of their own homes.

For the most part, anyway, they need not have worried: Nereids are notoriously treacherous creatures and in most cases the man who dallies with them lives to regret it—if he lives at all. A Melian peasant on his way home one night passed by some Nereids in a cave and was bidden to join them, which he did, spending the night feasting, drinking, dancing, and making love. When morning came the nymphs sent him home shattered and impotent. Several years ago a Greek informed Richard and Eva Blum (who quote the account in their *The Dangerous Hour: The Lore of Crisis and Mystery in Rural Greece*), "A neighbor of ours told us that his brother and his brother's wife were walking one night. Suddenly the Nereids got hold of him, seizing him by the arms, and dragged him along with them. His wife lost him, so the Nereids carried him away. Some days later he was found dead by a fountain; his body was covered with black spots from maltreatment."

On the other hand, a Nereid occasionally will do well by a man if she has fallen in love with him, which apparently does not happen very often. "Only in one case," Lawson writes in his important study of Greek traditions, "have I heard of a nymph's continued intimacy with a man throughout his life, and that strangely enough not in a folk story but in recent experience." The man in question, though he was married and had a family, had carried on the affair since youth; his lover was a Nereid who lived in a nearby cave. In his early days he had been extremely poor but now he was a wealthy man and the mayor of his village—all because, so it was said, the nymph had enriched his crops and protected his flocks from disease.

One trespasses on Nereid territory at one's own peril. Since the Nereids claim certain trees, springs, sections of rivers, wells, caves, and mountaintops as their own, the rural Greek is never particularly safe from them; and anyway they have been known to knock on doors to entreat men and women to follow them on urgent missions, which usually result in the injury or death of those guileless enough to take the nymphs at their word. Those they do not kill the Nereids leave mute, blind, epileptic, or castrated. One who has suffered death, illness, or abduction at their hands is said to have been "seized." (The Irish use the word *taken* to describe the same general phenomenon.)

But the Nereids are fond of human children and even in ancient times had acquired a reputation for kidnapping those they found particularly desirable. On a tombstone dating back to the first days of Greek civilization these words are recorded: "Tearful Hades with the help of Oreads made away with me, and this mournful tomb that has been builded nigh unto the Nymphs contains me." Nereids on kidnapping forays travel on whirlwinds (called "the fairy wind" in other countries), snatch up their victims (not always children) and take them away, sometimes leaving their dead bodies behind; as in other cultures the land of the dead and the land of the fairies occasionally overlap. The invocation "Honey and milk in your path!" is supposed to be an effective safeguard against the nymphs in flight, for they reputedly favor honey in their eating and, moreover, in common with fairies anywhere, demand ritualistic respect.

Again like other fairies, the Nereids love music and dancing (in Greece a girl who dances unusually well is said to "dance like a Nereid") and often appear in great numbers, playing violins, mandolins, and zithers, and making a strange, haunting music. "I remember sitting at the window in 1938," a peasant told the Blums. "It was about midnight when I heard the Nereids . . . passing by with drums and violins. They were dancing, and going towards their square where they always went to dance, a [village] square which is up towards the mountains. These Nereids did not harm anyone, but when you heard them you became frightened and you shivered."

(Beautiful but treacherous fairy women figure in other European traditions. In Denmark the Elf Woman "is young and of a fair and attractive countenance, but behind she is hollow like a dough-trough," Thomas Keightley wrote in his classic *The Fairy Mythology*. They appear under the moonlight, playing a stringed instrument and dancing, beguiling the hearts of young men to whom they may offer themselves. Germany's Wild Women live in stately palaces inside hollow hills, from which they emerge periodically to seduce men and steal children. In Brittany the Korrigan can predict the future, cure illnesses, travel at the speed of thought, and assume any shape they desire. Ordinarily, however, they are lovely young women by night, ugly hags by day. They dwell near springs, love to dance and make love, and steal children. They manage to accomplish all this despite the fact that they are only two feet tall.)

The Menehune (Hawaii). From time to time those Hawaiians curious enough to wonder about such things puzzle over the sudden appearance, in rural areas and sometimes along railroad tracks, of small, four-toed footprints shorter and narrower than a cigarette package. The existence of such tracks is hardly open to question; the controversy arises out of the problem of determining who or what is making the tracks. Typically, the folklorist does not concern himself with the question, since everyone knows that the Menehune (May-nay-hoo-nay) cannot exist.

And what are the Menehune? Little red people who stand between two and three feet in height, with a thick head of hair worn low on the forehead, they reside in trees and caves and in the mountains, venturing forth only between dusk and dawn. When they are not working (which evidently is their favorite pastime—they have a reputation for somewhat excessive seriousness), they are singing—their music, like all fairy music, is said to be beautiful—or engaged in competitive sports like wrestling and tug-of-war.

Hawaii's fairies have been in retreat ever since the coming of white men and Christianity but supposedly a few remain. "If you think that only children or the more poorly educated believe in the Menehune," James T. Fitzpatrick wrote in a 1967 issue of *Asian Adventure,* "you would be quite mistaken. People from all walks of life and of all income brackets in these islands take their Menehune quite seriously."

Those gifted with second sight have the best chance of seeing the little people, who, however, are not always visible. When encountered, the Menehune demand respect. To protect oneself in their presence, one is supposed to lie prone, as the ancient Hawaiians did in the presence of their chiefs.

The Little People (northwestern United States). The folklore of the Northwestern tribes is rich in traditions about diminutive beings but it is also a bit confusing. The confusion stems from the fact that two distinct types of entities figure in the legends. One of them are members of an apparently intelligent fairy race and the others are representative of a brutish, half-human, half-animal species which appears to have survived intact into our time: namely as the creatures known variously as "Bigfoot" and "Sasquatch," along with their innumerable kin in many parts of North America. This latter tradition, though a fascinating one in its own right, does not concern us here.

"The origin and the meaning of the numerous picture writings found on rocks along Lake Chelan and along the Columbia, John Day, Santiam, and other rivers of Washington and Oregon puzzle both Indians and archaeologists,"

Ella E. Clark notes in her *Indian Legends of the Pacific Northwest*. Elderly Yakimas believe that the writing was done by a mysterious race called the Wahteetas.

Full-grown Wahteetas were never more than two feet tall. They lived in the cliffs, clothing themselves in robes of rabbit hair, and at night skipped among the rocks in search of smooth stone surfaces on which they could print their enigmatic messages. They painted with four different colors: red, blue, white, and yellow. "They used to watch over the pictures and never let them grow dim," an old man told Lucullus McWhorter in 1912. "Often the Wahteetas repainted the rocks during the night. If you rubbed the picture paintings with any kind of coloring or any kind of mud, the next morning they would be all bright and fresh as ever. They were the laws of the Yakima, painted there by the ancient little people."

It was still possible to observe Wahteetas, according to the Yakimas, as late as the early twentieth century, but it was not a very good idea, since for adults it presaged death. By now the Wahteetas have disappeared, surviving only in the fading memories of a handful of aged Yakimas.

The Arapahos speak of the little people who perished many years ago in a forest fire. Though less than three feet tall, they were incredibly strong and were much feared, mostly because of their reputed taste for human flesh. Both the Shoshonis and the Bannocks maintain traditions concerning cannibalistic dwarfs who lived in caves in the Owyhee Range of Idaho and in the mountains of the Salmon River country.

The three-foot dwarfs of Flathead tradition were a gentler breed. In the early days, as the first inhabitants of the territory the Flatheads were later to occupy, they farmed and tended herds of tiny black horses. Eventually they retreated into the mountains, set up housing in caves, slept during the daylight hours and came out at night to dance and play.

The dwarfs of Rosebud Lake, who the Coeur d'Alenes tell us resided in the surrounding bushes and trees, are similarly of kindly disposition, though they are fond of practical jokes. Persons who approach them fall into a swoon; when they awaken they may find themselves hanging upside down from a tree or missing some of their clothing. The little people dress in brown suits and wear pointed hats of the same color.

"In the evening my family would sometimes hear sticks beating against the trunks of trees," a Coeur d'Alene related to Julia Nicodemus. "My grandparents would say, 'The dwarfs are hitting the trees.' We children would be afraid." At other times the fairies would wail all night long, much to the annoyance of human beings within listening range who were trying to sleep.

The "Stick Indians" (so called because the Nez Perces thought they lived deep in the forest) are also known for the strange sounds they make. They wear deer skins, kidnap people and livestock, and are very strong. They do not like to be seen (in fact they sometimes render themselves invisible), and the penalty for observing them can be a painful swelling of the face. Those who have seen the dwarfs describe them as physically unappealing, with small eyes, wrinkled faces, and uncombed long hair.

An Indian informant testified to their power. "One time when some people were huckleberrying near Mount Adams," he said, "they locked their baby in their car, for safety. No one else was in the car. While they were picking berries, they heard the baby cry. They went to the car and found that the baby was gone. Then they heard it cry from another direction. They went over there, and there they found it. The little people had taken the baby out of a locked car. This did happen."

Mircea Eliade states in *Shamanism: Archaic Techniques of Ecstasy:*

In the Great Basin we hear of a "little green man," only two feet tall, who carries a bow and arrows. He lives in the mountains and shoots his arrows into those who speak ill of him. The "little green man" is the guardian spirit of medicine men, of those who have become magicians solely by supernatural aid. The idea of a dwarf who grants power or serves as guardian spirit is extremely widespread west of the Rocky Mountains, in the tribes of the Plateau Groups (Thompson, Shuswap, etc.) and in northern California (Shasta, Atsugewi, Northern Maidu, and Yuki).

4

The first systematic study of Celtic fairylore was conducted by the Reverend Robert Kirk, the minister of Aberfoyle, Scotland, in the late seventeenth century. His *The Secret Commonwealth of Elves, Fauns and Fairies,* completed in 1691, remains one of the seminal works on the subject.

Kirk did not doubt the existence of fairies. He was not concerned, as a modern investigator would be, with defining popular superstition, but with delineating the nature and workings of a supernatural order whose reality he considered self-evident. If for no other reason, we must give Kirk credit for assuming the common sense and honesty of his informants. Evans-Wentz, the twentieth-century student, has suggested that Kirk himself was psychic and thus able to see the "good people."

Kirk concluded from his researches that fairies are an intermediate form between men and angels; that they have light, "fluid" bodies of the consistency of a condensed cloud, which enables them to appear and disappear at will, as well as to fly through the air or escape into their beautiful (and usually invisible) subterranean homes; that they can steal anything they like, from food to human babies; that their civilization parallels our own in many ways and they seem to live much like the people around them, adopting or imitating local customs; that they are ruled by a king and a queen, with the latter somewhat more powerful than the former; and that they are intelligent and curious and have no particular religion.

For his efforts Kirk came to a mysterious end. He is said to have angered the fairies, who do not like having their secrets advertised to the world, and one day in 1692 the clergyman dropped dead while strolling across alleged fairy territory. In 1909 Evans-Wentz interviewed the man who then held what long before had been Kirk's post at Aberfoyle, the Reverend William M. Taylor, who told him, "At the time of his disappearance, people said he was *taken* because the fairies were displeased with him for prying into their secrets. At all events, it seems likely that Kirk was taken ill very suddenly with something like apoplexy while on the Fairy Knoll, and died there. I have searched the presbytery books, and find no record of how Kirk's death really took place; but of course there is not the least doubt of his body being in the grave."

This last remark refers to a longstanding tradition that the fairies had snatched Kirk away *bodily* and that the reverend's coffin has nothing in it but stones. Tradition also holds that not long after he was "taken," Kirk appeared to a relative and said that the fairies had him in their power, "but," he went on, "I can be set free if you will have my cousin do what I tell him when I appear again at the christening of my child in the parsonage." The cousin in question was one Grahame of Duchray. True to his word, Kirk was there at the baptismal ceremony, but his presence so startled poor Grahame that he was unable to act on Kirk's order to throw a dagger over his head, and the reverend was lost forever.

Fairies, like UFO beings, come in all sizes and shapes, but, again like UFO beings, they are usually diminutive. Some are the size of dwarfs; others are Lilliputian in stature. Some are beautiful; others are ugly. Their temperament is at best uncertain, and they are better left alone. But they can be very kind if they wish to be.

In one such instance, reported in her *The Fairies in English Tradition and Literature,* the prominent British folklorist Katharine Briggs has related the experience of a friend, a clergyman's widow, who suffered from an injured foot. One day as she sat in Regents Park in London her foot was giving her particular trouble and she worried that the pain might be so great that walking home would be impossible. Suddenly she saw a tiny man in green who looked at her sympathetically and said, "Go home. We promise that your foot shan't pain you tonight." He vanished from sight; at the same time the pain in her foot vanished, too. She walked home with no trouble and slept soundly and painlessly all that night.

As we have seen, fairies are famous for their music. The late Dr. Thomas Wood, a composer and author, actually wrote down a fairy melody he claimed to have heard. As he told writer Harold T. Wilkins:

I was on Dartmoor in the summer of 1922 with a camping

party on the banks of the river Teign. . . . I used to go off after breakfast to be alone, to think and make notes for a book I was writing. This book was large and leather-bound and the manuscript weighed seven pounds. I had a blazer over my legs to keep off the horse flies and a ground sheet to keep away the damp. Ahead and below, mile after mile, ranged the great rolling stretches of Dartmoor. It lay shimmering in the heat. There were bracken and gorse, grassy paths for the ponies, and pools in the bog, fringed with reeds. Little streams ran laughing in the sun between the rocks. There were ancient stone circles, hut circles, and kistvaens—memorials of the past of an unknown race when the world was young—bare brown tors, all wild and untamable.

Wood was composing music for an opera and tapping out with his foot the time of the music when abruptly he heard a weird voice calling his name. *"Tommy! Tommy!"* As it got closer Wood looked around for its source but there was no one to be seen.

I picked up my field glasses and swept the moor to make sure. The moor was empty as the sky. Picnickers did not come here. The place was hard to find. . . . I knew I should see nothing! But that voice had sounded within twenty yards of me. It was not the voice of anyone over in the camp yonder. No one there called me Tommy and no one I could recall had a voice like that . . . small, clear, faintly mocking, pitched high. It was not a woman's voice, not a child's voice. It might be that of a youth, or a man's falsetto. Had I been honored by a visit from a pixy?

Wood returned to the spot the next day.

The weather was more steamingly hot than ever. Dartmoor was asleep. So were the bees, the hawks, the wind, the tors. An hour went by—an hour and a half. The shadows shifted. The sun moved. . . . And then I heard the last thing I expected to hear . . . *music in the air!* It was overhead, faint as a breath. It died away, came back louder, over me, swaying like a censer that dips. It lasted twenty minutes. Portable wireless sets were unknown in 1922. My field glasses assured me no picnickers were in sight. It was not a gramophone nor was it an illusory noise in my ears. This music was essentially harmonic, not a melody nor an air. It sounded like the weaving together of tenuous fairy sounds. I listened with every faculty drawn out to an intensity.

I am prepared to say on oath that what I wrote down is so close to the original that the authors themselves would not know the difference. . . . The music drifted into silence. No more came, then or since. I was reasonably certain that I had been deliberately encouraged to listen to the supernatural. The camp agreed with me. They knew their Dartmoor! And if you feel yourself skeptical—just you get yourself lost on this moor somewhere between Shovel Down and Tavy Head. That will teach you to respect the old ones!

Fairies seem to be infinitely malleable and almost as variable as human imagination itself. Evans-Wentz, Kirk, and others have remarked on how the shapes and personalities change from place to place, in each case mirroring the spirit and culture of the particular surrounding human community. But, as Miss Briggs writes, "Just as the landscape and the overhanging clouds change from county to county in these small but varied islands, so the fairies of each district vary subtly in mood and emphasis and color; but . . . everywhere the characteristics are broadly the same, the same stories are told about them; danger and beauty stream out of all of them."

Among the more malevolent aspects of fairy behavior is the little people's reported habit of abducting infants and replacing them with less than desirable children of their own. This belief, common to virtually all fairy traditions, springs in part from the unwillingness of certain parents to face up to the cruel truth that their baby has been born congenitally deformed or retarded. As late as May 17, 1884, according to the *London Daily Telegraph,* two women of Clonmel were arrested for beating a three-year-old boy in hopes that this kind of mistreatment would induce the fairies to return the "real child."

We are inclined to suspect that the changeling idea is another of the embellishments that attached themselves to the more real and unexplainable parts of the mystery. If it is at least possible that fairies might exist in some fashion (exactly how we will be explaining in the last chapter), we might consider that fairies, as a separate race who conducted their mysterious affairs in apparent secrecy, inevitably would have inspired speculation and gossip that departed considerably from reality. Significantly, some of the more intelligent and thoughtful folk informants who expressed belief in fairies to Evans-Wentz (and whose testimony is quoted in his *The Fairy-Faith*) at the same time were frankly skeptical of changeling stories.

5

There is another class of tales we may have to take more seriously, namely those dealing with fairy children. The following, a sworn statement by a Swedish clergyman of the seventeenth century, which appeared in Thomas Keightley's *The Fairy Mythology*, is only one of a number of strikingly similar claims:

In the year 1660, when I and my wife had gone to my farm, which is three quarters of a mile from Ragunda parsonage, and we were sitting there and talking awhile, late in the evening, there came a little man in at the door, who begged of my wife to go and aid his wife, who was just in the pains of labor. The fellow was of small size, of a dark complexion, and dressed in old grey clothes. My wife and I sat awhile, and wondered at the man; for we were aware that he was a Troll, and we had heard tell that such like, called by the peasantry Vettar (spirits), always used to keep in the farmhouses, when people left them in harvest-time. But when he had urged his request four or five times, and we thought on what evil the country folk say that they have at times suffered from the Vettar, when they have chanced to swear at them, or with uncivil words bid them to go to hell, I took the resolution to read some prayers over my wife, and to bless her, and bid her in God's name go with him. She took in haste some old linen with her, and went along with him, and I remained sitting there. When she returned, she told me that when she went with the man out at the gate, it seemed to her as if she was carried for a time along in the wind, and so she came to a room, on one side of which was a little dark chamber, in which his wife lay in bed in great agony. My wife went up to her, and, after a little while, aided her till she brought forth the child after the same manner as other human beings. The man then offered her food, and when she refused it, he thanked her, and accompanied her out, and then she was carried along, in the same way in the wind, and after a while came again to the gate, just at ten o'clock. Meanwhile, a quantity of old pieces and clippings of silver were laid on a shelf, in the sitting-room, and my wife found them next day, when she was putting the room in order. It is supposed that they were laid there by the Vettar. That it in truth so happened, I witness, by inscribing my name. Ragunda, the 12th of April, 1671.

—*Pet. Rahm*

Not much is said here of the fairy realm, which Mrs. Rahm had to enter in order to act as midwife to the fairy child, but other accounts are more explicit. Practically all of these purported visits seem to occur in some kind of trance or dream state. One of the early Celtic tales of the otherworld, preserved in the medieval folk ballad "Thomas Rymer," relates how the title character (in reality, the thirteenth century Scotch poet Thomas of Erceldoune) *was resting under a tree* when the queen of Elfland appeared and abducted him into her dominion, where he lived for seven years. The American legend of Rip Van Winkle has its hero sleeping when he "awakens" to find the elves around him. The Chippewa Indians, curiously enough, personified sleep as an entity called *Weeng*, which was never observed and apparently was only as real as sleep itself; however, as Henry Rowe Schoolcraft wrote in an early study of Chippewa folklore, "*Weeng* seldom acts directly in inducing sleep but he exercises dominion over hosts of gnomelike beings, who are everywhere present, and are constantly on the alert." Evidently these beings *had* been observed. "The forms of these gnomes are believed to be those of *ininees,* little or fairy men."

By far the most impressive account of a visit to fairyland comes not from folktale hearsay but from the written testimony of responsible, educated men who were determined to preserve an accurate record of an incredible event. However one prefers to interpret her story, there is no doubting that Anne Jefferies really existed—she was born in 1626 and died about 1698. Nor is there any reason to question the sincerity of Miss Jefferies' claim that she had spent time with the fairies in their native habitat.

At the age of nineteen Anne, described as a daring girl

of high intelligence, went to work as a servant for the Moses Pitt family of Cornwall, England. In her spare time she talked constantly of the fairies, whom, she said, she wanted to meet. People who knew her thought she was crazy. It was not that they didn't believe in fairies; just that the very thought of the little people made them shudder.

Undaunted, Anne would go about after sundown, searching through the trees and wildflowers, and singing:

> Fairy fair and fairy bright
> Come and be my chosen sprite.
> Moon shines bright, waters run clear
> I am here, but where's my fairy dear?

Months went by. Then late one morning, as she sat knitting in the arbor in her employer's garden, she heard someone pushing aside the branches as if to look at her. Thinking that it was her sweetheart, she went about her work and pretended not to notice. Then she heard a suppressed laugh and another rustle among the branches.

A trifle annoyed that her sweetheart had not shown himself, she called out, "You may stay there till the cuney [moss] grows on the gate, ere I'll come to 'ee." At this a peculiar musical laughter erupted and Anne realized that the caller, whoever he might be, was not her boyfriend. Hearing the gate opening behind her, she waited apprehensively to see who it was.

It turned out to be six little men, all bright-eyed and handsome and dressed in green. The most dashing one, who wore a red feather in his cap, stepped forward, bowed, and spoke to Anne as if she were an old friend.

Greatly charmed, Anne put down her hand, expecting the little man to shake it. Instead he jumped into her palm and she lifted him into her lap. Without further ado he proceeded to fondle her breasts and kiss her lips. Anne responded happily to the little's man attentions and things went well until presently he summoned his companions, who clambered up her dress and joined in, smothering her with kisses.

Then one ran his fingers over her eyes, which suddenly felt as if they had been pricked by a pin. The next thing she knew, she had lost her sight, but before she could make any sense of this abrupt turn of events she seemed to be whirling through the air at great speed. After a while one of her companions said something that sounded like, "Tear away!" and as quickly as her sight had left her it returned.

Anne found herself in a beautiful and brilliant land that might as well have been the Garden of Eden or the psychedelic vision of a twentieth-century acidhead. Palaces of silver and gold rose above lush green forests, and everywhere flowers grew, their fragrance scenting the air, where brightly colored birds sang sweetly. Gold and silver fish swam in clear lakes. Hundreds of men and women were engaged in different kinds of activities. Some were merely strolling about; others were involved in sports. Still more were dancing.

As Anne took in all this she noticed, to her pleasant surprise, that the "little people" were no longer little, but as tall as she, and sometimes more so. She found that she was dressed in grand and sparkling clothing. Her six companions remained by her side and constantly attended her, though her continued preference for the one who had first spoken to her seemed to make the others jealous. Eventually these two sneaked away into a luxurious garden, where, hidden among the flowers, they made love. Afterward, lying with her lover amid the Eden-like splendor of the fairy world, Anne hoped that she would live like this forever.

But suddenly loud noises interrupted their revery and they spotted the five other fairies, at the head of a huge crowd, coming after them in a violent rage. Anne's lover drew his sword to defend her but he was beaten down and fell wounded at her feet. The fairy who had blinded her again put his hands over her eyes, and all went dark. She felt the same whirling sensation and heard a sound like "a thousand flies buzzing about her."

While Anne was still having her fairy vision, some friends discovered her in the arbor in "a kind of convulsive fit," Humphrey Martin, one of the group, wrote Moses Pitt's son (also named Moses Pitt) some years later. "But when we found her in this condition we brought her into the house and put her to bed, and took great care of her. As soon as she recovered out of her fit, she cried out,

'They are just gone out of the window. Do you not see them?' . . . As soon as she recovered a little strength, she constantly went to church. She took mighty delight in devotion, and in hearing the Word of God read and preached, although she herself could not read." (Hunt, *Popular Romances of the West of England*)

If this were the end of the story we could easily dismiss it as a psychotic episode and nothing more. Unfortunately things are not that simple.

For a time Anne refused to reveal anything about her adventure in fairyland, but finally she confided some of it to friends and the story spread rapidly.

The younger Moses Pitt, in a letter to Dr. Edward Fowler, Lord Bishop of Gloucester, cited in Hunt's *Popular Romances*, remembered:

People of all distempers, sicknesses, sores, and ages came not only so far off as the Land's End, but also from London, and were cured by her. She took no moneys of them, nor any reward that ever I knew or heard of, yet had she moneys at all times sufficient to supply her wants. She neither made nor bought any medicines or salves that ever I saw or heard of, yet wanted them not as she had occasion. *She forsook eating our victuals, and was fed by these fairies from that harvest time to the next Christmas day;* upon which day she came to our table and said, because it was that day, she would eat some roast beef with us, the which she did—I myself being then at the table.

The fairies constantly waited on Anne and vied for her favor. From them she attained the power to render herself invisible. Once they gave her a silver cup, which she presented to four-year-old Mary Martyn as a gift.

Resuming Pitt's account:

She gave me a piece of her [fairy] bread, which I did eat, and I think it was the most delicious bread that ever I did eat, either before or since. . . .

One John Tregeagle, Esq., who was steward to John Earl of Radnor, being a justice of peace in Cornwall, sent his warrant for Anne, and sent her to Bodmin jail, and there kept her a long time.

[Earlier the fairies had warned her that she would be apprehended.] She asked them if she should hide herself. They answered no; she should fear nothing, but go with the constable. So she went with the constable to the justice and he sent her to Bodmin jail, and ordered the prisoner-keeper that she should be kept without victuals, and she was so kept, and yet she lived, and that without complaining. But poor Anne lay in jail for a considerable time after; and also Justice Tregeagle, who was her great prosecutor, kept her in his house some time as a prisoner, and that without victuals.

When at last Anne was freed she took a job near Padstow and sometime after married William Warren. Evidently it was during this period that she and the fairies parted company, either because churchmen had convinced her that the little people were allied with the devil or because she did not consider them worth another stretch in prison. In 1693 she flatly refused to discuss the subject, for any amount of money, with Humphrey Martin.

In concluding, Pitt told Dr. Fowler:

And now, my lord, if your lordship expects that I should give you an account when, and upon what occasion, these fairies forsook our Anne, I must tell your lordship I am ignorant of that. She herself can best tell, if she would be prevailed upon to do so; and the history of it, and the rest of the passages of her life, would be very acceptable and useful to the most curious and inquisitive part of mankind.

The Anne Jefferies case forces us to confront the disquieting possibility that some hallucinations possess a paranormal foundation. To place her experience in perspective we must view it in the context of shamanism, a phenomenon which commonly occurs in societies considerably more primitive than seventeenth century England's. In shamanism a member of the tribe, seeking to enter the company of spirits, prepares himself (or herself—shamans are as often women as men) for the experience in one fashion or another until finally, perceiving some sign that the spirits will receive him, he enters a trance or ecstatic state (usually seen by onlookers as a convulsive fit). While in this condition he experiences a sensation of "magical flight" which takes him to the supernatural realm, a wonderful otherworld which may be in the sky, under the ground, or some place else. There the spirits teach him, among other things, how to use herbs and other plants in the treatment of illness.

Even so cautious an observer as the noted French anthropologist Mircea Eliade concludes (in *Myths, Dreams, and Mysteries*) that "the reality of the extrasensory capacities and paranormal powers ascribed to the shamans and medicine men [is] . . . beyond doubt." Along with instances of telepathy, clairvoyance, precognition, and psychic healing documented by hard-headed anthropologists in the field, there are even, Eliade remarks, "disc-records of the 'voices of the spirits' of the shamans; these sounds had previously been ascribed to ventriloquism, but this seems improbable, for the voices clearly came from a source far from the apparatus in front of the shaman."

The relationship Anne's story bears to modern UFO contact claims is most revealing. A number of modern-day percipients speak of a "pricking" sensation at the onset of a UFO experience. In an incident that occurred in the Florida everglades on March 13, 1965, for example, James Flynn, approaching a landed object, felt as if he suddenly had been struck just above the right eye. The "blow" rendered him unconscious for twenty-four hours. No one has thought to put him under hypnotic probing to determine if anything happened to him during this period (conscious and unconscious memories of UFO sightings sometimes conflict, as the Hill, Schirmer, and others cases have demonstrated), but the results may be interesting.

Contactees occasionally remark on the "bee-buzzing" sound at the beginning and/or conclusion of their encounters. In addition, Anne's discovery that in fairyland the fairies were as tall as she is echoed in a bizarre report from the UFO-haunted Warminster, England, area, where on one occasion an investigator claimed to have been "taken" by tiny ufonauts who grew to normal size, then reduced the ufologist, and themselves, to *their* normal height.

This all tends to suggest that UFO contacts, with their attendant "visits to other planets," arise out of the same mechanism; that is, they, too, are hallucinatory trance visions whose accompanying "objective" paranormal manifestations serve to reinforce the notion that these visions are of a real place with real inhabitants. We will take up this complex question again later in this book.

A last comment on Anne Jefferies' story: If any part of it warrants skepticism, it is her fanatical religious conversion. Because it seems oddly out of character for a young lady so passionate and irreverent to become such an ostentatious Bible beater, we can only speculate that she assumed this pose in what proved to be an unsuccessful effort to keep her out of trouble with the authorities, who tended to view communion with the fairies as tantamount to traffic with Satan himself.

Detailing another aspect of this phenomenon, Lady Gregory devotes a long chapter of her *Visions and Beliefs* to stories, told to her by peasant informants, of people wasting away in trance states while supposedly their souls wandered through the land of the fairies and the dead. A typical tale was related by one Mrs. Donnely, about an aunt of hers who one night passed three men lying by a roadside near the town of Kinvara. One of them called out to her, "Go home, my poor woman." Another added, rather more ominously, "Go home if you can." She was sure that the second voice was that of her dead brother.

And from that day she began to waste away, and was wasting for seven years, until she died. And at the last some person said to her husband, "It's time for you to ask her what way she's been spending these seven years."

So he went into the room where she was on the bed and said, "I believe it's time to ask you now what way you have been spending these seven years." And she said, "I'll tell you presently when you come in again, but leave me now for a while." And he went back into the kitchen and took his pipe for to have a smoke before he'd go back and ask her again. And the servant girl that was in the house was the first to go into the room, and found her cold and dead before her.

They [the fairies] had took her away before she had the time to tell what she had been doing all those seven years.

As this story illustrates, the Irish in many cases do not differentiate between being dead and being "taken." Lady Gregory quotes an account from a Connemara man who told how a priest, called to a dying child's bedside, had shaken his head and muttered, "*The boys* have a hand in this." He was referring, of course, to the fairies. Presumably at his death, which came not long afterward, he entered the fairy realm.

(Several years ago, according to a newspaper account, an American woman was arrested for harboring her husband's dead body. "He isn't dead," she insisted. "He's visiting the space people.")

Stories of dead friends, relatives, and sweethearts encountered in fairyland are not at all rare. One informant even told Evans-Wentz of a peasant medium, one Ketty Rourk, who "could tell all that would happen . . . Sure some spirits were coming to her. She said they were the *gentry*: that the *gentry* are everywhere; and that my drowned uncles and grandfather and other dead are among them." One young man, a Mike Farrell, spent a year deathly ill; all that time, he later averred, he was living among the "gentry." Unlike the lady mentioned several paragraphs above, he lived to tell about it. "Uncle Dan," John McCann informed Evans-Wentz, "always believed he recognized in some of the *gentry* his drowned friends." The great-great grandmother of one of the authors resided in rural Ireland until the mid-nineteenth century; there she and her family lived in terror of the "Black Fairy," whose appearance inevitably presaged a death in the family. It came, apparently, to take the dead one's soul away.

But not all fairy flights are journeys just of the soul, apparently. According to the Reverend Joseph Glanville, a butler residing near Lord Orrery's seat in Ireland, one day happened upon the fairies and joined them in a feast. Afterwards they announced that they were going to keep him. Terrified, he fled to Lord Orrery's castle, where he was given police protection and watched carefully.

In the presence of several persons, two of them bishops, late one afternoon the butler was soon "to rise from the ground, whereupon Mr. Greatrakes [a well known seventeenth-century psychic and healer] and another lusty man clapped their hands over his shoulders, one of them before and the other behind, and weighed him down with all their strength, but he was forcibly taken up from them; for a considerable time he was carried in the air to and fro over their heads, several of the company still running under him to prevent him receiving hurt if he should fall." (*Sadducismus Triumphatus*, 1668.)

John Aubrey, in *Miscellanies* (1721), writes of a predecessor of Lord Duffus who supposedly was discovered in the French king's wine cellar with a silver cup in his hand. He explained that the day before he was walking near his house in the Shire of Murray when

> he heard the noise of a whirlwind, and of voices crying *Horse and Hattock* (this is the word which the fairies are said to use when they remove from any place) whereupon he cried *Horse and Hattock* also, and was immediately caught up and transported through the air by fairies to that place where, after he had drunk heartily, he fell asleep and before he awoke the rest of the company were gone, and had left him in the posture wherein he was found. It is said the King gave him the cup which was found in his hand, and dismissed him.

A correspondent of Aubrey's interviewed Lord Duffus, who confirmed that such a cup existed and was still in the family's possession. They called it the Fairy Cup. Lord Duffus said that he himself did not believe the story or its origin, which he had heard from his grandfather.

5

So what are we to make of all this?

On the one hand we have the utter failure of scholars to explain why the fairy tradition should have survived for so many centuries, right down in fact into our own time, if it is based solely on ancient memories, hearsay, and the like—which of course it is not. Surely we are not being unreasonable in asking why so many different kinds of people have insisted that they knew of the fairies *through their own personal experiences with them;* if such claims were rare, we could comfortably dismiss them as the products of deranged minds and lying tongues. Since they are *not* rare, we are faced with some decidedly uncomfortable questions whose answers—what we understand of them—appear to run counter to everything we like to think we "know" about the nature of the universe.

It is interesting to note, as we did earlier, that folklorists have been curiously reticent to try to account for fairy *sightings*, as opposed to the old, traditional tales. Reading the literature, one gets the distinct impression that scholars have consciously chosen not to think about this question. A recent work on fairylore does touch on the issue. Its author argues that such alleged sightings come from senile old people, incapable of separating fact from fantasy, recounting memories from their long-lost youth and getting the facts twisted beyond recognition. This is simply untrue, as proven by material elsewhere in the author's own book (and also proven, as the reader has seen, in these pages).

At the same time; the twentieth-century mind is understandably reluctant to take seriously something so naive as the idea of fairies. Surely fairies are no more than the last vestments of the childhood of the race, the twentieth-century thinker says, of concern only to small children and folklorists. If there were a fairyland, wouldn't science not only know it by now but have it measured and defined? How could it exist and yet leave practically no physical traces, especially if it is so widespread as tradition indicates? And how could anything so manifestly the creation of whimsy be real?

Valid questions, and ones equally relevant to the UFO mystery. Before we attempt some answers we must wend our way through a perplexing maze of data. We turn now to the aggravating affair of the Cottingley photographs.

6

"Should the incidents here narrated, and the photographs attached, hold their own against the criticism which they will excite, it is no exaggeration to say that they will mark an epoch in human thought," Sir Arthur Conan Doyle wrote in *The Strand Magazine* for December 1920.

The photographs did hold their own, but they hardly marked an epoch in anything beyond, perhaps, the annals of the obscure and esoteric. In fact the world, unable to deal with them comfortably, chose the easiest available alternative: it simply forgot them.

Today only a tiny handful of theosophists and students of the exotic have ever heard of the Cottingley photographs. In their time, it is true, they caused some stir, especially in

England, and three small books (the last appearing in 1945) have been written on the subject. Though recently two of these books have come back into print, their impact has been nil. The principals in the case all are dead and nowadays even the hardiest Fortean iconoclasts hesitate to suggest that the matter is unresolved and worthy of further consideration. After all, *photographs of fairies?* Really, now!

Unfortunately, the Cottingley photographs suffer the added disadvantage of not "looking real"—as if we are in any position to determine such questions. But one cannot help sympathizing with Katharine Briggs' observation that, while the case for the Cottingley fairies is extremely difficult to dismiss, nonetheless "as one looks at these photographs every feeling revolts against believing them to be genuine." There is no denying that the supposed fairies resemble nothing so much as paper cutouts, and that is precisely what several modern researchers with whom we have discussed the subject suspect them to be.

However, the gap that divides the subjective impression that these "fairies" are clumsy fakes from the objective truth that so far there is not the slightest evidence that they are has remained a considerable one, despite the best efforts of two generations of skeptics to close it. So, whatever one's personal reservations may be (and we admit that we are not free of them), for the time being, at least, the Cottingley photographs will have to take their place in the case for the reality of the fairy folk.

The episode begins in the summer of 1917, when a Mrs. Griffiths arrived in England from South Africa to live with her sister and her husband while Mr. Griffiths served as a soldier in France. Mrs. Griffiths brought along her ten-year-old daughter, Frances, and the two of them moved in with the Arthur Wright family, who resided in the village of Cottingley in the Bradford district of Yorkshire. Frances and her cousin, Elsie Wright, thirteen, hit it off immediately and spent a good share of their time playing together in a beautiful wooded area behind the cottage. It was there, they told their parents, that they met and befriended the glen fairies.

The parents of course did not believe the girls; not that they thought they were lying exactly, but they were sure that the "fairies" must be part of a fantasy world the children had invented to amuse themselves as they played. But at lunch one Saturday, when Mr. Wright chanced to engage in some banter about the fairies, Elsie retorted, "Look here, Father, if you'll let me have your camera and tell me how it works I'll get a photo of the fairies. We've been playing with them this morning." Her father laughed her off and said he didn't want to waste precious film on such foolishness. But when the girls persisted he at last relented, but gave them only one plate to work with.

Afterward he went out into the garden and within the hour Elsie and Frances returned. Elsie said, "We've got the photo, I believe. Will you look?" Mr. Wright promised he would get to it that evening. When he did, several hours later, he was surprised to see several dark figures—which he took to be white swans—suddenly appear on the plate. Still not terribly interested, he put the plate aside and told his daughter that he would make a print in the morning and then they would know just what the swans looked like.

However, whatever they might have been, they most definitely were *not* swans, as the astonished Mr. Wright discovered the next day. They looked exactly like several-inch-high winged women dressed in filmy clothing. The photograph showed Frances staring into the camera lens as four of the tiny creatures danced through the air in front of her. One of them was playing what seemed to be a long reed instrument.

Wright could not believe his eyes. Though Elsie had never lied to him before, he was certain that she must be deceiving him in some way, so he, his wife, and Mrs. Griffiths questioned the girls for some while, but could not get them to retract their story. Wright even went out to the glen on his own and poked around, hoping to find scraps of paper cuttings (curiously enough, Wright's first impression of what the "fairies" might really have been was identical to that of virtually every subsequent skeptic). Unsuccessful there, he and Mrs. Wright searched the girls' bedroom when they were away but found nothing to suggest how the pictures might have been taken. A month later Elsie and Frances took a second photograph, and then Wright forbade further use of the camera. The parents were concerned at the girls' continuing insistence that all they had said about the fairies was true, so the matter was dropped after a few prints had been made and the negatives were finally put away on a shelf.

Over a year later, in November 1918, Frances wrote to a friend in Woodstock, Cape Town, South Africa, enclosing a copy of the first photograph and noting matter-of-factly on the back that "Elsie and I are very friendly with the beck fairies." The letter itself, in part, ran thus:

... all think the war will be over in a few days, we are going to get our flags to hang up in our bedroom. I am sending you two photos, both of me, one is me in a bathing costume in our back yard, Uncle Arthur took that, while the other is me with some fairies up the beck, Elsie took that one. Rosebud [a doll] is as fat as ever and I have made her some new clothes. How are Teddy and dolly?

None of this leaked out to the public, though, until two years later. One morning in May 1920 Edward L. Gardner, an occult writer and a theosophist, received a letter from a friend who sent along the two Cottingley photographs (the second shows Elsie sitting and beckoning a winged, gnomelike figure to come up on her lap), explaining that after a lecture in which he had mentioned fairies a woman from the audience had approached him and handed him the photographs. "Maybe they're true after all," she said, "but my husband and I have never been able to believe it." The woman, of course, was Mrs. Wright.

Gardner subsequently wrote that he assumed the pictures were rather unimaginative fakes the first time he viewed them—again the skeptical initial impression. He asked for the negatives, not really expecting to hear anything more, but within several days they arrived, along with a letter from Mrs. Wright. Gardner took the negatives to a photographer named Snelling, but not before checking out his qualifications. The manager of the photographic firm for which Snelling had worked for many years (recently he had set up his own private studio) stated flatly, "What Snelling doesn't know about faked photography isn't worth knowing."

Rather to Gardner's surprise, Snelling, no believer in fairies, was impressed. *Quite* impressed, in fact. After careful examination over a one-week period, in the course of which he exhausted every possible alternative explanation, he concluded, "These two negatives are entirely genuine unfaked photographs of single exposure, open-air work, show movement in all the fairy figures, and there is no trace whatever of studio work involving card or paper models, dark backgrounds, painted figures, etc. In my opinion, they are both straight, untouched pictures."

Soon after, Gardner, in the company of Conan Doyle, brought the negatives to several photographic experts from Kodak, who admitted that there was nothing in them suggestive of fakery, "but that cannot be taken as conclusive evidence of genuineness." They said someone *might* have faked them using an extremely complicated, time-consuming process. As one of them remarked, "After all, as fairies couldn't be, the photographs must have been faked somehow." Kodak's testimony, though hedging and slightly ambiguous, generally served to confirm Snelling's analysis.

Gardner's subsequent interviews with the Wright family removed his last lingering doubts about the authenticity of the pictures. He found Elsie honest, straightforward, and able to reply in a satisfactory manner to the many questions he put to her. He visited the glen where the photographs had been shot and also talked for some time with the parents, who were just now beginning to consider the possibility that the pictures might be real. The Wrights refused to accept any money for them—"If the photographs are genuine," Mr. Wright said, "then they shouldn't be soiled by being paid for"—and further insisted that neither their name nor their place of residence be mentioned in Conan Doyle's upcoming article in *The Strand*.

Before he left Cottingley, Gardner made arrangements for more fairy photographs to be taken. He went off to Scarborough to see the Griffiths family, who had remained in England after the war, interviewed Frances, and saw to it that she and her cousin would be spending the last two weeks of August together in Cottingley.

When the time came, Gardner supplied the girls with a camera, sent them on their way, and waited for the results.* For the next two weeks the weather was rainy and miserable, affording Elsie and Frances only two afternoons on which the sun shone enough to allow the proper lighting conditions for decent photographs. Consequently only three were taken. One shows a fairy leaping just inches from Frances's face; the second has a fairy poised on bush leaves, offering a posy to Elsie, and the third shows eleven fairy figures standing and walking around something resembling a sheath or cocoon suspended in the middle of the grass. The girls did not know what it was. "Fairy observers of Scotland and the New Forest, however, were familiar with it," Gardner wrote years later in his book on the Cottingley controversy, "and described it as a magnetic bath, woven very quickly by the fairies and used after dull weather, in the autumn especially. The interior seems to be magnetized in some manner that stimulates and pleases."

After *The Strand* had publicized the story, the *Daily News & Westminster Gazette* commissioned one of its reporters, a Yorkshire man, to "break the fraud." He roamed the county until he had uncovered the Wrights' real identity (Doyle in his article had called them the "Carpenters"), then zeroed in for what he thought would be the kill—only to retreat when, baffled and confused, he found no evidence of fraud or forgery anywhere. He frankly confessed in the resulting newspaper articles that he had no explana-

---

*"Often I have been asked why I didn't stay with them and see the attempt through. The answer is, unfortunately, not convincing to everybody, but those who have some knowledge of the habits of the nature sprites will admit its validity. Had I been present it is exceedingly unlikely that anything would have presented itself to be photographed. The fact is, as the girls themselves knew well, that the fairy life will not 'come out' from the shrubs and plants around unless the human visitor is of a sympathetic quality. Such a visitor needs to be not merely sympathetic in mentality, for that is of little use; he must have a warm emotional sympathy, childlike in its innocence and simplicity. The girls thought I might get used to the fairies, or rather, they to me, in a month or two, but I had my doubts whether I could cultivate the necessary quality even in that time. At any rate, it was no good attempting it then."
—Gardner, in *Fairies: The Cottingley Photographs and Their Sequel* (1945).

tion for the figures in the photographs, unless, of course, fairies exist.

In August 1921 Mr. and Mrs. Geoffrey Hodson traveled to Cottingley, where they arranged for new pictures to be taken and got Elsie and Frances together once again. This time, however, the fairies refused to be photographed. Nevertheless Hodson, a reputed clairvoyant, accompanied the girls on their forays out into the glen and afterward claimed that he and they had seen dozens of supernatural beings, including fairies, elves, gnomes, brownies, and water nymphs. Here is one excerpt from his notes, which appeared in Gardner's *Fairies: The Cottingley Photographs and Their Sequel*:

In the field we saw figures about the size of the gnome. They were making weird grimaces and grotesque contortions at the group. One in particular took great delight in knocking his knees together. These forms appeared to Elsie singly, one dissolving and another appearing in its place. I, however, saw them in a group, with one figure more prominently visible than the rest. Elsie saw also a gnome like the one in the photograph, but not so bright, and not colored. I saw a group of female figures playing a game somewhat resembling the children's game of oranges-and-lemons. They played in a ring, and the game then resembled the grand chain in the lancers. One fairy stood more or less motionless in the center of the ring while the remainder, who appeared to be decked with flowers and to show colors not normally their own, danced around her. Some next joined hands and made an archway for the others, who moved in and out as in a maze. I noticed that the result of the game appeared to be the forming of a vortex of force, which streamed upwards to a distance of about four or five feet from the ground. I also noticed that in those parts of the field where the grass was thicker and darker there appeared to be correspondingly extra activity among the fairy creatures.

On November 25, 1922, the *Cape Argus*, a South African paper, reprinted Frances's letter of November 1918 (quoted earlier), the first time the document had come to light. As the paper observed:

The plain fact surely is that, however skeptical you may be

about the existence of fairies, the production of this letter . . . is a valuable piece of evidence in support of Sir A. C. Doyle's story. And for this reason. It was not until 1920 that this photograph began to attract attention. Yet for two years before Sir Arthur had seen this photograph, a similar photograph had been lying at Woodstock, Cape Town, sent from one girl friend to another with far less comment than was displayed in writing about their several dolls! . . . Isn't the very intimate and insignificant detail of it, the very offhand manner in which a world phenomenon is dismissed in a couple of lines—isn't all this the best kind of evidence possible that, two years before Conan Doyle ever started this controversy, Frances Griffiths believed implicitly in the existence of fairies? So implicitly indeed as to dismiss them with no more surprise or emphasis than she discussed her dad, her dolls, and the war?

And so there the matter rests. All the questions it raises are still unresolved after all these years.

In retrospect it is most difficult to tell where, if anywhere, the story breaks down, and so it is not surprising that those who attempted to refute it ended up frustrated. Certainly there is nothing in the behavior of any of the principals—Elsie, Frances, and Mr. and Mrs. Wright—to encourage suspicion. If they did not fake the photographs, then no one did, since our mysterious hoaxer would have had to secure their cooperation for the stunt to work. And what was the motive? Notoriety and financial advancement, as we have seen, can be safely ruled out.

On the negative side, folklorists have argued that the supposed fairies are more the fairies of children's literature than of folk tradition. Winged fairies are a literary invention; elsewhere, i.e., in the tradition, they are very, very rare. Moreover, critics have been quick to observe, the female Cottingley fairies wear the kinds of hairdos and clothing that was fashionable in England in 1917 and 1920, when the pictures were taken.

But these may not be legitmate objections, in view of the fact that students of fairylore from Reverend Kirk on have remarked on the way fairies mimic the customs of human society around them. In their physical form (and, as we have noted, the physical forms of fairies are infinitely malleable) the Cottingley manifestations seem to have conformed to the expectations of two educated nonpeasant girls raised outside the fairy faith and aware of it only in the distorted, romanticized version contained in children's books.

Here we are approaching the crux of the entire fairy situation. Interestingly enough, one folklorist, wrestling with the Cottingley problem and unwilling to admit that it might prove the existence of fairies, finally concluded that "it seems as if the matter must wait for further evidence of the effect of the mind upon mechanical devices"—throwing the question right into the lap of psychical research. Apparently our scholarly friend is talking about "thought projections" of the Ted Serios variety. (Serios is a Chicago man whose reputed ability to project mental images onto camera film has sparked considerable controversy over the past decade. For a comprehensive examination of the affair, see Dr. Jule Eisenbud's *The World of Ted Serios*.)

Of course the question is rather more difficult than that, since Elsie and Frances (as well as, later, Geoffrey Hodson) claimed to have *seen* the fairies, too. But in any case we believe we are just beginning to find a perspective in which to place the enigma of the fairies.

7

We began this chapter with two modern reports which seem to represent fusions of the fairy and the UFO myths. Afterward we tended to treat the former as a basically archaic phenomenon, or as an occasional hallucination of small children in our own time (one could reasonably contend that these latter are dreams conjured up by exposure to fairy tales and Disney movies). At any rate, it was treated as something—outside the testimony of certifiable loonies—that no longer exists in its pure form. That is not the case, as several recent accounts show.

The first of these appears in *FSR Case Histories* for June 1972. The author, prominent English ufologist Gordon Creighton, wrote that a full report of the incidents, which allegedly took place "on a farm less than a hundred miles from London," was given to him in confidence. He promised to publish all the details as soon as he could secure permission to do so. To date this has not happened. In reply to our own inquiry, Creighton promised that he would let us know if there were any new developments, but we have yet to hear from him. So all we have for now is his summary, which follows:

1. Farm workers and villagers have reported, on several occasions, that they have observed "gnomes" in broad daylight, in the fields.
2. Two women of the village frequently "saw gnomes dancing on the kitchen table." They described the creatures as being about one third of the normal human size.
3. The owner of the local farm has frequently complained that tractors (petrol-driven) and other farm machines (all also petrol-driven) constantly break down in certain specific spots.
4. He also complains that there are areas in the fields where nothing will grow.
5. During a visit by investigators in 1966, one of the party had a nasty experience, being overcome with nausea and violent trembling. The investigator had to be carried back to the car. The same investigator was also aware of a "strong vibration" or "powerful throbbing" in the air, which caused the person's body to sway rapidly backward and forward. The "beating in the air" or "throbbing" was described as "suggestive of invisible wings."
6. Cars of visitors have also stalled mysteriously and one investigator, visiting the farm alone on his bicycle, was unaccountably caused to have a nasty skid which precipitated him into a ditch.

The area in question has been under human inhabitation since Roman times. There is a long-standing local tradition about fairies. A former vicar once tried to make a scientific investigation, but failed to achieve any progress, owing to the reticence of the villagers, who feared that the "fairies" might go away if too much prying went on.

Much of the tract of ground affected seems to be old river-bottom land, reclaimed during the last twenty to twenty-five years. There seem to have been rumors of "fairy people" associated with the site at least as far back as the time of the reclamation. This reclaimed field seems to be the center of the zone in which crops will not grow, machines break down or engines fail mysteriously, and other strange mishaps occur.

Virtually all of these phenomena have been tied to

UFOs, as readers with a ufological background will already have recognized. What makes their appearance here so fascinating, though, is that clearly they are not occurring in a UFO context. There seems to be no doubt at all that these beings are the fairies of ancient tradition. Events like this provide us with especially conclusive evidence that in a sense our modern-day ufonauts are Space Age fairies.

The next story was printed in an article by American folk singer Artie Traum in the November 1972 *Crawdaddy*, a magazine of the youth counterculture. Traum was visiting Scotland during the summer of 1972, walking along a nearly deserted peninsula in the Western Highlands, when

> . . . I thought I heard a tiny voice in my ear. . . . I wasn't sure . . . it was like a chant . . . a bunch of voices. Then what they projected into me became clear. The song got louder, I heard pipes and fiddles and the almost annoying chant of "Run, man, run." I started running through the fields, dodging the sheep, the music fresh in my ears. I suddenly felt incredibly high, my head soared, I was a bird, or a cloud, propelled by the chorus of tiny voices. At the end of the field, I entered the woods and in that dark place the voices stopped. But I kept running. Jumping over rocks and between trees, through ferns up to my waist, until I fell over, my ankle painfully caught in a hole in the ground. I was groaning, clutching at my foot, almost passing out, thinking: Christ, it's broken, I'm helpless, and the faint rush of a breath passing hot over my head. I stopped moaning and looked around. There was crackling in the ferns, great motion. God, I'll be devoured, I thought, and in the panic pulled my leg out of the hole. Slowly limping down the hill, pulling my throbbing leg along with me, but afraid to step. I had no sense of direction, but I kept moving. Then I was sinking ankle-deep in bog. My hands full of smelly mud and aware that my head was swarming with voices, thousands of words making no sense. I knew that my mistake was going into the forest, so I made my way uphill to where I thought the meadow was, longing to hear the chanting, soothing chaos of open air. . . .

In a letter to Jerome Clark, Traum wrote that he was at a loss to explain the incident. Note its resemblance to Dr. Thomas Wood's Dartmoor experience fifty years earlier.

The following is taken from a nature column by Austin Hatton in London's *Sunday Telegraph* for April 28, 1974:

I do not believe in fairies. I do not believe in ghosts. But for once I feel that the supernatural has set a trap for me. In a way I hope that it has: then I can stop worrying about something that seems to have no real explanation.

My pilgrim's walk took me across land that at one time felt the shuffling feet of those struggling from the Isle of Ely to the revered acres of Little Walsingham. A thirty-yard stretch of bare sandy soil had, by the searing winds, been given all the consistency of concrete. About ten feet wide, this patch was as smooth as a motorway, and except for one weird feature, was barren. In the center, perfectly formed and dried hard, was the print of a bare foot.

Nowhere else on this dried ground could I find any other mark. Not a single explanatory indentation. The stretch of ground was too wide for anybody, especially with such a small foot, to have jumped across it, using only one foot to mark the soil when it was soft, in one gigantic leap.

Finally, we mention in passing recent reports—unfortunately too fragmented and incomplete for us to deal seriously with them here—about certain weird events at Findhorn, a Scottish community where artists and hippie types have taken up residence alongside the native rustics. As we understand it, the effort apparently is to revive traditional crafts and culture, including the ancient mystical reverence for nature. So far the experiment has been successful, though now that the word is getting out it is perhaps fated to become a counterculture mecca, which should destroy it in short order. Anyway, according to William Irwin Thompson, who mentions it briefly, and with no obvious facetious intent, in his *Passages About Earth*, the residents of Findhorn scarcely bat an eyelash when they happen upon a wood elf, an angel, or a similarly unlikely manifestation while strolling through the forest.

To all appearances these people are not speaking metaphorically, but then of course one never knows. Whatever the case, the growing "back to the land" movement, expressive of a deeply rooted pastoral longing which rejects the premise that science and reason alone can save our souls, may well bring back the age-old inhabitants of field and stream. As folklorist Robert Hunt wrote of an informant a century ago, "Bard Lechog, who always had faith in the fairies, believed that they will come again to be seen of men and women. For he thought they had their periods...."

VOICES FROM HEAVEN: THE RELIGIOUS IMPULSE

> Even more striking was their capacity for seeing apparitions in the sky of a kind denied to us—galloping horses, dragons, or armies in battle. These counterparts of our flying saucers might assume bizarre forms: for example, the vision seen by two country women shortly before sunset on April 16, 1651, of a battle in the sky, followed by angels of "a bluish color and about the bigness of a capon, having faces (as they thought) like owls." But usually they illustrate that in hallucination, no less than in ordinary vision, human perception is governed by stereotypes inherited from the particular society in which men live.
> —Keith Thomas, in *Religion and the Decline of Magic*

1

On a number of occasions as I (Jerome Clark) was growing up, in two small towns in southwestern Minnesota, I heard first- and second-hand accounts of angelic visitations. I remember practically nothing about them now but I do recall the impressions they made on me. At first, as a deeply religious and thoroughly impressionable little boy awaiting the imminent Second Coming, I took the stories literally and saw them as proof of God's intimate concern with the doings of us mortals.

By the time I got to high school, however, I had shed my early Christian faith and went about, in the fashion of any new convert, proudly proclaiming my atheism, much to the scandalization of those who had never before seen one in the flesh, and daring all comers to engage me in debate.

Consequently I spent a good share of my postadolescent

energy in long, fruitless arguments with local fundamentalists, some of whom had taken it upon themselves to save my soul from Satan's clutches. It was then that I began hearing once again about angelic visitations, about how so-and-so had seen one by somebody's deathbed, or how one had saved X's life, or whatever. I dismissed these tales out of hand, of course, even though I did not dispute the possibility of paranormal events—at least secular ones. Since a considerable number of these bore all the marks of unverifiable rumors and folk tales, my skepticism was not always unwarranted.

But other cases—which I finally dealt with, in the grand tradition of skeptics anywhere, by not thinking about—troubled me (needless to say, I never openly admitted this to anybody). Certain of the stories came from individuals whose critical faculties in religious matters might not have been the most acute—so I felt—but who otherwise seemed level-headed enough. They spoke with evident sincerity and often with high intelligence, and they named others who had been present when the supposed incidents had taken place.

None of this made any sense to me until years later when a close friend, under the influence of a powerful (and quite illegal) psychedelic drug, had his own "vision of heaven." The experience was a profound one, the more so for being so totally unexpected; like me, my friend had been raised a Christian but had not considered himself one for years. He had rather assumed that his chemically ignited imagination would have propelled him somewhere other than to the heaven of his Sunday-school days, complete with shining saints and singing angels. But as his psyche reeled from the shock of a strange new stimulus (LSD), is garbed itself in familiar symbols in order to keep the conscious part of his mind from disintegrating under the rapid influx of exotic material which he would not have been able to assimilate in any other form.

In their *The Varieties of Psychedelic Experience* Masters and Houston report that of 206 LSD subjects they observed, ninety-six percent had "seen" religious images, including Christ, saints, angels, and demons. They comment, "Of the four percent of the subjects who did not report any religious imagery at all, these persons were, with two exceptions, completely imageless or imagined only geometric forms. This would seem to indicate that if a subject is able to imagine at all, then some kind of 'religious' imagery is almost certain to occur as a part of the total eidetic image content."

Subsequent research done at the Maryland Psychiatric Research Center in Catonsville, where dying patients were given doses of LSD, substantiates the accuracy of this observation. A typical subject related that he "came up to the beautiful and the wonderful . . . passing among billions and millions of minute spirits like myself," until he found Jesus, with whom he merged into a single identity.

The point is that even in this supposedly post-Christian period of history the archetypal images which Christianity bequeathed us are very much a part of our psychic life. No doubt they will be with us for a long time to come. Confronted with the incomprehensible (whether it manifests itself in the psychedelic experience or the paranormal experience), the psyche invariably will speak to us in a language we know, even if we ourselves, as individuals, no longer speak that language.

In what follows we have chosen to confine ourselves to "miraculous" events which occurred in a Christian frame of reference. Certainly "miracles" take place in other religious contexts, but because this is not a book about all the varieties of paranormal religious experience (a subject to which many lengthy volumes could be devoted), for very practical reasons we must confine ourselves to the sole example of Christianity. For our purposes it should suffice.

2

Gustav Davidson is not the sort of credulous eccentric one might take the compiler of something called *A Dictionary of Angels* to be. To the contrary, the introduction to this book (published in 1967) shows him to be an eminently rational and good-humored scholar with a taste for the exotic. So these words of his are rather surprising:

At this stage of the quest I was literally bedeviled by angels. They stalked and leaguered me, by night and day. I could not tell the evil from the good, demons from daevas, satans from seraphim. . . . I moved, indeed, in a twilight zone of tall presences, through enchanted forests lit with the sinister splendor of fallen divinities. . . . I remember one occasion—it was winter and getting dark—returning home from a neighboring farm. I had cut across an unfamiliar field. Suddenly a nightmarish shape loomed up in front of me, barring my progress. After a paralyzing moment I managed to fight my way past the phantom. The next morning I could not be sure . . . whether I had encountered a ghost, an angel, a demon, or God. There were other such moments and other such encounters, when I passed from terror to trance, from intimations of realms unguessed at to the uneasy conviction that, beyond the reach of our senses, beyond the arch of all our experience, sacred and profane, there was only—to use an expression of Paul's in I Timothy 4—"fable and endless genealogy."

Deeply troubled by these "impossible" visions, Davidson finally arrived at a conclusion he could live with:

A professed belief in angels would, inevitably, involve me in a belief in the supernatural, and that was the golden snare I did not wish to be caught in. Without committing myself religiously I could conceive of the possibility of there being, in dimensions and worlds other than our own, powers and intelligences outside our present apprehension, and in this sense angels are not to be ruled out as a part of reality—always remembering that *we create what we believe.* Indeed, I am prepared to say that if enough of us believe in angels, then angels exist.

In 1884 a book comparable to Davidson's, the Reverend E. Cobham Brewer's *A Dictionary of Miracles,* appeared. An exhaustive summary that ranges from biblical times to the late nineteenth century, much of it is so thoroughly unbelievable that at times one can read it as an irrefutable argument for the collective insanity of the human race. But parts of it are oddly disconcerting, echoing events in our own day, and it is these which attract our attention.

For example, there is this angelic vision of St. Francisca's (1384–1440), recorded in the *Acts of Her Canonization* (1606):

She says he was of incredible beauty, his countenance being whiter than snow and redder than the blush rose; his eyes were always uplifted towards heaven; his long curly hair was in color like burnished gold; his robe, which extended to the ground, was sometimes white, sometimes blue, and at other times a shining red. From his face proceeded a radiance so luminous, she could see to read her matins thereby even at midnight.

According to Bede's *Church History* and other sources, St. Cuthbert, a seventh-century figure, sometimes entertained angels unawares. Brewer writes:

Eatas, abbot of Mailros, being called to govern the new abbey of Rippon, took Cuthbert with him, and committed to him the very difficult task of entertaining strangers. Once at least, in the execution of this office, St. Cuthbert had the honor of entertaining an angel, who, in return of his hospitality, left on the table three loaves of bread, of such exquisite whiteness and taste, there could be no doubt of their being "bread from heaven."

The reader will recall Moses Pitt's comments on Anne Jefferies' "fairy bread": "the most delicious that ever I did eat."

St. Hildegardes (1098–1179), who wrote many volumes allegedly dictated to her by the Holy Ghost, told papal investigators:

From infancy to the present day, being now seventy years old, I have received without cessation visions and divine revelations. In these divine communications I seem to be carried through the air to regions far, far away, and I see in my mind's eye the marvels shown to me. I do not see them with my bodily eye, nor hear what is said by my bodily ears, nor do I discover them by the agency of any of my bodily senses, nor do they come into my thoughts, nor are they dreams, or trances, or ecstasies; but I see them with my eyes open, while I am wide awake, sometimes in the night, and sometimes by day. What I see, I see in my soul; and what I hear, I hear in my inner self.

In *Confessions of St. Patrick* (373–464) we read of a

vision oddly like another destined to occur almost fifteen hundred years later:

> One night I saw before me a celestial visitant, holding a book in his hand. He said to me, "I am Victricius"; and he gave me the book, which was, in fact, a collection of letters. On the first page I read these words, "A voice from Ireland." As I read on, methought I heard the woodmen of Foclutum addressing me, and saying, "We beseech you, O man of God, come back to us, and teach us about the Savior." I was moved to tears by this appeal, and the vision ceased. Next night I heard celestial voices singing the songs of heaven, but saw no one, nor can I at all tell where the voices came from. I fell to prayer, and heard a voice whisper in my ear, "I am He who gave My life to redeem thine." I felt as if someone had entered into me, and knew it was the Holy Ghost. Next day I told the vision to a friend, and he replied, "One day you will be bishop of Ireland." This remark threw me into a consternation, miserable sinner that I was; nevertheless, it came to pass.

Centuries later a young French girl would receive another call from heaven, but her own divinely ordained mission would end less happily. Joan of Arc (Jeanne d'Arc), who was born on January 6, 1412, at Domremy, spent her first thirteen years as a devout, unassuming country girl. When she was not helping her mother with the domestic chores she played with her friends out in the woods, where a colony of fairies reputedly dwelled (a fact, as it turned out, of considerable significance; in 1431, when ecclesiastical authorities had her burned at the stake, one of their trumped-up charges was that she had trafficked with the fairies, i.e., the devil).

But at the age of thirteen Joan was called into history. One day a "luminous cloud" appeared before her and a voice told her, "Jeanne, you are destined to lead a different kind of life and to accomplish miraculous things, for you are she who has been chosen by the King of Heaven to restore the Kingdom of France, and to aid and protect King Charles, who has been driven from his domains. You shall put on masculine clothes; you shall bear arms and become the head of the army; all things shall be guided by your counsel." At that, cloud and voice vanished.

The manifestations would remain with Joan for the rest of her life. Years later, at her trial, she would testify, "I seldom hear the voice without seeing a light. That light always appears on the side from which I hear the voice." At first she was frightened and doubtful, suspecting that the devil was playing a trick on her; before long, however, her visitor, who soon became visible to her, convinced her that he was the archangel St. Michael. He usually arrived in the company of two others, St. Margaret and St. Catherine, in a "cloud of heavenly light." Joan claimed also to have seen hundreds of other angels over the years, including Gabriel, but these three were her most frequent contacts. She always refused to describe the beings in detail; all we know is that they wore crowns and exuded a pleasant odor, and that at least St. Michael had wings.

Joan's subsequent history is amply documented in scores of books, so we will not rehash it here. Suffice it to say that over a period of a year or so (1429–30) she led the French to a series of brilliant victories over the invading English. She seemed to possess the extrasensory powers of clairvoyance and precognition, which made her an even more formidable figure in the eyes of her enemies. In May 1430 she was captured, as her voices had prophesied, and turned over to the English. Charles VII, for whom she had fought so bravely, expressed his gratitude by indifferently leaving her to her fate.

Even in prison the angels visited her, as often as three times a day. On March 1, 1431, repeating one of their messages, she announced that within seven years the English would lose "a bigger prize than Orleans." Six years and eight months later, on November 12, 1437, Paris fell out of English hands.

Joan never lived to see her prophecy fulfilled. On May 30, 1431, she died at the stake. Accounts differ as to whether at the end she complained that her voices had betrayed her. At any rate, her clerical rehabilitation began twenty-four years afterward and culminated finally in 1909 with Pope Pius X's declaring her a saint.

For well over five centuries the matter of Joan's "voices" has provoked controversy among historians. Attempts to depict her as mentally deranged have failed, and to this day no convincing, "rational" explanation has emerged.

The issue is best summed up by V. Sackville-West (who, we should note, identifies herself as a skeptic in religious matters) in her biography *Saint Joan of Arc*:

> She makes us think, and she makes us question; she uncovers the dark places into which we may fear to look. We read, and, having read, are left with the essential queries: Does God on occasion manifest Himself by direct methods? Is the visible world the only world we have to consider? Is it possible for mortal man to get into touch with beings of another world? Is it possible that unearthly guidance may be vouchsafed to assist our human fallibility? . . . It is best to admit straight away that we can give no satisfactory answer to the general question.

Nor can we easily explain just what happened to one Joseph Smith of Palmyra, New York, between 1820 and '29. Like St. Patrick before him, Smith reportedly received a book from an angel; like St. Joan, he died a martyr's death.

His first uncanny experience took place when he was fourteen years old. Suffering from various religious uncertainties, he had retired into the woods to pray. While doing so he suddenly found himself paralyzed and unable to speak. He watched, terrified, as a brilliant pillar of light descended toward him; when it touched his head he abruptly lost his fear. Two glowing figures hovering slightly above the ground in front of him spoke gently and a long conversation ensued. Smith asked them which of the contending Protestant sects he should join. "None," they replied. "One is as worthless as the other."

Afterward the boy "came to himself" and discovered that he was lying on his back, looking up toward the stars.

Three years went by before Smith received another visitation. On the night of September 21, 1823, as he lay in bed, praying fervently, a light appeared in his room. Its glow increased until the room was as bright as it would have been at noon. In its midst Smith saw a figure standing in the air by his bedside. According to Thomas O'Dea's *The Mormons,* Smith testified:

> He had on a loose robe of most exquisite whiteness. It was a whiteness beyond anything earthly I had ever seen; nor do

I believe that any earthly thing could be made to appear so exceedingly white and brilliant. His hands were naked, and his arms also, a little above the wrists; so, also, were his feet naked, as were his legs, a little above the ankles. His head and neck were also bare. I could discover that he had no other clothing on but this robe, as it was open, so that I could see into his bosom.

Not only was his robe exceedingly white, but his whole person was glorious beyond description, and his countenance truly like lightning. The room was exceedingly light, but not so very bright as immediately around his person. When I first looked upon him, I was afraid; but the fear soon left me.

The entity identified itself as Moroni, a messenger from God, who wanted Smith to know he had a great mission to fulfill—one that would make him both loved and hated all over the world. Smith was to uncover a book, written on gold plates, which lay buried somewhere nearby. This book, a history of the ancient inhabitants of America, explained how Jesus had appeared here to establish a new Gospel. He would translate the work with the "Urim" and "Thummin," two stones attached to a breastplate buried with the book. Moroni said that the seers of olden times had used this device.

(The words *Urim* and *Thummin* mean "light and perfection." In the Old Testament—see Exodus 28—the high priest would consult the transparent stones, which he bore on his breastplate, when the king wanted the answer to some question of great national importance. We do not know precisely how the divination was accomplished.)

As the angel continued talking, warning Smith that if he showed the plates to anyone without specific permission he would be killed, the young man saw a vision which revealed the location of the plates. Then the light started to recede until only Moroni still shone. At this point Smith saw a "conduit open right up into heaven," into which the apparition rapidly ascended. The room was dark once more.

But only momentarily. The light returned and, amazingly, *the entire scene was repeated*—Moroni even used the same words he had spoken before. But at the end he added some dire prophecies about the impending end of the world. Then, much to Smith's understandable astonishment, it happened a third time, except that at the conclusion Moroni cautioned him not to sell the plates to enrich himself.

By now it was daylight. Smith rolled out of bed and set about his daily tasks. But he was so exhausted that his father told him to go home and get some rest. On the way, as he tried to cross a fence, he passed out and landed unconscious on the ground—only to experience Moroni's visitation for the fourth time. This time the angel's only unfamiliar words directed him to inform his father of his visions.

His father, agreeing that his son had had a genuine message from heaven, urged Joseph to go dig up the plates. Young Smith found them resting under a large stone on a hill near Manchester, New York, but when he attempted to remove them Moroni materialized to inform him that they would not be available for four more years, but that he should come to the spot on that date (September 22) each year until then and Moroni would meet with him.

Finally, in 1827, the angel handed over the plates and the magic stones, which Smith would wear like spectacles while he translated the document. Apparently word of Smith's dealings had gotten around, because, as he would write, "The most strenuous exertions were used to get [the gold plates] from me. The persecution became more bitter and severe than before, and multitudes were on the alert continually to get them from me if possible. But by the wisdom of God, they remained safe in my hands, until I had accomplished by them what was required at my hand." He returned them to Moroni after he had completed the translation.

Smith, who was virtually illiterate, dictated the translation to one Oliver Cowdery, who wrote down the words. Cowdery and two other men subsequently swore out a statement which declared, in part, "that an angel of God came down from heaven, and he brought and laid before our eyes, that we beheld and saw the plates, and the engravings thereon; and we know that it is by the grace of God the Father, and our Lord Jesus Christ, that we beheld and bear record that these things are true." Eight others, three of them members of the Smith family, swore that they had seen and handled the plates. One of them,

Hyrum Smith, would be martyred with his brother just a few years later.

Whatever the truth about Smith's vision and the gold plates, there is no question that the resulting *Book of Mormon*, based on the prophet's translation, is a remarkable document probably quite beyond the inventive powers of the poorly educated young man. Some nineteenth-century critics tried to prove that the document is really a reworking of a romance by Solomon Spaulding, but modern scholars discount this theory. Moreover, Smith's sincerity is evidenced in his refusal to recant his beliefs even in the face of the kind of savage persecution that finally ended in his death at the hands of a lynch mob in Carthage, Illinois, on June 27, 1844.

At the time of Smith's demise the Church of Jesus Christ of the Latter-day Saints had attracted forty thousand members. Today there are three million Mormons worldwide.

Smith and his followers were far from being the only sect of the period to claim angelic contacts. For instance, the Shakers, a now virtually extinct group whose disavowal of sexual intercourse made its survival beyond the first generation of converts a rather difficult proposition, recorded scores of visitations during the late 1830s and 1840s. Most occurred in trance states and involved only a single percipient, but sometimes a number of persons "saw" the visions collectively.

In one such case, on October 6, 1842, twenty-year-old Emily Babcock emerged from a meetinghouse after Sabbath worship to hear a trumpet blast. Looking up, she "beheld an Angel standing on the top of the center building holding in his right hand a trumpet and in his left a roll or book." Eight others testified in a signed statement that they, too, had seen the celestial visitor.

Often Shakers reported receiving angels who brought presents of clothing, jewelry, and food. The recipients would wear spectacles which supposedly enabled them to see these exchanges more clearly. But baffled onlookers frequently complained that these "spectacles" were as invisible as the angels and the gifts. Toward the end, after most of the excitement had died down, several Shaker mediums transcribed many thick volumes of communications from angels, saints, and Old Testament patriarchs.

All of which leads us to suspect that Smith's gold plates, along with their Urim and Thummin, were as incorporeal as Moroni himself. In all probability the other "witnesses" were telepathically tuned in to Smith's visions and with him they imagined *The Book of Mormon* to be an independent document rather than the purely psychic product of the still not very well understood mechanisms of "automatic writing." It seems likely that Smith, like mediums, shamans, and other visionaries, dictated *The Book* while in a trance state. That does not explain where its contents came from, needless to say. The possible answer to that and many related questions will have to wait until the last chapter.

3

The Roman Catholic Church holds it as an article of faith that the Virgin Mary has returned to earth on a number of occasions, mostly, it would appear, to converse with innocent young peasant children. The number of reported appearances exceeds by some considerable margin those that the Church is willing to accept as valid, and even those comparative few it does embrace meet with virtually total disbelief outside the confines of the faithful.

Yet, like it or not, they happen, and uncomfortably we observe as some of the wildest episodes from Catholic folklore are reenacted in our own enlightened age. At Fatima, Portugal, in 1917 three children playing near a stream saw a flash of light; immediately following, a woman in a dress "as white as snow" with a golden halo around her head materialized in a globe of fire, delivered a message, and vanished. On June 13, July 13, and September 13 the children saw her again. On the last date a fair-sized crowd had gathered; but the Lady was visible only to the children. Some of the others, however, viewed an "airplane of light" which dropped strange flakes. These flakes dissolved when touched.

The next month, as a mass gathering of the devout and the doubting stood watching, the "sun"—actually, according to accounts, some kind of disc-shaped object—came through the clouds and proceeded to "dance," changing color from yellow to green to blue and finally to deep blood-red before falling to earth, amid rising temperatures. *Not everyone saw this happen*, and once again only the children could see the Lady, who as usual gave them messages.

This amazing tale, whose relationship to the UFO enigma (including even the ghostly "angel hair," here described as "flakes") is obvious, is ably dealt with in Jacques Vallee's *Anatomy of a Phenomenon* and Paul Thomas's *Flying Saucers Through the Ages*, both of which we recommend to readers interested in a fuller account of this by now classic quasi-UFO incident.

The "dancing sun" motif exists in other Christian tales, such as one cited by Otto F. Swire in *The Outer Hebrides and Their Legends* in which the event occurs on Easter morning as a celebration of the Resurrection. From the peak of Ben More, as at Fatima, the "sun" changes color from green to purple to "deep blood-red" to intense white and finally to white-gold "like the Glory of God Himself." Also, Father Joseph A. Pelletier asserts, "Pope Pius XII saw the miracle of Fatima, the dancing sun, four times in the Vatican gardens thirty years after the original event took place in Portugal."

An illuminating essay by Peter Rogerson (*Merseyside UFO Bulletin*, Vol. 4, No. 2) relates this and attendant Virgin manifestations to pre-Christian myths of the "sun maiden" who figures originally in Eastern solar-oriented religions; she later appears as a fairy woman and then as the Mother of Christ, the "son of the Sun." Rogerson explains that she "can seduce men, and take them to the unknown country, or . . . impart to them messages of great import."

The famous miracle at Lourdes, France, seems to substantiate his contention that these alleged occurrences partake of elements out of pagan belief. In this instance we find unmistakable allusions to the Naiad (or Nereid)/Elf-woman tradition, which survives as an imperfect folk memory of a prehistoric nature religion (see, for example, Lawson's already-cited *Modern Greek Folklore and Ancient Greek Religion*).

We are told that on February 11, 1858, three girls on a stick-gathering expedition came to the banks of the river.

Two of them crossed it, but fourteen-year-old Bernadetta Soubirous, described as a "sickly child," at first stayed behind, fearing the cold, but after a while decided to follow her companions. Sitting by the riverside, she removed one shoe. Suddenly a gust of wind caused her to look up, a little puzzled because otherwise it was an absolutely calm day. She proceeded to untie the other shoe and again the wind abruptly blew.

Convinced that something strange was afoot, she glanced around her until her eye caught a brilliantly luminous light in a cave not far away. (Lourdes is surrounded by the Hautes Pyrenees.) Inside the cave stood the apparition of a beautiful young woman dressed in a dazzling white robe. Recognizing her as the Virgin, Bernadetta fell to her knees and tried to make the sign of the cross but discovered that she was paralyzed. The Lady signed herself with a golden cross, and this action seemed to free Bernadetta from her state of immobility. The vision beckoned to the girl, who was too frightened to come forward. At this juncture the Lady vanished.

Subsequent appearances attracted thousands of people to the spot, where they watched the child, apparently in a sort of trance state, converse with the Virgin, who remained invisible to everyone else. Under the Lady's direction Bernadetta cut a small hole in the ground near the cave. From it flowed a stream of water with reported miraculous healing powers. Since then vast numbers of sick persons have made pilgrimages to Lourdes to bathe in these waters, which do seem genuinely to possess unexplained curative qualities. In 1862 a four-year ecclesiastical investigation concluded that Bernadetta's visitor was in fact, as she claimed, "the Immaculate Conception," the Virgin Mary, who could be worshipped as the *Notre-Dames de Lourdes*.

Returning to the essentials of the story, we note these significant elements: 1.) *The mysterious gusts of wind,* so strongly reminiscent of the "fairy wind"; 2.) *the beautiful young woman in the cave by the river*—fairy women traditionally live in caves and are usually seen by streams; 3.) *the percipient's paralysis,* which some rural folk would call being "fairy-stricken"; 4.) *her trance state,* in which, as we have seen, most significant fairy encounters take place; 5.) *the miraculous healing water*—Anne Jefferies was only one individual of many who brought curative powers back from fairyland.

The major difference lies in the matter of the varying temperaments attributed to these feminine manifestations. Nereids and the assorted other "wild women" of European tradition were generally credited with scandalous behavior (uninhibited sexuality) at best and malicious conduct (murder) at worst. Most likely this was the case because the Nereids personified longstanding pagan beliefs which the Church struggled vigorously to suppress; nonetheless their image—and the rudiments of paganism—survived in the folk imagination. Eventually Christianity's influence forced the peasantry to connect them with the forces of evil. And so evil forces they became. We will try to explain how this may happen—how these kinds of phenomena can exist both subjectively and objectively—toward the conclusion of this book.

As a devout Catholic, Bernadetta, on the other hand, immediately assumed the woman of the vision to be the Virgin. Without having had to think consciously about the matter, she believed implicitly that a beautiful lady encountered in nature under miraculous circumstances could be none other than the Virgin herself. So the vision took on that identity; at the same time, as but one incarnation of an archetype thousands of years in the making, it could not divest itself of elements suggestive of its ancient lineage, i.e., the wind, the cave, the trance, etc. Thus Bernadetta's vision is saying, in effect, "This is only one face of many I have worn, and though I change, yet I remain the same."

Over a century and a half earlier, during the reign of Louis XIV, the apparition wore another face. Rogerson cites this weird incident involving a man named Marechal Ferraut, who spotted a strange light while riding home one evening through a dark forest in Provence. Rogerson quotes Elliott O'Donnell's *Family Ghosts*:

Between this tree [a blasted oak] and a sapling, the intervening space consisting of about a dozen yards, stood a tall figure absolutely still and apparently inanimate. It seemed at first to be shaped out of a transparent cloud. . . . However, rapidly becoming more and more substantial, it soon developed into a very beautiful woman. She was dressed in white, the most splendid jewels glittered on her arms and breast, and something like a tiara upon her lovely golden hair. . . .

Ferraut's glowing cloud reminds us of Joan of Arc's angelic visitants, who stepped out of a "luminous cloud"; furthermore, like Ferraut's, they appeared in the forest. In common with Bernadetta Soubirous and others, Ferraut was gripped with paralysis.

This time, however, the mysterious woman identified herself not as a saint but as a spirit of the king's late wife. She commanded Ferraut to deliver a message to the king, underscoring her words with terrible threats about what would happen to him if he disobeyed her. But Ferraut, who was more frightened of the king, had to meet her twice more before he carried out the mission.

What the message contained we don't know, since the king is said to have paid his informant a substantial sum to insure his silence. All we do know is that part of it concerned an apparition the king himself had seen in the same forest thirty years previous.

In a Maine coast village near Machiasport an even more bizarre incident took place. Late in August 1799 sea captain Paul Blaisdel heard a strange voice, and in January 1800 a beautiful woman dressed in white, floating just above the ground in front of the flabbergasted sailor, identified herself as Mrs. George Butler, and summoned her "father" and "husband" to the scene to prove the point. She had come, she said, to effect the marriage of George Butler to the captain's daughter Lydia. The two eventually were wed.

But in the meantime a whole series of incredible events shook Captain Blaisdel's house. The apparition herded large numbers of people (as many as two hundred in one instance) into the cellar, where it harangued them with sermons and prophecies (all of which proved accurate), speaking in a "shrill but mild and pleasant" voice. It would arrive as a shapeless mass of light, then grow into the figure of a woman and pass among the spectators, talking incessantly. When it was finished, it would resume its original shapelessness, "expand everywhere," and vanish instantly.

This story has been preserved in a rare old book published in 1859. The Reverend Abraham Cummings, author of *Immortality Proved by the Testimony of Sense,* was initially a skeptic. Then he went to the Blaisdel residence to investigate for himself. William Oliver Stevens, recounting Cummings' experience, writes in *Unbidden Guests*:

> About twelve rods ahead of him there was a slight knoll or rise in the ground and he could see a group of white rocks on the slope, showing dimly against the dark turf. . . . Two or three minutes later he looked up. . . . One of those two white rocks had risen off the ground, and had now taken the shape of a globe of light with a rosy tinge. As he went toward it he kept his eye on it for fear it might disappear, but he had not gone more than five paces when the glowing mass flashed right to where he was [and] resolved itself into the shape and dress of a woman, but small, the size of a child of seven. He thought: "You are not tall enough for the woman who has been appearing among us." Immediately the figure expanded to normal size . . . and now she appeared glorious, with rays of light shining from her head all about, and reaching to the ground.

The 1960s produced two major manifestations of the Virgin. The first, in the Cantabrian mountains of northwestern Spain, involved four young girls—three of them age twelve, the other, eleven—from the village of Garabandal. At 8:30 P.M. on June 18, 1961, a "brilliant angel" appeared in the wake of a mysterious clap of thunder. The first to see it was Conchita (Maria Concepcion) Gonzalez; the others observed it almost immediately afterward. After eight more appearances in June, the angel finally spoke on July 1. "Do you know why I have come?" he is supposed to have said. "It is to announce to you that tomorrow, Sunday, the Virgin Mary will appear to you as Our Lady of Mount Carmel."

The next day, as predicted, the Virgin and the angel came to the children. (The angel made occasional, infrequent appearances after that.) The girls told them about their everyday life and the two heavenly visitors laughed at some of the childish remarks. In later visits Mary let the children kiss her and even hold the infant Jesus, whom she sometimes brought with her.

Her messages were mostly of a religious nature, and not terribly interesting to the rest of us. As a general rule they were complaints about the growing indifference to the Church. Later, as pilgrims flocked to Garabandal, through the children she offered private words of encouragement to the troubled and afflicted. (As usual, only the children could see the Virgin.) Finally, according to Conchita's diary, as it is recorded in Father Pelletier's *Our Lady Comes to Garabandal*:

> The Blessed Virgin advised me of a great miracle, saying that God, Our Lord, would perform it through her intercession. Just as the chastisement will be very, very great, in keeping with our deserts, so too, the miracle will be extremely great, in keeping with the needs of the world.
>
> The Blessed Virgin has told me the date of the miracle and what it will consist of. I am supposed to announce it eight days in advance, so that people will come. The Pope will see it from wherever he is, and Padre Pio also. The sick who are present at the miracle will be cured and the sinners will be converted.
>
> There will be no doubt in the mind of anyone who sees this great miracle which God, Our Lord, will perform through the intercession of the Blessed Virgin. And now as we await this great day of the miracle, let us see if the world changes and the chastisement is averted.

Father Pelletier states that Padre Pio, the famous stigmatist, saw a preview of the miracle before his death. So did Father Luis Andreu, S. J. (who also had a vision of the Virgin), six hours before he died on August 8, 1961. Two years later God himself is supposed to have told Conchita that the miracle would "convert the whole world." The Lady added on January 1, 1965, that a "divine warning" would precede the great miracle.

Apparently the children received much or all of this in ecstatic or trance states, in common with saints and shamans everywhere and at all times. They also gave evidence of telepathic abilities in seeming to know the innermost thoughts of strangers who had come to watch or worship.

From Father Pelletier's account:

A miracle to confirm the apparitions was requested by the girls early in the apparitions. One was given to them, one that Conchita called a "little miracle," *un milagrucu*, using a diminutive proper to the Santander region. A visible host appeared suddenly and mysteriously on Conchita's tongue at 1:40 in the morning on July 19, 1962. This precise miracle was announced fifteen days in advance by Conchita at the bidding of the archangel Saint Michael, who gave her the Communion. Many people were on hand for the event and one man, who was standing inches from Conchita, took some pictures of it.

Another "miracle" brings us back to flying discs and dancing suns. London's *Sunday Express* for June 4, 1972, reported that forty British men and women visiting Garabandal had seen a bizarre sight in the sky. One of them, Marina Foley, said, "The sun looked like a flat, white disc and it was spinning in a clockwise direction and pulsating to and fro."

"We found we could stare at the sun without sunglasses," Gwendoline Hurndall said. "The outline of a cross had been seen and I just saw a part of it before it vanished. Then the sun began to spin like a Catherine-wheel, first one way and then the other. Then it started to jump like a yoyo for a few minutes before going back to its spinning again."

The witnesses also saw the sun go through a series of startling color changes.

The Virgin appeared for the last time on November 13, 1965. After kissing a number of religious objects which believers had handed to Conchita for that purpose, the Lady said, "I have come for all my children, so that I may draw them closer to my heart. . . . Talk to me about my children. I hold them all beneath my mantle. . . . I shall always be with you and with all my children." Then she was gone.

4

The most impressive visitation in history began on the night of April 2–3, 1968, in Zeitoun, a northern suburb of Cairo, Egypt. Two auto mechanics working in a garage across the street from the Church of St. Mary saw what they first took to be the figure of a white-robed nun standing on the top of the large dome at the center of the roof. Because the figure was holding on to the stone cross atop the dome, they thought that it might be someone about to jump. One of the men quickly summoned the priest while the other called for the police emergency squad.

As everyone found out soon enough, the Virgin Mary had come back to Egypt. During the next year she—and other equally weird manifestations—were seen by hundreds of thousands of people. Some of the many witnesses, who included Catholics, Protestants, Moslems, and atheists, took photographs which show the Virgin surrounded by a brilliant circular light. The best short account of the long and complicated affair is contained in *Our Lady Returns to Egypt,* by Jerome Palmer, O.S.B. In it Father Palmer cites the testimony of Bishop Gregorius, Prelate for Higher Studies, Coptic Culture, and Scientific Research:

The events have no equal in the past, neither in the East nor in the West. St. Mary has appeared in many different forms since April 2, 1968. She is still appearing from time to time [as of January 1969]. The most glorious apparitions took place between April 27 and May 15.

Before the apparitions took place some birds that look like pigeons—I don't know what they are—appear in different formations. Sometimes two appear on the dome just as if they had come out of it. However, the dome is closed; the windows do not open. Everyone watches to see where they come from. They might be seen flying eastward, then wheeling about and flying to the west, and while one watches them, they suddenly disappear.

I remember particularly on June 9, the birthday of Our Lady (in Coptic calendars), I was at Zeitoun when I saw two pigeons very white, very bright, luminous, radiating light. I was determined to watch them. They became tiny flakes of cloud and seemed to enter heaven. They do not flap their wings; they glide. In a flash they appeared; and disappeared in the same way. They did not fly away but above and around the center dome. They stay quite near and are close to the church when they vanish. Whatever formation they take, they keep. Sometimes as many as seven of them fly in the formation of a cross. They appear and disappear in this formation. They fly very swiftly. They are not light on one side only, but are completely lighted. One does not see feathers at all—just something bright. They are radiating creatures, larger in size than a dove or a pigeon. Sometimes as one of them flies lower, it gets larger and larger. People realize these are not pigeons. They are there to honor St. Mary, and usually appear sometime before an apparition.

These mysterious birds—which most Zeitoun witnesses called "doves," the name by which they are usually known—often manifest themselves in "miraculous" events like the one cited. The first references to them appear in the New Testament, where one descends from heaven at Christ's baptism; supposedly it is a symbol of the Holy Ghost. For other, postbiblical, accounts, see Brewer's book mentioned earlier.

I have myself seen not less [sic] than ten forms of the apparition. Once I saw an opening in the sky, like the opening in the sanctuary in the Coptic Church. St. Mary appeared in this opening. She appeared larger than natural size, young, beautiful, all in light. It was the color of the sky in Egypt. She wore something on her head like a veil. She looked down towards the cross on the main dome. She looked like the Sorrowful Mother. She did not look happy. She stood for as much as two or three hours in the same spot.

People who went to Zeitoun on Saturday, May 4, at 9 P.M. saw her in radiance until 5 A.M. on Sunday, May 5. For eight hours she was visible to thousands and thousands of people. I was there myself that night. Many went home to get their families and friends. Most of those present were Moslems.

Sometimes Our Lady has appeared aside or in the palm tree in the churchyard. Our Lord has also been seen as an Infant. She holds Him to identify herself. Jesus is always on her left arm. According to Eastern custom, the Queen should always be on the right side of the King. Sometimes He is wearing a crown, sometimes not. The same is true of St. Mary. She may appear several times in the same night, once with the crown and again without it. But she is always like a queen, very beautiful, very healthy, standing upright. She moves about, enabling all to see her. She moves very slowly. At times she has the olive branch in her right hand. Sometimes she lifts both hands in blessing.

The most wonderful scene I experienced was one under the northeast dome, above the icon of Our Lady. It occurred on the feast of the Flight of the Holy Family, June 1. About nine or nine-thirty at night a light appeared in the center of the opening beneath the small dome. The light took the shape of a sphere, moving up and down. Then very slowly it moved out toward the supporting archway and took the form of St. Mary. It lasted two or three minutes, and as usual the people shouted to her. She usually acknowledges their greetings with both hands, or with one, if she should be holding the olive branch or the Christ Child. She looks somewhat happy and smiling, but somewhat sad, always kindly. She then returned to the dome, and the figure became again a round ball of light and gradually faded into darkness.

After about ten minutes the cycle started again. I saw it several times between 10 P.M. and 3:30 A.M., at about ten-minute intervals. As she would disappear under one dome and darkness had come, she would appear under another of the domes, or over the entrance into the courtyard. It was St. Mary in complete form that I saw, head to foot, very bright, not bluish, yet not hurting the eyes. It actually seemed to soothe the eyes. No features were visible. No features could be distinguished, but the outline was that of a very beautiful figure. This scene I saw countless times.

There is also the phenomenon of the incense. The smoke of incense, very bright, comes out of the large dome in unbelievable quantities. The cloud goes up to ten or twenty meters or more. It is dark red. There is no other cloud in the sky but the one over the dome. It then takes the form of St. Mary, as stars appear and disappear over the church.

In virtually every story we have examined so far, we read references to brilliant, luminous lights, often globular in shape, associated with religious experience. From the New Testament, for example (Acts ii:1–3):

When the day of Pentecost was fully come, [the disciples] were all with one accord in one place; and suddenly there came a sound from heaven as of a rushing mighty wind, and it filled all the house where they were sitting; and there appeared unto them cloven tongues like as of fire, and it sat upon each of them.

Richard Maurice Bucke, author of the classic *Cosmic Consciousness,* wrote that "light" is invariably seen or sensed in the mystical experience. Certainly religious tradition seems to bear this out. To cite some specific cases:

—A "pillar of fire" allegedly settled on the head of St. Brigit (436–523) and restored sight to her one blind eye.

—Fellow nuns saw a "globe of fire" descend on St. Gertrude (626–659).

—At his ordination, just as the bishop of Paris pronounced the words "receive the Holy Ghost," St. John of Matha (1160–1213) was covered by a "pillar of fire." After the service, asked if he had had a vision, the young priest said, "I saw the angel of the Savior, sitting on a cloud of glory. His face was brighter than the sun, his robes were white as snow, and he bore on his breast a cross of two colors, red and azure. At his feet I beheld two slaves laden with chains; one was a Moor, the other a Christian. The hands of the angel were crossed, the right hand toward the Christian, and the left toward the Moor. That, father, is what I saw."

—Jeanne Marie de Maille (1332–1414) was encompassed by a "globe of fire" after she prayed for the heavenly fire the apostles had received at Pentecost.

—When St. John Nepomuck was born (1630), "marvelous flames of light" danced around his cradle.

While we could easily enough dismiss all this as naive legend, modern accounts are more difficult to contend with. In an 1877 issue of *Spiritual Magazine* we find this testimony from a leading official of the Corporation of London:

Having heard that fire had descended on several of the great Irish assemblies during the Revivals [of 1859], I, when in Ireland, made inquiry and conversed with those who had witnessed it. During the open-air meetings, when some 600–1,000 people were present, a kind of cloud of fire approached in the air, hovered and dipped over the people, rose and floated on some distance, again hovered on that which was found afterwards to be another revival meeting, and so it continued. The light was very bright and was seen by all, producing awe.

Dipping momentarily back into the more distant past once again, we note that while St. Columba of Rieti was in the grips of a five-day ecstasy during which she "visited" heaven and conversed with Jesus and the angels, her priest saw a globe of fire hovering above the woman's house. Later Columba told him it was the "star of the Magi" and that it had filled her chamber with light, leaving behind a beautifully scented perfume.

St. Gregory the Great, a sixth-century figure, reportedly fled to the mountains when he heard that the Church fathers were probably going to appoint him pope. Searchers found him when a "pillar of fire" in the sky led them to where he was hiding.

Fourteen hundred years later, in 1905, a hysterical religious revival swept Wales. Mrs. Mary Jones of Egryn, Merionethshire, became one of its principal figures. She received the call to preach, she claimed, through guidance from angelic beings whom she met in ecstatic visions. More impressive to outside observers, including those who had not been caught up in the national madness, was the fact that mysterious aerial lights seemed to follow Mrs. Jones around. (We are indebted to English researcher Roger Sandell for uncovering the following reports.)

In an interview published in the *Barmouth Advertiser* for February 2, 1905, Mrs. Jones said, as her interviewer, the Reverend E. Lewis, recounted, "She had seen, almost from the first, each evening, a light between her and the hills. It had revealed to her what to expect at the meetings." Lewis added, "That some mysterious lights have been seen on the shore in the past few weeks is beyond doubt. Nor is this the first time for this bay to be visited. They have been reported before, especially one winter in 1649."

On February 13 the *Daily Mail* carried a story by a reporter who had visited the village looking for the lights. His quest was rewarded when

At twenty past eight I saw what appeared to be a ball of fire above the roof of the chapel. It came from nowhere and sprang into existence instantaneously. It seemed to be about twice the height of the chapel, about fifty feet. Suddenly it disappeared, after having lasted a minute and a half. . . .

[Fifteen minutes later] two lights flared out, one on each side of the chapel. They seemed about a hundred feet apart. I made a rough guess that they were a hundred feet above the roof of the chapel. They shone brilliantly for thirty seconds and then began to flicker.

As the reporter walked back to Barmouth, he witnessed yet another strange sight:

It was about three hundred feet up the hillside and about five hundred feet from where I stood. It shone dazzlingly with a deep yellow brightness. It looked like a solid bulb of light six inches in diameter and was tiring to look at.

On the eleventh, at 11:48 P.M., a miner near Llywyon saw a "large meteor" passing from east to west across an overcast sky.

It attained its greatest brilliancy whilst over Barmouth [he wrote in the *Barmouth Advertiser*, February 23], when three or four balls of fire fell out of the main body which, showing through the clouds, appeared peculiarly grand, and the light was then so intense that I could distinguish objects more clearly than by the full moon. The meteor was nearer horizontal in its flight and more brilliant than any I have hitherto seen.

Somewhere around this time a reporter was present in Mrs. Jones's house when a light appeared. Conceivably he saw the same thing the miner observed—he said the sky was overcast when "apparently a couple of miles away flashed a brilliant white light in the form of an enormous star." He noted of other sightings made at different times: "The lights were seen by dozens at Portmadoc, as the Reverend Llewelyn Morgan will testify. At Aberdovey the lights were seen by a group accompanying Mrs. Jones to the chapel."

Even more puzzling is this incident, described in the February 16 *Advertiser* by reporter Beriah G. Evans:

Having proceeded a little over a mile along the road, all walking abreast, I saw three brilliant rays of light strike across the road from mountain to sea, throwing the stone wall twenty or thirty yards in front into bold relief, every stone plainly visible. There was not a living soul there, nor house, from which it could have come. Another half mile and a blood-red light, apparently within a foot of the ground, appeared to me in the center of the village street just before us. I said nothing till I reached the spot. Then it disappeared as suddenly and mysteriously as it had come.

"Mrs. Jones," I said, "unless I am mistaken, your light still accompanies us."

"Yes," she replied, "I kept silent to see whether you had perceived it yourselves."

Then I learned to my astonishment that none of my three companions had seen it. That is the simple story of my experience. Why I alone, apart from Mrs. Jones, should have seen the light, I shall not attempt to explain.

Apparently there were two different types of light phenomena: one objective, the other subjective—a matter whose full significance we will better understand when we examine it in the context of the UFO question.

One of the most fantastic manifestations of this whole curious affair seems to have been objective in nature, amazingly enough. After one of Mrs. Jones's February meetings, two men, one of them a prominent farmer, saw a "gigantic human form rising over a hedgerow. Then a ball of fire appeared above and a long ray of light pierced the figure, which vanished" (*Barmouth Advertiser*, February 23).

Another incident appears to have been objective as well. The Reverend H. D. Jones, a local Baptist minister, and others were walking back to Egryn from a revival meeting in nearby Llandebr; meanwhile Mrs. Jones (not related to the clergyman) and some of her followers drove alongside in a car. According to Reverend Jones (*Advertiser*, March 23):

After proceeding some distance the mysterious light suddenly appeared in the roadway a few yards in front of the car, around which it played, sometimes in front, others behind. When we reached the crossroads the road towards Egryn makes a sudden turn to the left and, on reaching this point, instead of proceeding straight on, the light at once made its way in the direction of Egryn in front of the car. Up till then it had been a single light but here it changed. After going some little distance up the road to Egryn a small red ball of fire appeared around which danced two attendant white lights, playing around it. Meanwhile the car proceeded on its journey, leaving the lights behind. Those then suddenly again combined in one and rushed at a rapid pace after the car, which it then overtook. For over a mile did we thus keep it in view.

Finally, there is this curious item from the March 30 *Advertiser*:

In the neighborhood dwells an exceptionally intelligent young woman of the peasant stock, whose bedroom has been visited three nights in succession by a man dressed in black. This figure has delivered a message to the girl which she is frightened to relate.

Before we mutter "hallucination" and forget the matter, we must see it as part of the "men in black" phenomenon of modern UFO lore.

Weird luminous phenomena have been reported frequently in the literature of psychical research. In a number of instances investigators have found the causes to be phosphorous or electrical gadgetry. Other cases, however, are not so easily explained, such as these two accounts by two prominent men who researched the mediumship of D. D. Home, the remarkable nineteenth-century psychic. The first is from Sir William Crookes' *Researches into the Phenomena of Spiritualism,* as it appears in Fodor's *Encyclopedia of Psychic Science*:

Under the strictest test conditions I have seen a solid luminous body, the size and nearly the shape of a turkey's egg, float noiselessly about the room, at one time higher than anyone present could reach on tiptoe, and then gently descending to the floor. It was visible for more than ten minutes, and before it faded away it struck the table three times with a sound like that of a hard, solid body. During this time the medium was lying back, apparently insensible, in an easy chair. . . .

I have seen luminous points of light darting about and settling on the heads of different persons; I have had questions answered by the flashing of a bright light a desired number of times in front of my face. I have had an alphabetic communication given me by luminous flashes occurring before me in the air, whilst my hand was moving out amongst them. In the light, I have seen a luminous cloud hover over a heliotrope on a side table, break a sprig off, and carry the sprig to a lady.

From Lord Adare's *Experiments in Spiritualism with D. D. Home,* also appearing in Fodor's *Encyclopedia*:

We all then observed a light, resembling a little star, near the chimney piece, moving to and fro; it then disappeared. Mr. Home said: "Ask them in the name of the Father, the Son, and the Holy Ghost, if this is the work of God." I repeated the words very earnestly; the light shone out, making three little flashes, each one about a foot higher above the floor than the preceding.

6

In his *Mind over Space* the late Dr. Nandor Fodor, referring to the phenomenon of transportation (or teleportation, to use its more common name), observed that the "disappearance or reappearance [of the percipient] may take place amidst luminous or cloudlike phenomena." The most obvious example is the Old Testament tale of Elijah, who was taken by a "chariot of fire and horses of fire."

"Records of similar disappearances throughout the centuries," he says, "indicate that the vortex of power that appears to accomplish the stupendous feat of human transportation does sometimes produce a luminous phenomenon which may give the impression of fire."

Teleportation, along with the related power of levitation, appears so frequently in history that even the most skeptical of scholars have had a hard time discounting its occasional occurrences. Reliable witnesses have reported instances of it all over the world, in many different kinds of religious and secular contexts. It usually takes place when the percipient is in a trance or dream state. St. John-Joseph de la Croix (1654–1734), for example, would enter a trance so deep that he appeared dead. In this condition he "visited" heaven, where he conversed with Jesus, the Virgin Mary, and others. Meanwhile, friends who remained behind in the conventional world would see his body surrounded by light; sometimes he would float up to the ceiling.

Oliver Leroy, author of *Levitation,* notes that about 230 saints have been credited with these powers. Some of them, like Francis Xaverius, Ammon, and Raphael, claimed that angels had borne them. Anne Catherine Emmerich, the stigmatic visionary, maintained that her "guardian angel" would lift her off her feet while she cleaned the church vestry; thus, she said, "I would clean and arrange everything in places where it was humanly impossible." Leroy writes:

Upon one occasion Joseph of Copertino, having recovered his senses on the top of a tree, could not come down again—a ladder had to be brought; Mother duBourg sank abruptly on her praying desk; Mary of Jesus Crucified, awakened from ecstasy, could hardly climb down the lime tree on top of which she was standing.

This incredible story, told of Marie d'Agreda, Superior of the Convent of the Immaculate Conception in Spain (d. 1665), is taken from Alonso de Benarides' *Revised Memorial of 1634*:

[While] she was one day praying for the savages in New Mexico, our Lord gave her to see them and bade her instruct them. In one of her ecstasies she found herself among the Indians and gave them rosaries which she had in her room, and which could not be found afterwards. She made five hundred visits. Whether "she was transported in the body she could not tell." But she managed to fulfill her mission and when the missionary who was sent out to Mexico met the Indians, he found that the Indians were already instructed and, as they said, by a woman who had been among them frequently. The statement was so surprising that Father Alonso de Benarides made a special visit to Spain, and was sent by Father Bernadin of Sienna, General of the Order of Agroda, where he met Marie, who recognized him as having seen him with other monks in America. She mentioned the day, the hour, the place, where she had seen them, and she spoke of Mexico like a person who had long lived in it.

St. Teresa of Avila described the feeling of rapture as "a cloud or a strong eagle rising upwards and carrying you away on its wings. . . . My soul was carried away, and almost always my head with it—and now and then the whole body as well, so that it was lifted up from the ground." Afterward she would be thoroughly exhausted physically.

There is a curious suggestion in her words of the duality of the experience—it could be either subjective or objective. In the first, "visionary" aspect it is the soul that rises. But under some circumstances the body ascends as well. Perhaps we could call this "mind before matter." The motivating power here, as in other cases, is clearly psychokinetic. The frequent manifestation of levitation/teleportation phenomena in poltergeist cases, where we see PK expressed in rather pure form, tends to confirm our suggestion.

7

Let us now return to where we started, with visions of angels and saints which occur in modern days but which remain, unlike Fatima and Garabandal, essentially private experiences which seldom achieve publicity. Many of these take place at the bedsides of dying persons, where, as Wainwright Evans remarks in an article on the subject, "not the least remarkable thing . . . is that the dying person is, to all appearances, fully rational, in normal possession of his senses, aware of his surroundings, and not to be classed as delirious or drug-ridden at all."

Evans bases his remarks on a recent survey conducted by Dr. Karlis Osis of the Research Division of the Parapsychology Foundation. Osis, who collected 1,370 cases from doctors and nurses around the country, found that cloudy-minded patients usually "saw" living people who were not there, the clear-minded dead people and unidentifiable apparitions. (One sixth of these latter patients died within ten minutes; of the remainder, one third passed on in an hour, and two thirds of the others within a day. A very few lingered a week to a month longer.) Since, according to a British study, persons *in normal health* who have hallucinations usually "see" living individuals, Dr. Osis comments, "It would appear that the predominance of hallucinations of the dead is not a function of being unconscious or delirious, but has deeper roots."

Still, Osis's statistics reveal that 28.1% of the dying persons in the survey "saw" living persons, which tends to call the survival interpretation into question. We agree with him, however, that the phenomenon is significant and that hallucination, at least as we ordinarily understand it, is not the sole cause. Perhaps what happens is that the knowledge (or, at any rate, sense) of impending death discharges the kind of psychic energy that catapults the mind into that "otherworld" which we shape with the contents of the unconscious. In that experience, which the saints underwent in their visions of heaven (and which, as we have seen, were sometimes accompanied by seemingly "objective" psychophysical effects), the materials of both the personal and the collective unconscious come into play. Osis's patients "saw" deceased friends and relatives, and the landscapes of heaven, a place of beauty, peace, and quiet.

The following case is interesting because it illustrates the archetypal nature of these visions. Like certain ostensible UFO occupant reports which could just as easily be interpreted as fairy visitations, this story of "angels" reminds us of Irish tales of the little people's vigils at the sides of deathbeds:

A little lad, robust, fun-loving, free, until he was eight years old, began then to fail in the body and to mature in mind, until his spiritual nature seemed to have absorbed mental and physical, in development for another world. One evening, as it began to draw toward the first day of the week, half sitting, half lying, in his great easy chair, he said to his eldest sister, who was watching by him, "I think this is the last night I shall spend with you." He spoke in a perfectly calm and ordinary tone. His sister, fearing that he was dying, called in her mother, but continued to stand over him and pressed her hand upon his brow. He immediately reached up his hand as though in trouble, saying, "Don't put your hand there, H———, I don't see out of my eyes as you do. You've got your hand where my sight comes in," then lying back with closed eyes, laboring hard for breath, he suddenly exclaimed, "Oh, what a beautiful sight! See those little angels."

"What are they doing?" asked the sister.

"Oh, they have hold of hands, and wreaths on their heads, and they are dancing in a circle around me. Oh, how happy they look and they are whispering to each other. One of them says I have been a good little boy and they would like to have me come with them." He lay still awhile and then, seemingly delighted, exclaimed, "See there come some other, older angels—two at one end and two at the other."

"Do you know any of them?"

"Yes, Uncle E. [who had died about six months before], but there are a whole row of older ones now standing behind the little ones."

"Do they say anything to you?"

"Yes, but I can't tell you as they tell me, for they sing it beautifully. We can't sing so."

The child identified one of the spirits as "Sally" and said that she was his aunt. Sally had been dead for thirty years and the boy had never before heard of her. He died three months later, according to Gail Hamilton, from whose *X Rays* we have taken the above account.

As the reader will have noticed, all the fairy elements are there—the little people holding hands, dancing in a ring, and singing a beautiful song, not to mention the dead human beings appearing in their midst—but of course at the same time it makes sense in traditionally Christian terms as well.

Dr. James Hyslop, the great psychical researcher of the late nineteenth and early twentieth centuries, was given this story by a correspondent:

The night before my brother died, I was up with him from a little after two until five o'clock. We knew he was seriously ill, but had no idea that the end was so near. In fact he was in bed only three days before he died. While I was with him he turned to me and asked if I saw the beautiful woman in white that stood by the window. Thinking him delirious and not wishing to excite him, I replied that I did. "Isn't she beautiful!" he exclaimed. Then later, "I think you'd better close the window. I'm afraid she is cold." . . . He also asked if I heard the wonderful music and spoke of seeing flowers. I went to my room at five, and at quarter past six he called me, saying, "I think I can get up today and go into your room." I rose and went to him, reaching him just in time to see his eyelids flutter and close.

We have, of course, encountered apparitions of a beautiful woman in white before. The following incident, submitted by Richard Hodgson to a turn-of-the-century issue of the *Journal of the Society for Psychical Research,* also contains several familiar elements. It is unusual, though, in the fact that the percipient is not the dying person.

Mr. G. while holding his dying wife's hand saw forming at the door "three separate and distinct clouds in strata." These clouds gradually approached the bed and engulfed it. Mr. G. said, "Then, gazing through the mist I beheld standing at the head of my dying wife a woman's figure." He also saw "two figures in white" which "knelt by my wife's side, apparently leaning towards her, other figures hovered about the bed, more or less distinct. Above my wife and connected with a cord proceeding from her forehead, over the left eye, there floated in a horizontal position a nude, white figure, apparently her 'astral body.' " After observing this figure for several hours, he witnessed his wife's actual death. "With a gasp, the astral figure struggling, my wife ceased to breathe . . . with her last breath, as the soul left the body, the cord was severed. Suddenly the astral figure vanished." All the figures disappeared at that moment.

The December 1970 issue of *Fate* contains a fascinating article by a man who experienced a trance vision of Christ while he hovered precariously between life and death, the victim of a very serious respiratory ailment. The author had told the story to a May 1970 convention of the Spiritual Frontiers Fellowship in Chicago. Curtis and Mary Fuller of *Fate,* who were in attendance, approached him afterward to ask him if he would publish his experience in their magazine. He agreed to do so on condition that he be identified only as "a practicing psychiatrist" and a graduate of the Medical College of Virginia.

The incident took place in December 1943 at Camp Barkeley, near Abilene, Texas. Mr. X had suffered a relapse of the disease which had kept him in the hospital for a week just a short while before. On the night of the nineteenth he completely lost consciousness and did not open his eyes again until the twenty-fourth. During that period the hospital staff virtually gave him up for dead. (St. John-Joseph de la Croix, St. Ignatius, and others who entertained heavenly visions were thought dead. The same is true of some persons who visited fairyland, as we saw in the previous chapter.)

In the meantime, X felt as if he had "left his body," a phenomenon well known to students of psychic phenomena. Occultists call it "astral projection"; parapsychologists prefer "out-of-the-body experience" (OOBE) or "traveling clairvoyance." Apparently it involves a special kind of psychological dissociation, in which the percipient participates directly in clairvoyant vision; that is, he "rationalizes" the material which comes to him through the clairvoyant vision by imagining that he personally is there in some fashion. Since one part of his mind knows that that is not the case, he "sees" his immobile body while his "soul"—actually that fragment of the psyche which has received the extrasensory stimulus—roams free through the ordinary world and sometimes-not-so-ordinary worlds. (Robert A. Monroe's *Journeys Out of the Body* is an especially fascinating account describing one man's many OOBE.)

X "left" the hospital room and found himself rapidly approaching a small town and a man walking down a dark street. Confused, X asked the stranger where he was, but the man gave no indication that he had seen or heard him. X ended up back at the hospital, trying to "find" his body, which lay under a sheet (the doctors had pronounced him dead). Finally he recognized his fraternity ring on the hand sticking out under the blanket. At this point X himself thought he might be dead.

As I was sitting there [he wrote] I thought the little fifteen-watt bulb was getting brighter and brighter. Then I realized it wasn't the bulb. The intensity of this light was such that if you turned on twenty million arc-welder's lights you'd have some idea of the intensity of light that had come into that room. And three things took place all at once. I have to describe them in series but they all happened in a flash.

Out of the center of this light stepped a Being of pure light. Something inside my spiritual being, which was sitting on the bed because my physical being still lay on the bed, said, "Stand up, you're in the presence of the Son of God."

X said that the figure impressed him as being powerful beyond description, yet at the same time it radiated "absolute, indescribable love." He was sure it "knew everything about me, good and bad, and yet totally accepted and loved me." It should be obvious that X could as well be—and undoubtedly is—talking of the psyche in its whole aspect, with the unconscious (which possesses all knowledge of the individual, assumes his worth implicitly, and tries to "save" him) addressing him in language the conscious mind can understand; in this instance, fittingly enough, the symbol of the Savior himself.

"Jesus" asked him what he had done with his life and kindly chose to ignore X's flabbergasted response that he was an Eagle Scout. When the question was repeated, X recalled various good deeds from his past. At the same time he knew that he never wanted to leave "Jesus's" company again.

Suddenly in a "wave of light" the two sped through space until they arrived at a large city, where they observed people going about the business of life. In a red-light district "human beings at the bars were being 'possessed' by the discarnate alcoholics who jumped inside their bodies when their electrical fields or auras were relaxed and began to open." More prosaically, X is describing, in Jungian terms, the "shadow" aspect of the unconscious, where our darkest, least worthy impulses wait to seek expression when our psychic defenses are weakened or disordered.

Elsewhere in town "beings of light," with benevolent intentions, tried to communicate with people but no one seemed to hear them. These represent, most probably, the muted voice of the unconscious in its striving for psychic unity and the attainment of self. The message, once again, is an old one: we have gained the world at the expense of our souls.

There was another wave of light and another whole realm was superimposed on our physical realm which, for lack of a better term, I'll call the mental realm. I believe this must have been the realm where all the great songs, paintings, symphonies, and inventions come from. I went into centers of higher learning—we would call them universities in this physical realm.... I recall one room in a library large enough to hold the entire University of Virginia. And this one room was full of holy books of which the Bible, as we know it, was just one translation. I take it that this room contained the books on the religions of the universe. And again I insist, we have a one-god universe.

It is interesting to see how in this instance the unconscious slyly tells X that his vision arises out of the same kinds of imaginative impulses that help fulfill our lives and keep us from exclusive dependence on the purely physical phenomena of existence. In other words, the same instincts and capacities that make human beings produce art lead them to create the "supernatural" otherworld. which compensates for the unsatisfying, confining limitations of the "natural" world. The "one god" who oversees all this is the human psyche.

With another wave of light, out in space was another whole dimension, another whole realm. Here was a city of pure light. I didn't see any golden streets, but what I did see was even more amazing. The beings who came and went from this city of pure light were like the Being who was conducting me. He did say, "I am the first fruit of many that are to follow." . . . Then the whole thing was gone! We suddenly were back in the hospital room in Texas!

X has come to the golden land: heaven in his terms, nirvana, fairyland, Venus in other people's. It is a place mystics have often visited. Almost invariably it comes to them in a flash of light, with an accompanying profound awareness of the meaning of all life, the continuity of all experience, the immortality of the soul, the primacy of love in the universe. In its ultimate expression it is devoid of concrete symbols; there is only, in Walt Whitman's words, "ineffable light, light rare, untellable, lighting the very light beyond all signs, descriptions, languages." It appears to be a tapping of the World-Soul, the collective psyche at its full potential, where all dualities are united and the limitations of perception and language are transcended.

X has not achieved the total experience of "cosmic consciousness"—his vision is contained within the boundaries of cultural symbol—but clearly he is moving toward it, experiencing it, as so many other persons have, in the form of a naive metaphor which he mistakenly took to be literal truth. Visionary events move toward the ineffable, and their symbols are not to be confused with their substance. Interpreting them literally (as X does, concluding that the biblical view of things is the correct one) is like trying to understand the meaning of a sentence by reducing it to the words that comprise it. The words in themselves are not what is meant; they exist only to direct us elsewhere to something greater and far more significant.

As if to prove the point, most of the "many that are to follow" came in different guises after the end of World War II. First, however, we must turn back several decades to consider the curious case of the phantom airships.

THE AIRSHIPS:
THE TECHNOLOGICAL IMPULSE

> The faint suspicion of a giant mystery, much larger than our current preoccupation with life on other plants, much deeper than housewives' reports of zigzagging lights: Perhaps we can resolve the point by trying to understand what these tales, these myths, these legends are doing to us. What images are they designed to convey? What hidden needs are they fulfilling?
> —Jacques Vallee, in *Passport to Magonia: From Folklore to Flying Saucers*

1

March 26, 1880, was a quiet night in tiny Galisteo, New Mexico. The train from Santa Fe had come and gone and the operator, his day's work finished, routinely locked up the depot and set out with a couple of friends on a short walk before retiring.

Suddenly voices cut through the silence—voices which sounded as though they were coming from the sky. At first the listeners thought their source must be persons in the nearby Ortiz Mountains. But when the voices got louder and closer the men on the ground looked up and abruptly changed their minds.

An object, "monstrous in size," was rapidly approaching from the west, flying so low that the observers could see elegantly written characters on the outside of the car. Inside, the occupants, numbering ten or so and apparently of normal appearance, were laughing and shouting in an unknown language, with sounds of music occasionally drifting out into the air. The craft itself was "fish-shaped," i.e., like a cigar with a tail, and was driven by a huge "fan" or propeller.

As it passed overhead a passenger tossed several items from the car. The depot agent and his friends recovered one of them almost immediately, a beautiful flower with a slip of fine silklike paper containing some characters which reminded the men of ones they had seen on Japanese tea chests.

Soon afterward the aerial machine ascended far into the sky and rapidly sailed away toward the east.

The next morning searchers found a cup which the witnesses had seen thrown out of the craft but been unable to locate in the evening darkness. "It is of very peculiar workmanship," the *Santa Fe Daily New Mexican* reported, "entirely different to anything used in this country." The operator took it and the flower and put them on display.

Before the day was over, however, this physical evidence of the passage of an early unidentified flying object had vanished. In the evening a mysterious gentleman identified only as a "collector of curiosities" appeared in town, examined the finds, suggested that they were of Asiatic origin, and offered a sum of money so considerable that the owner had no choice but to accept. The "collector" scooped up his purchases and was not seen again.

2

The story of aviation does not begin on December 17, 1903, of course. Long before Orville Wright's fabled twelve-second hop at Kitty Hawk, scientists and inventors had struggled to unlock the secrets of powered flight and to build what an 1897 issue of *Scientific American* called the "true flying machine; that is, one which is hundreds of times heavier than the air upon which it rests, by reason of its dynamic impact, and not by the aid of any balloon or gas bag whatsoever."

Since the last part of the eighteenth century adventurers had traveled aloft in balloons, an often dangerous mode of transportation because the aeronaut was at the mercy of the elements. A sudden, unexpected gust of wind could be, and often was, fatal to these pioneers.

In 1851 an engine-powered, egg-shaped craft called the dirigible was tested for the first time; not until 1885, though, could it be maneuvered in the air. The first crosscountry dirigible flight took place in France in 1903, with the craft covering a distance of thirty-nine miles. But dirigibles did not appear in the United States until 1904, when Thomas Scott Baldwin tested his *California Arrow* in August of that year.

But nothing in the early history of flight tells us just what a huge airborne cigar was doing over New Mexico in 1880, especially when it "appeared to be entirely under the control of the occupants, and appeared to be guided by a large fanlike apparatus," and also could ascend with rather startling abruptness. Its "monstrous" size and its propeller clearly indicate that it was something that should have had no business existing: a heavier-than-air flying machine.

Consider the testimony of British authority Charles H. Gibbs-Smith:

Speaking as an aeronautical historian who specializes in the periods before 1910, I can say with certainty that the only airborne vehicles, carrying passengers, which could possibly have been seen anywhere in North America . . . were free-flying spherical balloons, and it is highly unlikely for these to be mistaken for anything else. No form of dirigible (i.e., a gasbag propelled by an airscrew) or heavier-than-air flying machine was flying—or indeed *could* fly—at this time in America.

During the 1850s mysterious "airships" regularly crossed the skies of Germany, saddling the latter nineteenth century with what would prove to be one of its most recurrent, baffling problems.

And it was just before that, around the year 1848, that a remarkable, enigmatic young German named C. A. A. Dellschau immigrated to the United States.

Dellschau's own testimony places him in Sonora, California, a mining town, during the 1850s. Where he might have gone in the decades after that we do not know. We do know, however, that around the turn of the century he took up residence in Houston, Texas, married a widow, and lived in virtual seclusion. He had no friends; by all accounts, his quarrelsome disposition kept other persons at a distance. Dismissed as an eccentric by the few who knew him, Dellschau spent most of his time in his study, where he devoted hours to the compilation of a series of scrapbooks filled with clippings, drawings, and cryptic notations. He died in 1924 at the age of ninety-two.

Were it not for a chance discovery many years later, Dellschau's life, like most people's would have passed with scarcely a trace. But one day in March 1969 a ufologist named P. G. Navarro happened to stroll by an aviation exhibit at the University of St. Thomas, in Houston. Something caught his eye and he stopped to take a closer look.

What he saw were two large scrapbooks (Dellschau's) which contained old news stories and articles about attempts of various would-be inventors to construct heavier-than-air flying machines. But these were not nearly so interesting as Dellschau's drawings of strange-looking, cumbersome vessels which he claimed *actually had been flown at one time.*

Navarro, his curiosity aroused, eventually located ten more of Dellschau's scrapbooks and even talked with the man's stepdaughter, by now an old woman. He conducted as detailed an investigation as he possibly could under the circumstances, poring over the books and carefully making sense of Dellschau's notes, penned in English, German, and code. When he was through he had reconstructed an incredible story, which appeared in the winter 1970 issue of *Flying Saucer Digest.*

At least one thing was obvious: Dellschau was of two minds about his project. On one hand he wanted his "secrets" known; on the other, he was afraid to speak too directly, for reasons we shall get to shortly. So he compromised and wrote in a fashion aimed at discouraging all but the most determined student. Still Dellschau left much unanswered. Actually, in a very real sense, he left *everything* unanswered.

He was writing for an audience—if not one in his own day, then one at some period in the future. He addressed potential readers thus: "You will . . . Wonder Weaver . . . You will unriddle these writings. They are my stock of open knowledge. They . . . will end like all others . . . with good intentions but too weak-willed to assign and put to work."

According to Dellschau's notes, in the 1850s he and a

group of associates (about sixty in all) gathered in Sonora, California, where they formed the "Aero Club" and constructed and flew heavier-than-air machines. They performed their experiments, he says, in an open field near Columbia, a small town not far from Sonora. (Today an airstrip covers the field, which is the only spot in the predominately hilly region where planes can safely take off and land.)

The club performed its experiments in secrecy, and its members were not permitted to tell anyone of their work or to use the aircraft for their own purposes. One member who threatened to take his machine to the public in hopes of securing a fortune died in an aerial explosion—the victim, Dellschau hinted, of murder. Another, a "high-educated mechanic" identified as Gustav Freyer, was called to account by the club for withholding new information from them. Apparently this was no ordinary social organization.

The Aero Club was only a branch of a larger secret society whose initials Dellschau lists as "N Y M Z A." Of this society Dellschau wrote very little, except to observe that in 1858 a George Newell was its head in Sonora; otherwise he only alludes to orders from unnamed superiors who were overseeing the club's activities. These superiors were not from the government, for Dellschau wrote that once a government official who somehow knew of their work approached club members and tried to persuade them to sell their inventions for use as weapons of war. They were instructed to refuse the offer.

The group had a number of aircraft at its disposal, including among others August Shoetler's *Aero Dora,* Robert Nixon's *Aero Rondo,* and George Newell's *Aero Newell.* At first appearance it is hard to believe that anything resembling these machines ever could have flown. As Navarro remarks, "The heavy body of the machines seems to be radically out of proportion to the gas bag or balloon which is supposed to lift the contraption. Considering the large amount of gas (usually hydrogen or helium) that is required to lift one of today's dirigibles or even a small blimp, it is inconceivable that the small quantity of gas used in Dellschau's airships would be sufficient to lift it."

That is, if it were an ordinary gas, which this wasn't. According to Dellschau, it was a substance called "NB" which had the capacity to "negate weight." Fantastic as it may seem, our narrator is talking about antigravity.

Dellschau recorded all this in a curiously pessimistic tone. One strange paragraph reads, "We are all together in our graves. We get together in my house. We eat and drink and are joyful. We do mental work, but everybody is forlorn, as they feel they are fighting a losing battle. But little likelihood is there that fate shall bring forth the right man."

Dellschau wrote of the human race, and even the planet Earth, as if he stood apart from them. One peculiar paragraph, written originally in Dellschau's oddly archaic German, says, "Your Christian love reaches for the Wanderplace, and wanders away from Earth. Planets there are enough where Christian love shall be as we say so nicely in the Book Selag." A drawing elsewhere shows the figure of a devil opening up a crack in the fabric of the sky above one of the *Aeros*. The overall impression conveyed to us is of a man who knew secrets that forever would render him an outsider, isolated from the community of mankind.

4

On November 1, 1896, the *Detroit Free Press* reported that in the near future a New York inventor would construct and fly an "aerial torpedo boat." About two weeks later, on November 17, the *Sacramento Bee* reprinted a telegram it had received from a New York man who said he and a couple of friends would board an airship of his invention and fly it to California. But that very night all hell broke loose and the Great Airship Scare of 1896–97 was off to an unbelievable start.

The next day the *Bee* related the following in the first paragraph of a long article:

Last evening between the hours of six and seven o'clock, in the year of our Lord 1896, a most startling exhibition was seen in the sky in this city of Sacramento. People standing on the sidewalks at certain points in the city between the hours stated, saw coming through the sky over the housetops what appeared to them to be merely an electric arc lamp propelled by some mysterious force. It came out of the east and sailed unevenly toward the southwest, dropping now nearer to the earth, and now suddenly rising into the air again, as if the force that was whirling it through space was sensible of the dangers of collision with objects upon the earth.

There were hundreds of witnesses. Those who got the closest look at the object said that it was huge and cigar-shaped, with four large wings attached to an aluminum body. Some insisted that they heard voices and raucous laughter emanating from the ship. Presumably these people never had heard of Galisteo Junction's merry pranksters. R. L. Lowry and a companion allegedly saw four men driving the craft via a wheel-like apparatus. The observers heard one of the aeronauts say, 'We hope to be in San Francisco by tomorrow noon.' " J. H. Vogel, who was in the vicinity, confirmed the story and added that the vessel was "egg-shaped."

The next afternoon an airship passed over Oak Park, California, leaving a trail of smoke, and before long San Francisco, Oakland, and other cities and towns in the north-central part of the state had their own stories to fill newspaper columns with.

Several persons stepped forward to tell of earlier sightings, one of them a fruit rancher from near Bowman, in Placer County, who said that he and members of his family had watched an airship fly by at 100 mph late in October. Even more incredible was the testimony of William Jordan of San Rafael, who published this letter in the *San Francisco Call* on November 23rd:

The mysterious light mentioned in your valuable paper this morning as seen by several citizens in different parts of the state, and which seem to mystify yourself as well as your readers, is nothing more than an airship, and of this fact I am perfectly cognizant. I think now that I am released of my obligation of secrecy, which I have kept for nearly three months, as the experiment in aerial navigation is a fixed fact and the public, or a few of the public at least, have seen its workings in the air.

In the latter part of last August I was hunting in the

Tamalpais range of mountains, between the high peak and Bolinas Bay. I wounded a deer, and in chasing it I ran into a circular brush pile about ten feet in hight [sic] in a part of the mountain seldom visited even by hunters.

I was somewhat astonished, and my curiosity prompted me to approach it, when I encountered a man who sang out: "What are you doing here and what do you want?" I replied that "I had wounded a deer and was chasing it." He said "that they had been camping here for a month or so and had not seen a deer, but if you think your deer is in the neighborhood I will assist you in finding it as we need a little meat in camp."

This man went with me and in less than five hundred yards found my deer. We carried it into the brush corral. And what a sight—a perfect machine shop and an almost completed ship. I was sworn to secrecy and have kept it till this moment. Six men were at work on the "aerial ship." It is this ship that a few people have seen at night on its trial trip. It returns to its home before daylight and will continue to do so until perfected.

The most baffling part of the whole flap, which lasted well into December, was the role played by "E. H. Benjamin," a dentist whose name newspapers sometimes enclosed in quotation marks, as though they had reason to doubt his identity. It was either Benjamin or his uncle who approached the San Francisco lawyer George D. Collins that November and asked him to represent his interests in the patenting of an airship. He told the incredulous Collins that he had come from Maine to California seven years before in order to conduct his experiments without danger of interruption.

Collins told reporters that his client (whom he never identified by name), a very wealthy man, did his experimenting near Oroville, where he had taken Collins to view his invention—an enormous construction 150 feet long. "It is built on the aeroplane system and has two canvas wings eighteen feet wide and a rudder shaped like a bird's tail," the attorney said. "I saw the thing ascend about ninety feet under perfect control."

On the seventeenth, Collins went on, the airship had flown the sixty miles between Oroville and Sacramento in forty-five minutes. But this was not the first flight the inventor had made. For two weeks he had been flying nightly in attempts to perfect the craft's navigational apparatus.

From the *Sacramento Bee*, November 23:

> Oroville, Nov 23—The rumor that the airship which is alleged to have passed over Sacramento was constructed near this town, seems to have a grain of truth in it. The parties who could give information if they would are extremely reticent. They give evasive answers, or assert they know absolutely nothing about it.
>
> Not a single person that saw or knew of an airship being constructed near here can be found, and yet there is a rumor that some man has been experimenting with different kinds of gas and testing those which are lighter than air. The experiments were made some miles east of the town and no one is able to give any names of the parties, who are evidently strangers and seeking to avoid publicity.

The *San Francisco Call* established that Benjamin, a native of Carmel, Maine, had been seen in the Oroville area, visiting a wealthy uncle and confiding to friends that he had invented something which would "revolutionize the world."

Several days into the controversy, Collins was dropped as the inventor's lawyer because he was talking too much. W. H. H. Hart, a former state attorney general and one of the most respected men in California, took over Collins's job. In subsequent interviews Hart related that *two* airships existed, one in the East and the other in California. "I have been concerned in the Eastern invention for some time personally," he said. "The idea is to consolidate both interests."

The Western craft would be used as a weapon of war. "From what I have seen of it," he said, "I have not the least doubt that it will carry four men and one thousand pounds of dynamite. I am quite convinced that two or three men could destroy the city of Havana in forty-eight hours."

Hart represented both airship inventors, who worked out of California and New Jersey. The former instructed Hart to say "that if the Cubans would give him $10 million he would wipe out the Spanish stronghold." This was not the last time airships and Cuba would be spoken of in the same breath, as we shall see later.

One day early in December a stranger appeared at a place of business in Fresno, California, and inquired for a George Jennings. Covered with dust, the man looked as though he had traveled a long distance. No one recognized him until Jennings stepped out of a back room and greeted the visitor like an old friend. The two men engaged in whispered conversation and the dozen persons standing close by were nonplussed to overhear the word *airship* more than once.

Later Jennings talked freely to a reporter for the *Fresno Semi-Weekly Expositor,* balking only at giving his friend's name. The following account appeared in the paper's December 7, 1896, issue:

"It is true the airship is in Fresno County," he said. "Just where I do not know myself. It is also true that the man who was in here a short time ago is one of the inventors. He told me that the trip to this country was involuntary upon the part of the men in the airship. In other words the machine came itself and they couldn't stop it. His statement was that they were flying, as usual, around Contra Costa county hills and rose to a height of about one thousand feet. Suddenly the airship struck a current of air and refused to answer its steering gear. It was borne rapidly southward against all efforts to change its course until suddenly the current of air seemed to lessen and the machine once more became manageable. The men aboard at once descended and flew about, looking for a hiding place, which they at length found.

"My friend has told me that the airship was made principally of aluminum and that the rising and falling was accomplished by improved aeroplanes, while the motive power was electricity. He says the machine is perfect except for the fact that at times it refuses to steer in a given direction and that it will not stand still in the air. He has gone to San Francisco and will return with some material and men probably tonight. He said if the news from Washington* was satisfactory he would bring his

---

*An important detail. Collins's mysterious inventor informed the lawyer that he either had conducted or planned to conduct

airship over to Fresno and where everyone could see it."

Jennings said he was sure that individuals in the nearby towns of Watertown and Selma must have observed the craft as it limped through the county in search of a hiding place. Sure enough, the day before his encounter with the supposed aeronaut, the *San Francisco Call* had published a letter from five Watertown men who said they had seen an enormous airship nearly collide with a cornice on the city's post office building the evening of November 20. The craft had an "intensely brilliant" light and the witnesses could see human forms aboard the ship.

During the early morning hours of December 2 two fishermen, Giuseppe Valinziano and Luigi Valdivia, watched as an airship descended from the sky and alighted on the ocean waves several hundred yards away. The craft floated easily and its three occupants seemed to be in full control. They directed the ship to the beach. From there they dragged it into the woods.

---

business with the Patent Office in Washington, D.C. (Our source is not clear on this point.) However, Gordon Lore and Harold Deneault, authors of *Mysteries of the Skies: UFOs in Perspective*, searched carefully through the Patent Office files for 1896–97 and found two "airship" patents.

The first was granted to C. A. Smith of San Francisco on August 11, 1896. Smith surfaced during the airship flap later in the year, saying he had been "experimenting on air machines" for close to fifty years but denying any connection with the sightings then being made. He claimed that he *would* have a ship ready for crosscountry flight by the next April—by which time, oddly enough, a new airship scare arose in the midwestern and eastern states. It is not really very likely, though, that Smith's craft ever actually flew.

Henry Heintz of Elkton, South Dakota, was given the other patent on April 20, 1897, for a canoe structure held by girders to a cylindrical balloon the same length. Attached to the bottom of the hull was a searchlight. Since searchlights figure prominently in many airship reports, Lore and Deneault leave open the question of Heintz's relationship to the mystery, evidently unaware of a 1903 admission from the would-be inventor that "my models Nos. 1, 2, 3, 4, 5, and 6 . . . did not act as satisfactorily as I had expected" (*Aeronautical World*, Vol. I, Glenville, Ohio, pp. 171–72). He goes on to express more hope for No. 7, which he was building at the time of writing. As Clint Williams concludes, "We must assume that Heintz was more active at the drawing board than in the field of blue."

Excited, the two men drew in their nets and started for shore. But the surf was rough enough to make landing difficult and only after several attempts did they succeed in bringing their boat to land.

Their struggle attracted the attention of the aeronauts. As soon as the fishing vessel had hit the beach, one of the strangers approached and ordered them to be on their way. But Valinziano, who would have none of it, pressed the man for information. In reply the flier spoke evasively; but he was more specific in his threat to use force if the two tried to get off the boat. Finally, unable to intimidate the persistent duo, he walked back into the woods to consult with his companions. Ffteen minutes later he emerged and beckoned Valinziano and Valdivia to follow him.

All three of the aeronauts met them at the edge of the trees. One, whom the others addressed as "captain," did most of the talking.

"I suppose your curiosity has been aroused by our rather unusual method of traveling," he said. "I am not yet ready to make my discovery known to the public, but hope to be able to do so as soon as some slight changes are made in its construction. Until such time I must refuse to allow anyone to make a close inspection. You are welcome to get such view of the ship as you can from a distance, but any attempt at closer inspection will meet with forcible resistance." He refused to say anything about the ship's construction or its intended destination. He stated only that the trip was "experimental."

As he talked, the other two worked busily on repairing the ship. The fishermen noticed that the craft was well stocked with provisions and when it came time to eat they were invited to dine with the crew.

Afterward Valinziano and Valdivia prepared to leave, but the captain urged them to stay, promising them a ride aboard the airship when they had completed repairs. Several hours passed. Finally the captain said that it would be impossible to finish their work in time to fly that night and let them go. By now they had begun to suspect that he had detained them because he wanted to prevent them from alerting others to their presence.

One of the last 1896 stories came out of Camptonville, a little town in northern California, where at 9:00 P.M. on

December 7 a young woman's screams notified residents of the appearance of a giant airship which seemed to be descending on Ramm's Hill, two miles away. Five young men who went out to investigate discovered its sole occupant, a bearded individual who acted both deaf and mute.

Frustrated at first by the failure of normal communication, the party decided to write their questions on a sheet of paper. In reply the aeronaut took an "alphabet" from his pocket and spelled out his answers. He said he had flown from the Montezuma Mountains, where his wife and two children lived. He would answer no other inquiries.

The young men left. The aeronaut remained until four o'clock the next afternoon, when he sailed away, leaving not a trace behind.

Soon after that the airships disappeared from California, the "inventors" were heard from no more, and everything returned to normal—but not for long. The most astounding part was yet to come.

5

"The airship as a practical invention is believed to be so nearly ripe that a story of its appearance in the sky is not necessarily to be received with disrespect," *Harper's Weekly* commented in its issue for April 24, 1897.

Not in any case unless one chose to assume that thousands of Americans had lost their senses, a disquieting notion some scientists, editors, and professional skeptics seemed to have no trouble embracing. Professor George Hough, an astronomer from Northwestern University, spent a good share of his time assuring people that the "airship" was nothing more than the star Alpha Orionis as perceived by drunks, fools, and hysterics. Most newspapers ridiculed reports until they finally were forced to desist for fear of offending the growing numbers of readers who had seen the craft themselves.

California's airship was the first to receive widespread publicity but that same month, November 1896, an unidentified flying object passed through central Nebraska and sightings in the state continued into the next May. Delaware farmers saw airships as early as January 1897.

It took a sighting in Omaha involving hundreds of witnesses to put the airships back into the headlines, however. The object, a large, bright light "too big for a balloon," appeared on the night of March 29, 1897, flew low, and was visible for over half an hour.

From then on America was inundated with airships. The reports came primarily though not exclusively from midwestern states, and descriptions of the ships varied. To cite several random examples:

Everest, Kansas, April 1: "The basket or car seemed to be twenty-five to thirty feet long, shaped like an Indian canoe. Four light wings extended from the car; two wings were triangular. A large dark hulk was discernible immediately above the car and was generally supposed by the watchers to be an inflated gas bag" (*Kansas City Times*).

Chicago, April 11: "The lower portion of the airship was thin, and made of some light white metal like aluminum. The upper portion was dark and long like a big cigar, pointed in front and with some kind of arrangement in the rear to which cables are attached" (*Chicago Times-Herald.*

Texas, April 16: ". . . shaped like a Mexican cigar, large in the middle, and small at both ends, with great wings, resembling those of an enormous butterfly. It was brilliantly illuminated by the rays of two great searchlights, and was sailing in a southeasterly direction, with the velocity of wind, presenting a magnificent appearance" (*New York Sun*).

(The brilliant searchlights so often reported in airship sightings by themselves suggest that we are dealing with something far out of the ordinary. Though the arc light had been invented in the nineteenth century, searchlights which used it were encumbered with many heavy batteries or a large steam- or gasoline-powered generator. The aircraft of the period could not possibly have carried anything so heavy. The other available lights were dim incandescent ones which would not have produced the blinding glare witnesses saw. It was not until the mid-1960s that military and commercial airplanes regularly carried powerful strobe lights and the newer, more brilliant landing lights.)

There were numerous reports of occupants, usually of normal-looking men and women glimpsed inside the ships as they sailed by. One of the most interesting was made by M. G. Sisson, postmaster at Greenfield, Illinois, on the afternoon of April 19. While walking his dog through the woods he allegedly spotted an airship 150 feet above him —a phenomenon he found less unsettling than the sight of a woman who stood on a deck in front of the craft, catching pigeons with a net. When she saw him she quickly stepped inside and the craft flew away.

Later that day Thomas Bradburg of Hagaman, about nine miles east of Greenfield, supposedly discovered a partly written letter which appeared to have been dropped from the airship. Under a printed letterhead reading "Airship Co., Oakland, Cal."* it went:

> We are having a delightful time and plenty to eat. Mollie's scheme for running down birds and catching them with a net works excellently; we feast daily upon pigeon pie.
>
> Since starting out we have greatly increased the velocity of the ship. The following figures will give some idea of the speed which we are now able to make: St. Louis, April 15, 8:30 P.M.; Chicago, same evening, 9:33; Kansas City, one hour and forty minutes later.

This was only one of many such "messages" supposedly released from airships. Although at this late date there really is no way to tell for certain, it is likely that the vast majority were hoaxes. We mention the Hagaman document only because of its possible tie-in with Sisson's sighting (of course the one relevant question—had Bradburg heard Sisson's story before he "found" the letter?—is unanswerable) and because its mention of Oakland, California, as the inventor's place of residence takes us back to the controversies of November 1896.

But the events of 1896, incredible as they were, are relatively uncomplicated compared to what happened in 1897. California's celebrated controversy concerned only one

---

*Curiously, around 1897 the "National Airship Company" of San Francisco sold 250,000 shares of stock in itself in an attempt to raise a million dollars to fund the construction of a 1,000-foot airship. The airship was supposed to carry five hundred passengers on regular flights from New York to London. Neither the airship nor the scheme got off the ground, however.

alleged inventor, but April 1897 produced a rash of conflicting claims about a host of different men. Obviously someone was lying. Sometimes it was the "witnesses." Sometimes it was the newspapers. And sometimes it may have been the airship occupants themselves.

Let us first examine a number of contact claims of the period:

Springfield, Illinois, April 15: Adolph Winkle and John Hulle, farmhands, allegedly saw an airship land two miles outside the city and talked with its occupants, two men and a woman, who said they would "make a report to the government when Cuba is declared free."

Harrisburg, Arkansas, April 21: At 1:00 A.M. a strange noise roused "ex-Senator Harris" from sleep and through his bedroom window he saw an airship descending to the ground. The occupants, two young men, a woman, and an elderly man with a dark waist-length beard, got out and helped themselves to a supply of fresh well water. Overcome by curiosity, Harris went outside and engaged the old man in a long conversation, during which the latter claimed he had inherited the secret of antigravity from his late uncle. "Weight is no object to me," he said. "I suspend all gravity by placing a small wire around an object. . . .

"I was making preparations to go over to Cuba and kill off the Spanish army if hostilities had not ceased," he continued, "but now my plans are changed and I may go to the aid of the Armenians." He would accomplish all this with a gun which would fire, he said, "sixty-three thousand times per minute." (!)

He offered Harris a ride, which the ex-senator refused, and then the crew reentered their craft and disappeared into the night.

Conroe, Texas, April 22–23: Around midnight four men, one of them proprietor G. L. Witherspoon, were playing dominoes in the restaurant section of the town hotel when three strangers came upon the scene. They said they had landed their airship not far away and come into town for supper "by way of a change," then went on to report that they had flown from San Francisco en route to Cuba. Witherspoon and his friends declined an offer to examine the ship, suspecting that they were the victims of a practical joke. But about an hour later, after the visitors had left, a brilliantly lighted airship passed over Conroe.

Stephensville, Texas, late April: Alerted by "prominent farmer" C. L. McIllhaney that an airship had alighted in a field on his farm three miles from town, a large delegation of Stephensville's leading citizens—our source lists all their names—set out to see for themselves. They found a sixty-foot cigar-shaped craft and its two occupants, who gave their names as S. E. Tillman and A. E. Dolbear. The pair explained that they were making an experimental trip to test the ship for certain New York financiers. Turning down requests from onlookers who wanted to examine the craft, the aeronauts boarded the machine and sailed off.

Chattanooga, Tennessee, late April: Several Chattanooga citizens reportedly encountered a landed airship "in the exact shape of a shad, minus head and tail," resting on a mountainside near the city. Its two occupants were at work repairing it. One, who identified himself as "Professor Charles Davidson," said that they had left Sacramento a month before and had spent the time touring the country.

Jenny Lind, Arkansas, May 4: At 7:30 that evening an airship passed over town and three men leaped on their bicycles and pursued it until it landed by a spring next to a mountain. Its pilots, who introduced themselves as George Autzerlitz and Joseph Eddleman, talked with the three for a while, saying they subsisted on birds which they would overtake in flight and capture. Before leaving the aeronauts offered any one of them a free ride and ended up taking James Davis to Huntington, fifteen miles away.

(This story appeared in the *St. Louis Post-Dispatch* in the form of a letter from two Jenny Lind residents, who urged the paper to contact R. M. McDowell, general manager of the Western Coal and Mining Company in St. Louis. McDowell told the *Post-Dispatch,* "Yes, I know all those persons. I have extensive works at Jenny Lind. I don't understand the letter, though. It is very strange.")

Hot Springs, Arkansas, May 6: John J. Sumpter, Jr., and John McLemore, police officers, testified in an affadavit that they had seen a sixty-foot airship land that dark, rainy night. There were three occupants, a young man and woman and an older man with a long dark beard. The latter approached the lawmen, carrying a lantern, while the young man filled a large sack with water, and the woman stayed in the shadows, apparently not wishing to be observed. The old man said that they would stop off at Nashville after traveling the country. The officers turned down an offer for a ride and then left on other business. When they returned forty minutes later, the ship was gone.

(The *Fort Smith Daily News Record* noted that while Sumpter and McLemore were subjected to a great deal of ridicule, "they, however, most seriously maintain that it is absolutely true, and their earnestness is puzzling many, who, while unable to accept the story as a fact, yet see that the men are not jesting.")

Are these stories to be taken seriously? If they are hoaxes, at least they are not obvious ones, and there certainly were plenty of obvious ones in circulation during the three months of the 1897 airship scare. What makes the incidents, or alleged incidents, detailed above so fascinating is that they do have a certain consistency. Three of them note the presence of a lone young woman with one or two young men; two of them, including the suspicious-sounding Harrisburg contact, have an elderly man sporting a long dark beard. (Our source for the Springfield, Illinois, case does not tell us what the aeronauts looked like but it is possible that this landing is related to those at Harrisburg and Hot Springs, Arkansas.)

In two other accounts the occupants point to Sacramento and San Francisco as their place of origin. Another mentions New York. All these cities figure prominently in the November–December 1896 affair as locations either where the craft were seen or where they supposedly had been constructed. And then there is the business of the birds (the Jenny Lind report), reminiscent of M. G. Sisson's sighting.

As we have said before, however, *somebody* has to be lying. The extravagant claims and predictions the occupants allegedly made are clearly phony and often contradictory—just as they usually are even in apparently authentic claims of contact with "space brothers" in our own age. If it is not our claimants who are doing the lying, then it is the enigmatic people they conversed with, whose loquaciousness was designed not to elucidate but to obfuscate.

Even if every one of these stories is no more than the work of a prankster's imagination, though, that does not alter the fact that for the most part (the lesser part we shall examine shortly) the craft were piloted and probably built by human beings, as opposed to the hairy humanoids and golden-maned Venusians of modern flying saucer lore. But just who were they? And what ever happened to their marvelous inventions?

6

While 1897 newspapers printed reams of speculation about the supposed identity of the inventor, very little of this material seems based on anything more substantial than rumor and hearsay. Amid all the nonsense, however, are several bits and pieces which cause us to wonder just what was going on in those days and who knew what about it. For examples:

About 11:00 P.M. on April 19, in the Beaumont, Texas, area, farmer J. R. Ligon and his son Charley sighted a landed airship in an adjacent pasture. Investigating, they found four men moving around the machine and one of them, who said his name was Wilson, asked for and received a supply of water from the farmer's house.

Twenty-three hours later, at Uvalde, Texas, Sheriff H. W. Baylor spoke briefly with the three-man crew of an airship which had alighted outside the town. One of them gave his name as Wilson and identified himself as a native of Goshen, New York. Then he asked about a Captain Akers, whom he said he had known in Fort Worth in 1877 and who he understood lived in the area. After getting water from Baylor's pump the aeronauts reentered their craft and took off.

The *Galveston Daily News* located Captain Akers, who told them, "I can say that while living in Fort Worth in '76 and '77 I was well acquainted with a man by the name of Wilson from New York State and was on very friendly terms with him. He was of a mechanical turn of mind and was then working on aerial navigation and something that would astonish the world. He was a finely educated man, then about twenty-four years of age, and seemed to have money with which to prosecute his investigations, devoting his whole time to them. From conversations we had while in Fort Worth, I think that Mr. Wilson, having succeeded in constructing a practical airship, would probably hunt me up to show me that he was not so wild in his claims as I then supposed. I will say further that I have known Sheriff Baylor many years and know that any statement he may make can be relied on as exactly correct." (*Galveston Daily News,* April 28, 1897)

Another candidate whose nomination for airship inventor we shall have to consider carefully is described in the *Omaha Globe-Democrat* for April 10:

> The indications are that John O. Preast of this county is the author of the mysterious machine. Preast is a unique character, spending his time at his country residence near Omaha in experimenting with airships, constructing models, and studying all the subjects incidental to the theories of applied mechanics along the line of providing a vessel that will propel itself through the air. He has consumed the past ten years in this way, and the walls of his home are covered with drawings of queer-shaped things, some resembling giant birds, while others look like a big cigar, all of which he says represent models of airships. He is a man of superior education. He came to Omaha from Germany twenty years ago, and has lived the life of a recluse. Mr. Preast refuses to admit that the ship reported in different sections of the state is his invention, but some time since he told several persons that he would surprise the world with a working model in 1897. . . . The two times in the past week that the light has been seen at Omaha it disappeared near Preast's home, hovering over the place and then appearing to go out.

A November 1896 *San Francisco Call* informs us that the airship "closely resembles a bird." But what interests us more about this Mr. Preast is how much he reminds us of someone else: the equally mysterious C. A. A. Dellschau, whom we already have discussed. Both men were recluses, German immigrants, compulsive students of aviation who spent untold hours making drawings of odd-looking aircraft.

And who is this "Wilson"? Could he be the "Wilson" of

"Tosh Wilson and Co." (crew?) to whom Dellschau refers cryptically in one of the scrapbooks he compiled in his home in Texas around the time of the airship flap?

A wild guess, perhaps. Nonetheless we have some other puzzles to ponder. Germany is pivotal to the airship question because that is where the objects first appeared in the 1850s. Unfortunately we do not have access to these German reports, which might well answer a lot of questions for us; but how odd it is the number of German names that crop up in Dellschau's list of men allegedly involved with the Aero Club: Gustav Freyer, August Schoetler, Jacob Mischer, Ernest Krause, Julius Koch, A. B. Kahn, and many others. Note also the many German names (like Tillman, Dolbear, Autzerlitz, Eddleman, etc.) that crop up in connection with 1897 airship incidents.

We have the testimony of lawyer W. H. H. Hart, among others, that airships had been invented in California. As we have observed already, Hart claimed to have seen the airships and known the men who built them, and there is no reason to doubt the word of this former attorney general, especially since airships made their first major appearances in the Golden State—in the same general area, in fact, where Dellschau's supposed flying club had tested its *Aeros* some years before. Moreover, indications are that there was an Eastern airship, as Hart also asserted, though usually it is New York, not New Jersey, that our sources cite as its home state. "Wilson" may have been affiliated with the Eastern airship people.

Whatever the truth or untruth of Dellschau's story, very probably some kind of secret society or organization of aeronauts lived and worked in the United States and possibly Germany as well during the nineteenth century. The mysterious "collector of curiosities" who showed up in Galisteo Junction, New Mexico, in 1880 the day after an airship had flown over and who stole away with the evidence it had left behind may have been associated with the organization. Certainly the Californians George Collins and W. H. H. Hart dealt with must have been.

Just how many airships took part in the 1896–97 flaps is of course impossible to estimate, but it would have taken several dozen aeronauts to pilot the various craft reported in different parts of the country. All of them presumably would have been involved with the society and sworn to secrecy, since no one ever stepped forward to answer satisfactorily the many questions raised by the sudden appearances of airships. When aeronauts did volunteer information, they mouthed mostly drivel, although some slight strains of truth may have run through their stories. "Wilson," for example, seems to have been who he said he was, but he does not tell us much else. The airship's occupants, one gathers, did not want us to know who they were or what they were up to.

For instance, no one got a straight answer from them about the airship's source of power. The words *gas* and *electricity* dot a number of accounts and once, as noted earlier, *antigravity* crops up. Most airships carried both large gas bags and powerful searchlights, but at the same time the craft look so unwieldy that one wonders how they flew, particularly when they could also hover and move straight up and down. Maybe Dellschau's antigravity gas "NB" is as good an explanation as any other we're likely to find.

7

Now let us examine a story an entirely different from those we have been studying. This one was published in the *St. Louis Post-Dispatch* for April 19, in the form of a letter from W. H. Hopkins, a St. Louis resident whose job as general traveling agent for the Hartford Steam Boiler Inspection and Insurance Company had taken him out of town that week. The incident in question supposedly occurred on April 16:

. . . I was wandering through hills east of Springfield, Missouri, and coming to the brow of a hill overlooking a small clearing in the valley a short distance below me I saw a sight that rooted me to the spot with amazement for some time. I could not believe my eyes at first, and shook myself to see if I was not dreaming. There in the clearing rested a vessel similar in outline to the airship shown in the *Post-Dispatch* of a few days ago, and said to have been taken in Illinois. . . .

Near the vessel was the most beautiful being I ever beheld. She was rather under medium size, but of the most exquisite form and features such as would put to shame the forms as sculptured by the ancient Greeks. She was dressed in nature's garb and her golden hair, wavy and glossy, hung to her waist, unconfined excepting by a band of glistening jewels that bound it back from her forehead. The jewels threw out rays of light as she moved her head. She was plucking the little flowers that were just blossoming from the sod, with exclamations of delight and in a language I could not understand. Her voice was like low, silvery bells and her laughter rang out like their chimes. In one hand she carried a fan of curious design that she fanned herself vigorously with, though to me the air was not warm and I wore an overcoat.

In the shade of the vessel lay a man of noble proportions and majestic countenance. His hair of dark auburn fell to his shoulders in wavy masses and his full beard, of the same color but lighter in shade, reached to his breast. He also was fanning himself with a curious fan as if the heat oppressed him. . . .

After gazing for a while I moved forward, and the woman, hearing the rustle of leaves, looked around. A moment she stood looking at me with wonder and astonishment in her beautiful blue eyes, then, with a shriek of fear, she rushed to the man, who sprung to his feet, threw his arm around her, and glared at me in a threatening manner.

I stopped and, taking my handkerchief from my pocket, waved it in the air. A few minutes we stood. I then spoke some words of apology for intruding, but he seemed not to understand, and replied in a threatening tone and words which I could not make out. I tried by signs to make him understand, and finally he left her, trembling and trying to hold him back, and came toward me. I extended my hand. He looked at it for a moment, astonishment depicted in his dark brown eyes, and finally he extended his own and touched mine. I took his and carried it to my lips. I tried by signs to make them understand I meant no harm. Finally his face lighted up with pleasure, and he turned and spoke to the woman. She came hesitatingly forward, her form undulating with exquisite grace. I took her hand and kissed it fervently. The color rose to her cheeks and she drew it hastily away.

I asked them by signs where they came from, but it was difficult to make them understand. Finally they seemed to do so and smiling they gazed upwards for a moment, as if looking for some particular point, and then pointed upwards, pronouncing a word which, to my imagination, sounded like "Mars."

I pointed to the ship and expressed my wonder in my countenance. He took me by the hand and led me towards it. In the side was a small door. I looked in. There was a luxurious couch covered with robes of the most beautiful stuff and texture, such as I had never seen before. From the ceiling was suspended a curious ball, from which extended a strip of metal, which he struck to make it vibrate. Instantly the ball was illuminated with a soft, white light, which lit up the whole interior. It was most beautifully decorated with scenes such as I had never seen before.

At the stern was another large ball of metal, supported in a strong framework, and connected to the shaft of the propeller at the stern was a similar mechanism attached to each propeller and smaller balls attached to a point of metal that extended from each side of the vessel and from the prow. And connected to each ball was a thin strip of metal similar to the lamp. He struck each one and when they vibrated the balls commenced to revolve with intense rapidity, and did not cease till he stopped them with a kind of brake. As they revolved intense lights, stronger than any arclight I ever saw, shone out from the points at the sides and at the prow, but they were of different colors. The one at the prow was an intense white light. On one side was green and the other red.

The two had been examining me with the greatest curiosity in the meantime. They felt of my clothing, looked at my gray hair with surprise, and examined my watch with the greatest wonder. Signs are poor medium to exchange ideas and therefore we could express but little.

I pointed to the balls attached to the propellers. He gave each of the strips of metal a rap, those attached to the propellers under the vessel first. The balls began to revolve rapidly, and I felt the vessel begin to rise, and I sprang out, and none too soon, for the vessel rose as lightly as a bird, and shot away like an arrow, and in a few minutes was out of sight. The two stood laughing and waving their hands to me, she a vision of loveliness and he of manly vigor.

Incredible? Certainly. A skeptical *Post-Dispatch* reporter brought the letter to Hopkins's employer, C. C. Gardner, who read it carefully and then said, "This is wonderful. That is Mr. Hopkins's handwriting and he is now in their territory. He was also at Springfield on the day named. He is a traveling agent for the company."

Asked if he believed Hopkins's story, Gardner nodded vigorously. "Indeed I do," he said. "Strange as it seems, I am compelled to believe it. Mr. Hopkins is not a romancer. He never courts notoriety. What he writes he has seen and he believes it is his duty to make the facts public. He does not drink a drop. He has been connected with this company for a long time and is most reliable. What he writes you can publish as being absolutely true."

Other employees at the firm also spoke highly of Hopkins.

The reporter also searched out Hopkins's wife and two daughters. "It's the truth if he wrote it," Mrs. Hopkins affirmed, "and I believe every word." So did the girls.

Mrs. Hopkins rejected out of hand the possibility of a hoax. "What, a man fifty years of age writing such a letter without it being true! No, sir, every line of it is true. Mr. Hopkins is a member of the Maple Avenue Methodist Evangelical Church and has many friends in the West End. He undoubtedly wishes to acquaint his friends with the marvel he has seen and so uses the *Post-Dispatch* as the medium of communication.

"Mr. Hopkins left home a week ago. Before he left he ridiculed the idea of an airship having been seen. But now I suppose he is convinced it is not a myth. Truly, it is wonderful."

Even if we do not prefer to interpret literally the suggestion that the Springfield aeronauts hailed from the planet Mars, we can hardly deny the incident's otherworldly overtones. Actually the whole affair is more reminiscent of many post-World War II UFO contact claims than of most of the other 1897 landing reports. Just what does it mean?

For one thing, it is a curious blending of scientific and magical elements. The airship links the story to the late nineteenth-century Industrial Age concerns which we see reflected in most other parts of the airship saga. Otherwise Hopkins's tale resembles a visionary experience of fairy-folk who have forsaken supernatural modes of transportation for mechanical ones. Since, as folklore attests, fairies imitate the human society around them (to the extent of using horsecarts and other such contrivances) perhaps we should not begrudge them airships.

Seriously, however, the archetypal foundation of the story is clear. The "Martians" are in fact the primeval couple of world mythology; to us their most prominent representatives are Adam and Eve. Traditionally the couple are depicted as physically beautiful, innocent, and immortal children of nature, living in a timeless paradisal realm sometimes reputed to be located in the sky. (Of this realm, Sir James G. Frazer wrote in *Folklore in the Old Testament,* it "stands for that original state of bliss to which, in this vale of tears, man longingly looks back, and which he hopes eventually to regain. It thus symbolizes both the remote memory and the distant hope of the human race.")

Hopkins is most specific on the subject of the couple's attractiveness, and their nudity and general demeanor certainly mark them as "innocent." Their immortality is implied in the way, as the account has it, they "looked at my gray hair with surprise." We are led to believe that their home in the sky is timeless (as heaven and fairyland are reported to be) because they "examined my watch with the greatest wonder," apparently with no idea of what it might be.

Surely this ranks as one of the first modern UFO contact cases, and inevitably it recalls John Rimmer's contention that the UFO functions as an "antiscientific symbol." The Springfield case also stands in sharp contrast to the other, more mundane 1896–97 landing reports, in which we hear much bloodthirsty talk of decimating whatever foreign elements the American public happened currently to hold in disfavor. We see here the first hints of the psychic revulsion against technology; put another way, we can interpret it as an early attempt of the unconscious to resist the growing domination of the conscious mind—to restore the balance, as it were, between the mysterious and the mechanical.

Other accounts connect the airships with today's UFOs.

On April 16, at Mount Vernon, Illinois, the city's mayor focused his telescope on the "airship." What he saw was something that resembled, in the words of the *Saginaw Courier-Herald,* "the body of a huge man swimming through the air with an electric light at his back." It goes without saying that no theory which assumes that terrestrial inventors were solely responsible for airship manifestations is going to explain a sighting like this one.

Nor, as far as that goes, one like the now famous "calf-napping" at LeRoy, Kansas, on April 19, first reported in the *Yates Center* [Kansas] *Farmers' Advocate* for April 23, 1897, and since then widely reprinted in modern books on UFOs. Chief witness Alexander Hamilton related that the airship was "occupied by six of the strangest beings I ever saw.... They were jabbering together but we could not understand a syllable they said." As soon as they were discovered they sailed away, with Hamilton's calf in tow.

"I went home," Hamilton said, "but every time I would drop to sleep, I would see the cursed thing with its big lights and hideous people. I don't know whether they are devils or angels or what ... I don't want any more to do with them."

Quite a contrast to Mr. Hopkins's attractive young couple. We are reminded of the various types of UFO beings reported in our own time—unpleasant-looking creatures that flee from sight as well as strikingly handsome "men" and beautiful "women" who usually behave in friendly fashion toward human beings who approach them.

On April 25 the *Daily Texarkanian* (Texarkana, Arkansas) published the testimony of Judge Lawrence A. Byrne:

I was down on McKinney bayou Friday [April 23] looking after the surveying of a tract of land and, in passing through a thicket to an open space, saw a strange-looking object anchored to the ground. On approaching I found it to be the airship I have read so much about of late. It was manned by three men who spoke a foreign language, but judging from their looks, would take them to be Japs. They saw my astonishment and beckoned me to follow them, and on complying, I was shown through the ship.

Judge Byrne said that the machine was made of aluminum and "the gas to raise and lower the monster was pumped into an aluminum tank when the ship was to be raised and let out when to be lowered."

That is pretty much the sum total of his account, whose interest for us lies in his mention of "Japs"—evidently short men with Oriental features. Beings fitting this description figure in more than a few modern accounts, most notably the famous Barney and Betty Hill UFO abduction, which was the subject of John G. Fuller's *The Interrupted Journey*.

Our last case is by far the eeriest of all. From the *Houston Daily Post* of April 28:

Merkel, Texas, April 26—Some parties returning from church last night noticed a heavy object dragging along with a rope attached. They followed it until in crossing the railroad it caught on a rail. On looking up they saw what they supposed was the airship. It was not near enough to get an idea of the dimensions. A light could be seen protruding from several windows; one bright light in front like the headlight of a locomotive. After some ten minutes a man was seen descending the rope; he came near enough to be plainly seen. He wore a light blue sailor suit, was small in size. He stopped when he discovered parties at the anchor and cut the ropes below him and sailed off in a northeast direction. The anchor is now on exhibition at the blacksmith shop of Elliott and Miller and is attracting the attention of hundreds of people.

And in an ancient, obscure Irish manuscript, *Speculum Regali*, we read of an incident that supposedly occurred in the year 956:

There happened in the borough of Cloera, one Sunday while people were at mass, a marvel. In this town there is a church to the memory of St. Kinarus. It befell that a metal anchor was dropped from the sky, with a rope attached to it, and one of the sharp flukes caught in the wooden arch above the church door. The people rushed out of the church and saw in the sky a ship with men on board, floating at the end of the anchor cable, and they saw a man leap overboard and pull himself down the cable to the anchor as if to unhook it. He appeared as if he were swimming in water. The folk rushed up and tried to seize him; but the bishop forbade the people to hold the man for fear it might kill him. The man was freed and hurried up the cable to the ship, where the crew cut the rope and the ship rose and sailed away out of sight. But the anchor is in the church as a testimony to this singular occurrence.

As if that is not enough, around the year 1200 an anchor plummeted out of the sky, trailing a rope, and got caught in a mound of stones near a church in Bristol, England. As a mob of churchgoers congregated at the scene, a "sailor" came skitting down the rope to free it. According to Gervase of Tilbury's *Otia Imperialia,* the crowd seized the intruder and "he suffocated by the mist of our moist atmosphere and expired." His unseen comrades cut the rope and departed.

We do not pretend to understand why an incident of this nature should continually recur, but its occurrence amid the 1897 airship flap should prove conclusively that we are dealing with phenomena whose full implications boggle the mind. Something virtually incomprehensible was taking place in nineteenth-century America, and whatever conclusions we draw from it are bound to be not only fantastic but tentative, for the gaps in the story are often greater than the substance. With that necessary warning we proceed to consider a couple of possibilities.

8

As we have seen, most of the events of the 1896–97 period do not seem to possess the paranormal overtones we have come to associate with strange flying objects and related phenomena. While UFOs, as the next chapter will show, are at best only quasiphysical, the airships, on the other hand, appear to have been built of conventional materials. The airship pilots—most of them, anyway—were undeniably human. They gave no evidence of supernormal powers. In their contacts with witnesses they did not (with, of course, the exceptions noted above) follow the unmistakable modus operandi familiar to students of what has come to be called the Phenomenon. These incidents seem to break with the past (as manifested in fairy and religious phenomena) while at the same time they do not connect with the future (UFOs). Perhaps the one obvious similarity is in the fact that many of the aeronauts possessed, speaking euphemistically, a rather casual regard for the truth. Still, logic and the mass of evidence compel us to accept that they most likely were human scientists and inventors.

But the world of the nineteenth century had neither the knowledge nor the means to successfully fly heavier-than-air machines. Of that much we are certain. We are equally certain, conversely, that somebody was doing just that. Even if we reject Dellschau's claims as senile ravings, we still must confront the twin "impossible" facts of airships and human occupants.

Throughout history innumerable groups and societies, secret and otherwise, have banded together in acceptance of the idea that they were in one way or another in contact with "higher beings" who taught them things and oversaw their lives. Virtually all religions assume that their adherents were and are guided in this manner. So do cults of black and white magicians, spiritualists, flying saucer contactees, and many, many others. Some gifted scientists and inventors privately have believed that nonhuman entities helped them in their work.

Suppose that both in Germany and in the United States (specifically in California and New York) a secret cult of brilliant scientists, engineers, and inventors believed that it had established contact (perhaps through occult means —spiritualism, for example, was coming into prominence in the middle years of the nineteenth century) with paranormal forces which "told" them how to construct aerial vessels, ordering the group to keep its work under wraps. Presumably the German and American branches were in communication with one another, and around 1848 some of the Germans migrated in order to pool their efforts with those of their American cohorts. Setting up shop near Sonora, California, the group proceeded to conduct some incredible experiments.

Eventually there must have developed a degree of dissension and dissatisfaction in the ranks as members of the group came to realize that they might never be allowed to give their *Aeros* to the world. They may have hoped that someone—Dellschau calls him the "right man"—would arrive to find a way to defy the "superiors" and make the airship public property (not all that public, of course, since the group stood to collect an enormous fortune for their enterprise).

The Germans who stayed in their own country could have been responsible for that first 1850s airship flap. In the years after that, however, they, too, might have come to America, which now was the center of aviation action. One of them might have been John O. Preast.

While airships appeared over America from time to time in the years leading up to 1896, it was during that year the group chose to conduct widespread, sustained flights for whatever inscrutible reason. In order to maintain secrecy at a period when airships would for the first time be widely observed, the society agreed to plant a series of conflicting, confusing claims to mislead outsiders. The ploy worked brilliantly, of course.

Members of the organization, believing themselves to be under the domination of forces which apparently did possess some kind of at least shadowy reality, may have come to consider themselves pawns in a cosmic game, much in the fashion of modern contactees who have had their lives directed and sometimes destroyed by UFO beings. They may have actually thought that their purpose was to distract attention from the activities of their "superiors" (who must be viewed as late-nineteenth-century members of that psychic continuum to which fairies and today's ufonauts also belong).

If Dellschau was lying, which of course is certainly possible, then we must revise our theory only to exclude the German and Sonora angles. The existence of a secret society in contact with a paranormal agency can be inferred from a wide range of other evidence we have studied.

But to pursue our initial hypothesis to its conclusion, let us suppose that Dellschau retired to Houston late in the nineteenth century (as in fact he did), depressed and discouraged because it looked as though the whole amazing business forever would remain a secret. Still intimidated by the "superiors" and afraid to speak too directly, nonetheless he determined to leave the world a series of clues in hopes that one day a "Wonder Weaver" would find them and sew together the entire dazzling fabric.

Or let us consider an auxiliary theory:

Suppose that our secret group, failing to comprehend the real nature of the Phenomenon, never understood what it had unleashed on the world. Certainly its members knew that they were in the grip of a powerful force. But they did not know, to begin with, that this force is reflective, that it returns what it receives. As with other percipients since time immemorial, they were led to believe that they alone were privy to the secrets of the Phenomenon, though these "secrets" really had come out of themselves, been imprinted on the Phenomenon, and fed back to them.

In other words, it is quite possible that the information from which the group constructed its airships (if in fact it did so) came not so much from "higher intelligence," as the members apparently thought, but from the collective unconscious of the organization, which was composed of scientists and inventors who may not have consciously possessed sufficient knowledge to invent airships but who most certainly had the ability to do so *latently*.

Consider these words of C. G. Jung's (in *Man and His Symbols*): "Just as conscious contents can vanish into the unconscious, new contents, which have never yet been conscious, can *arise* from it." Jung points to the experiences of the French mathematician Poincare and the chemist Kekule, who made important scientific discoveries when sudden dreamlike "revelations" welled up from the unconscious. Likewise, the philosopher Descartes saw in a flash the "order of all sciences." Presumably the Phenomenon, which might have been triggered into manifestation by the airship group's tinkering with occultism, had a wealth of brilliant, raw psychic material from which to draw and to parrot back to its credulous audience. Unfortunately, as Dellschau and company were to discover, dreams passing themselves off as objectively real manifestations have only limited effect and ultimately are negative in their consequences.

If with the Dellschau group machine had arisen out of mystery, so the sudden appearance of the airships before a startled American public caused the opposite effect. The last half of the nineteenth century had seen tremendous changes in American life: the settling of the continent, the destruction of the wilderness, the rise of the Industrial Age, the move toward urbanization. This rapid transition from a simpler agrarian life proved a traumatic experience for most people, and while the new technology imposed a culture whose values were rooted in science, reason, and materialism, a considerable share of the psychically ravaged populace rebelled. One clear manifestation was the explosion of spiritualistic beliefs; another was the revival of fundamentalism and the proliferation of offbeat religious sects.

Few Americans had any idea that the airships were, indirectly at any rate, a paranormal phenomenon. Most of them saw the craft as a sort of final triumph of technology, and something about which they must surely have entertained ambivalent feelings. All the talk about bombs and aerial machine guns, pointing toward a time when there would be no safety anywhere, must have been disconcerting in the extreme. Moreover, now the heavens had been violated; men had tainted even the domain of the angels.

The Phenomenon, always reflective, playing now to a much larger audience, proceeded to produce imitation airships whose occupants were creatures from dream and nightmare, archetypal forms out of the primeval memories of the collective unconscious. W. H. Hopkins found a Martian Adam and Eve in the Missouri hills. Alex Hamilton wasn't sure if they were "devils or angels or what"—but he did know that their home was somewhere in the sky. For there was no more room on the earth, now that she had given up her greatest secrets, for a realm of wonder, of magical enchantment or supernatural horror. Outer space, however . . .

From the mystery to the machine—so it had begun when the aeronauts' secret society probed the Phenomenon for technical information. It had ended when the machine gave way to the mystery, when gods and demons and angels resumed their ancient place in the sky. The stage had been set for the coming of Unidentified Flying Objects.

UFOs: THE MYSTERY IN THE MACHINE

> Such an object provokes, like nothing else, conscious and unconscious fantasies, the former giving rise to speculative conjectures and pure fabrications, and the latter supplying the mythological background inseparable from these provocative observations. Thus there arose a situation in which, with the best will in the world, one often did not know and could not discover whether a primary perception was followed by a phantasm or whether, conversely, a primary fantasy originating in the unconscious invaded the conscious mind with illusions and visions.
> —C. G. Jung, in *Flying Saucers: A Modern Myth of Things Seen in the Skies*

1

On the evening of May 3, 1969, Jose Antonio da Silva, age twenty-four, left his home on a fishing trip. He boarded a bus at Belo Horizonte, Brazil, and got off some time later on the Jaguara road, down which he hiked until he got to a place known as Bebedouro, in the municipal district of Matozinhos. By midnight he had reached his destination, a small lagoon. He set up a little tent along the lagoon's banks then decided to do some fishing before retiring.

At daybreak he awoke and cast his line into the water once again. The morning dragged on slowly, and the only fish he encountered were in the sardine can he opened at noon. Undiscouraged, he went on with his fishing, without an inkling of the incredible events about to occur.

By 3:00 P.M. Jose Antonio, thoroughly bored, sat there, semidozing, his thoughts so far adrift that he was scarcely aware of the sudden appearance of figures moving about behind him, speaking in a language he did not recognize. Only when he heard a cry "seemingly like a groan coming from deep down in the chest" did he realize that he was in the presence of something extraordinary. But before he could move, a partially concealed someone fired a "burst of fire" from out of the bushes and it hit him in the legs.

"The burst looked like fire," he said later, "but it wasn't, because it didn't burn my leg." The "fire," actually a beam of light, green in the middle and red at the edges, paralyzed him. A painful cramp gripped his legs, then a feeling of numbness, and he fell to his knees. Almost immediately two small figures with masks grabbed him under the arms and hauled him through the tangled thickets, which they negotiated with no apparent difficulty. His knees scraping the ground, Jose Antonio chose not to resist—he did not care to provoke his abductors into firing the light at his head.

Presently a third figure appeared. Jose Antonio (a soldier by profession) was sure that this was the one who had made the groaning sound before firing at him. All three of the beings carried "rifles" with large barrels rather on the order of a blunderbuss. In the center of the top side of each weapon was a trigger which when pulled backward caused the luminous beam to shoot out the barrel.

The beings, about four feet in height, were built more or less like small but robust human beings, though their legs were unusually thick. They wore shining, light-colored "spacesuits" and masks with two holes at eye-level. A tube of plasticlike material extended from the lower part of the mask, passed over the chest and under the armpit, and ended in a small metal container on each of their backs.

They carried Jose Antonio into a strange machine shaped like two saucers joined together by a thick, vertical cylinder. A series of rods, set at regular intervals, slanted down from under the upper plate into the base of the cylinder just before they reached the lower plate. The cylinder was gray, the plates were black, and the entire object stood about seven feet high.

Jose Antonio found himself in a quadrangular room illuminated by a brilliant "mercury vapor" light whose source he could not detect. The walls of the room seemed to be composed of some smooth, dark gray stone. His captors sat him down, forced a helmet on him, fastened him down, and positioned themselves one on each side. The third being entered and took the one remaining seat, in the center of the room. He pulled two levers and abruptly the craft left the ground.

Jose Antonio spent a considerable period of time—many hours, he thought, though he had no way of telling for sure—in growing physical and emotional discomfort. He listened as the beings conversed in an unpleasant "guttural" tone and he wondered miserably what lay in store for him. Meanwhile, he had difficulty breathing and the sharp edges of the helmet kept digging into his shoulders and the back of his neck.

Much later the machine seemed to rotate ninety degrees on its lateral axis and the seats automatically adjusted themselves to the new position. After another long period the craft and seats resumed their normal positions. Finally it landed with a "jarring sensation."

As the beings rose to free their captive from his seatbelt, they silently placed a bandage over the holes in his helmet. Then they carried him out by his armpits. Though still numb, his legs had begun to recover their normal strength and he thought he might be able to walk. But he did not dare to press the issue with the little men, who seemed very strong for their size.

In the darkness he could hear footsteps and masculine voices all speaking in the same weird language of his companions, who themselves remained silent. At last Jose Antonio was put down on a small, backless seat and was relieved of the bandage which had obscured his vision.

Sitting there, the helmet still on his head, he surveyed his surroundings. He was in a large quadrangular room, with four beings: his three captors, who now were removing their helmets, and one other, who was conversing animatedly with the trio. Jose Antonio took him to be their commander. Seeing him, the young man's spirits sank even lower. Now he was certain that he would never get back.

Like the others, the "commander" was extremely hairy. Both his red hair and his beard came down to his waist.

His pale skin contrasted with his thick, wide eyebrows. His large, round eyes, greenish in color, were set deep inside his head. He hardly ever blinked, and Jose Antonio did not notice any eyelashes.

The being's nose was long, pointed, and large. His ears were unusually big, too, and more rounded at the top than those of a human being. Of the mouths of this and the other humanoids, Jose Antonio told investigators, "They looked like fishes' mouths. I didn't see a tooth in any of them. When they opened their mouths, I didn't see one." (R. L. Johannis, you may recall, claimed that his "little green men" had oral cavities which were "very much like the mouth of a fish.")

The chief's apparently happy disposition helped the young man to relax for a while. Other little men came and went—at one point there were as many as a dozen in evidence—conferring with the leader and taking orders from him.

Whatever passing comfort Jose Antonio got from the scene was shattered, however, when he happened to glance to his left and gaze upon an incredible and terrifying sight. On a low shelf, seemingly fashioned out of stone, lay the bodies of four human men stretched out side by side. Naked, rigid, and positioned on their backs, the bodies bore no visible wounds but it was obvious that they were dead. One was a well-built Negro and another had light brown skin. Two others, more slightly built, were Caucasian, one of them very blond, "like a foreigner."

As the little beings went about their business Jose Antonio gloomily studied what he could see of the room. Like the interior of the flying vehicle, it appeared to be made of stone and was uniformly gray-colored. And he recognized the same "mercury vapor" light again without visible source. To the left of the corpses, he noticed color pictures of familiar earthly sights: nature scenes, a small town, transportation vehicles. On the floor not far away he saw a somewhat cylindrical apparatus which reminded him slightly of a racing car.

At this point a being carefully undid Jose Antonio's cloth bundle, the one the young man had used to carry his fishing tackle. He assumed that the third being of the abducting party had scooped it up from where it had been dropped and brought it with him.

The little men excitedly examined the contents. They set aside one of everything for which there was a duplicate and put what was left—except for an identity card, whose loss eventually would cause Jose Antonio some trouble—back into the bundle. They even returned his sardine can.

He wondered if the identity card had tipped them off that he was a soldier, because as soon as they had seen it, one picked up his weapon and shot a beam of light against a wall, leaving a mark on the affected area.

Flourishing something that looked like a pencil, the commander tried to communicate with Jose Antonio with words and gestures. At last he drew pictures on a white slate and the young Brazilian got the impression that the being expected him to provide terrestrial weapons for the humanoids. He responded negatively but the chief would not leave the subject, much to the other's discomfort. (Oddly, Brazilian researcher Hulvio Brant Aleixo, who along with others investigated this fantastic story, notes, "Jose Antonio has repeatedly refused to reveal to us other passages in the 'conversation' on this subject.")

Next, one of the little beings handed him a heavy stone cube. The hollowed-out upper part contained a dark green liquid which the chief urged his captive to drink. Finally, after observing someone else partake of the stuff, Jose Antonio complied. It tasted bitter but somehow it made him feel better—and seemed to improve his understanding of what the commander was trying to tell him.

The commander went on to draw a series of sketches referring, Jose Antonio could see, to day and night, to the terrestrial year, and to two groups of years, one composed of three, the other of seven. He is proposing to take me to the earth, the young man thought, where I shall remain for three years, collecting information for him. Then he will send for me to come to them, where I shall remain studying for seven years. And then finally they will land on earth, with me as a guide.

Nervously fingering the rosary he had been wearing rolled around his waist, he gestured disapproval. Enraged, the chief ripped the crucifix out of his hand. A bead dropped to the floor and rolled away. A bystander retrieved it and then passed around it and the crucifix.

Then the most incredible part of an already incredible series of events occurred. Out of nowhere Jose Antonio saw appear in front of him a human figure who stood motionless, gazing at him in friendly fashion. The figure, about five and a half feet tall, was Caucasian, slender, bearded with long fair hair, and dressed in a friar's cassock. Amazingly, the little men seemed totally oblivious to his presence.

The apparition spoke in clear Portuguese and gave him certain "revelations" which he was to keep to himself until handed fresh instructions, which might not be for several years.

On the matter of this vision [Brant Aleixo wrote in *Flying Saucer Review*, November-December 1973] the soldier has displayed tremendous resistance to questioning, especially as regards the message received by him, which he considers to be a secret. Even these details of the physical description of the individual seen in the vision were given by him only with the greatest reluctance, for he maintains that these details could suffice for the identification of the person.

We asked him how it could be possible for the secret to be discovered merely from a simple description of the features of someone whom we did not know and would never meet. He gave us to understand, however, that it *would* be possible to recognize the person, and that it *would not* be impossible that we should meet him. Asked whether the vision was of Jesus, Jose Antonio promptly replied that it was not. As to whether it was some saint, he was unwilling to reply, merely smiling and changing the subject of conversation. After repeated interviews we managed to obtain some indications regarding the contents of the message.

The apparition vanished suddenly. The instant it had done so, the humanoids started to quarrel with each other. The commander stepped forward and with the two original captors, who had never left the soldier's side, saw to it that the bandage was again placed over the helmet's eye openings. Jose Antonio felt himself being carried away and taken somewhere else. Once there, the beings removed the blindfold and he saw that he was inside the ship.

Long afterward the craft landed with a thump, and as his captors removed his helmet and unfastened his seatbelt Jose Antonio nearly lost consciousness; he was aware only that the beings were carrying him through the darkness.

As dawn broke, perhaps an hour later, his head cleared at last. Hearing running water nearby, he crawled with his bundle to a stream, filled his water bottle, and drank heartily. Then he caught several small fish and ate them.

His surroundings were unfamiliar to him. All he knew was that the beings had deposited him on the edge of a stone quarry, beside a ravine. He limped away to the nearest paved road, flagged down a passerby, and found out that he was twenty miles from Vitoria, capital of the state of Espirito Santo. Astonished, Jose Antonio asked what the date was. It was May 9. He had been away four and a half days.

At first he considered going on to Minas Gerais, where the traveler had told him the road led, but then he decided against it, fearing trouble with the police because he had no identity card. He wondered if he should retreat to the woods and try to live on the wildlife.

As he walked, several motorists stopped and offered him rides, but he always refused, even though his right knee was swollen painfully and he was having difficulty staying on his feet. Moreover, he had three open wounds, caused by the helmet, on the nape of his neck and just below his shoulders. Finally he accepted a lift, which took him near the town of Colatina. There he approached some children to inquire about the nearest train station—he had vowed now to return home to Belo Horizonte regardless of possible consequences—but probably because of his strange appearance (he was dirty and unshaven) the children merely jeered at him, then added injury to insult by pelting him with rocks.

Jose Antonio followed the tracks to the Colatina depot, where, waiting for the arrival of the train, he befriended the agent, who took him home for a meal with his family. The young man also met an old settler, who kindly offered him a job, which he could not accept. Before he left for home, Jose Antonio bought a ticket for a youth who had no money. He noted that the beings had returned all but Cr$100 of the Cr$35,000 he had carried in his pockets.

At 7:25 A.M. the next day he got off the train at the Belo Horizonte station. Geraldo Lopes da Silva, a railway security official, challenged him for his papers, which of course Jose Antonio could not produce. Lopes took him into custody and listened in disbelief to the young man's incredible tale. The official grilled him for a while until at last, unable to get him to contradict himself, he reluctantly concluded that this evidently sincere young soldier really had undergone a bizarre experience. He called a reporter from the Radio Guarani local station. After the reporter's interview Jose Antonio was sent off to his barracks.

Major Celio Ferreira, deputy-commandant of the Guards Battalion of the Minas Gerais Military Police, whom Jose Antonio served as orderly, was relieved to see the young man. The day before, the concerned officer had even organized search parties to look for him. He took Jose Antonio into his own home for the next twenty-four hours in order to let him get rest, food, and medicine. On the morning of May 11, the young man, still lame in one leg, rejoined his family.

That same evening a team of Brazil's top ufologists conducted the first of what eventually would be twenty interviews with Jose Antonio. Exactly a week later he would reenact for them the incident at the site where it had supposedly occurred. Brant Aleixo remarks that the interviews took place "without any significant variations being observed either in his account or in his behavior."

2

If any further evidence were needed to connect UFOs with the kinds of supernatural manifestations we examined in preceding chapters, this astounding story provides it. What appears on the surface to be a tale (whether hallucination, hoax, or actual experience) of a kidnapping by possibly hostile spacemen proves, on more careful analysis, to be something quite different.

Perhaps we should not make too much of the fact that nowhere in this account do the little men specifically identify themselves as extraterrestrials. Certainly the implication is there and we really cannot blame Jose Antonio da Silva for assuming that he had been flown to another planet. Nonetheless, all the contactee knew was that he had been taken aboard a strange craft, which seemed to leave the ground, and that he had been led into a cave, which could have been anywhere, including the earth.

The Tzeltal Indians of Mexico, for example, do not connect the *ikals* with space people, but they do associate them with spherical flying objects. The *ikals* are three feet tall, hairy, and black. They live in caves, from which they periodically emerge to attack or kidnap individuals. They render their victims helpless by paralyzing them.

There is a longstanding tradition that "demons" live in caves under the earth, and the belief takes many forms. The Judeo-Christian myth of hell, usually understood to be a subterranean realm, is one obvious manifestation. When Gervase of Tilbury, a medieval chronicler who was also a monk, described the following incident, he naturally saw it as a visitation by an emissary of the devil.

In 1138, at the Brunia Monastery in the Trier region of old Prussia, wine began to disappear from its storage place in the cellar. Eventually the culprit succeeded in spilling on the floor the contents of an entire keg, all because he had forgotten to stop the bunghole after tapping the cask. Certain that one of the monks was imbibing on the sly, the steward complained to the abbot, who in turn went downstairs to anoint the cellar with holy water, lock the door securely, and place a saint's relic above the entrance.

Early the next morning the abbot and his monks unlocked the door, and discovered that another keg had been tapped, leaving the floor sticky with its contents. A sudden movement in the shadows caught the abbot's attention and two of the monks jumped the intruder and brought him into the light.

The thief, so we are told, proved to be a strange, dark-skinned dwarf. He maintained complete silence, ignoring questions about how he had managed to sneak into the cellar. A search of the room revealed at least part of the answer—it appeared that he had entered through a small tunnel that led down into the earth.

In the weeks that followed the monks attempted to draw their visitor into Christian society but the little fellow would not speak a word. He spent his time sitting cross-legged on a bed, looking straight ahead, and refusing all offers of food and drink.

Then one day the dwarf was shown to a visiting bishop, who rose in fear and shouted that the creature was a demon which must be expelled at once. At this, Gervase concludes, "the demon ran in alarm from the holy words. He went to the cellar and returned to his underworld tribe."

This charming folk tale demonstrates one consistent feature of these subterranean dwarfs: they have no time for Christianity, as Jose Antonio was to find.

Related to all this, of course, is the "Shaver Mystery," which spawned one of the odder cults of these odd times. Richard S. Shaver, who surfaced in 1945, for several years flooded *Amazing Stories,* then edited by Ray Palmer, with supposedly true stories of his adventures under the earth's surface with an extremely unpleasant group of humanoids. Before the wonder had run its course, *Amazing*'s circulation had jumped by fifty thousand readers. Letters poured into the magazine's editorial office from persons who claimed similar experiences. All this served only to outrage the science fiction establishment, and editor Palmer ended up leaving to cofound *Fate* with Curtis Fuller in 1948.

Life (May 21, 1951) summed up the content of Shaver's story thus:

> The Shaver Mystery concerned a race of malformed subhuman creatures called deros (from detrimental robots) who inhabited a vast system of underground cities all over the world. The original name of their habitat was Lemuria, and they had once been slaves of a Lemurian master race. But this master race had long since disappeared from the earth, leaving the ignorant and malicious deros in control of its great cities and wonderful machines. Since then the deros occupied themselves mainly in persecuting the human race who lived on the crust of the earth above them . . . from shipwrecks to sprained ankles. . . . They performed most of their harassments by telepathy, rays, and other remote-control devices from their subterranean homes. . . .

The psychological roots of the Shaver Mystery are almost too obvious for comment. In Freudian terms the subterranean world is the id; in Jungian, the shadow. Whatever one chooses to call it, it is that part of the psyche which lies near the surface of consciousness and whose contents we repress because they are socially and morally repugnant. Without this repression civilization itself would disintegrate. At times, under conditions of social upheaval, this dark side of the psyche has escaped its bonds, and before it could be contained death and destruction on an unimaginable scale have ravaged the earth. The people of Nazi Germany succumbed to this affliction and it is hardly surprising that Hitler and many of his cronies believed that the earth is hollow, with its subterranean regions populated by a cruel and powerful race of supermen.

A happier manifestation of the dwarfs-in-the-caves myth is found, as noted earlier, in fairylore. In some ways Jose Antonio's kidnappers are not really very different from the "good people" who took away Reverend Kirk. Evans-Wentz writes in his *The Fairy-Faith*:

> Mrs. J. MacGregor, who keeps the key to the old churchyard where there is a tomb to Kirk, though many say there is nothing in it but a coffin filled with stones, told me Kirk was taken into the Fairy Knoll, which she pointed to just across a little valley in front of us, and is there yet, for the hill is full of caverns and in them the "good people" have their homes.

Someone Evans-Wentz identifies only as an Irish peasant seer told him that the "gentry" are "a military-aristocratic class, tall and noble-appearing." But, he said, "they are able to appear in different forms. One once appeared to me, and seemed only four feet high, and stoutly built. He said, 'I am bigger than I appear to you now. We can make the old young, the big small, the small big.'" They could also strike people down with paralysis.

As evidence of their somewhat militaristic nature, we have these words from T. C. Kermode, another of Evans-Wentz's informants. Kermode, a member of the House of Keys, the Lower House of the Manx Parliament, said:

> About forty years ago, one October night, I and another young man were going to a kind of Manx harvest-home at Cronk-a-Voddy. On the Glen Helen road, just at the Beary Farm, as we walked along talking, my friend happened to look across the river and saw a circle of light, which I have

now come to regard as the "astral light" or the light of nature, as it is called by mystics, and in which spirits become visible. The spot where the light appeared was a flat space surrounded on the sides away from the river by banks formed by low hills; and into this space and the circle of light, from the surrounding sides apparently, I saw come in twos and threes a great crowd of little beings smaller than Tom Thumb and his wife. All of them, who appeared like soldiers, were dressed in red. They moved back and forth amid the circle of light, as they formed into order like troops drilling. I advised getting nearer to them, but my friend said, "No, I'm going to the party." Then after we had looked at them a few minutes my friend struck the roadside wall with a stick and shouted, and we lost the vision and the light vanished.

Kermode added that many Manx people had spoken to him of the fairies over the years. "They consider the fairies a complete nation or world in themselves, distinct from our world, but having habits and instincts like ours," he explained. "Social organization among them is said to be similar to that among men, and they have their soldiers and commanders."

Our shape-changing friends appeared at least once with "their heavy brown hair . . . streaming down to their waist," according to one of Evans-Wentz's accounts. "Their skin was as white as the swan of the wave." There their resemblance to Jose Antonio's ufonauts ends: the fairies were beautiful and their voices melodious.

However, the *farfadets* of France were hairy dwarfs, with uncertain tempers, who lived in underground tunnels. One night in the 1850s a group of women talking by the shores of the Egray River saw the *farfadets* pulling a "chariot with whining wheels."

The *nains* (dwarfs) of Brittany are a "hideous race of beings with dark or even black hairy bodies, with voices like old men, and with little sparkling black eyes." But in America, when the Cherokees migrated to Tennessee, they found there a strange race of pale-skinned, "moon-eyed" people who could not stand the daylight. The Indians drove them out.

The fairies John Keely, et. al., chased across the West Limerick countryside (see chapter two) possessed "hard, hairy faces like men," and "though they passed through hedges, ditches, and marshes, they appeared neat and clean all the time." Jose Antonio's hairy humanoids dashed over tangled thickets with no difficulty whatever. Just four years earlier, on January 26, 1965, seven teenaged boys from the Brands Flats, Virginia, area allegedly pursued three silver-suited humanoids across a muddy field. The mud slowed their flight not at all and they left no footprints.

In common with many others who have been swept away into the otherworld, Jose Antonio found himself among dead mortals. As befits this materialistic age, here the dead were really dead.

Among the inhabitants of the subterranean realms the Christian deities are held in decided disfavor, as our Brazilian captive discovered when the commander treated his crucifix and rosary beads with malicious irreverence. (In another Brazilian abduction case, which occurred on August 20, 1962, at Duas Pontes, Minas Gerais, the victim started praying after the apparently invisible entities threatened to kidnap him. They responded by saying that his prayers would do no good because they were going to take him anyway. Unlike Jose Antonio, Rivalino Mafra da Silva was never seen again. The incident took place hours after Rivalino had seen dwarfish beings near his house.) The implied threat of divine intervention did not deter the entity from revealing his plan to keep Jose Antonio for seven years, the customary period of time abductees spend in fairyland.

It is hardly surprising, then, that when unexpectedly the divine did intervene the beings were oblivious to its presence. The appearance of this vision adds a whole new dimension to the story, of course. Except for its location it is a tale we have heard many times before: a saint or angel suddenly manifests itself (often in a cave) and passes on secret revelations to its astounded listener, usually a devout Catholic. The entities always speak in the language of the percipient. Sometimes such events take place in the presence of mysterious aerial objects.

Jose Antonio's divine vision offers us a valuable clue to certain other archetypal foundations of the story, which from the religious standpoint symbolizes the journey into hell. Tradition has it that not only demons but the unsaved dead (sometimes defined as those denied eternal life) populate the underworld. From time to time, in pursuit of their evil ends, the demons make pacts with living mortals. Of course those who consent to such an agreement lose their souls—i.e., the chance to be saved from death.

Jose Antonio, in refusing the commander when the latter asked him to amass terrestrial weapons for the humanoid soldiers, may have saved himself from the fate of the four whose bodies he saw in the cave. It was not by coincidence that the saint appeared just at that crucial moment when Jose Antonio had resisted temptation at what seemed to be great personal peril; when, moreover, the commander had attempted to force the courageous young man to believe that the religious faith which sustained him was worthless and ineffectual.

The saint's disappearance in some way seemed to signal the end of the ordeal. We are told that the "instant" the vision vanished, the humanoid order began to fall apart. The beings started quarreling with one another and in the uproar Jose Antonio was whisked away to eventually be freed. By resisting evil and keeping his religious faith, in other words, he had achieved salvation.

We can also unravel the psychological meaning of the story. In the psyche's language, J. E. Cirlot writes (*A Dictionary of Symbols*), "the Journey into Hell symbolizes the descent into the unconscious, or the awareness of all the potentialities of being—cosmic and psychological—that are needed in order to reach the Paradisiac heights." The "Paradisiac heights" are attained when one achieves individuation, or comes to self-actualization through the balancing of the conscious and unconscious parts of the mind. (See chapter one.)

That Jose Antonio's experience was in fact a "descent into the unconscious" is implied in the curious persistence of certain archetypal symbols in his story. Once again we have the motif of three ufonauts to notify us that this will be a spiritual adventure; with their captive they make a quaternity, thus taking on " 'corporeity' and a form adequate to physical creation," i.e., the possibility of effecting action in the outside "conscious" world. (Plato: "The ternary is the number pertaining to the idea; the quaternity is the number connected with the realization of the idea.")

But they come wearing "masks" (space helmets) to shield themselves from the light of conscious reality—just as contents of the unconscious come to consciousness garbed in symbolic disguise. Jose Antonio is shielded from an opposite reason: to protect him from psychic injury as he descends into the unknown depths of the unconscious.

The brilliant light whose source he cannot detect is the light traditionally associated with the spirit. It appears in all kinds of visionary experience, especially those with religious or quasireligious overtones (for examples, see virtually every incident recorded in chapter three), and is almost invariably reported by those who experience "cosmic consciousness." As the late Aldous Huxley commented in an essay on the subject, in these episodes

> there can be both negative, bad light, and good light. In *Paradise Lost* Milton talks about the illumination of hell, which he says is darkness visible. This I think is probably a very good psychological description of the kind of sinister light which sometimes visionaries do see, and it is a light which I think many schizophrenics see. In Dr. Sechehaye's volume *Journal d'une Schizophrene*, her patient describes precisely this appalling light which she lives in: it is a kind of hellish light, it is a light like the glare inside a factory, the hideous glare of modern electric lighting gleaming upon machines. But on the other hand, those who go into a positive experience say this light is of incredible beauty and significance.

Undifferentiated light, in which light floods everything the visionary "sees," is invariably associated with the "full-blown mystical experience," which is extremely positive in nature. "And," Huxley adds, "there is the experience of differentiated light, that is to say of objects, of people, of landscapes which seem to be impregnated and shining with their own light." Such visions can be either positive or negative.

The quadrangular shape of the interiors of both the UFO and the cave signifies the boundaries of the soul and seems to suggest that here the conscious and unconscious are meeting in a kind of no-man's land. Significantly, Jung held that the dwarf is an archetypal "guardian of the threshold of the unconscious." Thus we see the humanoid crew as symbolic guides directing Jose Antonio on this journey of the soul.

The dwarf has another traditional meaning. Quoting Cirlot:

> Now, smallness may be taken also as a sign of deformity, of the abnormal and inferior; this is the explanation, then, of the "dancing Shiva" appearing as an image of a deity dancing upon the prostrate body of a demon-dwarf who symbolizes the "blindness of life," or the ignorance of man (his "pettiness"). Victory over this demon signifies true wisdom.

Certainly there is nothing noble or admirable about these humanoids. They are concerned chiefly with warfare, it appears, and their behavior is at best childish—one shoots a beam of light against the opposite wall for no reason other than to show off, and later the entire group end up shouting at one another like youngsters on a playground. In addition, they apparently are capable of murder.

The commander points to signs marking three and seven, and then the unit ten. Jose Antonio believes that these refer to years. But in the language of archetypes seven comprises the union of the ternary (spiritual possibility) and the quaternity (external achievement growing out of the ternary's resolution of the duality conflict). Representing perfect order, it symbolizes, among other things, "the capital sins and their opposing virtues." Ten is symbolic of unity, "the totality of the universe—both metaphysical and material" (Cirlot).

The commander, then, is tempting Jose Antonio to join forces with him, to merge the conscious with the unconscious for purposes of achievement in the outside world. But something is wrong here, the young man has discovered—four men, two dark-complected, two light-skinned, lie dead, telling him that the dwarf has nothing to offer but the death of the soul. Jose Antonio wisely refuses to participate in this psychic suicide.

In the valley of the shadow—and he is in that destructive "shadow" realm of the unconscious—he fears no evil, and as it turns out, God (or, at any rate, a representative) is with him. The presumably benign intentions of the divine visitor offset the evil ones of its demonic counterpart. From this encounter with this archetypal messenger from a nobler region of the unconscious, Jose Antonio receives true wisdom as the percipient of heavenly revelation. Afterward, of course, he returns to the surface and consciousness.

Thus the story symbolizes the victory of the conscious mind over the destructive aspect of the unconscious. Here the ancient archetypes are only thinly disguised; the Space Age trappings merely serve to clothe a fable that is as old as man himself.

3

Well, you say, all that is fine and good, but did the incident actually *happen*?

We can best approach this vital question by considering briefly a central problem of UFO investigation: the absence of really *conclusive* evidence that the objects are what they appear to be—namely, spaceships from other planets. Certainly people are reporting something. This something occasionally leaves marks on the ground; sometimes it is photographed or tracked on radar screens; sometimes it stops car engines; sometimes it injures or kills people; sometimes it spews forth various physical materials, which invariably prove to be conventional earthly substances (the sole exception is the mysterious "angel hair," which, like the "ectoplasm" of spiritualist literature, to which apparently it is related, disintegrates within a very short period of time; consequently no one has ever been able to study it carefully).

We have a few cases in which ufonauts supposedly have given individuals physical items of different kinds. Most such instances are transparent hoaxes—even the credulous souls who used to congregate at the contactee-oriented flying saucer conclave at Giant Rock, California, recognized that the hair of a "Venusian dog" one now-mercifully-forgotten claimant was merchandising bore a striking resemblance to the quite terrestrial hair attached to the fellow's own mongrel hound.

The late Joe Simonton, whose sincerity no serious investigator ever questioned, accepted three cookies from the crew of a UFO which had landed on his Wisconsin farm.

(See Vallee's *Passport to Magonia,* pp. 23–31, for a discussion of the parallels between this remarkable incident and certain motifs of fairy folklore.) The cookies, alas, tasted like cardboard—Anne Jefferies and St. Cuthbert, who found otherworldly food incomparably tasty, would have been appalled—and chemical analysis showed them to be composed of ordinary corn and wheat flour. Those inclined to conclude that Simonton baked them himself to perpetuate a pointless hoax should consider these words of astronomer J. Allen Hynek, then the Air Force's chief scientific consultant on ufological matters, whose investigation convinced him that "there is no real question that Mr. Simonton felt that his contact had been a real experience."

The myriad rumors of crashed discs in the southwestern desert plainly have risen out of the awful frustration that faces the "scientific ufologists." If the UFOs will not come across with the "proof" of their extraterrestrial origin, then the imagination, fired by wishful thinking, will fill the gap. All that is proved, in the end, is that the "scientific ufologists" have made no more of a case than the skeptics have. However, one debunker, the famous Cornell University astronomer Carl Sagan, recently demonstrated convincingly that if spaceships are visiting the earth (as well as other solar systems) in the numbers UFO sightings suggest, then their builders must be using many times the amount of metal and plastic existing in the known universe. Sagan is only repeating something ufologist Tom Comella (who wrote as "Peter Kor") said several years before in the May 1966 issue of *Flying Saucers:* "The saucer evidence reveals more different types of objects and beings than the physical spaceship theory can logically account for."

Otto O. Binder, in an article published in *Saga's UFO Report* for spring 1974, lists an assortment of descriptions of the "little men" who figure in some landing reports. The list is by no means a complete one:

All black
Blue and bearded
Green skin and hair
Shining yellow eyes, black face, and glowing green torso
Dun, like potato bags

Fish-scale skin, legs with golden glow
Striped clothing
Bright red faces
Pure white skin . . .
Hairy bodies
Glowing orange eyes
Misshapen bald head
No arms
Slit mouth, nostril holes
Three-fingered hands
Shriveled face, white hair
Pumpkin head
Eight-fingered hands
Large chests
Huge heads
Furry, clawed hands
Thin, hooked nose
Heads like potatoes
One-eyed
Elephantine ears
Fingerless hands
Twisted legs.

This list, which could have been much longer, deals only with humanoids, without touching on long-haired "Venusians," man-apes, man-birds, giant birds, robots (including one reported instance of three six-inch beer-can-shaped objects walking about on fins), a giant "sugar lump," "human cadavers," headless things with or without wings, and even a few individuals with normal human features—again, a far from complete list. (Readers interested in a fuller accounting should consult Charles Bowen's anthology *The Humanoids,* a comprehensive survey of occupant reports to 1966.) The unflappable Mr. Binder sees all of this, in the words of the article's title, as "Clues That Prove UFOs Come from Different Galaxies." (!)

John A. Keel, a veteran critic of ETH whose work we have long admired, has observed (*Flying Saucer Review,* July-August 1969):

One of the many troublesome negative factors is the *fact* that although thousands of UFO photos have been taken in the past twenty years, only a dozen or so taken in different parts of the world depict identical objects. If the objects were more uniform in design (and origin) there would now be hundreds of identical pictures. Thus, on the strength of the pictorial evidence alone we can conclude that a wide, almost endless, variety of objects is involved. . . .

The U. S. Air Force [made] . . . an effort to study all of the sighting reports in the early 1950s. Project Blue Book Report No. 14 contained 240 charts, graphs, and tables breaking down the known and unknown reports into many categories. If you study the report carefully you will see some of the reasons for the official conclusions. The sightings were too numerous and too frequent to be the work of a single technological source. The descriptions, including those of the coveted "reliable witnesses," were too varied to support the notion that they were simply and purely manufactured machines. An attempt to develop a "model UFO" from the descriptions in 434 "unknown" cases met with failure. There was no single basic uniformity in all these reports. Therefore, either every object was individually constructed and utilized only once, *or . . . none of the objects really existed at all.*

(Keel's words were echoed recently by ETH partisan Wendelle C. Stevens, who has collected over a thousand UFO photographs. He says, "If the old adage 'A picture is worth a thousand words' [were true in this instance], then a thousand photos surely represents a staggering weight of evidence, and one would think that conclusions would be almost automatic. This, however, is not the case. There seems to be an almost infinite variety of shapes, colors, densities, sounds, speeds, and effects. In all these thousand-odd cases, there are less [sic] than five where two different reports seem to relate to an identical craft.")

Keel has probably spent more time in the field than any other private researcher. This fact has afforded him the opportunity to view the UFO mystery from the inside, and not from the distorted perspective of most UFO literature, written usually to enhance belief in interplanetary visitors, which blithely ignores the evidence inconsiderate enough not to fit the authors' preconceptions.

In his work Keel employed a technique developed by British psychical researcher G. N. M. Tyrrell to enable the investigator to separate "objective" and "subjective" reports of apparitions. Keel's main concern was with landing and contact cases. "Although I traveled widely and interviewed countless witnesses and percipients," he wrote (*FSR,* May-June 1971), "I was discouraged to find that remarkably few were able to meet these requirements"—i.e., those which would have indicated that the experiences were "real." Nonetheless, ordinary dreams, hallucinations, and hoaxes could not explain most of these incidents either, for the persons involved often had other, "objective" UFO experiences which independent witnesses confirmed; sometimes they were plagued by poltergeists and mysterious callers who seemed in some way to be connected with the UFO "intelligences"; and their ESP faculties increased dramatically.

Under close scrutiny even some ostensibly "real" stories break down. A recent example is the widely publicized contact claim from Pascagoula, Mississippi, where on the evening of October 11, 1973, metallic beings with clawlike "hands" supposedly hauled Charles Hickson and Calvin Parker aboard an oblong UFO and subjected them to a physical examination.

As the story goes, the two men were fishing off a pier on the Pascagoula River when they heard a buzzing sound. Its source, a pulsating blue light, rapidly approached them until it stopped to hover a foot or two above the ground some thirty to forty yards away. Something like a door suddenly appeared in the side of the UFO and three "things" floated out toward them. Grabbing the terrified witnesses under the arms, the ufonauts glided back into the craft. The door disappeared as soon as they were inside. A brilliant, almost blinding light with no apparent source illuminated the interior.

The creatures placed Hickson and Parker in separate rooms. "There were no seats, no chairs," Hickson later told police; "they just moved me around. I couldn't resist them, I just floated—felt no sensation, no pain. They kept me in that position for a little while, then they'd raise me up." Meanwhile a "big eye" about the size of a football floated up, down, and around his body like some sort of examining instrument.

Hickson, who did most of the talking in subsequent interviews with lawmen and reporters (Parker had suffered a nervous breakdown from the experience and had to be hospitalized), then found himself alone, his body paralyzed except for his eyes, which he could move freely. After about twenty minutes or so the beings returned; then, again carrying him and Parker under the arms, they gently floated to the pier where the men had been fishing. They sailed back into the UFO, which, in Hickson's words, "seemed gone almost instantly and it sure didn't look like a plane taking off."

This incident took place in the middle of a major UFO flap. Dozens of people in the area had reported seeing unusual aerial objects in previous weeks. The night of the alleged abduction two men saw a UFO with blue lights along the nearby Singing River and a clergyman observed a similar phenomenon hovering over the Pascagoula River near where Hickson and Parker reported their encounter.

The two, for their part, underwent intensive grilling by the authorities. They stuck to their stories. Subsequently Hickson took a lie-detector test and both were subjected to hypnotic probing. By every indication the men were telling the truth.

However, things turned out to be rather more complex than first appearances suggested. Ralph Blum, whose personal interviews with the witnesses convinced him of their sincerity, has pointed out in his *Beyond Earth: Man's Contact with UFOs*:

[An] apparent inconsistency I have not been able to resolve is the fact that the craft Charlie Hickson was "floated aboard" in Pascagoula was not reported by even one of the cars crossing the Highway 90 bridge, just a stone's throw from the old Shaupeter shipyard. Nor was its arrival or departure recorded by the "zoomar security cameras" that Ingills Shipyard reportedly uses to scan the river at night. And yet according to Charlie Hickson he was aboard the craft some twenty to thirty minutes, and according to Dr. Hynek, Charlie's experience was "very real and frightening." But the truth is, we still don't know the exact nature of his experience.

That is certainly true, but its dreamlike qualities are unmistakable. Everyone who dreams—which includes all of us—will recognize the "floating" element in the story. The absence inside the craft of seats, chairs, or anything at all besides the "eye" and the ufonauts is reminiscent of most dream perception, in which few details—and these mostly the very important ones around which the dream's "plot" revolves—are "visible." Most dreams seem to be enacted in a nebulous realm where there is little scenic detail or color variation. This is especially the case in fantastic dreams (which nightmares often are) whose elements, generally speaking, are not fashioned out of personal memory or experience.

Even more telling are these words of Hickson's: "I just floated—felt no sensation, no pain. . . . I couldn't move. Just my eyes could move." Lyall Watson writes in *Supernature*:

> In paradoxical sleep [the state in which dreams occur] the brain produces more rapid waves, almost like those of wakefulness, the eyes move rapidly to and fro, and the heartbeat becomes irregular, but despite all this mental activity going on, the muscles of the body . . . are more relaxed and the sleeper is much more difficult to awake. The relaxation of the muscles amounts almost to paralysis, with even reflex twitches being eliminated, so the nightmares in which we struggle to escape but are unable to move are a true reflection of our physical condition.

Hickson and Parker reported that the beings carried them back to the exact spot where they had been before their experience. More likely, as they began slowly to awaken from their mutual nightmare, their unconscious minds, aware of the men's true physical location, incorporated that knowledge into the fabric of the dream. This sort of blending of external reality and dream image commonly occurs as the mind and body start to emerge from sleep.

Finally, the "mystery" of the UFO's abrupt disappearance has a simple enough solution: the dreamers woke up.

Parapsychological research on the question reveals that the unconscious regularly receives telepathic signals; apparently it is only rarely that these signals break through to the conscious mind. Thus, in the dream state, where the unconscious is in charge, individuals are particularly susceptible to telepathic input. We suspect, therefore, that Hickson and Parker shared a telepathic dream in which the former acted as sender and the latter as receiver.

A fantastic idea, perhaps, but the only possible explanation given the ostensibly incompatible facts that 1.) the two men sincerely believed the abduction occurred and 2.) the abduction did not really occur.

Hickson and Parker were certainly capable of effecting the kind of telepathic exchange we are suggesting, for it is known that telepathy usually takes place between those who share emotional ties, such as friends, relatives, or lovers. Often a crisis situation, where strong emotions (fright, for example) predominate, will trigger the ESP faculty. Here the sudden manifestation of the X Factor (whose precise nature we shall explore in the next chapter) struck such terror into the two that Hickson, the dominant personality in the relationship, telepathically transferred into Parker's psyche the contents of a nightmare vision.

In an essay entitled "C. G. Jung and Parapsychology," appearing in J. R. Smythies' *Science and ESP*, Aniela Jaffe remarks:

> Since in archetypal situations man usually reacts with strong emotions, it would seem as if the emotion itself favors such happenings [of an extrasensory nature]. In fact, during or because of emotion, the threshold of consciousness is lowered; the unconscious and its contents—the archetypes—break into consciousness and may begin to prevail. In other words: man falls into the realm of the relative space-timelessness of the unconscious so that synchronistic events may take place more easily than in a firm state of consciousness.

Here the "archetypal situation" is the confrontation with the unknown and its traumatic consequences. The "archetypes [which] break into consciousness" manifest themselves as demons or monsters from another world. In *Flying Saucers* Jung discusses the significance of the "eye" archetype in relation to the UFO myth; in fact, he even recounts a dream experience in which a woman "saw" an eye in a sky full of saucers.

Like other percipients who cannot assimilate the influx of traumatically unacceptable stimuli, Hickson fainted, broadcasting a telepathic signal so powerful that it caused Hickson to reel over as well. Ostrander and Schroeder devote an entire chapter of *Psychic Discoveries Behind the*

Iron Curtain to Soviet research into parallel events, which they term "The Telepathic Knockout." Sometimes, as in a July 30, 1970, incident in New York City, where nineteen persons mysteriously collapsed, the "telepathic whammy" may claim a sizable number of victims. Psychologists, who not do understand the phenomenon very well, call it "mass hysteria."

If you find the idea of telepathically shared dreams or hallucinations difficult to credit, perhaps you should listen to Dr. Rudolf von Urban, Dr. Alexander Pilcz, and some of their colleagues, who conducted a study of the famous Indian Rope Trick. As they and several hundred others watched, the Fakir threw a coil of rope into the air. Then they saw a small boy climb up the rope and vanish. Soon afterward parts of his dismembered body fell to the ground in full view of the astonished (and no doubt sickened) observers. The Fakir scooped these remains into a basket, ascended the rope, and came back down, smiling, with the beaming boy. The crowd was duly impressed.

But subsequently, when the scientists developed the motion-picture film with which they had recorded the event, they discovered that in reality the Fakir had simply thrown the rope into the air and let it fall back down to the ground in the manner of any ordinary rope. He and his young assistant stood impassively by the rope while everyone else imagined a considerably different event. The entire incident took place in total silence. The Fakir had not told them what to expect.

Noted parapsychologist Andrija Puharich, who recounts the story in *Beyond Telepathy,* concludes, "Presumably the hallucination originated with the Fakir as the agent or sender. . . . We must assume that the hallucination was telepathically inspired and therefore extended to the several hundred people present as receivers of this delusion."

The Pascagoula case recalls some features of the religious visions cited in chapter three. Here we have a mysterious, luminous flying object which not everybody can see (though similar but "objective" phenomena had appeared elsewhere in the area, these had been widely and indiscriminately observed). The phantom light is related in some way to a visionary experience in which the inevitable "blinding light" figures.

The major difference, however, is that, whereas Hickson and Parker seem to have had a dream, most of the religious percipients entered trance or ecstatic states, something else altogether. These latter involve a much deeper altering of consciousness—they bear some considerable resemblance to the psychedelic vision, to cite a familiar example—and in them the percipient may freely participate in communication and other activity. He may receive "wisdom" from some kind of archetypally clothed teacher who may prophesy about future events or lament the human race's moral limitations. Moreover, the percipient "sees" the magical otherworld in all its often-ornate detail. Whatever "paralysis" he may feel initially usually vanishes soon after the event is set in motion. And finally, while in trance or ecstasy, he may experience—objectively—either levitation or teleportation.

Seen in the context of paranormal flight, incidentally, Hickson and Parker's floating dreams take on new significance. They express the impulse toward such activity, though not its fulfillment, which can be accomplished only in the more profoundly psychically charged states of trance or ecstasy. In the latter, the unconscious is able to tap the latent but powerful psychokinetic (PK) function.

Exactly how and why this should happen, we of course have no idea. We can only repeat these words of the great psychoanalyst and psychical researcher Nandor Fodor, who after years of grappling with the question could conclude only this:

> We have some evidence that the demands of life are higher than physics admits; that the life force is capable of making physical laws yield to it. A tiny mushroom may crack a marble slab if that is the only way to sunshine and air. We do not know what is the force that accomplishes such remarkable feats. It should be sufficient to know that such a force exists.

4

Which brings us back to the abduction of Jose Antonio da Silva and to the question we raised earlier: What was the nature of his experience?

We have seen that visionary perception often is initiated

when the percipient "sees" a light and feels paralyzed. Just before that, however, at the onset of trance, he may drift off as D. D. Home did: "I feel for two or three minutes in a dreamy state, then I become quite dizzy, and then I lose all consciousness. When I awake I find my feet and limbs cold and it is difficult to restore the circulation." The Reverend Stainton Moses, who often watched the medium go into trance, added these observations: "By degrees Mr. Home's hands and arms began to twitch and move involuntarily. I should say that he has been partly paralyzed, drags one of his legs, moves with difficulty, stoops, and can endure very little physical exertion." Home, unlike many other percipients who enter the otherworld (whether "seen" as the spirit realm, heaven, hell, or fairyland), inevitably suffered amnesia upon recovery. In this altered state of consciousness, in lighted rooms and in the presence of such eminent Victorians as Sir Oliver Lodge and Sir William Crookes, Home occasionally floated about or out of the seance room.

In other cases of levitation/teleportation, involving individuals with apparently genuine mediumistic abilities, the percipients have claimed that they were carried by luminous spirits, angels, or fairies. (See chapters two and three.) At the conclusion of the adventure, the travelers almost invariably felt exhausted, numb, lame, and thirsty. They lie in a semiconscious condition for a while, most often an hour or two, before regaining sufficient strength to face the conventional world once again. It may take longer for them to regain full use of their limbs.

In some ways this parallels symptoms of epileptic seizure, which begins with gradual disorientation, a slow withdrawal from ordinary perception. The victim sometimes gets dizzy and loses his sense of balance; at the same time a subjective "pins and needles" kind of numbness attacks all or part of his body. He "sees" sparks or flashes of light. While in reality his hearing has been impaired, still he "hears" nonexistent sounds and/or voices. Complete blindness, or blindness of a part of the visual field, has been reported in a number of cases. Simple or complex hallucinations (depending on the severity of the attack) may follow, though sometimes the victim will not remember when he regains consciousness.

We are reminded of religious ecstasies in which epileptic-like seizures gripped various saints while their souls wandered through the heavenly regions. Unfortunately for those seeking simple explanations, these apparently purely subjective experiences were accompanied by objective paranormal phenomena. Friends found Anne Jefferies in "a kind of convulsive fit" while she herself thought that she was among the fairies. Her subsequent well-attested talent for miraculous healing suggests that her hallucinations were not ordinary ones by any means. The medium Eusapia Paladino fell "into true convulsions" or "hysterical" fits, according to Cesare Lombroso, "when the more important phenomena occur."

This is how, in our opinion, the "abduction at Bebedouro" really occurred:

For some reason—call it the instigation of the X Factor—at about 3:00 P.M. on May 4, 1969, Jose Antonio entered a state of altered consciousness, most likely a trance with an accompanying convulsive fit. Remember that the experience started as the young soldier sat in a kind of drowsy, distracted state in which "voices" suddenly spoke, followed very shortly thereafter by the familiar burst or flash of light which benumbed his legs and made him lose his balance. Soon he lost part of his eyesight (a fact represented symbolically in the image of the helmet which obscured a portion of his vision). As we have already examined the archetypal foundations of the dream, we will not repeat our speculations here.

Jose Antonio's hallucination was sufficiently traumatic, its psychic content sufficiently profound, to open regions of the unconscious few persons ever tap, and incredibly, in an explosion of pyschokinetic energy the young man was teleported over two hundred miles to the place where he found himself. Quite possibly *two* such "transportations" occurred (in the hallucination, remember, there were two journeys, one from his original location, the other from the cave to the Vitoria region). These entered his visionary perception as flights aboard a UFO, just as others before him had related their miraculous experiences to other kinds of supernatural beings suited to their own particular cultural frames of reference. Wherever he went before returning to normal consciousness—perhaps some part of the thinly populated wilderness that covers much of Brazil—evidently no one came upon his body.

Like someone recovering from trance and/or teleportation, Jose Antonio lay semiconscious for at least an hour before regaining the strength necessary to hobble down the road. We can account for his wounds in any number of ways. For example, he may have hurt himself while unconscious and incorporated the injuries into the hallucination. However, we find more tempting a hypothesis which ties these to the stigmata which have afflicted religious mystics, mostly Roman Catholic clerics, who while in trance/ecstasy envision Christ, who causes his wounds from the cross to appear on the visionary's hands and feet. It is an uncontested fact that the affected parts show every evidence of having been penetrated by large, thick nails.

Fodor has told of a case from his own psychiatric practice in which a neurotic woman suffering from a father complex became the focus for poltergeist activity. On one occasion she dreamed that her dead father had carved a cross on one of her breasts. She awoke suddenly to find herself bleeding profusely in that area. When she wiped the blood away she found the image of a cross.

Even more to the point is a story published in *UFO Percipients* (*Flying Saucer Review* Special Issue No. 3, published September 1969). The author, psychical researcher H. S. W. Chibbett, writes that in November 1947 he hypnotized a woman friend, a medium identified only as Mrs. X, who proceeded to relate a fantastic story.

She said that she was on what seemed to be another planet, standing before a "beautifully ornamented . . . archway leading down into the earth." Walking beneath it, she heard a whirring, dynamolike sound which she discovered emanated from another opening. This one led into a cave full of machinery. Suddenly two men clad in spacesuits grabbed her and dragged her off into the cave, where a bald man was sitting in front of a switchboard, addressing someone repeatedly as "H6AQ . . . H6AQ . . ."

Turning to the women, the man asked, "Another bird?"

"Then there was a blank," Mrs. X told Chibbett. "I think you were trying to get me back.

"The next thing I remember was lying on the floor, and they had my shoulder exposed. They looked at the mark, you know, of [apparently a birthmark or scar], and then the man jumped back quickly and said: 'No—not this one!' They immediately covered my shoulder.

"The man then said: 'You can take back what you want—but next time it will be on the face!'

"He bared my right leg (the women holding me down), and pulled from his belt what appeared to be a kind of gun. As he held it, beneath his thumb was a knob. He gave a funny sort of laugh—like a hen cackling—and pointed the instrument at my leg. He pressed the stud. I saw nothing emerge from the muzzle, but I felt a terrible searing pain like a burn, and heard a hissing noise. And I saw him inscribe the symbols on my leg, etched in red. The man then told me it would never go."

Mrs. X had not recounted these "events" as they "happened," but only after Chibbett had brought her out of the hypnotic state. Shortly after being put under, she had stopped answering his questions. Finally she had whispered something about "guards" and pointed to her right leg. Chibbett drew down her stocking, glanced at a strange marking on her leg, and awakened her immediately. Only then did he hear what supposedly had gone on.

Later [he wrote in his notebook the same day], I examined the stigmata on her leg closely. The letters and numerals were clearly outlined in red (H6AQ), and did not appear to be on the surface of the skin, but beneath it. When the skin was depressed, the symbols showed up more clearly. Beneath them was another mark, much fainter. It looked like a bow and arrow. These marks were also seen by W. T. and G. H., who were present on this occasion.

Of course there is no chance that Mrs. X's experience occurred anywhere but in her psyche. Whatever its inspiration, its components are surely imaginary. The percipient, who thought that she had been on Mars, said, "My captors were not speaking English, but curiously enough I was able to understand what they were saying." Yet the "Martian" draws a purely terrestrial radio code signal on her leg!

But what is important here is the mere *fact* of the stigmatic marking, which proves that the PK function of the mind will sometimes oblige us with "evidence" to "validate" an individual's belief in an unreal experience.

Secondarily, we must not overlook this very important consideration: In this undoubted nonevent Mrs. X's unconscious mind fashioned its tale out of the same basic archetypal idea that Jose Antonio's used: *the notion that dangerous, demonic beings dwell under the surface of this or another plant.* The moral, it should go without saying, is not that therefore this is literally the case; to the contrary, in fact. It serves to illustrate the truth of an axiom long known to psychiatrists, which holds that a concocted, fictitious dream is as valid a measure of an individual's psyche as one that is truthfully recalled. As flowers of the imagination, they are rooted in the same psychic soil.

We do not mean in any way to impugn Mrs. X's integrity, which we have no reason to question. What we contend is that, in common with hoaxes, her story is without real foundation. But that does not stop it from sounding like other tales whose validity as objective accounts of actual experiences no "scientific ufologist" would ever presume to doubt.

In several published articles on the late-nineteenth-century UFO scare, Jerome Clark reported the story, published in an 1897 newspaper, of an alleged airship landing near Linn Grove, Iowa. Since then the report has appeared in a number of UFO books, and in fact it was included in the first draft of this book.

But early in 1974 an informant who had lived in Linn Grove in 1897 told Clark that he had never heard of the supposed incident. Neither, as it developed, did others who had resided in the little town back then (some were actual relatives of the "witnesses" cited in the press account). Apparently a reporter invented the story, using the names of real people without their knowledge or permission.

Nonetheless no UFO student can help being impressed by some of the details, especially those that mention "two queer-looking persons" with enormously long beards who tossed two boulders of "unknown composition" out of their craft and sailed away. Not only does this tie in generally with the bearded ufonauts of the mid-twentieth century; more specifically, it anticipates Jose Antonio's hairy humanoids with their stone-and-rock fetish. But even though the stimuli that brought the reports into being may be very different, both still draw from the same psychic reservoir, where devils and fairies guard the waters of the unconscious.

Even so seasoned a researcher as John Keel was taken in by a North Carolina landing report which eventually proved to be a hoax—but not before he had written an article stating his conviction that the story was authentic because it conformed even in minute detail to a number of other incidents, many of them unpublicized, which he had investigated.

Likewise, Eileen Buckle devoted an entire book, *The Scoriton Mystery,* to what subsequently proved to be a spurious incident. The hoaxer, now deceased, knew only a little about UFOs, in fact just barely enough to concoct the tale and give it shape. Nonetheless there is no denying that the account is extraordinarily convincing as Miss Buckle presents it—in the book's pages the phony "contactee" regales us with detail after obscure detail which one would have thought only ufologists of many years' standing would know anything about. On top of that, during the course of their investigation the author and her coworker, Norman Oliver (it was Oliver, incidentally, who later would unmask the fraud) underwent various odd paranormal experiences which seemed to validate the hoaxer's claims.

So inevitably we must pose a terrible question. Of what can we possibly be certain when liars, lunatics, dreamers, and honest sober citizens all appear to be talking in the same language?

And that takes us to the heart of the contactee dilemma.

5

The first publicized flying saucer contactee was the late George Adamski, who claimed that on November 20, 1952, he met with a spaceman named Orthon, a Venusian with long golden hair and of slightly Oriental appearance. Curiously, the being must have been something of an androgyne—Adamski at first thought him "an unusually beautiful woman." Adamski, an occultist who in the late 1940s had published a privately printed book on "cosmic philosophy," had gone out to the California desert with six followers for the express purpose of meeting with a saucer. Not long after their arrival, a large cigar-shaped UFO supposedly sailed over a nearby mountain ridge, drifted toward them, and hovered not far from the ground.

Guided by some kind of vague telepathic impulse, Adamski wandered off alone, until a "flash in the sky" alerted him to the presence of a smaller craft descending half a mile away. He ran to the scene, where he encountered the extraterrestrial, who proceeded to give him a long and boring lecture on the dangers of atomic explosions.

Sometime in the course of all this Adamski allegedly snapped a picture of the landed "scoutcraft"—from a distance, unfortunately, sufficient to make the uninitiated confuse the "scoutcraft" with a mountain rock.

In 1953, with British saucer enthusiast Desmond Leslie, Adamski published *Flying Saucers Have Landed*. Two years later *Inside the Space Ships,* detailing contacts with Venusians, Martians, Saturnians, and others, rolled off the presses complete with pictures "shot in outer space from scoutcraft portholes." Meanwhile Adamski hopped from one lecture and one country to another, enthralling the cultists, who proclaimed him the most important man on the planet, and enraging the conservative ufologists, who complained, quite correctly, that his antics were making the idea of interplanetary UFOs look ridiculous.

Adamski remained a highly controversial figure right up till his death in April 1965. Oddly enough, though, in view of all the emotional energy he generated in his last twelve and a half years, he passed rapidly into oblivion and is all but forgotten now by serious ufologists. Why this happened is anybody's guess. Perhaps it is because ufology has changed drastically over the past ten years. With the flood of dramatic new reports, with the growing complexity of the enigma, with the ongoing debate between the old-line, conservative "scientific ufologists" and the irreverent, radical "new ufologists," UFO research is simply a much more engaging pursuit than it was in the 1950s, when Adamski had his heyday.

Perhaps, too, it happened because in the end everyone came to share the usually unspoken realization that the full truth about George Adamski would never be known. In those days most of the more sober UFO students rejected his story out of hand and even went so far as to deny that it deserved investigation at all. That left matters in the hands of the credulous, whose accounts, of course, are highly suspect.

We might as well confess our personal distaste for Adamski and his claims. It is born in part out of memories of confrontations with his partisans, whom we always found to be a singularly unpleasant assortment of fanatics. One of them, a cultured European woman who ought to have known better, once accused Jerome Clark of possession by evil spirits because he could not swallow whole the exotic fare the "space brothers" dished out.

Aside from that probably irrelevant consideration, there are other more telling reasons that compel us to question Adamski's sincerity. For one thing, the man allowed his followers to call him "Professor Adamski" and to identify him as an astronomer from Mount Palomar, when in fact, in the days before he started to make a living off his flying saucer income, he worked as a waiter in a restaurant at the foot of the mountain serving hamburgers and BLTs to tourists visiting the famous observatory. His "scientific credentials" consisted of an interest in star-gazing and an apparent passion for science fiction. We know the latter because Ray Palmer has maintained for years that back in 1946, when he edited *Amazing Stories,* he rejected a manuscript Adamski had submitted. The story, which did not pretend to be anything but fantasy, concerned Jesus Christ's landing on earth in a spaceship. In 1953, when Palmer read *Flying Saucers Have Landed,* he was amazed to discover that the new story was really the old one updated, with Jesus now a Venusian and the spaceship a flying saucer.

In addition, the original "six witnesses" leave something to be desired. As early critics quickly pointed out, their testimony is not totally unambiguous and it contains clear hints that wishful thinking has colored their vision; remember, they supported Adamski's concept of "cosmic philosophy" (as did the "space brothers," who mouthed the same tedious drivel back to the "professor"). Furthermore, two of the "witnesses" later became contactees themselves. One, the late "Dr." George Hunt Williamson, who called himself an anthropologist, went on to pen a series of especially unconvincing volumes which combined wild contact claims with preposterous Von Daniken-like speculations about mankind's ancient history. An enterprising contributor to Jim Moseley's *Saucer News* probed Williamson's academic background and determined that the man was no more a "doctor" and an "anthropologist" than Adamski was a "professor" and an "astronomer."

But unfortunately, it seems axiomatic that in ufological matters practically nothing lends itself to easy resolution, and the Adamski controversy is no exception.

Most of Adamski's photographs show a peculiar "UFO" shaped rather like a bell with a "conning tower" above and "three-ball landing gear" below. Since at that time, so far as anyone knew, nobody besides Adamski claimed to have seen such a UFO, the skeptics hooted.

But on the night of October 7, 1953, residents of Norwich, England, saw a strange light sailing overhead. During the four minutes it was visible, two of the observers, Mr. and Mrs. F. W. Potter, focused their three-and-a-half-inch refracting telescope on the object. Afterward Mr. Potter drew a sketch which he handed over to the editor of the *Eastern Evening News*. The next night the paper printed it next to one of Adamski's photographs (*Landed* had only recently been published in Great Britain). The two resembled each other strikingly, though Potter's lacked the spherical "landing" apparatus. But the craft withdrew these during flight, according to Adamski; thus this ostensible omission actually served to further confirm the contactee's allegations.

It is very curious, however, that the Potters had not only read Adamski's book but enthusiastically embraced it. No one has ever called their honesty into dispute. But we can only wonder at the coincidence: not only does this rare type of UFO appear before two of the relative few familiar with the Adamski/Leslie volume, but it arrives just when they are out star-gazing through their telescope, so that they alone get a closeup view.

Early the next year, on the morning of February 15, 1954, thirteen-year-old Stephen Darbishire, responding to a "persistent nagging feeling," started walking up the hill behind his house at Coniston, Lancashire, with his eight-year-old cousin, Adrian Mayer. Suddenly a shining object drifted slowly downward out of a gap in the clouds. Stephen, who had brought along his small Kodak in hopes of photographing birds, snapped two pictures of the UFO as it dipped between the hills less than one hundred yards away. He later explained that it was made of a "plasticlike metal which light could travel through but I could not see through it"—translucent, in other words.

So closely does it resemble Adamski's "scoutcraft" that the man himself could have taken the pictures which Stephen developed. Further, of his original saucer Adamski had written, "I could not see through it any more than one can see through the glass bricks that are popular in some of the newer office buildings and homes, which permit more light to enter than would solid walls. It was translucent and of exquisite color."

Eventually Leonard G. Cramp, an engineer, made an orthographic comparison of the Coniston UFO and Adamski's scoutcraft photographs and found that they showed objects of identical dimensions. He published his findings in *Space, Gravity and the Flying Saucer*. Since then a number of people, contactees and noncontactees, have reported seeing similar UFOs.

The golden-haired "Venusian" kind of ufonaut figures in many post-1952 landing reports. The great majority of witnesses, who include unlettered South American peasants, could not possibly have heard of George Adamski; as a matter of fact, some had never even heard of UFOs. For example, when on December 9, 1954, Brazilian farmer Olmira da Costa e Rosa saw three men with long blond hair and slanted eyes standing in his maize field, he took them for members of the United States Air Force! They had arrived, incidentally, in a machine shaped like an "explorer's hat"—which is one way one might describe the scoutcraft.

Adamski's death sparked one final controversy: the Scoriton affair, to which we referred in the previous section. The matter is extremely complicated and we see no point in going into it here in any but the briefest form. Suffice it to say that the incident, an almost certain hoax, involved the supposed return of a reincarnated Adamski in the company of two Venusians. Since Adamski had confided to a very small group of friends that he would reappear like this and the "witness" had no way of knowing that fact, even ordinarily more cautious ufologists could not help being impressed; and when investigators encountered ostensibly confirmatory paranormal manifestations, the claim seemed hardly open to question any longer. Thus the story's eventual collapse stunned researchers.

Perhaps in the Scoriton fraud we have a key clue to the mystery of George Adamski. If at their core UFO events are subjective, products of unconscious needs, then UFO fact and fiction may be inseparable, for they draw on the same creative source: the human psyche and the archetypes of the collective unconscious. The unconscious will not be denied, however much we may attempt to banish its "irrational" contents from our lives; still they rise to the surface to let us know that we cannot ignore them. The archetypal forms intrude into our sphere in our art and literature, our popular entertainments, our religions, everywhere—not least of all in our dreams and in our fantasies.

"We create what we believe," says Gustav Davidson. Perhaps we should rephrase that to read, "We create what we *need* to believe." Davidson happened to be speaking of angels. So, in this particular instance, are we. According to critic Robert Hughes:

The physical shape of angels is only a metaphor, but the spiritual experience to which the now-dead form refers is still very much alive. That is the process of revelation, of stepping between levels of awareness. . . . As the rigid boxes of nineteenth-century positivism disappear from our culture and our lives and the new epiphanies of consciousness unfold themselves, it is possible that we shall return to that receptiveness in which earlier civilizations saw their angels. Except that, inevitably, we will call them something else.

If it is true that in 1946 George Adamski was putting Christ inside a spaceship, then he was a man with a keen prophetic understanding of the manner in which men of the mid-twentieth century would attempt to reconcile the supernatural with the supertechnological. This world and the otherworld must learn to coexist, even in an age which worships machines and decries mysteries.

Out of ancient Christian and modern secular symbols Adamski invented a tale which naively attempted to unite the two main polarized elements of our time, here expressed as religion and reason. Six years later he would do the same thing, only this time turning Jesus into an extraterrestrial angel. It hardly matters whether Adamski had such flying saucer visions as he describes, or whether he imagined them one day and proceeded to peddle them to the world as literal fact. What does matter is that without knowing it he found a Space Age faith for us, something we desperately sought and would have found in time. But Adamski happened to be there first because his was the perfect temperament. He was a student of the physical and spiritual mysteries of the cosmos, a visionary with a telescope. He was among that handful of individuals who are truly of their time.

Fittingly the vision, or a part of it, next appeared to the Potters, who already had taken the new revelation into their hearts. Next it came, as miracles so often do, to children. Stephen Darbishire received the call in the familiar fashion—an inexplicable impulse drove him to the hillside, where the vision performed deliberately for him. Now the child would force a troubled, doubting world to accept the new celestial order with actual "proof" of its presence here on earth.

The revelation, once given, spread all over the world, to the farflung places where it manifested itself to all manner of people, believers and skeptics, educated and ignorant, even to those who had never heard of it and who, when it happened, could scarcely comprehend it. And when word of all these miraculous events returned to the faithful in their Western European and American conclaves, they would simply nod and ask the obvious: "Could there be any further doubt?"

6

There certainly is no doubt that Howard Menger's claims sound ridiculous when first encountered. Years ago, when we read his *From Outer Space to You,* we did not consider for a moment that the book could be anything but bad science fiction. Now, older and presumably wiser, we are not so sure. But if nothing else, it demonstrates with uncommon clarity that the elements of the flying saucer myth are far older than most ufologists realize.

For reasons of space we will not review his entire story, which is essentially pretty standard contactee fare involving contacts with an assortment of blond, golden-haired Venusians, dark-complected Martians, and beautiful Saturnian women who all express concern about our wayward habits, including the often-heard complaint about our tinkering with the "balance of the universe." All absurd, naturally, but typical, and reminiscent of many other stories before and since. It contains all the marks of visionary experience. The interiors of the spacecraft he seems sincerely to believe he boarded, for example, are bathed in the familiar brilliant light with no visible source, and so on.

At any rate, what interests us is Menger's initiation into the otherworld of the space people. As a child growing up in rural northern New Jersey, Menger states, he began having "flashbacks," brief visionary glances of another realm. "About this time we [Menger and his younger brother Alton] began to see the discs in the sky. . . . My playmates did not always see them, but I sensed just when to look up." One day a shining circular object landed in the field where the two Menger boys were playing. Above it a larger object, also circular, hovered silently. Suddenly it vanished and soon the disc on the ground disappeared "in a blinding flash of light."

After a time Howard took to wandering off alone deep into the woods, where he invariably gravitated to a certain spot where he could rest by a creek, feeling strangely peaceful and contented. Then one day in 1932, when he was ten, he saw a beautiful woman sitting on a rock by the stream. She had long blond hair and wore a translucent "ski suit" outfit. When she turned to Howard she emanated "warmth, love, and physical attraction," and the boy lost his initial fright.

"She seemed to radiate and glow as she sat on the rock," Menger would write many years later. ". . . I seemed to be encompassed by the very glow, almost visible, that emanated from her presence. Somehow the entire area surrounding us appeared to take on a greater kind of radiance."

Approaching him, she took his hands in hers and explained that her "people" had watched him for a long time because "we are contacting our own." Howard quickly discovered that she knew all his thoughts. She talked to him for a time about things he did not understand; at one point, a sad expression on her face, she predicted "a great change." There would be pointless wars, destruction, and misunderstanding among human beings. "As you grow older," she said, "you will know your purpose. You will help other people grow to know their purpose, too." She would see him again but not for a long time, she said. In the meantime her people, who were "far away" but "always around—watching for you, guiding you," would be contacting him.

While serving in Hawaii during World War II, a "strong impulse" led Menger to drive alone to a cavern area several miles from the base. There he got out of his jeep and walked through the dense underbrush toward the caves, where he met a beautiful woman with long dark hair and dark eyes. She was dressed in a flowing tunic. Menger was struck with awe at her spirituality but at the same time she aroused him sexually—a fact she acknowledged by saying, "It's only a natural thing. . . . It flows from you to me as from me to you." ("The space people, though far superior to us physically, mentally, and in spiritual developments, are still much like us," Menger explains. ". . . At such a meeting one knows innately that one's every thought is bared under powerful telepathic observation . . . one suddenly realizes he cannot hide anything.")

The woman made predictions about Menger's immediate future. When he asked her where she was from, she said Mars. After further conversation they parted.

With the war over, Menger returned to civilian life to start a sign-painting business. One day in June 1946 he was gripped with an impulse to return to the "enchanted area" where fourteen years before the blond woman had appeared. He drove to his parents' home in High Bridge, New Jersey, and plunged deep into the woods.

When nothing happened, Menger got tired of waiting

and decided to leave. He relates what then suddenly took place:

> Then I jumped a foot off the ground and let out an exclamation. There was a tremendous flash of light and the sense of heat on the back of my neck. I turned. Above the vast western section of the field a huge fireball moved at tremendous speed.
> It looked like a huge spinning sun, shining, pulsating, and changing colors. It hovered over the field, as I stood watching it, seemingly transfixed.
> The pulsating color changes diminished and the fireball turned into a metallic-looking craft, surrounded by portholes.
> It descended slowly to the ground. When it was almost on the ground I could make out the form clearly. It appeared to be bell-shaped, and reflected the sunlight like a mirror.

We trust that readers will not be surprised to learn just who stepped out of this "dancing sun" vision: none other, needless to say, than his fairy queen/Virgin/spacewoman friend, dressed in a garment "which seemed to glow." She arrived in the company of two handsome, fair-skinned men with long blond hair.

Until she touched his hand, Menger says that he could not move. At her touch, however, he regained control of his body movement and "a feeling of relaxation and well-being consumed me." She appeared not to have aged at all in the years since they had last seen each other. As always in these encounters, her spiritual presence moved him profoundly while contrarily he could not conceal the "strong physical attraction one finds impossible to allay when in the presence of these women." Again she could read his mind and again she made various prophecies, telling him among other things that he would join with twelve other persons who would assist him in his missionary work, which was to restore the "universal laws and wisdom" to the human race.

She and her two companions reentered the ship, which ascended several hundred feet into the air before vanishing in a flash of light.

The psychological foundations of this story are almost too obvious for comment. Here the "sun maiden" represents the anima, which opens the door to the unconscious just as the "spacewoman" initiates Menger into the otherworld. As an archetype she symbolizes the "eternal woman" as men perceive her, personifying the uniting of the heretofore polarized elements of sensuality and spirituality (or body and mind, or matter and spirit, or—ultimately—conscious and unconscious). She is associated with the mandala (whose shape and radiance symbolize wholeness). Surely it is highly significant that, like so many UFO percipients, Menger first observes a shining globe ("In what may be called the early stages of the visionary experience, people do see with the closed eyes things which are exactly like Mandalas."—Aldous Huxley); only later does it become, as Menger unconsciously rearranges the manifestation into something comfortable to the twentieth-century mindset, a Venusian scoutcraft.

From the vehicle a trio of beings emerge, symbolizing three of the four component aspects of the psyche(Menger, as ego, is the fourth). As we know well by now, the ternary represents spiritual possibility, the quaternity the realization of that possibility (which is born out of the ternary's victory over duality) in conscious life. Thus the messengers come to tell Menger his "mission": he must lead men and women back to "universal law and wisdom," i.e., the psychic laws that govern all of us even if we attempt to ignore them.

When the celestial visitors prophesy that Menger will have twelve followers, we hardly need explain where *that* idea comes from. However, as Cirlot remarks, "The first ten numbers in the Greek system . . . pertain to the spirit: they are entities, archetypes and symbols. The rest are the products of combinations of these numbers." Twelve, of course, is composed of three units of four; therefore it simply restates the notion of spiritual possibility which is accomplished, with the aid of the conscious mind, in the physical world. In Jungian thought, Christ is believed to have been an individual who had achieved self-actualization, that is, psychic completion through the uniting of conscious and unconscious, and consequently of all duality. And so, since this occurs so rarely, in the eyes of many he appeared to have godlike power.

We find further evidence that Menger's visitors came from inner, not outer, space in a variety of pronouncements, such as: "We are contacting our own"; "The space people, though far superior . . . are very much like us"; "It flows from you to me as from me to you" (the spacewoman to Menger); "We are far away" but "always around—watching for you, guiding you"; "You will grow to know your purpose." These statements refer mostly to the unconscious's constant observation of the conscious mind, its attempt to direct the latter, and the consequent exchange of content between the two.

Now if this were all we had to concern ourselves with we could dismiss Menger's claims as plainly and simply hallucinatory and relegate them to files marked "psychopathology." But as usual we are going to find things vastly more complicated.

In *UFOs: Operation Trojan Horse*, for example, John Keel writes, "I have talked with several different people who were around High Bridge in 1956–57 [when Menger's contact experience was in its most intense phase]. One of them is Ivan T. Sanderson, who lives nearby and who knew Howard before, during, and after these episodes. Something strange was definitely happening to Menger and the people around him at that time."

Through the efforts of Berthold Eric Schwarz, who is both a ufologist and a psychiatrist, we have the testimony of one of the people to whom Keel refers. Dr. Schwarz explains in a *Flying Saucer Review* article (July–August 1972) that he heard of "B. C.," a fifty-three-year-old salesman with university training, while investigating a "silent contactee" case. ("Silent contactee" is a phrase coined by Keel to denote claimants who have never publicized their experiences. Usually ufologists come upon them only by accident. Apparently there are thousands of such cases that will forever remain obscure.)

B. C., who had been active in ufology for a six- to ninemonth period in 1958, had spent considerable time with Menger on his farm. From that experience he concluded that some of the contactee's claims were spurious; at the same time, on the other hand, B. C. saw things there that were completely inexplicable. Other persons Schwarz interviewed confirmed B. C.'s story and some even told of weird events they themselves had witnessed at the Menger farm. B. C. related:

The contactee's son [Robert], aged twelve, was dying of brain cancer. The parents had given up on doctors and were using advice from the "spacemen." The boy was close to the end. My friend Rob and I went up there to see if there was anything we could do.

We were sitting in the kitchen and the boy was in the other room with the nurse, who was on twenty-four-hour duty. The sick boy then called urgently. His mother rushed into the room and we followed. The nurse took his pulse; it was very slow. The boy had a convulsion and a light started to show up above his head. It began as a light blue, and was about eight inches from the wall but not casting any light on the wall. It was like a bar of light. It pulsated and grew whiter, and then it faded. The whole light manifestation lasted about one and a half minutes.

The nurse left to call the doctor. Rob and I were alarmed. When the boy relaxed the light was white. By the time the doctor came there was no light and the boy was all right. When I saw the light, I turned my head sideways to make sure that it was not an optical illusion which would travel with me, but it was still there. I asked Rob what he had seen in the last several minutes and he described it to me the same way.

The night of the column of light, I saw four men in luminous uniforms. They were about three hundred feet away on a hilltop in the pasture. They stood in front of a dark grove of trees behind a fence. It was a moonlit night. They were on the edge of the rise, walking and glowing. If they were stooges, it would have been a very strange and expensive hoax. The sick boy's mother was with us: the other children were too young and too small to fake this. The father was in the house, as was everyone else whom we had met when we first came. The father might have been grieving over his very ill son and flipped, but this would be hard to accept. It was not very cold that night.

On one occasion, according to another individual who had been a friend of Robert's, Menger had taken his son out into the pasture to meet the space people and get their help. But the boy, who was totally blind from the brain tumor, could not see them. His distraught father became hysterical and struck him.

Still, when the light would appear above his bed, as it

did on more than one occasion, Robert could "see" a number of "people" around his bedside. "They are from the planet Orion and are coming to take me away," he explained. Everyone was puzzled since the father knew nothing of Orion or anything related to it. (Menger's space contacts always identified themselves as inhabitants of planets in this solar system.)

The boy's composure in the face of death impressed all those who came to visit him, but then Robert had always been a remarkable boy. In his book Menger states that at the age of three his son sang all the verses of "Ol' Man River" before an audience of adults. Schwarz's informants added that Robert, though only twelve when he died, could spreak brilliantly on a number of subjects, and many people, including an unnamed "high-ranking Jesuit from Washington, D.C.," came to interview him and converse with him at length.

Schwarz conducted a three-hour psychiatric examination of Robert's mother, who proved to be healthy, honest, and intelligent. (She and her husband had separated late in the 1950s.) She described some of her own UFO experiences, one of them with luminous beings that "could almost be seen through—and that seemed to hop around like the astronauts" on a moonwalk.

From the interviews of her and of others [Schwarz wrote], it would seem reasonable to suppose that the elements of later fraud and presumed serious psychopathy involving her husband, the publicized contactee, were an entirely different matter and a tragic story in themselves.

It is of interest that despite some dreadful life experiences, the woman's children have all done well in the world. The mother handled the truth and reality of the valid, early, family UFO experiences in a factual way—even if she had no explanation. The later alleged UFO material involving her husband alone, which she believed was fraudulent, she also handled on a reality plane. It can be conjectured that if she had not assumed such a course, her children (and she herself) would not have survived without serious emotional decompensation.

Schwarz also talked with a physicist, now a department chairman at a university, who, at a distance of only about six or eight feet, observed a small disc-shaped object in a ravine near Menger's farm. It changed colors continually in the fifteen to twenty minutes it remained in view.

Howard Menger has long since split the flying saucer scene. On the *Long John Nebel* television show in New York City one evening in the early 1960s, Menger virtually recanted his story, mumbling that the saucers might have been "psychic," the space people "visions," the whole experience "metaphorical." Later, in letters to his publisher, Gray Barker of Saucerian Books, he labeled his own work "fiction-fact" and implied that he had participated in a CIA experiment to test public reaction to the idea of extraterrestrial visitors. The Pentagon had supplied him with faked UFO pictures to help him put across the hoax.

In 1967 Menger surfaced one last time to address the faithful at the Congress of Scientific Ufologists in New York. This time he said nothing about CIA tricks or metaphorical spaceships; instead he rambled for a while on peripheral topics until finally he said, "I often wonder what would happen to these people who say, 'Well, what proof do you have? If I could see a flying saucer or someone step out of a craft, boy, I would make sure the people knew about it.' Well, I just wonder about that. If you realize what people go through when this happens to them. If you really think you have guts enough to come out and tell people. Of course, nowadays it might be a little easier, but in the early fifties it was very, very rough, especially when you are in business and you are trying to act like a reputable citizen and bring up a family and, you know, things like this in your community."

Today Menger is reportedly living in another state, supporting himself at his old sign-painting job.

The Menger affair, riddled as it is with mythic and archetypal material, tells us much about the real nature of the UFO mystery. We have already remarked on the many contexts in which "sun maiden" types appear. The events that surround his son Robert's tragic death have their parallels in fairylore, religion, and the literature of psychical research, as we have seen.

(Incidentally, a 1960 Australian contact claim may put the younger Menger's puzzling reference to "people from Orion" into some kind of weird perspective. The claimant, a milkman on his rounds at Wanda Beach, south of Sydney, reportedly came upon two slant-eyed, spacesuited men standing beside a landed UFO. Through a translating device they told him that they had come from somewhere near the "galactic center" to assist the people of the solar system in repelling an approaching invasion fleet from the Orion region. The Orion group had long wanted to claim the earth, the ufonauts said, but the vigilance of our immediate planetary neighbors—presumably Venusians, Martians, et. al.—so far had thwarted the invaders' plans.)

John Keel probably knows as much about the contact experience as anybody, having conducted in-depth, firsthand studies of dozens of claimants both famous and obscure. In an essay published in his private newsletter *Anomaly* (September 1969), he makes these revealing observations:

Following contact, one of two emotional responses frequently takes place: 1.) Expansion of awareness and perception. 2.) Rapid deterioration of personality.

The euphoric-type experience can sometimes produce a combination of these responses. We have now closely investigated and studied approximately two hundred involved percipients. In several cases we were able to isolate potential contactees before their main experiences began. They were kept under constant study through all the stages of initial "contact" and their reactions were carefully recorded and compared. The following information has been derived from those studies.

The "expansion" (1.) percipient gradually develops a higher IQ and heightened perceptions in all areas. ESP abilities are frequently enhanced. The unconscious mind seems to release all kinds of hidden data into the conscious mind, sometimes through dreams and sometimes through sudden flashes of acute perception. In a few cases it was noted that visual and auditory acuity were also noticeably affected. These percipients were able to see slightly above the normal visible spectrum and were able to hear sounds in the ultrasonic range. These changes can occur very suddenly, even within twenty-four hours after initial contact.

The type 2 percipient may briefly enjoy heightened perceptions but this is usually followed by a slow deterioration of personality. Persons who were fundamentally honest before contact begin to suffer from confabulation. The UFO event dominates their life and they willingly engage in any lie or subterfuge necessary to substantiate their story. Since they are consumed by total belief, they can successfully pass lie-detector tests. Specific sensory information is so deeply implanted in their mind that they are able to recite their UFO experiences word-for-word months, or even years, later.

The type 2 percipient (and some type 1s) may develop obsessive-compulsive characteristics and become completely preoccupied with the contact experience. Such individuals devote a large part of their time to spreading the "message" of the UFO occupants even though this may lead to the loss of their jobs and the eventual disintegration of their family life. They become "space age messiahs" and willingly endure ridicule and hardship to advance the "cause."

Keel's comments may not explain *why* percipients react differently to the contact experience, but at least we can place Howard and Robert Menger in some sort of context. (Many of these same observations, by the way, could be made about spiritualist mediums.) Since the mechanisms causing contact hallucinations remain totally mysterious, anything we might say must necessarily be highly speculative. We really have no idea whether the varying responses can be traced to the percipients' personality structure or to something else, like biochemical/electrical disturbances in the brain. It may be that the "light" so widely reported in mystical and paranormal perception has to do with brainwave disturbance. We leave this question open in hopes that someone knowledgeable in this area will elect to pursue it.

As Menger himself implied, though, individuals who admit to such culturally unacceptable experiences are opening themselves up to all kinds of difficulties with their fellows. Even those who have had considerably less dramatic UFO encounters than Menger's—Lonnie Zamora and Dale Spaur come to mind offhand—have been driven out of jobs, marriages, and home towns by the sheer force of hostile public opinion. Not many persons possess strength enough to withstand this deadly social fallout.

7

We do not mean to convey the impression that all supposed space contacts are of the Adamski/Menger variety, with Venusians holding center stage while the friendly folk of Mars, Jupiter, and the other planets of our solar system take occasional bit parts. The fact is, as Keel notes, "we have been informed by seemingly sincere contactees . . . that the saucers come from unknown planets named Clarion, Maser, Schare, Blaau, Tythan, Korendor, Orion, Fowser, Zomdic, Aenstria, and a dozen other absurd places."

Nonetheless there is a disproportionate number of Venusian contacts, just as in spiritualistic circles the "guides" may assume all kinds of identities but tend to gravitate toward certain favorites, such as alleged spirits of American Indians. The Venusian claims usually contain the strongest religious overtones. In the incident we are about to examine, they even called themselves "angels," an identification so stunningly unsubtle that the story in which they appear is bound to be more than usually interesting. In fact the case of Paul Solem tells us a great deal about the nature of the UFO mystery itself.

Solem's first sighting and contact, he would claim, took place one day in June 1948 when he, his wife, and his brother-in-law observed three glowing objects speeding toward them over a field at his Howe, Idaho, ranch. On impulse Solem directed a mental question to the presumed occupants. To his surprise a "voice" inside his head replied, "We are from another planet. You will hear from us later."

More than four years went by before Solem heard anything, however. In the fall of 1952, seeing a multicolored light in the sky over his ranch, he followed the UFO for three miles until it landed in the Lost River Sinks. As it came to rest on the ground, the lights dimmed and went out and Solem saw a metallic disc reflected in the moonlight. Next to it was a person whom he first took to be a woman but who turned out to be a man with long blond hair, clothed in a white uniform.

The ufonaut, now speaking orally rather than telepathically, asked to be addressed as "Paul 2." He told Solem that as a Venusian he held the rank of "angel" and that Solem himself, a Venusian in a former existence, had been a spiritual teacher on that planet. In this life his task would be to work with the Indians of North and South America in preparing for the building of the City of Zion, a post-apocalyptic utopian social order in which money would be outlawed and all persons would live communally.

Solem later asserted that this was only the first of many communications with Venusians. Solem is somewhat vague about his whereabouts during the next seventeen years, but says that he traveled the western states; talking with Indians and other contactees, gathering small groups of followers, and generally shying away from publicity. At least two of those seventeen years Solem spent in the Idaho State Mental Hospital, according to a report compiled by the Prescott, Arizona, sheriff's office. He was put there in September 1967 while serving a six-month sentence in Idaho Falls for "misusing a telephone to annoy a person." The Idaho Falls arrest had been Solem's third since 1958.

Solem first came into public view in July 1969 when a series of campfire meetings at the edge of Fort Hall Indian Reservation in Idaho attracted the attention of local newspapers. Solem, accompanied by several Indians, spoke to the crowds about a coming mass migration of Indians north from Mexico and Central and South America. As foretold in Hopi prophecy, the migration, led by a 130-year-old Indian named Etchata Etchana, will come in the wake of a huge fire and explosion which will herald the coming of the "True White Brother." The True White Brother will be carrying a set of stone tablets to match those given the Hopi forty-five hundred years ago by the Great Spirit. On this, the Day of Purification, only those who have remained true to the old ways will survive.

In a meeting attended by Barbara Boren of the *Idaho State Journal* on the evening of July 12, Solem "called" the UFO beings, who replied (through Solem), "Paul, you are doing the best you can to get the message across." The skeptical reporter admitted that she saw two "starlike moving lights" high in the air.

Not long afterward Solem left for Hotevilla, Arizona, where he said the Venusians had ordered him to go. There he met with the chief of the Hopi Traditionalist Sun Clan, 108-year-old Dan Katchongva (or Qochhongva, meaning "White Cloud Above Horizon"), who went on to preside over a stormy gathering in which the younger members laughed at Solem's claims. Chief Dan himself, however, defended the contactee.

"This man speaks the truth," he said. "This is all part of our religion."

One Hopi who did not laugh was Titus Lamson. Five or six months previously he had seen a brilliantly lighted object sail over Hotevilla, moving in a westerly direction. A saucer-shaped construction with a dome and aerial on top, it became transparent as he watched it. Inside, he could see the back of someone dressed in a gray "ski-jump outfit." The man, who had blond hair reaching to his shoulders, was facing an instrument panel.

The craft descended slowly until it nearly touched the ground, and then disappeared over a ridge. Lamson set out to search for it with a flashlight but could not find it.

To Traditionalist Hopi like Lamson and Chief Dan, beings from other planets play an important role in the lore of their people. Thousands of years ago, according to Hopi belief, survivors of a vast flood which had decimated the tribe split and migrated in four different directions: north, south, east, and west. Only one group managed to complete the migration, which led them all the way to the North Pole and—under the guidance of a brilliant "star" —back to what is now Old Oraibi, Arizona.

The "star" was the vehicle in which the Great Spirit Maasau traveled. When Maasau came to earth, he drew a petroglyph on Second Mesa which showed a maiden with the traditional butterfly hairdo in a wingless, dome-shaped aerial vessel. This signified, he said, the coming of Purification Day (similar to the Christian Day of Judgment), when the faithful would fly to other planets in "ships without wings." The Great Spirit went on to explain that other worlds are inhabited and that Hopi prayers are received there.

Over the years the Hopis were taught by the *kachinas*, spiritlike beings from other planets, who instructed the Indians in agricultural techniques and gave them the philosophical and moral guidelines that were to shape

Hopi culture. Eventually the *kachinas* withdrew to the San Francisco mountains, where Hopis believe they still reside.

In his *Book of the Hopi* Frank Waters recounts the story of six Hopis who refused military service in World War II (the word *Hopi* means "peace," and members of the tribe still loyal to the traditional beliefs will not bear arms against fellow human beings) and who as a consequence were sentenced to three years' hard labor at a Tucson prison camp. The men ended up working on a road gang near Mount Lemon, suffering hardships so considerable that finally one of the group, Paul Siwingyawma, asked their Guardian Spirit for a sign that they were doing right. Waters writes:

Finally one night the sign came: a ball of fire coming from the north. All the Hopis were awakened to watch it. The great fireball moved through the forest without burning anything, passed through the gap in the mountain, and went south to the mountain east of Tucson. Then it slowly returned on the same route. Four nights in succession the vision appeared. Then the Hopis knew it was the manifestation of Masaw, the Guardian Spirit of the land, and a great strength entered them.

The issue of Solem's contacts and their relationship to the Hopi prophecy split the clan. Chief Dan viewed the matter philosophically, remarking that the division itself was fulfilling the prophecy that there would be three divisions among the Hopi before the coming of the True White Brother. The first division, in 1906, had been between the Traditionalists and the Modernists (the "Hostiles" and the "Friendlies")—the former were forced to leave Orabi and settle in nearby Hotevilla. What now was occurring was the second division.

For his part Solem left a few weeks later for Prescott to work with Indians and whites to further the message.

This was the state of affairs when some months later—in August 1970—a deluge of flying saucer sightings hit Prescott. The sightings began early in the month, shortly after Chief Dan had ordered ten thousand copies of the Hopi prophecy to be distributed to world leaders. Solem and his Hopi friends insisted that this was no mere coincidence, that in fact the UFOs had come to confirm the accuracy of the prophecy.

Whatever the truth, there seems no question that residents of Prescott were reporting more than their share of unusual aerial phenomena and that Solem had a way of attracting the saucers to himself.

In a dramatic demonstration made in the presence of editor Joe Kraus of the *Prescott Courier* on the evening of August 7, the contactee had stood off by himself, gazing into the sky, mentally "calling" the ufonauts. After fifteen minutes he announced, "They're here. I can't see them yet but I know they are here. One just said, 'We're here, Paul!' There are several people in the saucer. I can hear them talking."

Not more than two minutes later, Kraus reported in the lead story in the August 9 *Courier,* "a star appeared in the sky that wasn't there before. . . . It rose in the sky, stopped, hovered, wavered to one side, and then continued across the sky, repeating the maneuvers. . . . A flying saucer? Yes, if we could believe our eyes."

As the witnesses watched, Solem repeated words that he allegedly received through mental communication with a being aboard the ship:

"My name is Paul 2, fourth in command of all ships that enter the atmosphere of the planet called Earth. We come to lend credence and as a sign or token that the Hopi prophecy was of a divine nature. Great sorrow and fear will be coming to this planet very soon and few will escape it. Our leader as spoken of in Hopi prophecy is already here on Earth in mortality and is known as the Apostle John, the same as in the New Testament. The white brother shall be introduced by a huge fire and the earth shall quake at his arrival. We are of the ten lost tribes and we will return several nights unless there is contempt for us."

When Solem finished speaking, the "star" disappeared.

Kraus concluded, "Paul Solem is either a hypnotist, magician, has a vivid imagination, or he is telling the truth. Whatever, he is dedicated to his work."

Others in the area were seeing strange flying objects as well. The Reverend John Foster, a Baptist minister visiting from Phoenix, reported seeing an erratic pulsating light moving across the sky. Others saw objects zigzagging through the air and executing incredible maneuvers. *Courier* photographer Chuck Roberts took a picture of a UFO crossing the path of the satellite Pegasus.

Perhaps the most spectacular sighting was described by Mrs. Irene Wood:

"We were on a hill on De Merse Street and at 8:15 P.M. we saw a huge brilliant mass of light looking as big as three moons coming very fast from just over Thumb Butte. It seemed almost over Prescott and went to the east. It halted and a huge mass detached itself and fell straight down behind the hills.

"We came back in the house and at 8:30 we saw another smaller object that was reddish color with a glow. No blinking lights either. It came from exactly the same position and went the same route as the first. But when it got to the place where the first mass had detached its load, it let down six small red objects. There were no breakages apparent. Just as the thing hovered the six fell and they were spaced exactly the same distance apart. At one time we saw four of these things in the sky at one time."

On the night of August 9 about a hundred persons watched Solem "contact" the saucers, which obligingly appeared shortly afterward.

The next day Chief Dan, his counselor, Ralph Tawangyawma, and interpreter Caroline Tawangyawma arrived in Prescott to see the UFOs for themselves. Solem told them that the spaceships would show up if the sky cleared.

It did not do so until the last night Chief Dan and his companions were in Prescott. At 10:30 P.M., when the rainclouds broke, Solem went outside to attempt contact, and in a short while those still inside heard him yell, "Here they come!" A group of fifteen persons waiting at the door saw a bright object come sailing by.

In the words of witness Nonnie Skidmore, "The craft came in a rolling motion like a moon and was about five hundred to eight hundred feet off the ground. It came from north to south, then turned by the side of the house due west. It climbed and turned off its light like a lightbulb."

Two young Indians—Alvis Smith, an Apache, and Joe Manuel, a Pima—who had been talking with Chief Dan came forth publicly to confirm the account, as did a white couple who had made their own sighting separately.

On the seventeenth Solem announced that he no longer would contact UFOs in the Prescott area and that as a result sightings would diminish. They did.

Several days later the *Courier,* looking back on the flap, reported that a hoax had been responsible for sightings on the previous Sunday night: someone had dropped lighted plastic bags from an airplane.

"It should be noted, however," Joe Kraus went on, "that Paul Solem . . . did not make any attempt to contact UFOs that evening as members of the *Courier* staff were with him. . . . The changing colors, the zigzags, the contacts which Paul Solem claimed he made and which were observed by several hundred witnesses including *Courier* staff members did not seem to us to appear as a satellite or a plastic balloon. There may be other explanations. If there are we have yet to find anyone to come forward with this information."

In the months that followed Solem continued to live in Prescott, traveling occasionally with Chief Dan and others to Indian reservations to try to convince the inhabitants of the imminent coming of the True White Brother. In October they went to Santo Domingo Pueblo in New Mexico, where the chief repeated the message once again:

"We have seen the flying saucers and have heard their message to us," he said. "We know they are real as their pictures were drawn upon stone for all to see near Old Oraibi in the very beginning.

"We know the faithful are to be gathered to escape Purification Day. We give you our testimony and all that we tell you is true so you have no excuse that you were not told."

Nevertheless things had begun to disintegrate for Solem, Chief Dan, and those who were linking the saucers and the prophecy. A further split in the ranks of the Traditionalists lessened their numbers. Chief Dan believed that this was the prophesied "third division" that would open the way for the migration and the great "earth eruption" to follow.

In November, Solem reported, the Venusians complained to him that the message had not spread as it should have. Solem said that he would hold another meeting soon.

"This one will be in broad daylight," he said, "and we'll have reporters and cameramen from the big networks so there won't be any question any longer. This time we'll try to bring the ship to within a hundred feet."

"You do understand all of this, don't you?" Mrs. Nonnie Skidmore, corresponding secretary to Chief Dan, asked Jerome Clark at the time. "This is the greatest event in the entire solar system right now."

Solem's Venusians promised to stage four major demonstrations in Prescott, the first to occur on Easter Sunday 1971 over a field owned by a Tim Chapman. As the critical day drew near, excitement grew and virtually the entire community seemed willing to admit that the "greatest event in the entire solar system" might be about to take place right on their doorstep. Certainly enough was riding on the outcome: the credibility not only of Solem and the Traditionalist Hopis, but apparently of the ancient Hopi prophecy itself.

When Solem arrived at the field Easter morning he was furious when he saw that bulldozers had been working there. The Chapmans agreed to put the bulldozers out of sight and the fifteen hundred persons there assembled, including numerous reporters and television cameramen, waited anxiously for the appearance of the flying saucers.

Which, it goes without saying, never appeared.

Solem and his associates were mortified. Solem blamed the presence of the bulldozers for the nonappearance of the UFOs, threatened to sue the Chapmans, and canceled the other landings. That week he left Prescott and dropped out of sight. He has not been seen since.

Soon afterward the Hopi Tribal Council deposed Chief Dan from his position as head of the Sun Clan, on the grounds that his relationship with Paul Solem had hurt the image of the Hopis. Mrs. Skidmore, who had taken the penniless Solem into her home (Mr. Skidmore finally moved out when his wife failed to act on his ultimatum that Solem leave), was left with a pile of the contactee's unpaid bills.

Prescott, Arizona, seemed almost predestined to play host to a fiasco like the Paul Solem affair. During the 1950s contactees like Truman Bethurum and George Hunt Williamson had set up shop there, and in addition the ancient Hopi teachings about benevolent gods from outer space helped make Solem's contactee doctrine palatable to a sizable share of the area's population.

Another major contributing factor was Solem's personal situation, which rendered him uniquely vulnerable to the grandiose pronouncements of his Venusian "friends." The Venusians filled what otherwise appears to have been a life plagued with mistakes and failures: trouble with the law, marital difficulties (his wife had left him long before he came to Prescott), financial and psychiatric problems. When Paul 2 told him he had been a "spiritual teacher" on Venus in a previous existence, Paul 1 must have been pleased. He was someone important after all and now he had purpose and direction.

The Venusians led the contactee to Prescott, where he would be in a position to prove to the world that he was a major figure on the planet, not just a bankrupt ex-rancher and ex-mental patient. When one of us talked with him late in 1970 Solem exuded an air of happiness and self-confident expectation, rather like that of a man who believes, as Solem obviously did, that he is on the verge of greatness.

But had he been alert enough he would have known who the "Venusians" really were, for they themselves as much as told him. Solem thought that the extraterrestrial was "Paul 2"; but perhaps the Venusian was really saying "Paul, too." Either way the meaning is clear. "He" was Solem's alter ego, a subpersonality split off from the contactee's unconscious mind and projected onto the outside world, where "he" seems to have an independent existence and be able to effect paranormal manifestations much in the manner of the "spirit guides" in the seance room. Sometimes "he", like the spirit guides, can be seen by others (Titus Lamson).

The "UFOs" were created out of the psychokinetic energy Solem unknowingly generated from himself (contactees, remember, frequently have powerful extrasensory abilities) and from the believers who surrounded him. We have seen other instances of this in non-UFO contexts, such as the luminous aerial phenomena which thrilled the followers of Mary Jones or drove Irish fundamentalists into new heights of hysteria.

But of course the "Venusians" would cooperate only up to a point. As Solem's egotism grew through the course of events, its demands escalated and through its agent, Paul 2, it made the fatal mistake of demanding more than it could possibly supply. The "Venusians" were real all right, in a way, but it was more true that they were figures in a childish fantasy, lies that had come to life, psychic manifestations of a delusion of grandeur. For humanity in general, they were the discarded waste products of the collective psyche. They had no power beyond their hold on a handful of true believers. In Prescott a long tradition of belief in extraterrestrials insured them an unusually receptive audience; but they were operating at the outer limits of their power and it was absolutely impossible for them to go farther. The charade had to end somewhere and it did, when the UFOs stopped appearing and the apocalyptic prophecies went unfulfilled. The world does not dance to a child's tune. It would not be supplanted by an order of things which only pretend to exist.

The Prescott affair shows how easily UFO manifestations can adopt themselves to prevailing cultural circumstances. Just as the Hopi religion itself had begun to blend with Christianity ("Maasau is really Jesus," a Hopi woman told us), so when the new revelation came with the Venusian spaceships it absorbed the archetypes of the Hopi and the Christian and assumed a form that people of the Space Age could accept. This process has occurred all through history as human beings dealt with changing circumstances by giving new faces to ancient forms. As Jung puts it in *Symbols of Transformation,* "The symbols [the psyche] creates are always grounded in the unconscious archetype, but their manifest forms are molded by the ideas acquired by the conscious mind." This is true in all human experience and it is certainly true in paranormal experience.

Perhaps the single most tragic aspect of the Solem incident is that it served to discredit the religious beliefs of the Hopi. The Hopis have developed one of the most complex, fascinating religious systems of any people and their prophecies appear to be something other than the delusions of "primitives." Long before they had any contacts with other peoples, their religion told them there are three other races composed of people with black, white, and yellow skins; it also predicted that the coming of the white man would bring on a long period of hardship for the People of Peace. It also told them of a great war that would be set off by peoples of the swastika and the sun, apparently Germany and Japan in World War II. In 1914, just before World War I, the Hopis sang a special song, one predicting the spread of evil over the world, during their important Wuwuchim ceremony. They did the same in 1940, before the United States became involved in World War II, and in 1961—the year the first small contingent of American "advisors" entered Vietnam, precipitating a major and calamitous involvement no one else could then foresee—the Hopis sang their song once again.

It is unlikely that Solem's "Venusians" had anything to do with the Hopi's *kachinas* beyond the possibility that belief in *kachinas* helped create the proper psychic environment in which the whole preposterous Prescott farce could be enacted. We would not be much surprised if the Hopis at one time in their history really did have extensive dealings with extraterrestrials. Although the speculations of the Von Daniken crowd seem to have done much to discredit the entire idea of early space visits among more serious-minded people, we should remember that such respected scientific figures as Dr. Sagan have expressed more cautiously stated versions of the same general theory, which holds that long ago intelligent beings from other planets taught primitive cultures the rudiments of civilized life. Long after they had gone back to wherever they had come from, memories of their appearance were preserved in tribal myths and legends. Sagan, however, does not believe, and neither do we, that these early, hypothetical extraterrestrials were related in any way to our modern UFOs.

As for Paul Solem, wherever he is these days, he might

do well to contemplate these words of St. John of the Cross (W. T. Stace, *The Teachings of the Mystics*):

I am really terrified by what passes among us in these days. Anyone who has barely begun to meditate, if he becomes conscious of words of this kind during his self-recollection, pronounces them forthwith to be the word of God; and convinced that they are so, goes about proclaiming, "God has told me this," or, "I have had that answer from God." But all is illusion and fancy; such a man has only been speaking to himself.

PARAUFOLOGY: UNDERSTANDING THE INCOMPREHENSIBLE

> This western Otherworld, if that is what we believe it to be—a poetical picture of the great subjective world—cannot be the realm of any one race of invisible beings to the exclusion of another. In it all alike—gods, fairies, demons, shades, and every sort of disembodied spirits—find their appropriate abode; for though it seems to surround and interpenetrate this planet even as the X-rays interpenetrate matter, it can have no other limits than those of the Universe itself.
> —W. Y. Evans-Wentz, in *The Fairy-Faith in Celtic Countries*

1

One day in the late 1940s a sign painter named Allen Noonan was busily working at his trade when, he says, "all of a sudden I was just gone. I just wasn't there. I went out of my earthly body and was taken in my astral body to appear before the Galactic Command at the Great Central Sun. I appeared before a Great White Throne. It was in a tremendously beautiful white building. I could see light all around me. I stood there before this tremendous light. And out of the great white light, a Voice spoke to me. It just came booming out. And it said: 'Will you agree to be the Savior of the World?'"

Noonan hesitated only momentarily, thinking gloomily of his probable eventual crucifixion, and answered, "Yes."

The Voice concluded, "You may die in the hands of your fellow men. Their sins shall remain with you until the Mother Comforter comes to deliver them."

Over the years Noonan experienced numerous other contacts, all of them in his "astral body," with the Ashtar

Command, an intermediate group between the Galactic Command and the United Planets Organization, which "operate in different dimensions of space and time." They communicate telepathically with thousands of earth people "whose consciousness has risen into the fourth dimension."

At the Giant Rock Flying Saucer Convention in October 1960, the UPO tipped Noonan off that they would send a spaceship over the crowd of fifteen hundred persons. Then:

At exactly 1:30 P.M. [Noonan wrote], I received another communication in my mind. The Space People told me to send an aura from the center of myself to the center of the sun. And when I asked them what this meant, they explained to me that it would be like sending out a radar beam. If I concentrated my mind on the sun, the Mother Ship would be able to pick up my communication and come in between us here on earth and the sun.

Noonan did what he was told and suddenly clouds started to form around the sun. Soon they merged into one great cloud which covered the sun and sent the saucer faithful into fits of wonder. Noonan explained that these clouds "were caused by the ionization of the propulsion systems of the smaller spacecraft that were leaving the Mother Ship.

"The Space Command flies in and out of the earth," Noonan says. "The earth is hollow and the Higher Command, the Galactic Command, already has bases inside the earth. There are great openings at each pole of the earth and what we call the 'Northern Lights' is only the Great Central Sun shining out of these openings."

In 1967, while being interviewed by Lloyd Mallan of *True,* Noonan went to the hotel window, looked out at a cloudless sky, and asked the reporter if he had any camera film left. "Perhaps," he said, "it will be possible for me to summon a scanner or two to appear." Mallan loaded his camera with a roll of infrared film and waited, expecting absolutely nothing.

"Ten minutes later," he wrote, "a chill went up and down my spine. Two saucer-shaped clouds had formed in trail between some buildings across the way. I shot a few pictures of them, knowing that they *must* be conventional lenticular clouds. But *why* did they form at the particular time that Noonan said they would, coming apparently out of nowhere in an otherwise clear sky? Frankly, I still cannot explain the phenomenon—although I am fairly sure that there is a natural explanation for it." Two of the pictures are reprinted in *The New Report on Flying Saucers,* published in 1967 by *True* magazine.

In *The Aquarian Revelations* Brad Steiger notes certain consistent features of contact reports:

> . . . A warm ray of "light" emanated from the craft and touched the contactee on the neck, the crown of the head, or the middle of the forehead. In certain instances, the contactee may have lost consciousness at this point and, upon awakening, may have discovered that he could not account from anywhere from a minute or two to an hour or two of his time.
> . . . The contactee who retained consciousness and communicated with either an attractive Space Brother or a "voice inside his head" has very often told that he has been selected because he is, in reality, someone very special. . . . After a period of a week to several months, the contactee who has received a cosmic charge to spread the Space Brothers' message feels himself prepared to go forth and preach the word.
> . . . Families and friends of the contactee report that he is literally a different and changed person after his alleged experience. Higher intelligence and perception are often mentioned, as well as a seeming increase in ESP or psychic abilities.

Sometimes the ufonauts inform the contactee that he was really born a Venusian, Martian, or whatever, either in this life or an earlier one. The idea evidently is to imply that contactee and contactor are somehow related, despite the apparent differences, and that the two in a sense are "one." Not infrequently the percipient becomes so dissociated that the two *do* become one—that is, the contactee assumes the identity of the "spaceman." To mention only one of many possible examples, in the late 1950s one Lee Childers surfaced with a typically ludicrous story of contacts with "Prince Neosom of the Titanic Solar System." It was not long after that that Childers himself claimed to be Prince Neosom—which, sadly enough, just happened to have been the truth all along.

The contact messages are much the same: Stop atomic tests, stop war, learn the "universal laws," prepare yourselves for the coming cataclysms. Actor Stuart Whitman, trapped in the twelfth floor of a New York hotel during the great power blackout of 1965, heard a "sound like a whippoorwill" outside his window. Its source turned out to be two luminous discs, one blue, the other orange. From them emanated a voice which, as Whitman told Vernon Scott, "said they were fearful of earth, because earthlings were messing around with unknown quantities and might disrupt the balance of the universe or their planet . . . the blackout was just a little demonstration of their power, and they could do a lot more with almost no effort. They said they could stop our whole planet from functioning."

Since no one else saw the objects, which should have been plainly visible over crowded New York streets, we can only assume that Whitman's was a visionary, subjective experience. Nonetheless, contactees from Brazil, Argentina, and other places have spoken of the space people's fear that we are "upsetting the balance of the universe."

On January 30, 1965, at about 2:00 A.M., Sid Padrick, a radio-TV technician, was walking along the Pacific Coast near Watsonville, California, when he heard what sounded like a jet roar and looked up to see the shadowy outline of a huge disc-shaped UFO. Panicking, he started running down the beach until a voice from the object assured him that its occupants meant him no harm. They invited him aboard and Padrick decided to take them up on the offer.

The crew, eight men and one woman, were basically human in appearance, though with rather pointed chins and noses and longish fingers. One of the group, who told Padrick that he could call him "Xeno" (Greek for *stranger*), guided him through the ship, which had two stories with seven rooms on each floor. Only Xeno talked to the contactee. "He had no accent whatsoever," Padrick said. "I believe they can adapt themselves to whatever condition they're working under. Yet he said he was the only one of the nine on board who could speak English. Every question I asked him, he would pause for about twenty-five or thirty seconds before he would answer—regardless of how minor it was. Perhaps he was getting instructions—mentally—in what response to give. . . .

"He told me they were from a planet in back of a planet which we observe—but we do not observe them. He did not say we couldn't observe them. He merely said we didn't observe them. . . .

"The walls, floors, and ceiling were all the same shade of pale bluish-white. There were no square corners anyplace. Everything was rounded, corners, doorways, seats, anything movable or even fixed. Corners of rooms were all rounded. The light seemed to come right through the walls. There was no direct lighting whatever. In other words, the whole wall was lit. . . .

"I was shown an oblong lens, which looked like it was part of a lens system. It had a magnified, three-dimensional effect. On it I saw an object which I was told was the 'Navigation Craft'—he never referred to it as a 'Mother Ship.' It looked somewhat cigar-shaped but rounder in the middle—more like a blimp. This was 2:45 or 3:00 A.M., *and the object was in sunlight,* so it had to be pretty far out—I imagine one thousand miles out, or better. I did not see any markings or portholes on it. . . .

"The spaceman said, 'As you know it, we have no sickness; we have no crime; we have no vice; we have no police force. We have no schools—our young are taught at an early age to do a job, which they do very well. Because of our long life expectancy, we have very strict birth control. We have no money. We live as one."

Their mission, Padrick said, "involves the religious or spiritual aspect. The spaceman took me to a room similar to a chapel but he referred to it only as the 'consultation room.' The color effect in that room was so pretty that I almost fainted when I went in—a mixture of many beautiful colors—I can't describe it. There were eight chairs, a stool, and what appeared to be an altar. He said, 'Would you like to pay your respects to the Supreme Deity?' When he said that, I almost fainted. I didn't even know how to accept it. I said to him, 'We have one, but we call it God. Are we talking about the same thing?' He replied, 'There is only One.' So I knelt on the little stool and did my usual prayer. I'm forty-five years old and until that night I had never felt the presence of the Supreme Being—but I did feel Him that night. It was a very relieved and very exciting feeling, something that would lift you up right out of your steps.

"I wouldn't even classify [Xeno] as a scientific person. It's obvious that they are on a very high scientific level, but their relationship with the Supreme Being means a lot more to them than their technical and scientific ability and knowledge. I would say that their religion and their science are all in one.

"He told me they do not measure time and distance as we know it, but rather in terms of light. When I asked him how fast they traveled through space, he answered that their speed was limited only by the speed at which they could transfer their energy source. He said this craft I was on was not propelled by its own power source, but rather through a power transmitted to them—on a light beam, or on a light source known to them. . . .

"This encounter has meant more to me than just a visit from people from outer space. It means that my life has been lifted way, way up beyond what I could ever have conceived of before."

Investigators discovered that most of those who knew Padrick held him in high regard and believed his story. Two other UFO sightings had been made in the area around the same time. A crew of Santa Clara County park rangers had seen "a disclike thing" over the Hecker mountains east of Watsonville on December 28, and Monterey Mayor George M. Clemins observed a bright object over Monterey Bay on the evening of January 29.

John Keel has written extensively on what he terms the "time cycle factor," a curious aspect of the contact phenomenon which we see reflected in Padrick's statement that "they don't measure time and distance as we know it." Ufonauts forever seem to be asking percipients how we measure our "time cycle" or else chiding us because we measure it incorrectly.

In one such instance, under hypnosis contactee "Raymond Shearer" (a Midwestern attorney whose real name is known to writer Warren Smith) revealed that a ufonaut "asked me what type of time we used. This was a strange question, but I realized that he was asking me about how we measured time. I explained about our days, months, and years. He said that we should learn to handle time correctly.

"He said time doesn't exist. His people have the ability to distort time as we know it by speeding it up, slowing it down, or stopping it. To do this, we have to remove the brainwashed ideas about time from our minds. A little baby, or a child, does not have any concepts of time. A minute will seem like an hour to them. A day can seem as if it is forever—and it is. As we grow older, we become more conscious of time. We lose this innocence. His people have been here many times, but we would never be able to visit them. Our ideas of time would prevent it."

Keel discusses another aspect of the question in his important article "The Time Cycle Factor" (*Flying Saucer Review*, May-June 1969):

> The two most commonly reported time distortion effects (TDE) are:
> 1. Time compression . . . The witness undergoes an experience of seemingly long duration but later discovers a comparatively short period of real time—or earth time—has passed. Experiments have shown that seemingly long and involved dreams often occupy only a few seconds or a few minutes of the sleeper's real time. Therefore we must examine time-compression experiences from a psychiatric approach as well as a physical approach.
> 2. Time lapses. Events in which the witness suffers partial or total amnesia and is unable to remember how he passed specific periods of time. Several cases have been reported to me in which the witnesses, who were usually in automobiles, saw an approaching object and then suffered a memory lapse although they had no awareness of losing consciousness or otherwise undergoing an unusual experience. Such witnesses complain that it took them two hours or more to drive distances of only a few miles. This type of experience also demands psychiatric examination.

Parallel events figure in fairy and religious lore. ("In heaven," an angel once told a visionary, "one day is like seven years on earth.") Keel goes on:

> Nearly every contactee is given a set of prophecies or pre-

dictions concerned not only with his or her immediate interests and future but with national affairs as well. Many of these predictions are very precise, pinpointing time, place, and so on, with incredible accuracy. I have collected many such predictions and have been impressed with their *proven* validity. Contactees told me, far in advance of the events, of the collapse of the bridge at Point Pleasant, W. Virginia, of the murders of Martin Luther King and Robert Kennedy, and of innumerable ship and aircraft disasters and major earthquakes. A small percentage of these predictions missed because the time coordinates were off. Collecting, documenting, and validating such predictions can lead to the development of an important body of evidence.

It is not quite true that all contactee prophecies come true. The prophecies that fail, however, are usually those that relate to some major UFO intervention in human affairs (such as mass landings or takeover of the earth) and/or the end of the world. Apocalyptic visions have long been a part of human life and their frequent occurrence in UFO contexts furnishes yet more reason to believe that the roots of the saucer myth are very deep indeed. Festinger, Riecken, and Schachter deal with this fascinating subject in *When Prophecy Fails,* in which they relate a Minnesota-based contact-cult's end-of-the-world fantasies to comparable beliefs among Christian sects of the last two thousand years. English ufologist Peter Rogerson has coined the word *apocalyptophilia* to describe the phenomenon.

2

Orfeo Angelucci comes as close as any contactee to letting us know what the UFO mystery is really about when in *The Secret of the Saucers* he quotes a ufonaut's pronouncement that everyone on earth has a "spiritual, unknown self which transcends the material world and consciousness and dwells eternally outside of the Time dimension in spiritual perfection within the unity of the oversoul." The sole purpose of human existence is to attain reunion with the "immortal consciousness."

Angelucci's contacts normally took place in somnambulistic states which sometimes lasted as long as a week. In them he would wander out into space in his "astral body," meeting with gentle extraterrestrials whose ships flew at the speed of light. "The Speed of Light is the Speed of Truth," they told him, and said "cosmic law" forbade their making spectacular landings on earth. Angelucci's experiences would begin with a "dulling of consciousness"—"a state," as Jung notes, "which is a very important precondition for the occurrence of spontaneous psychic phenomena." Once the contactee awoke from his sleep/trance state to discover an inflamed circle the size of a twenty-five-cent piece, with a dot in the center.

Angelucci is speaking of the individuation process, of the reconciliation of conscious and unconscious. The transcendent "spiritual, unknown self" is the unconscious in its collective aspect. "Space and time," Jolande Jacobi writes, "are categories that spring from consciousness, from its 'discriminating activity.' The time that prevails in the collective unconscious and its manifestations is the 'mythical time' in which past and future are one, that is to say, always the present." The stigma is a mandala figure, a symbol of the self, of absolute wholeness, of God Who is a "circle whose center is everywhere and the circumference nowhere."

Because the collective unconscious exists outside time and space, it can perceive the direction of events in a manner denied us in ordinary conscious perception. It is attuned to elements in the common psyche of humanity that are unknown and deeply mysterious. Nonetheless it occasionally manifests itself to us in dreams or visions which preview future occurrences. Parapsychologists call this effect "precognition." When the premonition arises out of the collective unconscious, it may be to alert us to the imminence of some major event of archetypal significance: the death of a political leader, a natural or man-made disaster, the outbreak of war, or something else of that magnitude.

When Sid Padrick said the ufonauts' mission "involves the religious or spiritual aspect," he is absolutely right, as a number of subtle hints in his story seem to imply. The UFO has nine occupants, and with Padrick it has ten (actually, as we shall demonstrate shortly, without him it probably would have been *none,* if it had been at all). Ten is an archetype of unity, "the totality of the universe—both physical and material." Thus in the contactee's vision the spacemen's "religion and their science are all in one." Moreover, every room in the ship is rounded, evoking in our minds images of circles or mandalas, with all that they suggest.

The seven rooms on each of the two floors inevitably imply the ancient notion of correspondences, expressed usually, "As above, so below." Remember that the seven "are the link between the Will of Heaven and events on earth [and] . . . are consulted in human destiny."

The cigar-shaped "navigation craft" to which we are led to believe the circular-shaped smaller craft will return may symbolize the masculine/feminine antithesis and its implied resolution. The cigar is not only a phallic form but it is in the light and in the sky, all traditionally masculine archetypes in both Eastern and Western thought; the disc-circle waits below on the earth in the coolness of night, resting by the ocean—earth, coolness, darkness, and waters have long been associated with the feminine principle.

The spacemen "live as one." Xeno, the stranger from outer space with the strangely human face, tells Padrick, "There is only One." Can there be any doubt as to what he is referring? "Our world has shrunk," Jung remarks, "and it is dawning on us that humanity is *one,* with *one* psyche." Only when human beings acknowledge that truth psychically and politically will they be able to save themselves.

And can there be any doubt where "Xeno" comes from? He speaks of light, which we recognize as an energy source of visionary imagination, as "a power transmitted to them" —from the human mind, of course. Xeno's home, "a planet in back of a planet which we observe," is an astronomical absurdity but a pretty clear description of the hidden world of the unconscious, which normally though not necessarily is obscured by the familiar world of the conscious.

As we have projected the contents of the unconscious onto the cosmos in the UFO myth, so we should not be surprised when the ufonauts tell us we are upsetting "the balance of the universe" when they really mean the balance of the human psyche. Their further warnings about the perils of nuclear war, pollution, and social injustice address the consequences of that psychic imbalance, which threatens literally to destroy us.

Allen Noonan's tale is full of archetypal motifs. The "Galactic Center," "the center of myself," "the center of the sun" all symbolize transcendence from earth to heaven, or the achievement of individuation. The "Mother Comforter" is an anima figure; in her incarnation as "Mother Ship" (with its dim suggestion of the "sun maiden") she mediates between conscious and unconscious—i.e., she could "pick up my communication and come between us here on earth and the sun." The "Mother Comforter" who "comes to deliver" Noonan's fellow men may symbolize the Great Mother of ancient myth, come to restore to the psychic life of mankind the neglected feminine/unconscious aspect. The subterranean saucers coming through opposite ends of the earth but sharing the "Great Central Sun" represent "the union of opposites through the middle path"; they also make it clear, as if it were not already quite apparent, that Noonan's spaceships and space people are purely psychic.

His PK talents link him to Paul Solem and other, more traditional mystics. We shall have more to say on this general question shortly.

While Noonan's message to the human race, once its symbolic content is understood, merits our consideration, at the same time—sadly and typically—the contactee himself, with his messianic delusions, has fallen victim to an experience whose true significance he failed to comprehend. Jung writes, "Consciousness commits the same grave mistake as the insane person: it understands the event as a concrete external happening and not as a subjective symbolical process. The result is that the external world gets into hopeless disorder and is actually 'destroyed,' so far as the patient loses his relationship to it."

3

Finally, all of this leads to a staggering conclusion which we shall call the First Law of Paraufology:

The UFO mystery is primarily subjective and its content primarily symbolic.

Not, as we have seen, that it is without objective aspects, but these apparently are only subsidiary manifestations whose cause can be traced to certain extrasensory functions of the brain. In the considerable majority of cases the contact experience, which comprises the core of the enigma, occurs in states of altered consciousness, during which the percipient undergoes a profound experience at the very deep collective level of the unconscious. The rather limited probing of contactees' psychiatric backgrounds conducted thus far (mostly by Schwarz, David Saunders, and R. Leo Sprinkle, all highly trained psychologists working independently) has failed to show any consistent pattern of precontact psychosis, although pathological traits like dissociation may develop afterward. So it appears that mental illness, contrary to the skeptics' frequent assertion, is not a significant contributing factor in the general run of these hallucinatory visions.

We see no alternative but to view the flying saucer contactee as a modern-day spiritualist medium, religious mystic, shaman, or visitor to fairyland. As we know, all these latter perceived an otherworld which may have seemed "real" enough but which could not possibly exist, and all of them got there in states of dream, trance, or ecstasy.

We find particularly striking confirmation for our contention that the UFO mystery is subjective and that its contents are archetypal from the dream of a European painter which Jung quotes in *Flying Saucers*.

"I found myself, together with other people, on the top of a hill," he wrote, "looking over a beautiful, broad, undulating landscape teeming with lush verdure." A flying saucer came out of the sky and landed nearby, causing everyone but the dreamer to flee. A woman stepped out of the craft and approached him. "The woman told me that they knew me well in that other world (from which she had come) and were watching how I fulfilled my task (mission?). She spoke in a stern, almost threatening tone and seemed to attach great importance to the charge laid upon me."

It is extremely unlikely that the painter, who had this

dream on September 12, 1957, had ever heard of Howard Menger, whose book did not appear until two years later. "The anima personifies the collective unconscious, the 'realm of the Mothers,' " Jung comments, "which, as experience shows, has a distinct tendency to influence the conscious conduct of life and, when this is not possible, to irrupt violently into consciousness in order to confront it with strange and seemingly incomprehensible contents."

Two other dreams Jung cites are equally interesting. Neither of the dreamers was knowledgeable in UFO matters. Yet in one the dreamer's face was "scorched" by the close approach of a saucer; in the other a disclike dancing "sun" appears and finally falls to earth.

There is a dark side to the myth of the otherworld which we must emphasize before going any further. We saw it suggested in Jose Antonio's encounter with the underworld demons and in portions of Mr. X's vision of the afterlife (at the end of chapter three), but for the most part we have tended to depict the collective unconscious as essentially benevolent in nature, the long-suffering victim of the conscious's "egomania," to coin a phrase. But this has not always been the case; in our current psychocultural malaise it may be easy to forget that the conscious mind had some quite valid reasons for breaking free and striking out on its own.

In a private communication our friend Peter Rogerson lays out the issue so succinctly that we would not presume to improve on his efforts. Therefore we are taking the liberty of quoting his remarks in their entirety. First, however, we ought to explain that what we have labeled the "otherworld" Rogerson calls, after Vallee, "Magonia" (Latin for "magicland"). He begins by alluding to the incidents at Roachdale, Indiana, and Louisiana, Missouri (see chapter one):

The stories of the monsters are very interesting. The "snowman" seems to be a "wildman" image. It represents man stripped of all the gloss of civilization, the liberation from the restraints of society and a return to an archaic elemental mode. The symbol may be that of the "beast within" as well as being the "spirit of the wilderness" which gives a "call of the wild" in everyone's soul. In Keel's first book there were one or two cases where cars stalled in the presence of these "creatures." Here there is made explicit the fundamental incompatability between the "elmental" forces within and the modern mechanical civilization. This symbol underlies many of the vehicle-stopping reports. The theme is of the UFO as an "outsider" to our nice little surface world, outside of rational control, in whose presence the products of our rational civilization cannot operate. The UFO possesses a number of features in common with the snowman: it contains hints of tremendous power, of total freedom from rules and restraint (the power of the UFO to deny the laws of physics is one of its most disturbing aspects).

This idea of the UFO and Fortean phenomena [unexplained physical and paraphysical events] as symbolic of the unconscious forces within ourselves allows us to understand some of the fervor behind the skepticism of government and science. The [U. S. Air Force] Project Bluebook and Condon Enquiry [the much-criticized University of Colorado government-sponsored UFO study, headed by the late Dr. Edward U. Condon, which after two years and half a million dollars concluded that UFOs are not worth studying] can be seen as magical acts, ritual exorcism of the "terrors of the dark," and a magical reaffirmation of the boundaries of the "cultural universe." It is the identical motivation of the soothing of a child's night fears by its parents. This serves to reassure the parents as much as the child of the permanence of the conscious, rational world.

The underlying force behind such actions is to defend the "ego," which is in perpetual danger of falling back into the mother-sea [of consciousness], to use William James's term. For "primitive" man this is accomplished by the performing of certain magical actions, by observing certain taboos, etc. Otherwise he is in imminent danger of "losing his soul," of being taken to Magonia. Today we have managed to build a much securer foothold in which the ego is secure. But under certain conditions the defenses collapse. These will be conditions of psychological or social stress. Often the gap widens, then closes (for example with crisis apparitions) but some time gaps are wider; it is then that such magical rituals as Condon are needed. If the ritual fails, then there is danger of whole communities being seized to Magonia, as happened in Nazi Germany. It is interesting to note that both Sechaveral Sitwell and Harry Price in their books on poltergeists compared Hitlerism to poltergeist outbreaks.

An important book in the understanding of contemporary mythology is Toffler's *Future Shock*. Toffler argues that the acceleration of change in the modern world has produced a cultural shock similar to that suffered by less sophisticated societies when confronted by the more sophisticated. Faced with an "unbearable present and unimaginable future," many people seek a liberation from the restraints of selfhood and sanity. At its most extreme example this leads to suicide or drug addiction; at less severe levels there is the need to create in-groups and build fantasy worlds. The various UFO cults are typical examples of this.

It is under these conditions of stress that the longing for Magonia develops. Magonia here is no longer a threat but a desired paradise, the land beyond the west, so near and yet so far. It is the "primal paradise"—the womb—a place of haven and refuge. Mircea Eliade has shown how much "religious" endeavor has been based on regaining this state. The success of the Von Daniken myth clearly lies in this longing for the lost golden age. Von Daniken also expresses another powerful mythological theme, that of the divine ancestors returning to reconstitute the golden age. This also lies at the heart of the "Atlantis risen" myth.

"If progress and materialism have made technology possible by ignoring all the other subtle forces in nature," William Irwin Thompson observes in *At the Edge of History,* "then the death of materialism will open man up to beasts and demons he has not feared since the Middle Ages." Thompson is thinking of the current mania for witchcraft, Satanism, and the sort of hysterical fundamentalism displayed in the Jesus movement. All of these eschew reason, order, and intellectual curiosity—the gifts of the conscious mind to man—and assume the primacy of the unconscious (though few participants in these movements possess the sophistication to recognize that that is what they are doing).

The otherworld, the realm of the collective unconscious, certainly does have the potential power to destroy us. In ufology we find this demonstrated symbolically in certain ominous incidents. Ufology's evil "men in black" (MIB) —one of the most common archetypal depictions of the devil has him as a man in black, incidentally and not so coincidentally—run about, threatening ufologists, contactees, and other UFO sighters, warning them of the imminent takeover of the earth. Keel tells us that the MIB virtually destroyed one prominent researcher when they convinced him that they do in fact control the world; if he cooperated with them, they said, they would give him the cure for cancer and see to it that he would win the Nobel Peace Prize in 1972. As always happens in deals with the devil, the ufologist ended up a broken man.

The MIB, modern-day incarnations of an archetype given shape in a darker, superstitious-ridden age, symbolize the uncontained unconscious which, as Stuart Whitman's ufonauts warned, "could stop the whole planet from functioning."

Another percipient handled the matter more wisely. Jose Antonio da Silva, representing the conscious mind, was asked to serve the unconscious "underworld" in its efforts to take over the earth. While acknowledging that "underworld's" power, at the same time he refused to be subservient to it. Through this he achieved a psychic balance which resulted in his being saved by a figure symbolizing the unity (and equality) of the two aspects of the mind: the apparition is at once of the otherworld and of this world.

The otherworld exists as a counterpart to the conscious, rational world of the five senses. It reminds us that magic and mystery are as much—*but not more*—a part of the life of man as are science and reason. Seen in that context, it is positive and necessary. Seen as the sole reality compared to which all else palls into insignificance, it can be incredibly destructive. "We could cut off half of the human race if we wanted to," the Irish *Sidhe* once said, meaning that potentially, given the circumstances, they could annihilate the conscious half of the psyche and with it the rational world.

What the UFO myth is saying to us is this:

Man is on the brink of catastrophe because our age has denied him the capacity for belief in the magical and the wonderful. It has destroyed the mystical, nonrational elements which traditionally tied him to nature and his fellows. It has emphasized rationality to the exclusion of intuition, equations to the exclusion of dreams, male to the exclusion of female, machines to the exclusion of mysteries.

The UFO phenomenon has absorbed many of the ancient archetypal forms in which human beings have traditionally needed to believe and which they have sought to complete their world. As William Woods expresses it in *A History of the Devil*:

> All stories, all religious doctrines exemplify in different ways the Greek sense of balance . . . for balance is justice. Balance is at the heart of truth. Balance, exemplified in the very cosmos, is an inviolable order, without which we should have nothing but chaos. . . . The very seasons are a balance of opposites. Whatever men believe, they believe because it fills up a hole in logic or continuity, or because they perceive in it a balance analogous to that in the everyday things they can observe with their own eyes.

If this balance is not soon restored, the UFO myth tells us, nature will have its way. The collective unconscious, too long repressed, will burst free, overwhelm the world, and usher in an era of madness, superstition, and terror—with all their sociopolitical accouterments: war, anarchy, fascism.

This is very clearly the meaning of Stuart Whitman's vision, incidentally. His ufonauts may have claimed credit for the New York power blackout but we need not believe them—subsequent investigations uncovered more mundane, though equally disturbing, causes which seem to suggest that our much-overextended technology is nearing the breaking point. Again, the ufonauts' meaning was metaphorical, not literal: man's present psychically unbalanced course cannot continue forever. When the unconscious can no longer be contained, its liberated contents will destroy all that the conscious mind has produced: the fruits of science and technology, civilized order, and the very process of reason itself. Under the new imbalance a spiritual dark age will blanket the earth.

In the way the UFO phenomenon symbolizes, often naively, the resolution of the great dualities which trouble our time—in it, as John Rimmer has demonstrated, magic and machine are one—it sounds a warning and yet it offers us hope. We can no longer afford to ignore its message to the hearts of all of us.

4

We now approach another very important question, to which the Second Law of Paraufology addresses itself:

The "objective" manifestations are psychokinetically generated byproducts of those unconscious processes which shape a culture's vision of the otherworld. Existing only temporarily, they are at best only quasiphysical.

In a 1923 essay entitled "An Experience in the Occult," the great German novelist Thomas Mann recounted the story of a seance he attended with medium Willi Schneider, a nineteen-year-old dental assistant. While Mann held the twisting, entranced youth, handkerchiefs and bells sailed about the room, a music box played, and the keys of a typewriter were struck by the fingers of Schneider's "spirit guide" Minna. Mann, an open-minded skeptic with no particular interest in the occult, wrote, "Any mechanical deception or sleight-of-hand tricks were humanly impossible." He concluded that the phenomena were caused by the medium's mind, which somehow translated its dreams into objective realities. "It was Hegel," Mann remarked, "who said that the idea, the spirit, is the ultimate source of all phenomena; and perhaps supranormal physiology is more apt than normal to demonstrate his statement."

More recently, in his famous *The Imprisoned Splendour,* Dr. Raynor C. Johnson postulates "a psychic aether or 'substance' which partakes of some of the qualities of matter (such as localization in space and retention of form), and which is yet capable of sustaining thought images and emotions: something, in short, which is a bridge between matter and mind."

What is being suggested here is something utterly incredible, of course, for which nothing in our ordinary understanding of the supposedly self-evident differences between the "objective" and the "subjective" has prepared us. How can we be expected to believe that a psychic fancy can have a corresponding physical manifestation?

Those conversant in the literature of psychical research are perhaps best prepared to comprehend the notion, for it is the foundation of a widely accepted hypothesis concerning the nature of the poltergeist. Its first proponent, the late Dr. Nandor Fodor, wrote in the *Journal of Clinical Psychopathology* for July 1945, "The poltergeist is not a ghost. It is a bundle of projected repressions." He theorized that the manifestation, far from being an alien intelligence, as had been assumed, is no more (and no less) than a psychokinetic enactment/expression of conflicts being played out inside an individual unconscious, often though by no means always that of a young person undergoing the tremendous psychological and physiological strains of puberty.

Parapsychologist William G. Roll describes the theory in its current form in his recent *The Poltergeist*:

If the psychological needs or tensions of a person can extend beyond his body to be released in physical events in his environment, then the usual picture we have of man and his relation to the physical world is incomplete. Gardner Murphy, the psychologist . . . has been president of both the British and American Societies for Psychical Research. In his presidential address to the first of these organizations, delivered in June 1949, Murphy said that it is no longer possible to think of human personality as a solitary and independent entity. Rather we should look at it "as a node or region of relative concentration in a field of vast and complex interpenetrating forces." In this field, "none of us is completely individualized any more than he is completely washed out in a cosmic sink of impersonality." If we accept this expanded view of human personality, we may suppose that a person's tension system extends beyond the biological organism into his physical environment. In other words, we can think of the psi field as consisting of psychic energy. This field surrounds its source, in our case the poltergeist agent, and interacts with physical objects in his environment, much as sunlight interacts with water molecules as it penetrates the ocean. In the course of this process, psychic energy is transformed, for instance, to kinetic or light energy.

Madame Alexandra David-Neel was a remarkable French woman who had been educated at the Sorbonne and who in the years after explored vast tracts of Tibet which no other white traveler had crossed before her. She was awarded a gold medal by the Geographical Society of Paris and was also a Knight of the Legion of Honor. In one of her books, *With Mystics and Magicians in Tibet,* Mme. David-Neel writes of the *tulpa,* described as a "visible and sometimes tangible thought-form independent of its creator."

While living with the Tibetan yogis, Mme. David-Neel, who had on occasion seen these entities come into existence, decided to create one which she conceived of as a short, fat, good-natured lama. After some months of studied concentration, the *tulpa* appeared and Mme. David-Neel took it with her when she and her retinue resumed their travels through the country.

"Now and then," she wrote, "it was not necessary for me to think of him to make him appear. The phantom performed various actions of the kind that are natural to travelers and that I had not commanded."

Unfortunately the situation got out of hand.

"A change gradually took place in my lama. The countenance I had given him altered; his chubby cheeks thinned and his expression became vaguely cunning and malevolent. He became more importunate. In short, he was escaping me. One day a shepherd who was bringing me butter *saw* the phantasm, which he took for a lama of flesh and bone."

Mme. David-Neel realized that she was going to have to destroy her creation before it could do harm.

"I succeeded," she said, "but only after working at it for six months. My lama was hard to kill. That I should have succeeded in obtaining a voluntary hallucination is not surprising. What is interesting in such cases of 'materialization' is that other persons see the form created by thought."

The implications of this are profound and disturbing.

Thus we are rather surprised that so far, to our knowledge, no one has considered the UFO phenomenon as a kind of "planetary poltergeist" usually generated by the psychic energy of the *collective* unconscious, and more rarely by the individual unconscious.

"The subconscious mind," Colin Wilson theorizes in *The Occult,* "is not simply a kind of deep-seat repository of sunken memories and atavistic desires, but of forces that can, under certain circumstances, manifest themselves in the physical world with a force that goes beyond anything the conscious can command. . . . [Here] we begin to get a shadowy outline of a theory of the occult that avoids both extremes of skepticism and credulity."

If the otherworld is really the domain of the collective unconscious imprinted on the "psi field," creating in each cultural frame of reference a dream world that is relatively fixed in the psychic realm, then occasionally—through a process of "psychic spillover"—its errant inhabitants may enter our realm. This happens when the PK function of the brain confronts the archetypal contents of the otherworld, and it apparently is a side-effect of only secondary importance.

Where peasants were kidnapped into fairyland and mystics were transported into heaven, today UFO contactees are whisked off to Venus, a world as full of scientific marvels as the others were of supernatural ones. These realms could not possibly exist in the objective world. But its "inhabitants," quasiphysical entities which can be touched and photographed and can leave the appropriate traces (in the UFO context these consist of effects engineered to lend credence to the idea of an interplanetary otherworld), emerge from the purely psychic source point; they are no more than fragmented pieces of the whole, mere hints of a vaster subreality which could not possibly manifest itself objectively in the external world without actually supplanting it. It is here, incidentally, that one can safely draw a firm line between the subjective and the objective. That is what Angelucci's ufonauts were alluding to when they said that "cosmic law" prevents spectacular mass UFO landings.

So while the "inhabitants" may be visible to any number of people, percipients almost invariably enter the otherworld *alone,* or at least (in a very few incidents) in the company of a very small number of psychically attuned companions. Here one experiences the totality of what is only implied in the "objective" manifestations. Here the psychic needs which, tapping PK energy, fashion fairies, apparitions of the Virgin Mary, and UFOs are completely satisfied and enacted in their fullest expression, before they dissolve into the necessarily invisible "archetypes as such" (Jung's expression, by which he separates the actual archetype from the archetypal image).

A Zuni Indian legend described by Frank Hamilton Cushing in an 1892 issue of *The Journal of American Folk-Lore* speaks of the shapeless psychic realm lying beneath consciousness and awaiting form and definition. It tells us metaphorically about the archetypes beneath the archetypal images and suggests that these images can manifest themselves in our conscious life and perception:

> It seems—as the words of the grandfathers say—that in the Underworld were many strange things and beings, even villages of men, long ago. But the people of those villages were *unborn-made*—more like the ghosts of the dead than ourselves, yet more like ourselves than are the ghosts of the dead, for as the dead are more finished of being than we are, they were less so, as smoke, being hazy, is less fine than mist, which is filmy; or as green corn, though raw, is soft, like cooked corn which is done (like the dead), both softer than ripe corn which, though raw, is hardened by age (as we are of meat).
>
> And also, these people were, you see, dead in a way, in that they had not yet begun to live; that is, as we live, in the daylight fashion.
>
> And so, it would seem, partly like ourselves, they had bodies, and partly like the dead they had no bodies, for being unfinished they were unfixed. And whereas the dead are like the wind, and take form from within of their own wills, these people are really like the smoke, taking form from without of the outward touching of things, even as growing and unripe grains and fruits do.
>
> Well, in consequence, it was passing strange what a state they were in! Their persons were much the reverse of our own, for wherein we are hard, they were soft—pliable. Wherein we are most completed, they were most unfinished; for not having even the organs of digestion, whereby we fare lustily, food in its solidity was to them destructive, whereas to us it is nourishing. When, therefore, they would eat, they dreaded most the food itself, taking thought not to touch it, and merely absorbing the mist thereof. As fishes fare chiefly on water and birds on air, so these people ate by gulping down the steam and savor of their cooked things while cooking or still hot; then they threw the real food away!

There is another dimension to this matter. We have seen that contactees and other percipients may develop powerful ESP abilities, increased intelligence, and new personalities. The reason seems to be that the experience of the otherworld is so psychically charged that it produces profound electrochemical changes in the structure of the brain. The very frequent references to brilliant light in these visions has led anthropologist Roger W. Wescott to theorize that consciousness itself is internal bioluminiscence. In *The Divine Animal* he proposes that "such endrocranial bioluminiscence [is] a literal form of light generated in, by, and for the brain. . . . Awareness itself may consist of the internal generation and reception of perceptible radiation—in a word, of light."

The hallucinations occur partly because the brain is not equipped to handle the abrupt and massive influx of materials from the collective unconscious, and partly because we can experience the archetypes only as images and symbols. The forms they assume are both ancient and modern: ancient in the sense that they always have been intrinsic parts of the psyche, modern in that we perceive them in the context of ideas the conscious mind has acquired.

No one knows just how it is that an individual comes to enter the otherworld. The "X Factor," however, seems to have to do with the lowering of the threshold of consciousness, when one's psychic barriers are relaxed and the ego is vulnerable. This can occur when one conscientiously seeks out the experience through the ritual use of psychedelic drugs, ecstasy, sleep, and other self-induced methods. Sometimes it can occur when one is engaged in some monotonous pursuit requiring minimal mental activity: driving a car along a deserted road at night, working at an undemanding job (Allen Noonan), fishing (Jose Antonio, Hickson and Parker) and so on. Sometimes the sudden appearance of an "objective" manifestation may provoke an agitated state in which one's hold on ordinary reality is so shaken that the ego is temporarily overwhelmed by the contents of the collective unconscious ("Raymond Shearer," Barney and Betty Hill).

Sometimes the psychic charge may be sufficient to create phenomena in the vicinity of the percipient where none were before. Hickson and Parker apparently entered the otherworld when they drifted off mentally while engaged in the quiet pursuit of fishing; the immediate cause of their UFO vision was the many sightings then being made in the area, which must have been on their minds at some level or another even though they themselves had not seen—and did not see—a saucer. At any rate, while in the otherworld one or both of them broadcast telepathic signals which several persons intercepted and which made them think that they had observed the UFO of the two men's dream. Noonan's and Solem's phenomena, on the other hand, were not telepathic hallucinations but objective quasiphysical PK effects. In some instances the percipient generates both PK and telepathic manifestations: Mary Jones, for one.

Another variety of psi phenomena the percipient may experience is paranormal healing, which he may undergo himself or bestow upon others, or both. Levitation and teleportation are two other "wild talents" of percipients. The latter of these explains how sincere contactees can come up with "physical evidence" which they believe they got from the otherworld but which really is from this world. The appearance of conventional objects as if from nowhere is a feature common in poltergeist cases. Mediums call these things "apports" which their "spirit friends" convey into the seance room in paranormal fashion as "evidence" of the reality of the "other side." UFO percipients somehow incorporate these objects, which the vision's psychic charge has caused the contactee unknowingly to apport from somewhere else in this world, into the fabric of the dream.

If our speculations about the nature of the UFO myth are correct, we can predict with certainty that the Age of Flying Saucers has only begun. As technology and the civilization it sustains plunge deeper into the abyss, as the prospect of the imminent collapse of all our familiar institutions looms ever greater, as in the olden days men will turn their eyes upward and ponder the meaning of the mysterious signs and portents in the heavens.

What conclusions will they draw? Will they dismiss them as aberrations of no consequence whatever? Will they see them as gods or demons come to reassert their ancient hold on the human heart? Or will they peer anxiously into the faces of the strangers who fly them—and see in them what they have long forgotten, what they have always known?

SELECTED BIBLIOGRAPHY

Books

Adamski, George, *Inside the Space Ships*. New York; Abelard-Schuman, 1955.
——— *Flying Saucers Farewell*, New York: Abelard-Schuman, 1961.
——— (with Desmond Leslie), *Flying Saucers Have Landed*, New York: British Book Centre, 1953.
Angelucci, Orfeo. *The Secret of the Saucers*. Wisconsin: Amherst Press, 1955.
Bloecher, Ted. *Report on the UFO Wave of 1947*. Washington, D.C., 1967.
Blum, Ralph. *Beyond Earth: Man's Contact with UFOs*. New York: Bantam, 1974.
Blum, Richard and Eva. *The Dangerous Hour: The Lore of Crisis and Mystery in Rural Greece*. New York: Scribner's, 1970.
Bowen, Charles (ed.). *The Humanoids*. Chicago: Regnery, 1970.
Brewer, E. Cobham. *A Dictionary of Miracles*. 1884.
Briggs, K. M. *The Fairies in English Tradition and Literature*. Chicago: University of Chicago, 1967.
Brown, Slater. *The Heyday of Spiritualism*. New York: Hawthorn, 1970.

Bucke, Richard Maurice. *Cosmic Consciousness.* New Hyde Park, New York: University, New York, 1961.

Buckle, Eileen. *The Scoriton Mystery.* London: Neville Spearman, 1967.

Campbell, Joseph (ed.). *The Portable Jung.* New York: Viking, 1971.

Cavendish, Richard (ed.). *Encyclopedia of the Unexplained.* New York: McGraw-Hill, 1974.

Child, Francis James. *The English and Scottish Popular Ballads.* 1882–98.

Cirlot, J. E. *A Dictionary of Symbols.* New York: Philosophical Library, 1962.

Clark, Ella E. *Indian Legends of the Pacific Northwest.* Berkeley: University of California, 1953.

Coleman, Bernard. *Ojibwa Myths and Legends.* Minneapolis: Ross and Haines, 1962.

David-Neel, Alexandra. *With Mystics and Magicians in Tibet.* New York: University, 1957.

Davidson, Gustav. *A Dictionary of Angels.* New York: Free Press, 1967.

de Laszlo, Violet S. (ed.). *Psyche and Symbol: A Selection from the Writings of C. G. Jung.* Garden City, New York: Doubleday Anchor, 1958.

Doyle, Arthur Conan. *The Coming of the Fairies.* New York: Weiser, 1972.

Ebon, Martin (ed.). *True Experiences with Ghosts.* New York: Signet, 1968.

Eisenbud, Jule. *The World of Ted Serios.* New York; Morrow, 1967.

Eliade, Mircea. *Myths, Dreams, and Mysteries.* New York: Harper, 1961.

———*Shamanism: Archaic Techniques of Ecstasy.* Princeton, New Jersey: Princeton University Press, 1972.

Evans-Wentz, W. Y. *The Fairy-Faith in Celtic Countries.* New York: University, 1966.

Fodor, Nandor. *The Haunted Mind.* New York: Garrett Publications, 1959.

———*Mind over Space.* New York: Citadel, 1962.

———(ed.). *Encyclopedia of Psychic Science.* New Hyde Park, New York: University, 1966.

———(with Hereward Carrington). *Haunted People.* New York: Dutton, 1951.

Fort, Charles. *The Books of Charles Fort.* New York: Holt, 1941.

Frazer, Sir James G. *Folklore in the Old Testament*. New York: Tudor, 1923.

Furst, Peter T. (ed.). *Flesh of the Gods: The Ritual Use of Hallucinogens*. New York: Praeger, 1972.

Gardner, Edward L. *Fairies: The Cottingley Photographs and Their Sequel*. London: Theosophical Publishing House, 1945.

Gill, W. W. *A Second Manx Scrapbook*. London: Arrowsmith, 1932.

Girvan, Waveney. *Flying Saucers and Common Sense*. New York: Citadel, 1955.

Green, Celia. *Out-of-the-Body Experiences*. New York: Ballantine, 1973.

Gregory, Lady Augusta. *Visions and Beliefs in the West of Ireland*. New York: Oxford University, 1970.

Hartland, Edwin Sidney (ed.). *County Folklore: Gloucestershire*. England: 1892.

Holiday, F. W. *The Dragon and the Disc*. New York: Norton, 1973.

Hunt, Robert. *Popular Romances of the West of England; or, The Drolls, Traditions, and Superstitions of Old Cornwall*. New York: B. Blom, 1968.

Hynek, J. Allen. *The UFO Experience: A Scientific Inquiry*. Chicago: Regnery, 1972.

Jacobi, Jolande. *Complex/Archetype/Symbol in the Psychology of C. G. Jung*. New York: Princeton, 1959.

———*The Psychology of C. G. Jung*. New Haven, Connecticut: Yale, 1973.

Jobes, Gertrude and James. *Outer Space: Myths, Name Meanings, Calendars*. New York: Scarecrow, 1964.

Johnson, Raynor C. *The Imprisoned Splendour*. New York: Harper, 1953.

———*Psychical Research*. New York: Funk & Wagnalls, 1968.

Jung, C. G. *Flying Saucers: A Modern Myth of Things Seen in the Skies*. New York: Harcourt, Brace and Company, 1959.

———*Memories, Dreams, Reflections*. New York: Random House, 1963.

———*Psychology and Religion*. New Haven, Connecticut: Yale University, 1955

———*Symbols of Transformation*. Princeton, New Jersey: Princeton University, 1967.

———*Collected Works*. Princeton, New Jersey: Princeton University, 1970.

———(ed.). *Man and His Symbols*. Garden City, New York: Doubleday, 1964.

Keel, John A. *UFOs: Operation Trojan Horse*. New York: Putnam's, 1970.

———*Strange Creatures from Time and Space*. Greenwich, Connecticut: Fawcett Gold Medal, 1970.

———*The Mothman Prophecies*. New York: Saturday Review/E. P. Dutton: 1975.

Keightley, Thomas. *The Fairy Mythology*. England: 1882.

Keyhoe, Donald E. *The Flying Saucers Are Real*. New York: Fawcett, 1950.

Kirk, Robert. *The Secret Commonwealth of Elves, Fauns and Fairies*. England: 1815.

Koestler, Arthur. *The Roots of Coincidence*. New York: Random House, 1972.

Lawson, John Cuthbert. *Modern Greek Folklore and Ancient Greek Religion*. New York: University, 1953.

Leach, Maria (ed.). *Funk & Wagnalls Standard Dictionary of Folklore, Mythology and Legend*, Vol. One. New York: Funk & Wagnalls, 1949.

Lore, Gordon, and Deneault Harold. *Mysteries of the Skies: UFOs in Perspective*. Englewood Cliffs, New Jersey: Prentice-Hall, 1968.

Lorenzen, Coral and Jim. *Flying Saucer Occupants*. New York: Signet, 1967.

Masters, R. E. L., and Houston, Jean. *The Varieties of Psychedelic Experience*. New York: Holt, Rinehart and Winston, 1966.

McCreery, Charles. *Psychical Phenomena and the Physical World*. New York: Ballantine, 1973.

Menger, Howard. *From Outer Space to You*. Clarksburg, West Virginia: Saucerian Books, 1959.

Monroe, Robert A. *Journeys Out of the Body*. Garden City, New York: Doubleday, 1971.

Murphy, Gardner, and Ballou, Robert O. (eds.). *William James on Psychical Research*. New York: Viking, 1960.

Norman, Eric. *The Under-People*. New York: Award, 1969.

O'Dea, Thomas F. *The Mormons*. Chicago: University of Chicago, 1957.

O'Donnell, Elliott. *Ghostland*. London: 1925.

Oliver, Norman. *Sequel to Scoriton*. London: 1968.

Ostrander, Sheila, and Schroeder, Lynn. *Psychic Discoveries Behind the Iron Curtain.* Englewood Cliffs, New Jersey: Prentice-Hall, 1970.

Palmer, Jerome. *Our Lady Returns to Egypt.* San Bernardino, California: Culligan, 1969.

Pauwels, Louis, and Bergier, Jacques. *The Dawn of Magic.* London: Gibbs & Phillips, 1963.

Pelletier, Joseph A. *Our Lady Comes to Garabandal.* Worcester, Massachusetts: Assumption Publications, 1971.

Puharich, Andrija. *Beyond Telepathy.* Garden City, New York: Doubleday, 1962.

———*Uri: A Journal of the Mystery of Uri Geller.* Garden City, New York: Doubleday Anchor, 1974.

Rogo, D. Scott. *A Psychic Study of the "Music of the Spheres" (NAD, Vol. 2).* Secaucus, New Jersey: University Books, 1972.

Roll, William G. *The Poltergeist.* New York: Signet, 1974.

Sackville-West, Victoria. *Saint Joan of Arc.* New York: Literary Guild, 1936.

Sanderson, Ivan T. *Uninvited Visitors.* New York: Cowles, 1967.

———*Invisible Residents.* New York: World, 1970.

Schwarz, Berthold E. *A Psychiatrist Looks at ESP.* New York: Signet, 1968.

Scott, Sir Walter. *Minstrelsy of the Scottish Border.* London: Oliver and Boyd, 1932.

Seligmann, Kurt. *Magic, Supernaturalism and Religion.* New York: Pantheon, 1948.

Smith, Joseph. *Book of Mormon.* Salt Lake City, Utah: The Church of Jesus Christ of the Latter-Day Saints, 1961.

Smythies, J. R. (ed.). *Science and ESP.* New York: Humanities, 1967.

Stace, W. T. (ed.). *The Teachings of the Mystics.* New York: Mentor, 1960.

Steiger, Brad. *The Aquarian Revelations.* New York: Dell, 1971.

———*Revelation: The Divine Fire.* Englewood Cliffs, New Jersey: Prentice-Hall, 1973.

———*Mysteries of Time and Space.* Englewood Cliffs, New Jersey: Prentice-Hall, 1974.

———(with Joan Whritenour). *New UFO Breakthrough.* New York: Award, 1968.

Stevens, William Oliver. *Unbidden Guests.* London: 1949.

Swire, Otto F. *The Outer Hebrides and Their Legends.* Edinburgh: 1966.

Tart, Charles T. (ed.). *Altered States of Consciousness.* Garden City, New York: Doubleday Anchor, 1972.

Thomas, Keith. *Religion and the Decline of Magic.* New York: Scribner's, 1971.

Thomas, Paul (pseud. of Paul Misraki). *Flying Saucers Through the Ages.* London: Neville Spearman, 1965.

Thompson, Stith. *The Folktale.* New York: Holt, Rinehart and Winston, 1946.

Thompson, William Irwin. *At the Edge of History.* New York: Harper & Row, 1971.

————*Passages About Earth: An Exploration of the New Planetary Culture.* New York: Harper & Row, 1974.

Tyrrel, G. N. M. *Apparitions.* New York: Macmillan, 1970.

Vallee, Jacques. *Anatomy of a Phenomenon.* Chicago: Regnery, 1965.

————*Passport to Magonia: From Folklore to Flying Saucers.* Chicago: Regnery, 1969.

Van Over, Raymond (ed.). *Psychology and Extrasensory Perception.* New York: Mentor, 1972.

Waters, Frank. *Book of the Hopi.* New York: Viking, 1963.

Watson, Lyall. *Supernature.* Garden City, New York: Doubleday, 1973.

White, John (ed.). *The Highest State of Consciousness.* Garden City, New York: Doubleday Anchor, 1972.

Wilhelm, Richard. *The Secret of the Golden Flower.* New York: Harcourt Brace, 1931.

Wilkins, Harold T. *Flying Saucers on the Attack.* New York: Citadel, 1954.

Wilson, Colin. *The Occult.* New York: Random House, 1971.

Wilson, Mona. *The Life of William Blake.* London: Rupert Hart-Davis, 1948.

Woods, William. *A History of the Devil.* New York: Putnam's, 1974.

Yeats, William Butler (ed.). *Irish Folk Stories and Fairy Tales,* New York: Grosset & Dunlap, 1971.

Magazines

Barry, John. "Fairies in Eire." *The Living Age,* November 1938.

Binder, Otto O. "Clues That Prove UFOs Come from Different Galaxies." *Saga's UFO Report,* spring 1974.

Bord, Colin. "Angels and UFOs." *Flying Saucer Review*, September-October 1972.

Bord, Janet. "UFOs in Folklore." *Flying Saucer Review* Vol. 20, No. 1 (1974).

Brant Aleixo, Hulvio. "Abduction at Bebedouro." *Flying Saucer Review*, November-December 1973.

Buckle, Eileen. "What the Children Saw." *FSR Case Histories*, August 1971.

Chibbett, H. S. W. "UFOs and Parapsychology." *Flying Saucer Review*, (Special Issue No. 3, entitled *UFO Percipients*) September 1969.

Clark, Jerome. "A Contact Claim." *Flying Saucer Review*, January-February 1965.

——— The Strange Case of the 1897 Airship." *Flying Saucer Review*, July-August 1966.

——— "The Old West's Strangest Mystery." *Real West*, May 1967.

——— "More on 1897." *Flying Saucer Review*, July-August 1967.

——— "Indian Prophecy and the Prescott UFOs." *Fate*, April 1971.

——— "On the Trail of Unidentified Furry Objects. *Fate*, August 1973.

——— "Exploring Fairy Folklore," *Fate*. September and October 1974.

——— (with Loren Coleman). "Anthropoids, Monsters and UFOs." *Flying Saucer Review*, January-February 1973.

——— (with Loren Coleman). "Mystery Airships of the 1800s." *Fate*, May, June, and July 1973.

——— (with Lucius Farish). "The 1897 Story." *Flying Saucer Review*, September-October and November-December 1968 and January-February 1969.

——— (with Lucius Farish). "The 'Ghost Rockets' of 1946." *Saga's UFO Report*, fall 1974.

Coleman, Loren, and Hall, Mark. "Some Bigfoot Traditions of the North American Indians." *The INFO Journal*, fall-winter 1970.

Creighton, Gordon. "Gnomery Down on the Farm." *FSR Case Histories*, June 1972.

——— "A Weird Case from the Past." *Flying Saucer Review*, July-August 1970.

Crowe, Richard. "Missouri Monster." *Fate*, December 1972.

Cushing, Frank Hamilton. "A Zuni Folk-Tale of the Under-

world." *Journal of American Folk-Lore*, January-March 1892.
Doyle, Arthur Conan. "Fairies Photographed." *The Strand Magazine*, December 1920.
Farish, Lucius. "An 1880 UFO." *Flying Saucer Review*, May-June 1965.
——— "Unidentified 'Airships' of the Gay Nineties." *Fate*, November 1966.
——— "The E. T. Concept in History." *Flying Saucer Review*, July-August 1973.
Fredrickson, Sven-Olof. "The Angelholm Landing Report." *Flying Saucer Review*, March-April 1972.
Hanlon, Donald B. "Texas Odyssey of 1897." *Flying Saucer Review*, September-October 1966.
——— (with Jacques Vallee). "Airships Over Texas." *Flying Saucer Review*, January-February 1967.
Harney, John. "Some Thoughts on Telepathy as a Possible Means of Communication with Extraterrestrial Intelligences." *Merseyside UFO Bulletin* 2:5 (September-October 1969).
Hughes, Robert. "The Glory of the Lord Shone Round About Them." *Time*, December 28, 1970.
Keel, John A. "The Principle of Transmogrification." *Flying Saucer Review*, July-August 1969.
——— "The Perfect Apparition." *Flying Saucer Review*, May-June 1971.
——— "Medical Aspects of Non-Events." *Anomaly*, September 1969.
——— "America's First UFO Experts." *Saga's UFO Report*, summer 1974.
——— "The Time Cycle Factor." *Flying Saucer Review*, May-June 1969.
Kor, Peter (pseud. of Tom Comella). "From the Critic's Corner." *Flying Saucers*, January 1963.
——— "Realm of the Saucers." *Flying Saucers*, May 1966.
Lord, Harry. "The Little Men of Leam Lane." *Flying Saucers*, December 1964.
Mann, Michael G. "Prince or King, He Isn't a Spaceman!" *Saucer News*, March 1960.
Mesnard, Joel. "The Little Singing Creatures at Arc-sous-Cicon." *Flying Saucer Review*, January-February 1973.
Navarro, P. G. "The 'Secret' Super-Intelligent People." *Flying Saucers*, November 1970.

———"Mr. Dellschau's Airship." *Flying Saucer Digest*, winter 1970.

Noonan, Allen. "I Went to Venus—and Beyond." *The New Report on Flying Saucers*, No. 2 (1967).

Padrick, Sid. "The Padrick 'Space Contact.'" *Little Listening Post*, fall 1965.

"Practicing Psychiatrist." "I Found Life Beyond Death." *Fate*, December 1970.

Rimmer, John A. "The UFO as an Anti-Scientific Symbol." *Merseyside UFO Bulletin* 2:4 (July-August 1969).

———"A Look at the Alternatives." *Merseyside UFO Bulletin* 3:1 (January-February 1970).

———"The UFO Is Alive and Well and Living in Fairyland." *Merseyside UFO Bulletin* 3:6 (December 1970).

———"Politics and Cultism." *Merseyside UFO Bulletin* 4:4 (September-October 1971).

Rogerson, Peter. "The UFO as an Integral Part of the Apocalyptophilia and Irrationality of the Mid Twentieth Century." *Merseyside UFO Bulletin* 4:1 (spring 1971).

———"The Sun Maiden" *Merseyside UFO Bulletin* 4:2 (June 1971).

———"Psychological Theories of UFOs." *Merseyside UFO Bulletin* 4:4 (September-October 1971).

———"The Mythology of UFO Events and Interpretations." *Merseyside UFO Bulletin* 5:3 (summer 1972).

Rogo, D. Scott. "Deathbed Visions and Survival." *Fate*, June 1972.

Sandell, Roger. "UFOs in Wales in 1905." *Flying Saucer Review*, July-August 1971.

———"More on Welsh UFOs in 1905." *Flying Saucer Review*, March-April 1972.

Sanderson, Stewart F. "The Cottingley Fairy Photographs: A Re-Appraisal of the Evidence." *Folklore*, summer 1973.

Schwarz, Berthold E. " 'Beauty of the Night.' " *Flying Saucer Review*, July-August 1972.

Smith, Warren. "The Inside Story of the Pascagoula UFO Kidnap." *Saga*, March 1974.

———"Contact with a UFO Crew." *Saga's UFO Report*, summer 1974.

Stevens, Wendelle C. "UFOs: Seeing Is Believing." *Saga's UFO Report*, fall 1974.

Stumbough, Virginia. "Fairies Were Real." *Fate*, November 1957.
Traum, Artie. "The Cambridge Festival: Some Notes on Guzzling English Beer, Scottish Legends, Supernatural Possession of Musicians & Americans Abroad." *Crawdaddy*, November 1972.
Umland, Rudolph. "Phantom Airships of the Nineties." *Prairie Schooner*, winter 1938.
Vest, Paul. "Could Fairies Be Real?" *Fate*, October 1951.
Wilkins, Harold T. "Pixie-Haunted Moor." *Fate*, July 1952.
Winder, R. H. B. "The Little Blue Man on Studham Common." *Flying Saucer Review*, July-August 1967.

A NOTE ON UFO AND FORTEAN PUBLICATIONS

Readers who want to pursue the matters *The Unidentified* has explored would do well to consult the following publications:

Flying Saucer Review (FSR Publications, Ltd., P.O. Box 25. Barnet, Herts. EN5 2NR, England) is the finest UFO journal in the English language, and one which no serious researcher can be without. *FSR* began in 1955 as a contactee-oriented publication but in the last decade, under the able editorship of Charles Bowen, has grown immeasurably in stature and sophistication. Its editors and most of its contributors take a paraphysical, non-ETH perspective, and increasingly the magazine has directed its attention to the psychological and paranormal aspects of the UFO experience. Bimonthly.

Merseyside UFO Bulletin (Peter Rogerson, 8 Braddon Avenue, Urmston, Manchester M31 1UE, England) regularly publishes the best theoretical writing on UFOs and related phenomena that we have ever seen. Its editors, a small group of young intellectuals, independently arrived at conclusions much like our own. Their publication never fails to be outrageous, irreverent, and exciting. Published irregularly several times a year.

The News (R. J. M. Rickard, PO Stores, Aldermaston, Berkshire, England) is an excellent bimonthly which carries on the work of the late Charles Fort, the American iconoclast who collected reams of material on such "damned" phenomena as monsters, falls from the sky, enigmatic antiquities, UFOs, and much else. In fact, it is associated with the International Fortean Organization (P.O. Box 367, Arlington, Virginia 22210), publishers of the quarterly *INFO Journal.*

Skylook (Dwight Connelly, 26 Edgewood Drive, Quincy, Illinois 62301) is the best American UFO magazine, quite informative despite its rather narrow, 1950s-ish view of the nature of the UFO mystery; it is, for example, just about the last refuge for those ultraconservative diehards who reject contact claims out of hand. Nonetheless the publication—and its parent organization, the Mutual UFO Network (Walter H. Andrus, director, 40 Christopher Court, Quincy, Illinois 62301)—have done a commendable job of investigating UFO incidents in this country and elsewhere. Monthly.

Saga's UFO Report (333 Johnson Avenue, Brooklyn, New York 11206) is the only mass-circulation magazine to deal exclusively with UFOs. For a commercial venture—i.e., one that must necessarily appeal to thirteen-year-olds and little old ladies as much as to "serious researchers"—it is surprisingly good. Its coverage of contact stories is especially strong. Discriminating readers can easily overlook *SUFOR*'s somewhat breathless advocacy of ETH and ancient astronauts for its many more worthy features. Quarterly.

Fate (3500 Western Avenue, Highland Park, Illinois 60035) publishes a wide range of articles on the "strange and unknown," including UFOs and other Fortean phenomena. A fine magazine, indispensable to anyone concerned with the paranormal. Monthly.

Pursuit is the quarterly journal of the Society for the Investigation of the Unexplained (R. D. 1, Columbia, New Jersey 07832). SITU carries on the work begun by Ivan T. Sanderson, and has gathered many of his most brilliant followers under its wind. *Pursuit,* therefore, has many thought-provoking articles reflecting the membership's high degree of good Fortean skepticism.

The Bigfoot News (P.O. Box 632, The Dalles, Oregon 97058) is a monthly roundup of the latest sightings of Bigfoot and expedition news from the Pacific Northwest, including Idaho and all of western Canada. Since the first issue, in October 1974, BF's publisher, Peter Byrne, has done a worthwhile service in filling the gap left with the ceasing of the publication of George Haas' *Bigfoot Bulletin* and Jim McClarin's *Manimals Newsletter.*

INDEX

Aero Club, 135–136
Alamo, unknown celestial body, 32
Aleixo, Hulvio Brant, 169
Airship Co., 145
Airship reports, 131–163
  and water, 141–142, 146, 147–148, 149
Akinesia—*see* Paralysis
Amnesia, 191, 231
Ancient astronauts, 25, 239
Angel hair—*see* Apports: angel hair
Angels, 66, 93–94ff. *See also* Entities
Anima, 28, 205–206, 237
Animal mutilations, 17–18, 157
Anti-gravity, 135–136, 146, 152
Apports, 248. *See also specific artifacts under* Fairies
  angel hair, 105, 181
  ectoplasm, 181
  objects from UFOs, 29, 131–132, 159, 182
Argentina, 228
Arizona, 214–216, 218, 220–222
Arkansas, 147, 148
Armies in the skies, 93
Ashtar Command, 225–226. *See also* Entities
Astral projection, defined, 126
Atlantis, 239
Aubrey, John, 79
Australia, 210

Automatic writing, 104
Baldwin, Thomas Scott, 137
Barker, Gray, 210
Bedroom apparitions, 12
Biblical figures—*see* Entities; Percipients; Saints
Bigfoot, 11, 63
Birds, 112–113, 145, 147, 148
Binder, Otto O., 182–183
Black Fairy, 78. *See also* Fairies: death
Bloecher, Ted, 31
Blum, Eva and Richard, 60
Blum, Judy and Ralph, 186
Bowen, Charles, iii, 47, 183
Brazil, 31, 33, 165, 177, 238
Brewer, E. Cobham, 96
Briggs, Katherine, 67, 81
British Interplanetary Society, 27
Bucke, Richard Maurice, 114
Buckle, Eileen, 54, 196
Burroughs, Edgar Rice, 79
California, 26, 134, 136–140, 142–143, 145–148, 150, 160, 228, 230
Callers, mysterious, 185
Campbell, Lady Archibald, 56
Caves, 25, 61, 64–69, 97–99, 167, 173–179, 193–195, 204. *See also* Hollow earth; Otherworld
Central Intelligence Agency (CIA), 210
Changeling, defined, 69–70. *See also* Fairies: kidnappings

Chapman, Tim, 220
Chibbett, H. S. W., 193
Cirlot, J. E., 38, 178, 180, 206
Clark, Ella E., 64
Collective unconscious, 31, 36–37n, 38ff, 225ff. *See also* Carl G. Jung
Comella, Tom, 182
Condon, Edward U., 238
Contactee, general overview, 227
Contactees—*see* Percipients
Cosmic consciousness, 129
Cottingley fairy photographs, 80–88
Cramp, Leonard G., 200
Crashes, UFOs—*see* Ufonauts: crash hoaxes
Creighton, Gordon, 46–47, 88
Crete, 59
Crowe, Richard T., iii, 13–14
Cuba, 140, 146
Cummings, Abraham, 109
Cushing, Frank Hamilton, 246
da Silva, Geraldo Lopes, 171
Death, 123–124, 164. *See also* Fairies: death
Delaware, 143
Deneault, Harold, 141
Denamark, 62
Deros, 174. *See also* Dwarf; Fairies; Little green men; Little people; Ufonauts
Devil, 239
Doernberger, Walter, 27
Doyle, Sir Arthur Conan, 23, 80, 84–87
Dragons in the sky, 93
Dreaming—*see* Trance-state
Dryads, tree-nymphs, 60
Duffus, Lord, 79

Dwarf, psychological definitions of, 179–180. *See also* Fairies; Little people
Ecstasies—*see* Trance-state
Egypt, 111
Eisenbud, Jule, 88
Electromagnetic effects, 11, 28–29, 56, 90, 228, 238. *See also* Magnetic bath
Eliade, Mircea, 41, 66
Entities, and mysterious figures, names of
  Artemis, 60
  Apostle John, 217
  Auterlitz, George, 147, 151
  Benjamin, E. H., 138–139
  Black Fairy, 78
  Bostick, Captain, 26
  Butler, Mrs. George, 108–109
  Captain, 142
  Collector of curiosities, 132, 151
  Dellschau, C. A. A.—*see* Percipients
  Davidson, Professor Charles, 147
  Dolbear, A. E., 147, 151
  Eddleman, Joseph, 147, 151
  Freyer, Gustav, 135, 151
  Heintz, Henry, 140
  H6AQ, 193
  "Japs", 158
  Jesus, 116, 121, 126
  Kahn, A. B., 151
  Koch, Julius, 151
  Krause, Ernest, 151
  Lady of Fatima, 104
  Maasau, 215, 222
  Minna, 242
  Mischer, Jacob, 151
  Mollie, 145
  Morini, 101, 104

Newell, George, 135
Orthon, 196
Our Lady of Mount Carmel, 109–111
Paul Two, 214, 217, 221
Preast, John O., 150, 161
Prince Neosom, 227
Sally, 124
Saint Michael, 111
Schoetler, August, 135, 151
Smith, C. A., 141
Space Brothers, concept of, 148
Tillman, S. E., 147, 151
True White Brother, 214, 216, 219
Victricius, 98
Virgin Mary, 104ff, 246
Wilson, 149–152
Wilson, Tosh and Co., 150–151
Xeno, 228–230, 234
Epileptic seizures, similar to trance-state, 75, 191. *See also* Trance-state
Etchata, Etchata, 214
Evans, Wainwright, 122
Evans-Wentz, Walter Y., 19, 48, 66, 69, 78, 175, 225
Evidence, physical—*see* Apports; Electromagnetic effects
Extraterrestrial hypothesis (ETH), 9–10, 184, 223
Fairies, 23, 34–36, 45, 98, 192, 245. *See also* Deros; Dwarf; Entities; Little green men; Little people; Ufonauts; *and specific kinds of fairies*
bread, 74
children, 71
Cottingley photographs, 80–88

cups, 74, 79, 132
death, 77–78, 124
defined, 52
feast, 79
funeral, 50
healing powers, 74–76, 107
imitators of society, 81, 156
kidnappings, 61–62, 64–65, 66–67, 69, 78, 165–172, 175
music and sing-song voices, 62, 63, 67–68, 69, 90, 129, 152, 173
pygmy origin theory, 53
queen, concept of, 66, 203–205
ring, 50, 124
sexuality, 60–62, 72–73, 107, 204
shape changing, 48, 62–69, 175–176
wind, 37, 45, 61, 70, 79, 106
Farfadets, hairy dwarfs of France, 176
Farish, Lucius, iii, 26
Ferreira, Celio, 172
Fishing—*see* Trance-state
Fitzpatrick, James T., 63
Florida, 76
Flowers, 131–132, 153
Flying saucer people—*see* Entities; Ufonauts
Fodor, Nandor, 120, 190, 193, 242
Fort, Charles, ii
France, 45–46, 53, 62, 105, 107, 176
Frazer, James G., 156
Frederickson, Sven-Olof, 29
Fuller, Curtis, 125, 174
Fuller, Mary Margaret, iii, 125

Fuller, John G., 158
Galactic Command, 225. *See also* Entities.
Gardner, C. C., 154
Gardner, Edward L., 83–85
Garon, Jay, iii
Gentry, the, 52, 78
Germany, 27–28, 62, 133, 150–151, 160
Gernsback, Hugo, 27
Ghost rockets, 28
Gibbs-Smith, Charles H., 133
Gold plates, 101–103
Good people, the, 48, 52, 56
Great Britain, 20–24, 46–47, 51, 52–54, 67, 72, 76, 80–88, 88–91, 116–119, 159, 175, 199
Greece, 51, 59–61
Green men—*see* Little green men
Gregory, Lady Augusta, 48, 77
Hall, Mark A., iii
Hamilton, Gail, 124
Hands, 24, 33
Hart, W. H. H., 139
Hawaii, 62–63, 204
Healing, 74–76, 106–107, 110, 248
Hill people of Ireland, 49, 55, 240
Hitler, Adolf, 28, 238
Hoaxes—*see* Ufonauts: crash hoaxes
Hodgson, Richard, 125
Hodgson, William Hope, 27
Hollow earth, 226. *See also* Caves.
Honey, importance to fairies, 62
Horses
  hair and monsters, 18
  in the skies, 93
  tiny, 23
Hough, George, 143
Hughes, Robert, 201
Hunt, Robert, 92
Huxley, Aldous, 179
Hynek, J. Allen, 181, 185
Hyslop, James, 124
Idaho, 64, 213–214
Ikals, little people of Mexico, 173
Illinois, 103, 144–146, 156
Indiana, 12, 15, 237
Indians, American. *See also* Percipients: Paul Solem
  Apache, 219
  Araphoos, 64
  Bannocks, 64
  Cherokees, 176
  Chippewa, 71
  Coeur d'Alenes, 64
  Flatheads, 64
  Hopi, 215
  Nez Perces, 65
  Pima, 218
  Shoshoni, 64
  Spirit guides, 213
  Yakimas, 64
  Zuni, 246
Individuation, 38, 233, 235
Ininees, Chippewa fairies, 71
Inventors, mystery, 136, 137–139. *See also* Entities.
Iowa, 196–197
Ireland, 55–57, 116, 158
Italy, 32
Jacobi, Jolande, 233
Jaffe, Aniela, 188
James, William, 238
Jobes, Gertrude and James, 41
Johnson, Raynor C., 251
Jung, Carl G., 31, 38, 162, 165, 179, 188, 206, 222, 232, 234, 235–237, 246

Jupiter, beings from, 26
Kachinas, Hopi spirit-beings, 215–216, 223
Kansas, 143, 157
Keel, John A., iii, 21, 183–184, 196, 207, 211, 230–231, 238, 239
Keely, John—*see* Percipients
Keightley, Thomas, 61
Kidnappings—*see* Fairies: kidnappings
Kor, Peter, pseudonym, 182
Lang, Andrew, 50
Lawson, John Cuthbert, 50
Leach, MacEdward, 52
Lemuria, 174
Leprechauns, 50, 57. *See also* Little green men.
Leroy, Oliver, 121
Leslie, Desmond, 197
Levitation, 120–122, 190–191, 248
Lewis, E., 108
Little green men, 25, 33, 35, 37, 54, 56, 65, 72, 168, 182. *See also* Leprechauns; Little people; Ufonauts
Little people, 21–25, 31–37, 45–48, 166ff, 171, 176, 182–183. *See also* Deros; Dwarf; Entities; Fairies; Leprechauns; Little green men; Ufonauts
Lore, Gordon, 141
MacGregor, Mrs. J., 175
McWhorther, Lucullus, 64
Magnetic bath, 86
Magonia, defined, 237
Maine, 108–109, 139
Mandala, 27–28, 206, 233–234
Mars and Martians, 27, 154, 156, 194, 197, 203, 204, 227
Martin, Humphrey, 73, 75
Mass hysteria, 188
Mediums—*see* Percipients
Menehune, little people of Hawaii, 62–63
Men-in-black, 119, 239–240. *See also* Entities: Collector of curiosities
Mesnard, Joel, 46
Messages, 14, 99, 108, 110, 145, 170
MIB—*see* Men-in-black
Minnesota, 21, 93
Mississippi, 185
Missouri, 12–15, 152, 237
Momo, 12–14
Monroe, Robert A., 126
Mormons, 103
Moseley, James, 199
Mouths, slit-like, 33, 168, 183
Murphy, Gardner, 243
Naiads, water nymphs, 60
Nains, dwarfs of Brittany, 176
National Airship Company, 145
Navarro, P. G., iii, 134, 135
NB gas, 135, 152
Nebraska, 143–144, 150
Nereids, Greek nymphs, 50–51, 59–62, 105–107
Newcomb, Miss, 47
New Jersey, 139, 151, 203, 204, 207
New Mexico, 121, 131–133, 151, 219
New York, 100, 101, 146, 148, 149, 151, 241
New Zealand, 23
Nirvana, 129
Noises, strange, 13, 24, 146, 185

North Carolina, 196
NYMZA, secret society, 135
Oberth, Hermann, 28
O'Donnell, Elliott, 55, 107
Odors, rotten, 13, 16
Oklahoma, 30
Oreads, mountain nymphs, 60
Oregon, 64
Orion, planet, 209, 211, 213
Orque, unknown celestial body, 31
Osis, Karlis, 122
Ostrander, Shelia, 188
Otherworld, 52, 237, 240, 245. *See also* Caves
Out-of-body experiences, defined, 126
Palmer, Jerome, 112
Palmer, Ray, 174, 198
Paralysis, 21, 33, 35, 100, 106, 108, 166, 173, 175, 187, 191. *See also* Trance-state
and beams of light, 33–35, 45, 166, 174
Pelletier, Joseph A., 105, 110–111
Percipients (includes all contactees, mediums, witnesses coming in contact with the Phenomenon)
Adamski, George, 196–202, 213
Adare, Lord, 120
Akers, Captain, 149
Andreu, Luis, 110
Angelucci, Orfeo, 232, 245
Arnold, Kenneth, 31
Babcock, Emily, 103
Baring-Gould, S., 53
Baylor, H. W., 149
B.C., 201
Bell, Keith, 24
Bepoix, Patricia, 45

Bethurum, Truman, 221
Blackburn, Sean, 21
Blaisdel, Paul, 108–109
Blake, William, 49–50
Blot, Thomas, 26
Boren, Barbara, 214
Bowers, Mrs. Wallace, 10–11
Bradburg, Thomas, 145
Burdine, Carter, Bill and Herman, 17–18
Butler, Alex, 46, 49
Byrne, Lawrence A., 157
Carlsson, Gosta, 28–29
Childers, Lee, 201
Clemins, George M., 230
Cloncs, Leroy, 17
Coleman, Susan Reneé, 58
Collins, George D., 138–139, 151
Cowdery, Oliver, 102
Crookes, Sir William, 119, 191
Crowe, Richard T., 13
d'Agredá, Marie, 121
Darbishire, Stephen, 199–200, 202
da Costa e Rosa, Olmira, 203
da Silva, Jose Antonio, 165–178, 190, 192, 237, 240, 241
da Silva, Rivalino Mafra, 177
David-Neel, Madame Alexandra, 244
Davidson, Gustav, 96, 201
Davis, James, 147
de Benarides, Alonso, 121
de Maille, Jeanne Marie, 115
Dellschau, C. A. A., 133–136, 150–152, 160–163
duBourg, Mother, 121

Eliane, Mercia, 239
Elijah, 36, 120
Emmerick, Anne Catherine, 121
Evans, Beriah G.
Farrell, Mike, 77
Ferrant, Marechal, 107–108
Flynn, James, 70
Foley, Marina, 111
Foster, John, 217
Gerais, Minas, 177
Glanville, Joseph, 78
Gonzalez, Conchita, 101–104
Goodwin, I. J., 22
Grahame of Duchray, 67
Grant, Mrs. Biddy, 56
Gregorius, Bishop, 112–113
Griffiths, Frances, 81–88
Greatrakes, Mr., 78
Hamilton, Alexander, 157, 163
Hardy, Mrs., 23
Harris, ex-Senator, 146
Harrison, Edgar, Terry and Wally, 13
Hart, W. H. H., 151–152
Hatton, Austin, 91
Hickson, Charles, 185–190, 247
Higgins, Jose C., 32, 38–41
Hill, Barney and Betty, 158, 247
Hodson, Geoffrey, 86, 88
Home, D. D., 119–120, 191
Hopkins, W. H., 152–155, 163
Howard, Pat, 13
Hulle, John, 146

Jefferies, Anne, 71–77, 88, 107, 182, 192
Jennings, Georges, 140
Joan of Arc, 98–100, 108
Johannis, R. L., 32–37, 168
Jones, H. D., 118
Jones, Mary, 116–118, 137, 222, 248
Jordan, William, 129
Katchongva, Dan, 214–215, 216, 218–219, 220
Keely, John, 57, 174
Kermode, T. C., 177
Kircher, Athanasius, 26
Kirk, Robert, 66–67, 69, 175
Kraus, Joe, 217, 219
Lamberson, Tom, 21
Lamson, Titus, 215, 221
Lawson, J. C., 49–50
Lechog, Bard, 92
Ligon, Charley and J. R., 149
Lodge, Sir Oliver, 191
Lowry, R. L., 137
McCann, John, 78
McDowell, R. M., 147
McIllhaney, C. L., 146
McLemore, John, 147–148
Mairot, Marie-Reine, 46
Mallan, Lloyd, 226–227
Mann, Thomas, 242
Manuel, Joe, 219
Martyn, Mary, 74
Menger, Alton, 203
Menger, Howard, 202–212
Menger, Robert, 208–209, 210–211, 247–248
milkman, 211
miner, 117
Morgan, Llewelyn, 117
Moses, Stainton, 191

Noonan, Allen, 225, 235, 247–248
Padrick, Sid, 228, 233–234
Paladino, Eusapia, 192
Parker, Calvin, 185–190, 241
park rangers, 230
Pio, Padre, 110
Pitt, Moses, 72, 73–74, 97
Potter, Mr. and Mrs. F. W., 199, 202
Ravier, Joelle, 45–46, 49
reporter, 116–117
Roberts, Chuck, 218
Rogers, Keith, Lou, and Randy, 14
Rourk, Ketty, 78
saints—*see* Saints
Schneider, Willi, 242
Serios, Ted, 88
Shade, Lois, 14
Shaver, Richard S., 174–175
"Shearer, Raymond", 230, 247
Simonton, Joe, 181
Sisson, M. G., 144–146, 148
Siwingyawma, Paul, 216
Skidmore, Nonnie, 218, 220
Smith, Alvis, 218
Smith, Hyrum, 103
Smith, Joseph, 100–103
Solem, Paul, 213ff, 235, 248
Soubirous, Bernadetta, 106–107, 108
Spaur, Dale, 212
Sprankle, Margaret, 30
Steiger, Brad, 58
Sumpter, John J. Jr., 147–148
Swedenborg, Emanuel, 26
Swenson, Steve, 21
Swifte, Edmund Lenthal, 20
Tawangyawma, Caroline and Ralph, 218
Thomas of Erceldoune, 71
Traum, Artie, 90
Valdivia, Luigi, 142
Valinziano, Giuseppe, 142
Van Winkle, Rip, 71
Vogel, J. H., 137
Whitman, Stuart, 228, 240, 241
Williamson, George Hunt, 199, 221
Wilson, David, 24
Winkle, Adolph, 146
Witherspoon, G. L., 146
Wood, Irene, 218
Wood, Thomas, 67–68, 90
Wright, Elsie, 81–88
"X, Mr.", 125–129, 237
"X, Mrs.", 193
Zamora, Lonnie, 212
Photographs
  inside UFOs, 168
  of fairies, 80–88
  of UFOs, 184. *See also* Percipients: George Adamski
Pilcz, Alexander, 189
PK—*see* Psychokinetic
Plato, 39, 178
Poltergeist activity, 185, 193, 238, 243–245, 248
Portugal, 104
Price, Harry, 238
Psychic aether, 242. *See also* Apports
Psychokinetic, 122, 190, 195, 221, 235, 242–246
Puharich, Andrija, 189
Pymgies, 53

Rays—*see* Paralysis and beams of light
Red-heads, entities with, 28, 56–57, 168
Revivals of 1859, 115
Rimmer, John A., 10, 42–43, 156, 242
Rogerson, Peter, iii, 9, 105, 107, 232, 237
Roll, William G., 243
Rymer, Thomas, 45, 71
Sackville-West, V., 100
Sagan, Carl, 182, 233
Saints, as entities
  Michael, 111
Saints, as percipients
  Ammon, 121
  Brigit, 115
  Columba of Rieti, 116
  Cuthbert, 97, 182
  Gerude, 115
  Gregory the Great, 116
  Francisca, 97
  Francis Xaverius, 121
  Hildegardes, 97
  Ignatius, 126
  John-Joseph de la Croix, 120, 126
  John Nepomuck, 115
  John of Matha, 115
  John of the Cross, 224
  Joseph of Copertino, 121
  Mary of Jesus Crucified, 121
  Patrick, 97–98
  Raphael, 121
  Teresa of Avila, 122
Sandel, Roger, 116
Sanderson, Ivan Terence, 49, 207
Sasquatch, 63
Saturn and Saturnians, 197, 203
Saunders, David, 236
Schoolcraft, Henry Rowe, 71
Schroeder, Lynn, 189
Schroth, David, iii
Schwarz, Berthold Eric, 207–210, 236
Scoriton affair, 196, 201
Scott, Vernon, 228
Scott, Walter, 51
Selag, mystery book, 136
Seven, the number, 41, 77, 138, 169, 180, 229, 231, 234
Sexuality—*see* Fairies: sexuality
Shakers, 103
Shamanism, 76
Sidhe of Ireland, 49, 55, 240
Sitwell, Sachaveral, 238
Smith, Warren, 230
Sounds—*see* Noises
South Dakota, 141
Space cookies, 182. *See also* Apports
Spain, 109–111
Spaulding, Solomon, 103
Spiritualism, 160
Sprinkle, R. Leo, 236
Steiger, Brad, iii, 58, 227
Stevens, Wendelle, 188
Stevens, William Oliver, 109
Stick Indians, Nez Perces fairyfolk, 65
Stigmata, 193–195
  "caused" by UFO helmet, 171
Stone
  magic, 100–102
  quarry, 171
  tablets, 214
Subterranean world—*see* Caves; Otherworld
Sun Maiden, 105, 235. *See also* Fairies: queen; Entities: Virgin Mary

Sweden, 28, 70
Swire, Otto F., 105
Taylor, William M., 66
Telepathic whammy, 189
Teleportation, 26, 120–122, 190–191, 192, 248
Tennessee, 147–148, 177
Ten, the number, 180, 233–234
Texas, 27, 126, 134, 144, 146–147, 149, 150, 158, 161
Thomas, Keith, 93
Thomas, Paul, 105
Thompson, William Irwin, 91, 239
Three, the number, 28, 169
Thought-forms, 244. *See also* Apports; Trance-state
Thummin, magic stone, 101, 104
Tibet, 244
Time cycle factor, Keelian concept of, 230–231
Titantic Solar System, 234. *See also* Entities
Trance-state, 33, 35, 76–77, 104, 106, 110, 120, 121, 125–126, 146, 162, 165–166, 185, 187–192, 232–233, 237, 247. *See also* Paralysis
Trumpet, 103
Tulpa, tangible thought-form, 244
Twelve, the number, 206
Tyrrell, G. N. M., 184
Underworld—*see* Caves; Otherworld
Union of Soviet Social Republics, 27–28
United Planets Organization, 226. *See also* Entities
United States Air Force, 184

Ufonauts, 21, 28–31, 121, 138ff, 166ff. *See also* Entities; Fairies; Little green men; Little people
  breathing and heat problems, 33, 152–153, 158
  crash hoaxes, 27, 181
  lying, 148
  Spaniard pilot theory, 29
Urim, magic stone, 101, 104
Vallee, Jacques, 27, 105, 131, 182, 237
Venus and Venusians, 26, 197, 200–201, 203, 213, 220, 227, 245
Verne, Jules, 27
Vettar, spirits of Sweden, 70
Virginia, 177
von Braun, Wernher, 27
von Daniken, Eric, 239
von Franz, M. L., 38
von Urban, Rudolf, 188
Washington, 10, 21, 64
Watch, examined by entities, 153–154, 156
Waters, Frank, 216
Wells, H. G., 27
Wescott, Roger W., 247
Whipsnade Park Zoo, 47
White, Betty Lou, iii
Williams, Clint, iii, 141
Wilkins, Harold T., 68–69
Wilson, Colin, 245
Wind, fairy—*see* Fairies: wind
Winder, R. H. B., 48
Witnesses—*see* Percipients
Woodall, William, 16–18
Woods, William, 241
Wright, Orville, 132
Writing, automatic—*see* Automatic writing; Messages
Xeno—*see* Entities: Xeno

Book Two:
CREATURES OF THE OUTER EDGE

To John Keel, pioneer.

There is not wanting a feast of broad, joyous humor, in this stranger phantasmagoria, where pit and stage, and man and animal, and earth and air, are jumbled in confusion worse confounded.

—Thomas Carlyle

CONTENTS

Introduction	11
Chapter One: Mystery Animals	15
Chapter Two: The Bigfeet	28
Chapter Three: The Manimals	51
Chapter Four: Phantom Cats and Dogs	117
Chapter Five: Things with Wings	165
Chapter Six: Phantasms	195
Epilogue: 1977—A Year Filled with Monsters	208

CREATURES OF THE OUTER EDGE

INTRODUCTION

This is a catalogue of absurd marvels. It is a compilation of impossible events, hundreds of them, stories so ridiculously unlikely that they sound like demented jokes.

The only trouble is, they all happened. Or anyway, they are supposed to have happened, and by the time you have finished reading the last page, you probably will agree that some incredibly strange occurrences which appear to make no sense whatever are going on all around us.

This book is an effort to record a great many data which otherwise would go unnoticed by any but that small and devoted band, among whom the authors proudly number themselves, who call themselves Forteans, after Charles Fort (1874-1932). Fort was the first person to record in any systematic way all manner of decidedly unusual events which practically nobody besides direct witnesses had any idea were occurring. Fort discovered that not only were they occurring, but they were doing so with astonishing frequency.

One of the many subjects which fascinated him was the phenomenon of mystery animals—weird creatures which seem not to belong in this world at all. Sightings of such beasts have increased dramatically since Fort's time. *Creatures of the Outer Edge* is an effort to update the master's work by describing what people are reporting today. Beyond noting some of the general patterns in the sightings, we have kept speculation to a minimum until the last chapter, preferring for the most part to let the cases speak for themselves. And these cases have much to say that is surprising, often shocking. You will very likely discover mystery animals are not what you think they are. As we track these bizarre creatures, we will discover that their trail leads to some unexpected places. We will find that the farther we pursue them, the more impenetrably mysterious they become.

We would like to thank the following people for their generous assistance:

Curtis and Mary Fuller of *Fate*; Terry Catchpole of *Oui*; R.J.M. Rickard of *Fortean Times*; Charles Bowen of *Flying Saucer Review*; Peter Rogerson of *MUFOB*; Paul Willis of *The INFO Journal*; Rod B. Dyke of *UFO Newsclipping Service*; Mark A. Hall, Ron Dobbins, Tim Church, John A. Keel, Don Worley, Lucius Farish, Brad Steiger, Tom Adams, Jim McClarin, John Green, the late George Haas, Dr. James Ulness, Dr. Warren Smerud, Richard Crowe, Dr. Berthold Eric Schwarz, and Robert Jones; plus hundreds of other Forteans, witnesses, newspaper reporters, game wardens and librarians across the nation who have put up with almost twenty years of our questions and queries; plus, of course, Penny, Toni, and Libbet, as well as our mutually supportive families!

                                   Jerome Clark
                                   Loren Coleman, M.S.W.

Illinois
Massachusetts

CHAPTER ONE

Mystery Animals

Some awfully strange things are wandering through our world—things which are supposed to exist only in dreams and nightmares, things which all the laws of reason assure us are flatly impossible. Things which, for a great variety of reasons, are distinctly unwelcome but which nonetheless resolutely refuse to go away.

Two of them appeared in the 1920s, if we are to credit the testimonies of psychical researchers of the period, who claimed to have encountered them during a series of seances. The medium was a man known to us only through the pseudonym "Franek Kluski," a Polish engineer, poet, and writer whom parapsychologists regard as one of the most remarkable psychics of all time. "Kluski" is supposed to have had a spirit guide who called himself Hirkill.

"Accompanying [Hirkill] always was a rapacious beast, the size of a very big dog, of a tawny color, with slender neck, mouth full of large teeth, eyes which glowed in the darkness like a cat's, and which reminded the company of a maneless lion," an article in *Psychic Science* (April 1926) tells us. "It was occasionally wild in its behavior, especially if persons were afraid of it, and neither the human nor the animal apparition was much welcomed by the sitters. . . . The lion, as we may call him, liked to lick the sitters with a moist and prickly tongue, and gave forth the odor of a great feline, and even after the seance, the sitters, especially the medium, were impregnated with this acrid scent as if they had made a long stay in a menagerie among wild beasts."

We have the further testimony of Dr. Gustave Geley, who described another kind of beast which manifested itself during some of "Kluski's" seances:

> This being which we have termed Pithecanthropus has shown itself several times at our seances. One of us, at the seance on November 20, 1920, felt its large, shaggy head press hard on his right shoulder and against his cheek. The head was covered with thick, coarse hair. A smell came from it like that of a deer or a wet dog. When one of the sitters put out his hand, the Pithecanthropus seized it and licked it slowly three times. Its tongue was large and soft. At other times, we all felt our legs touched by what seemed to be frolicsome dogs.

And Col. Norbert Ochorowicz wrote:

> This ape was of such great strength that it could easily move a heavy bookcase filled with books through the room, carry a sofa over the heads of the sitters, or lift the heaviest persons in their chairs into the air to the height of a tall person. Though the ape's behavior sometimes

caused fear, and indicated a low level of intelligence, it was never malignant. Indeed, it often expressed goodwill, gentleness and readiness to obey. . . . After a long stay, a strong animal smell was noticed.

Over forty years later an even more unlikely series of events was taking place in Salem, Ohio, a small community near Youngstown. The episode began one morning in the spring of 1968 when Mrs. Alice Allison happened to glance out a window and observed something hovering over her buckeye tree, which stood about thirty feet high. "It looked like an airplane without wings," she told investigator Mark Swift. "It sounded like a helicopter but it had no propellers." It was black and unlighted, but the top half of the front part was a clear dome, inside which she could see an occupant.

"He was a man and wore a khaki-colored shirt," she said. "He had olive-colored skin, which was slightly tanned, and his eyes were slanted." She thought he might be worried that the craft was about to crash, since it was making sputtering sounds and rocking back and forth in the air.

Mrs. Allison's seven-year-old son Bruce also observed the object, though not the occupant, because he was viewing the phenomenon from the rear.

After about twenty minutes the object finally flew off slowly in a southwesterly direction.

Around that same time the family often saw a large catlike creature, about three feet high and three and a half feet long. Sometimes it would sit out in the driveway, where once, after a rain, the Allisons found three-inch footprints. On another occasion they discovered claw marks half an inch deep and six inches long in a tree near the house.

Both they and the neighbors heard the creature. "My daughter woke up one night and it was growling and panting so loud it seemed as if it were at the foot of the bed," Mrs. Allison said. Catlike prints, far too large to have been made by a domestic cat, appeared on top of a neighbor's car. A check with the nearest zoo in Cleveland, seventy miles away, failed to uncover any reports of escaped animals. The animals known scientifically as *Felis concolor* and popularly as the panther, the cougar, or the mountain lion has been extinct in Ohio for well over a century.

But that was not all. Ever since the appearances of the mystery cat, the Allisons have been sure that *another* strange creature resides in the nearby woods. "I don't know what it was," Mrs. Allison remarked, "but it was big enough to be a man, a big man. It would stand out in the woods and watch the house. All you could see was a black outline, but it definitely wasn't a bear."

Once, as they entered the driveway, they saw the thing dashing into the woods. Bruce recalled, "It's not like a person running through the woods —you trip over stumps, branches, and rocks. It ran so fast it didn't even look like it touched the ground. During the summer you could go out into the woods and see where it had been lying. Right before it started to get cold, you could see this big spot. One night we heard our tomcat fighting with something and after that we never saw it again, but we can still feel its presence. It's out there!"

The Allisons' married daughter, though she had never actually seen the creature, had heard its growling from time to time. Once, in 1971, however, her husband had been driving to work and was just pulling out of Salem Heights when suddenly something like a "very large man" leaped in front of the car and put its hand up against the vehicle as if to avoid being hit. The car thumped hard against the figure, but when the driver jumped out of the car, there was nothing there—only a big dent in the fender and some black hairs sticking to it.

It should be noted here that for a number of years Ohio has reluctantly hosted sightings of creatures or large "monster men" usually described as somewhat apelike and covered with long black hair.

Since the original UFO incident the Allisons have been plagued with odd poltergeistlike phenomena. In addition, they have had further UFO sightings, though none so dramatic as the first.

We cite the alleged experiences of "Kluski" and the Allisons because between them they cover all the perimeters of the "Goblin Universe" (to borrow Dr. John Napier's delightful phrase)—at least those parts of it which define the territory we shall be exploring in the pages ahead.

That territory, the "outer edge" of our title, stretches along the fringes of reality. It is a place where all manner of bizarre events occur. On the surface these events do not seem to be related at all, which is why legions of dedicated people have separately busied themselves trying to prove the existences of 1.) spaceships from other worlds; 2.) psychic phenomena, poltergeists and apparitions; 3.) flesh-and-blood animals not yet known to science, such as the Bigfoot and the eastern panther. In most cases those people who have specialized in one area are only marginally aware of the work of the other specialists, and virtually all of them would deny vehemently that they are really dealing with one single larger phenomenon, only viewing it from different perspectives.

By now there is a large body of literature on the supposedly separate questions of UFOs, psi and unknown animals. Having read a considerable proportion of this literature—and then having conducted our own personal investigations of the phenomena in question—we have learned to be careful about taking the various "authorities," pronouncements at face value. We have discovered that one proposition is "proven" usually at the expense of another. Examining the Allisons' story, a ufologist would ignore the psi and mystery animal (MA) elements. A Bigfoot researcher, assuming he could bring himself to consider the possibility that hairy critters might exist outside the Pacific Northwest region (a notion most Sasquatch hunters firmly reject), would certainly suppress all references to such inconvenient manifestations as UFOs and poltergeists. And of course a parapsychologist would carefully weed out UFO and MA references.

The major point we shall be trying to make here is that all borderline phenomena are related in some mysterious fashion. In our earlier book, *The Unidentified* (Warner Books, 1975), we argued that UFO reports, fairy tales and religious visions arise from the same source. Whatever that source may be, its signals must be filtered through human consciousness and perception, which shape the manifestations to conform to certain archetypal forms that are both strange and yet oddly familiar to us. Strange because they appear supernatural or extraterrestrial, but familiar because, in a sense, *we have created them.* We have clothed them in the garb of cultural imagination; thus primitive societies which believe nature sprites control the processes of growth and fertility see fairies. People of the late 19th century who awaited the invention of powered flight saw airships with ostensibly human occupants. And our own Space Age culture, filled with visions of interstellar travel and interplanetary visitors, sees flying saucers and little men from other worlds.

That is not to say that these strange phenomena do not exist. These things are not hallucinations, at least as that term is usually understood, nor are all reports of them mere cases of mistaken identity.

In fact, the skeptics' position is demonstrably absurd.

It is not as if, as the present book will show, we are dealing with isolated incidents. Rather we are confronting a vast, and daily growing, tidal wave of reports of peculiar phenomena which threaten to drown us in a sea of madness. Yet most of these reports come not, as various authority figures would have us believe, from liars and lunatics, but from reputable citizens whose testimony on any other matter would not be open to question.

If these supposed incidents occurred only rarely, we would be justified in dismissing them as honest (and occasionally dishonest) mistakes. But as a matter of fact they occur thousands of times a year in all countries and on all levels of society, and almost invariably to persons who never before had any belief in, or even knowledge of, them. Practically every witness whose story comes to public attention (and most witnesses, fearing ridicule, keep their stories to themselves) says something to the effect that "I never would have believed it if it hadn't happened to me."

Not that that helps any, since these things, however they might manifest themselves, are not supposed to exist, and to say that one has seen them —or that one believes that others have seen them— is to identify oneself as ripe for the booby hatch. Yet by now there is such an abundance of reports that, if everyone who says he has seen something out of the ordinary is nuts, we will have to hospitalize a good share of the population.

Ironically, in the end it comes down to a question of "common sense." While these manifestations may seem to defy common sense, the notion that untold numbers of apparently sane, responsible people have reported things that are not real constitutes an even greater affront to common sense. Any serious effort to explain away all these reported manifestations (and very few of the scoffers have any idea of the magnitude of the problem) demands the formulation of a new theory of the human mind, one which holds as a basic tenet that insanity is far more widespread than even the most pessimistic observers of human behavior have ever imagined. It would also have to explain the very selective operation of this insanity, showing us how the individuals in question could give every appearance of sanity before the "sighting," and no further signs of derangement after it. It would also have to demonstrate that any number of people can collectively lose their grip on reality and imagine they were seeing the manifestation *at the same time*. And we would have to know how these hallucinations could leave peculiar tracks all over the landscape, or how animals could sense their presence and flee from them in terror.

On the other hand, acceptance of these stories creates other kinds of problems and some of the questions skeptics have raised are difficult indeed to answer. For example, if these things are real, why is there no conclusive proof of their existence? So far as reports of creatures—our main interest here—are concerned, why, if they are real, are there no bodies, no bones, no live specimens locked securely in zoos and laboratories? Why only certain kinds of physical evidence, invariably of a somewhat ambiguous nature—footprints, strands of hair or fur, possible feces samples, and not others? The "evidence" we have is always just enough to keep us from rejecting the reports as delusions but never enough to prove conclusively that unknown animals exist in our midst.

Elusiveness and ambiguity seem implicit in the manifestations. They refuse to be understood. The more closely we examine them, the more surely they escape our view. Just as soon as we think we have one of them isolated and categorized, it becomes something else, or suddenly shows up in what we presumptuously deem a thoroughly inappropriate context. Take, for instance, this bizarre little episode, cited by David Webb in his *1973— Year of the Humanoids:*

> September 9, Savannah, Georgia: "Ten big, black hairy dogs" emerged from a landed UFO in Laurel Grove Cemetery and ran through the cemetery. The UFO turned out its lights after landing. Several youths made the report.

Confronted with incidents of this type, proponents of the theory of extraterrestrial UFOs (a theory which makes the common mistake of assuming that unexplained phenomena are not continuous with one another but the products of a variety of separate, unrelated forces) invariably speculate that the creatures are "test animals"—an astoundingly anthropomorphic notion if there ever was one.* Actually "black dogs" are nothing new to our terrestrial environment, as students of folklore and demonology will readily attest. Known widely in British and North American tradition, these supernatural beasts are considered demonic creatures and are sometimes called "the hounds of hell." (Conan Doyle got the inspiration for his classic *The Hound of the Baskervilles* from just such legends.) Their appearance is often associated with death. Thus it is fitting that in the present instance the witness observes them in a graveyard. We will have more to say about black dogs in a later chapter.

* John Rimmer remarks, "As ufologists we seem prepared to accept that such matters as UFO propulsion methods, alien physiology, and advanced technologies may be so far advanced beyond anything we are able to comprehend that they will appear to us as 'magic.' Yet, paradoxically, we also seem prepared to assume that the beings behind such marvels are going to behave exactly like us when we meet them face to face." (*Merseyside UFO Bulletin*, December 1970).

To read an account like the one just cited as evidence that black dogs are "UFO occupants" is to miss the point. The overwhelming majority of black dog stories do not involve anything remotely similar to UFOs. But such reports do suggest something about the "reality" UFOs and black dogs—and poltergeists and phantom cats—inhabit.

That reality is the "reality" of dreams, which constantly reshuffle the contents of the unconscious mind and manufacture ever-changing syntheses of those contents, with all manner of seemingly unrelated ideas and images coming together briefly, then splitting apart, then merging again in other, even stranger forms. The motifs of fairylore and UFO phenomenology therefore become so hopelessly entwined that in some cases the investigator cannot tell whether he is dealing with reports of "elves" or of "extraterrestrials." If he decides one way or another, he arbitrarily isolates the event—"freezes" it, in other words, when in fact it is fluid.

Borderland phenomena do not recognize boundaries. If we insist upon containing them, defining their territory, we are only fooling ourselves. We must be prepared to accept the bewildering fact that they can be any number of things at one time: real and unreal, objective and subjective, technological and supernatural. For example, in the following incident, investigated by veteran ufologist Len Stringfield, we confront a creature that is biological in appearance and mechanical in behavior.

The main witness, Mrs. H., who lived in a trailer court in the Covedale area of Western Cincinnati, Ohio, awoke around 2:30 a.m., October 21, 1973, and arose from bed intending to get a drink of water. But an intense light coming through the curtains attracted her attention, and when she opened the curtains she was startled to see a row of six individual lights forming an arc about six feet from her window. The lights were a vivid silvery blue, self-luminous (casting no light on the ground below) and four feet off the ground.

Mrs. H. then saw another bright light, this one farther out in the asphalt parking court beyond her trailer. A car parked a few feet from the trailer obscured the bottom part of the light, but she could see enough of it to observe an "apelike creature" inside. The light seemed to move toward the rear of the parked car and the witness had the impression that the entity was "maybe doing something to the car."

At that point she dashed into her son Carl's bedroom and tried to rouse him. When she returned to the window, as she would later inform Stringfield, "The creature appeared to be farther away from the car, maybe thirty-five feet away," and this time encased in a "shield of light . . . looking like a light in an operating room." The shield was shaped like a bubble umbrella and the light was contained within the shield. It was large enough, Mrs. H. thought, to contain several other creatures of the same size.

The creature, which seemed to be looking toward a warehouse building to the left of the trailer, was gray in color. Its face was "featureless" except for a downward-sloping snout. Its arms were moving up and down slowly and very stiffly. The elbows never bent. The whole effect reminded Mrs. H. of the movements of a robot. Though she could see no machinery inside the glasslike enclosure, she thought the creature might be moving some kind of invisible lever.

Mrs. H. picked up the phone and called the police, who did not seem to take her seriously. While she was talking, a "loud, deep *boom*" sounded and when she and Carl looked again out the window the strange phenomenon was gone. They were not sure if the *boom* and the disappearance of the UFO were connected, since they were not watching when they heard the sound. And by this time the owner of the car in the lot had returned with his girl friend to "jump" the vehicle. They thought it might be possible that the car had made the sound when it started.

Since Stringfield was unable to locate the young couple, we do not know the answer to that particular question. Nonetheless there are other instances in which UFOs have vanished in the wake of just such an "explosion."

Another series of creature reports describe something that seems to have assumed two presumably mutually exclusive identities.

One day in August 1970, three Rantoul, Illinois, youths on an early-morning fishing trip to Kickapoo Creek picked up in their headlights an upright creature as big as a cow. It seemed unbothered by the lights and continued ambling along the edge of the creek.

That same week another person saw it near the Heyworth-Kickapoo Creek area, followed it, and found a string of opened mussel shells and half-eaten minnows.

On the night of August 11, Steve Rich, 18, George Taylor, 17, and Monti Shafer, 20, were hiking through land belonging to Farrell Finger, about two miles northeast of Waynesville and half a mile from Kickapoo Creek. At 9:15 p.m. Rich called the others' attention to the "thing" standing atop a cliff. It was between seven and eight feet tall, slightly hunched over, but not so hunched over as an ape would be. Its arms were proportionately as long as a man's. One of the youths fired an arrow at it, but when they returned to the cliff the next day, they found only the undamaged arrow—no footprints. But they did discover piles of broken shells.

These stories, in common with many others, ask us to believe that a shadowy creature which does not leave prints and which is not affected by human weapons nevertheless eats solid food like a conventional animal. We seem to have here a phenomenon that is at once a ghost and a living creature.

"One measures a circle, beginning anywhere," Charles Fort wrote in a memorable phrase several decades ago. He was writing, as we have been, of a continuous universe in which all things, in varying degrees, are part of something else. One starts measuring, in other words, at an arbitrary point.

We shall start tracing our own circle in the Pacific Northwest.

CHAPTER TWO

The Bigfeet

1.

For some years now the Bigfoot, the legendary hairy giant of California, Oregon, Washington and British Columbia, has captivated the imagination of the world. Its occasional appearances to startled campers, lumberjacks and hunters have inspired numerous books, articles, television shows and movies. Several men, including Peter Byrne of the International Wildlife Conservation Society, have tossed all concerns aside, taken up residence in the wilds, and devoted all their energies to the problem.

And problem it is, and right now that's about *all* it is. For all their efforts, the investigators have produced nothing, such as a body or a live specimen, that would conclusively establish the beast's existence. There are, of course, a great many reports, but the people who make them can offer little in the way of proof beyond their own testimonies.

The other "evidence," what there is of it, is also

open to question. So far it includes footprints, hairs, droppings, odors (which may linger either at the site or on clothing and hair), injuries or fatalities to other animals, several low-quality still photographs, a 16-mm color movie, tape recorded cries, handprints, footprints, hairprints, blood, damaged or disturbed property, food remains, bones, and an alleged —and much disputed—body frozen in ice.

Some of this evidence, especially of the more conclusive variety (the bones and the supposed frozen body), has been allegedly lost or destroyed. Some of it is almost certainly faked. Some of it has proven to be not from any such creature as described. Much of it has not been examined by people qualified to study it.

Even the classic story of Jacko, an apelike creature reportedly captured in British Columbia in 1884, appears to have been a hoax, according to no less an authority than John Green, who first discovered and publicized the original news account from *The Daily British Colonist*. The case for Jacko's existence from the very beginning rested solely on the one newspaper article, and as Green dug for further evidence over the years, he finally discovered the story to have been nothing more than a journalistic fabrication. In any case, as primatologist John Napier had already noted in his *Bigfoot: The Yeti and Sasquatch in Myth and Reality*, "The description [of Jacko] would fit an adult chimpanzee or even a juvenile male or adult female gorilla." Of course, as Napier conceded, "it is difficult to imagine what an African ape was doing swanning about in the middle of British Columbia." Since Green's exposure of the hoax, the answer seems simple enough: The hoaxer patterned his creation after the model of real apes.

Like others, the authors possess a healthy fear of being made to look like fools, so let us state at the outset that we do not categorically reject the possibility that a physical creature prowls the Northwestern backwoods. If that sounds like cowardly bet-hedging—well, that's precisely what it is. But maybe some day somebody will walk out of the forest, Bigfoot in tow, and the issue will be settled once and for all. In fact, we frankly rather hope that will be the case, if only for the sheer joy of watching certain jeering skeptics sitting down before plates heaped high with cooked crow.

Nonetheless, as time has passed we have both struggled to contain a growing suspicion that, in common with a lot of other things, Bigfoot may be something other than what it's cracked up to be, that the case for a flesh-and-blood critter has been made at the expense of certain kinds of "unacceptable" data which have necessarily had to be suppressed.

To start with, for example, there is the frustrating matter of the footprints, about which Napier, by no means unsympathetic to the idea of Bigfoot, has complained, "There seem to be two distinct types of Sasquatch track, and the differences between them appear to go beyond the range of normal variation expected within a single species of mammal. This in itself is bound to make one rather suspicious." Napier concludes that one or both must be fakes.

"What I find a great deal more interesting," Bigfoot hunter Ken Coon writes in a privately distributed paper, "Sasquatch Footprint Variations," "are the *extreme* variations in foot form." Clearly, it would seem, Dr. Napier does not know the full magnitude of the problem.

Coon describes a track found in San Diego County, California, after a physician and his family made several sightings of a hairy apelike creature. "It was fourteen inches long, ten inches across the front of the foot, tapered to a very narrow heel, and had only four toes. It did not appear that a toe had been lost, as the arrangement was such that the foot appeared to be designed for just four toes .... [These] prints were in no way similar to what we expect a Sasquatch track to look like, yet the descriptions of the creatures, except for the size, are very similar to common Sasquatch sightings, the San Diego creatures apparently somewhat shorter in stature."

All primates have five toes. The idea of a four-toed primate is, as Coon notes, ridiculous. Even more ridiculous are the *three*-toed prints left by a Bigfoot in the Antelope Valley of California. Coon says that two fellow Bigfoot hunters to whom he showed these prints were almost frantic in their insistence that they had to be the product of a hoax or a bear. Coon, a skilled investigator and former sheriff's captain, points out in reply:

> 1. I personally interviewed several of the alleged witnesses in the Antelope Valley sightings and heard taped interviews of others. Several of them and one young lady in particular were among the most convincing of any interviews of my experience.
> 2.) The footprints like the one in my possession were found at various times and places in the same areas where the sightings were taking place. I have seen photographs of tracks (series of prints) wherein the creature displayed a stride of 55 to 60 inches and great print depth.
> 3.) The likelihood of their being bear prints is eliminated by the fact that there were very long toes evident, great stride, no evidence of a quadrapedal gait and no claw marks. This is in addition to the size (14 inches), larger than any black bear. I know that bear prints do not always show claw marks and that bears sometimes superimpose one print partially on another, cre-

ating a huge print. But all of the details of the print together eliminate the possibility that an outsized grizzly was walking around Antelope Valley on his hind legs. This, by the way, is desert country.

4.) The tracks *could* have been faked as is always possible unless someone sees them being made as the Sasquatch walks by. But I believe the circumstances surrounding them makes that no more likely than in the case of any other alleged Sasquatch prints found to date.

2.

The problem of Bigfoot's real identity grows even more acute when we consider the testimony of the Northern Athabascan Indians of the Canadian plains and Alaska, who have a longstanding traditional belief in the *Nakani,* also called "Bad Indians," Bushmen, and other names. In the early fall of 1970 Bob Betts and Jim McClarin flew into the remote Athabascan village of Ruby on the Yukon River to investigate the question firsthand.

Betts and McClarin discovered that the people of Ruby were unwilling to talk about the Bushman. But after the two researchers had lived in the village for a number of days, the villagers came to trust them and at last the two began to hear about the hair-covered, manlike being which supposedly still inhabited certain areas along the Yukon River.

The Indians said the Bushman is seen only in the fall of the year, just as the Alaskan night is starting to get truly dark but before the cold winter sets in. Villager Bill Captain took Betts and McClarin to see Paul Peters, an Athabascan who lived ten miles downriver from Ruby and who claimed to have observed a Bushman himself in the fall of 1960 on the north shore of the river near his fish camp.

Peters had been working in front of his cabin, which sat on the north bank of the river about a hundred feet back from the water. He kept his sled dogs chained on the beach near his boat. When they began whining and acting strangely, Peters stopped the work he was doing and looked up to see what was bothering them. About a hundred yards down the shore from where his dogs were tied, he saw something walking along the rocky beach toward the dogs. The "something" looked like a man but was quite tall and covered with black hair. A few seconds after Peters spotted it, the Bushman lumbered off into the dense brush along the river bank. It had appeared to the witness to be about six and a half feet tall and very stocky and muscular.

The Indians along the Yukon say the Bushman is usually nocturnal, although it will make an occasional appearance during daylight hours. Betts and McClarin were told it did not stay in any one place but that it would "travel around." No one could tell them where the Bushman spent the rest of the year, although some villagers suggested that perhaps it migrated south and others thought maybe it hibernated in caves or underground holes. They were convinced, however, that the Bushman lurks around villages and fish camps waiting to steal children. In fact, they often used the threat of the Bushman's presence to keep children from wandering too far away from camp.

The local informants thought that the Bushman came around the villages in the fall because it was then that the Indians hung salmon on the drying racks. They were sure the strange creature ate the fish because sometimes the salmon disappeared from the smokehouses and racks during the night. One man from Kobuk told Betts and McClarin he had spread loose dirt around his smokehouse to see what kind of animal was stealing his salmon and the next morning found large humanlike tracks in the dirt. The tracks were bigger than any he had ever seen before.

The Bushman also had the unsettling habit of throwing sticks or rocks at people who unknowingly entered an area it inhabited. The fear of Bushmen was so great that several villagers had actually abandoned productive fishwheels after having rocks tossed at them from the brush. One such incident supposedly occurred in 1949 to a man named Robert Kennedy, who ran a fish camp 22 miles downriver from Ruby.

Kennedy, who in 1970 was in his sixties, told the two investigators that he had been at the fish camp alone and was sitting quietly on the river bank watching his fishwheel when suddenly a large rock came sailing through the air only a few feet over his head. Startled and scared, Kennedy grabbed his .30-.30 and fired several shots in the direction from which the rock had come. A few moments later another rock was thrown at him from the thick brush. Kennedy unchained several of his big huskies, which dashed up the hill and into the brush. After a brief commotion they returned from the hill, frightened and whining, and resisted their master's efforts to get them to go back up. Convinced that it had been a Bushman in the brush, Kennedy gathered his things together and abandoned his camp the next morning.

While McClarin and Betts were in Ruby, Patty Nollnar arrived from nearby Nulato and, hearing that they were interested in the Bushman, said that he and six other Nulato villagers had encountered such a creature only a few days before while they were spending the night on the bank of the Koyukuk River. The seven Indians, who had been out trapping muskrat about twenty miles up the Koyukuk from its confluence with the Yukon, were lying around their small fire when suddenly a rock was thrown at them from the trees nearby. In response, the men fired their rifles into the trees and brush around the campsite. No more rocks were thrown but the party, certain that a Bushman had been responsible, threw their gear into the boats and left the area.

The local informants also commented frequently on the Bushman's high-pitched whistle. One man, an employee at an area Air Force base who claimed he had heard it as a boy, compared it to the high-pitched whine of a jet engine starting.

So far there is nothing in these reports to upset the conventional wisdom that, if the Bigfoot (or Bushman) exists, it must be some kind of flesh-and-blood animal. That, however, is not the view the Athabascans hold.

They believe that the Bushman cannot be caught or killed, and they told Betts and McClarin that if they did have the misfortune to encounter a Bushman, it would "freeze" them motionless before they could use the movie cameras they carried. It was evident that the Bushman was feared as much as an unknown being with supernatural powers as a physical threat. From childhood the natives are taught by their elders to avoid any meeting with the Bushman; if such a meeting should be unavoidable, one should look down at the ground and pretend not to see it. Above all, the elders impress upon the children that they must respect the Bushman as being more powerful, both naturally and supernaturally, than the Indian. To go out actually in search of one, as Betts and McClarin were doing, was thought not only disrespectful but highly dangerous.

When asked about the origin of the Bushman, many of the informants said they had no idea where it came from and would not discuss the matter further. Others said the Bushmen were once natives like themselves who, during an extended period of starvation a long time ago, had gone into the woods to live a primitive existence like the wild animals. While most of these Indians were said to have died, others had reverted to an animal state, growing hair all over their bodies and becoming larger and stronger. They had lost their ability to make weapons, clothing, or fire and could no longer communicate in the language they once knew.

We don't think we need take seriously the myth of the creature's origin, since it is clearly an attempt to account for an otherwise inexplicable presence. Still, it is interesting to note that the Athabascans see the Bushmen as related to man and both inferior and superior to him: inferior in the sense that the Bushmen have reverted to an animal state, superior in the sense that they have achieved supernatural powers. This theme of the peculiar union of opposites runs through much of the monster lore we shall be examining.

But how seriously are we to take the Athabascan notion that the Bushman/Bigfoot is somehow paranormal? Betts and McClarin tended to interpret that part of the story as a folklore embellishment growing out of the Indians' fear of a real, if elusive, creature. Maybe—but then maybe not, for other Bigfoot witnesses have maintained that there is something decidedly "unnatural" about the creature.

3.

For example, we have the story, printed in the July 16, 1918, *Seattle Times,* of "mountain devils" which attacked a miner's cabin at Mt. St. Lawrence near Kelso, Washington. Supposedly these hairy creatures, which stood seven to eight feet tall, could make themselves invisible. Unfortunately that is all we know about this alleged episode.

We know far more about the experiences of one Fred Beck, participant in an incident which has become a classic of Bigfoot lore. Or at least an *edited* version of that incident has become well known. The familiar version has been carefully bowdlerized by later writers who have cited it as further evidence that an unknown flesh-and-blood hominoid exists in the wilderness of the Pacific Northwest. Beck's version, on the other hand, suggests something rather different. The following is based upon Beck's own account as detailed in as obscure, out-of-print booklet, *I Fought the Apeman of Mt. St. Helens,* which Beck and his son R. A. Beck published privately in 1967.

One night early in this century two young brothers working in a logging camp near Kelso, Washington, heard a rustling sound outside their tent. Peering anxiously outside, they were terrified to see a huge, hairy, upright figure watching them. Finally the creature lumbered back into the woods.

The Beck brothers, who had never heard of the Bigfoot, then known only to the Indians, were perplexed by the whole episode. Finally, one of them convinced himself the thing had been a bear. But Fred, the other brother, was not so sure. He had seen many bears in his time and he did not think this was one of them. Later on, in July 1924 to be precise, Fred Beck's suspicion that he had seen something far out of the ordinary would receive spectacular confirmation.

For six years prior to that date Beck and his partner had been prospecting for gold in the Mt. St. Helens and Lewis River area in southwestern Washington. In the beginning, before they built a cabin, they lived in a tent below a small mountain called

Pumy Butte. Nearby a creek flowed, and along it there was a moist sand bar about an acre in size where the prospectors would go to wash their dishes and get drinking water.

Early one morning one of them came running to the camp and urged his fellows to follow him back to the creek, where he showed them two huge, somewhat humanlike tracks sunk four inches deep in the center of the sand bar. There were no other tracks anywhere nearby. Either whatever made them had a 160-foot stride, the men reasoned, or "something dropped from the sky and went back up."

As time passed, the miners came upon other, similar tracks which they could not identify. The largest of them was nineteen inches long.

After they had built their cabin, Beck and the four other miners working their gold claim, the Vander White, would hear a strange "thudding, hollow thumping noise" in broad daylight. They could not find the cause, though they suspected one of their number might be playing tricks on them. That proved not to be the case, since even when the group were gathered together the sound continued all around them. They thought it sounded as if "there's a hollow drum in the earth somewhere and something is hitting it."

Those were not to be the last strange sounds they would hear, either. Early in July 1924, a shrill whistling, apparently emanating from atop a ridge, pierced the evening quiet. An answering whistle came from another ridge. These sounds, along with a booming "thumping" as if something were pounding its chest, continued every evening for a week.

By now thoroughly unnerved, the men had taken to carrying their rifles with them when they went to the spring about a hundred yards from the cabin.

Beck and a man identified as "Hank" were drawing water from the spring when suddenly Hank yelled and raised his gun. Beck looked up and saw, on the other side of a little canyon, a seven-foot apelike creature standing next to a pine tree. The creature, a hundred yards away from the two men, dodged behind the tree. When it poked its head around the tree, Hank fired three quick shots, spraying bark but apparently not hitting the creature, which disappeared from sight for a short while. It reappeared 200 yards down the canyon and this time Beck got off three shots before it was gone.

Hurriedly, Beck and Hank returned to the cabin and conferred with the other two men there (the third was elsewhere at the time). They agreed to abandon the cabin—but not until daybreak. It would be too risky, they felt, to try to make it to the car in the darkness. The four got their belongings together in preparation for the move, then settled down for a good night's sleep which, as it turned out, they did not get.

At midnight they awakened suddenly to a tremendous thud against the cabin wall. Some of the chinking which had been knocked loose from between the logs fell on Hank, who was pinned underneath it. Beck had to help him free himself. Then, as they heard what sounded like many feet tramping and running outside, they grabbed their guns, prepared for the worst. Hank peered through the open space left by the dislodged chinking (the cabin had no windows) and spotted three "apes" together. From the sound of things, there were many more.

The creatures proceeded to pelt the cabin with rocks. Though terribly frightened (the other two miners were huddling in the corner in a state of shock), Beck said they should fire on the creatures only if they physically attacked the cabin. This would show that the miners were only defending themselves.

But within a very short time the "apes" *were* attacking the cabin. Some of them jumped on the roof, evidently in an effort to batter it down. In response, Beck and Hank fired through the roof. They were also forced to brace the door with a long pole taken from the bunk bed, since the creatures were furiously attempting to smash it open. Beck and Hank riddled the door with bullets.

The attacks continued all night, punctuated occasionally by short quiet interludes. At one point a creature reached through the chinking space and grabbed an ax by the handle. Beck lunged forward, snatched the blade part and turned the ax upright so that the "ape" couldn't get it out. As he was doing so, a bullet from Hank's rifle narrowly missed his hand. The creature withdrew its arm and retreated.

Finally, just before daybreak, the attack ended. The embattled miners waited for daylight, then cautiously stepped outside, guns in hand. A few minutes later Beck spotted one of the creatures about eighty yards away, standing near the edge of the canyon. Taking careful aim, he shot three times and watched as it toppled over the cliff and fell down into the gorge 400 feet below.

As quickly as they could get out of there, the miners departed, heading for Spirit Lake, Washington, and leaving $200 in supplies and equipment behind. They never returned to claim it.

At Spirit Lake Hank told a forest ranger about the experience. After the group had come home to Kelso, the story leaked to the newspapers and caused a sensation. Reporters found giant tracks at the scene, but no other traces of the creatures the men believed they had shot at. The canyon where the episode allegedly occurred became known as "Ape Canyon" and still bears that name over fifty years later.

In his booklet Beck reveals that all his life, from his early childhood on, he had numerous psychic experiences, many of them involving supernatural "people." He says that they found the mine they were working in 1924 through guidance from two "spiritual beings," one a buckskin-clad Indian, the other a woman after whom they would name their mine (Vander White).

Of the "apemen," Beck writes, "they are not entirely of this world. . . . I was, for one, always conscious that we were dealing with supernatural beings and I know the other members of the party felt the same." Beck believes the creatures now known as Sasquatch or Bigfoot come from "another dimension" and are a link between human and animal consciousness. They are composed of a substance that ranges between the physical and the psychical, sometimes one more than the other, depending upon the degree of "materialization." Because of their peculiar nature none will ever be captured, nor will bodies ever be found.

Preposterous? The fantasies of an old man? Perhaps.

But we must note here that no one except those resolutely determined to reject *all* Bigfoot reports has ever questioned Beck's testimony about the Ape Canyon shoot-out. If we accept that much, then we cannot honestly reject the unpalatable portions, however much we might like to do so. And if we accept the reality of the isolated set of footprints, for instance, then we are forced to consider seriously Beck's contention that the Bigfeet "are not entirely of this world." Either this, or we must reject the Ape Canyon story entirely.

4.

It is not our intention to deal at great length with the Bigfoot question, which has been adequately documented elsewhere. Our purpose is simply to point out certain paranormal elements in several of the reports and to suggest the possibility that the Bigfoot may not be significantly different from the "manimals" which are being sighted in increasing numbers throughout the rest of the country.

The considerable majority of Bigfoot encounters, in common with their eastern counterparts, are of very short duration, involving no more than a few seconds to a few minutes. Most are isolated events, free of obviously paranormal content, and it is not hard to understand why the stimulus for the reports has usually been assumed to be something purely physical. Most Fortean phenomena, however, also appear to occur in isolation and that is why, as we observed in the last chapter, UFOs, MAs and psi have seemed to be separate concerns. Our interest in this book is in that significant minority of incidents that tie the various classes of phenomena together and suggest that they are continuous with one another.

In that regard, let us consider four relatively recent Bigfoot cases.

Vader, Washington, winter 1970-71 and spring 1971: On December 4, 1970, Mrs. Wallace Bowers heard her children calling for her to come outside. Upon doing so, she discovered mysterious footprints in the inch-deep snow covering her farm yard. "The footprints were *very* large, measuring sixteen inches, and five to seven inches wide," she told an investigator. "The night before, it had snowed, freezing hard afterwards. In comparison of weight, my husband's pickup truck never even went through the snow and ice upon his leaving for work; he leaves around 5:30 a.m., as he is a logger. The morning we discovered the giant tracks, or footprints, alongside his truck in the drive, the prints were like black on white, as whatever made them was so heavy it took the frozen snow with each step, *plus* leaving one and a half-inch impressions in the frozen gravel beneath."

Mrs. Bowers recalled that the family dog had acted oddly the night before, as if sensing the presence of an intruder. Vader is in the middle of Bigfoot country and the tracks in the snow resembled those attributed to the creature.

At 7:15 a.m. three days later, on the seventh, the Bowers children again called their mother, this time to the window, where they were watching a "bright star" which was moving across the sky. The object flew closer to the witnesses and for ten minutes they were able to view it carefully.

Its center appeared to be a dome around which a larger circle seemed to be revolving. It was deep orange in the center, with the light diffusing toward the outer edge, but with a definite bright rim.

Mrs. Bowers said it seemed tipped sideways slightly, rather like an airplane banking, and then it hovered briefly over the nearby Bonneville power lines. After it left the power lines, it changed from orange to a bright, clear light, and at one time seemed to make one last sweep closer, again turning orange. The children thought they saw a "gray shape" drop away from the UFO just before it vanished in the distance.

During the sighting Mrs. Bowers switched on the intercom in the house, only to hear a peculiar "sharp" sound. "And the funny thing is," she said, "we tried to use the intercom the night before and got that same sharp sound."

But that was not to be all. Later in the week (the UFO sighting occurred on a Monday), Mrs. Bowers was putting a log in the living room fireplace when she saw the curtains moving in the boys' bedroom, which was visible from where she stood.

"All the children were in the living room with me," she said. "All I could think of was getting them safely out of there. So I loaded them into the car and we left, but I definitely saw a shape in the bedroom as we drove away." They returned only after Mr. Bowers had come home from work.

"I feel sure that was probably a prowler," Mrs. Bowers said. "We've had trouble in our neighborhood and I don't think it's related to the others. But the footprints and the saucer—I don't know..."

Nonetheless, the "prowler" was a strange one: He took nothing. He rummaged through the bedrooms but afterward the Bowerses could find nothing gone. While it is of course impossible to prove anything, we cannot help thinking of the mysterious "gray shape" the children thought they saw, and then of the long tradition of bedroom apparitions. Very shortly we will encounter another case of "prowlers" who took nothing.

Subsequently, according to Mrs. Bowers, "We had several months of strange noises in the night, something very heavy thudding across the yard, but we never saw anything. Our house is so well insulated it is hard for us to even hear a car come into our drive. So it was really strange to be awakened by this thudding jar going across our yard. Every night, it was around the same time. It would wake us up between 2:00 and 3:00 a.m."

Balls Ferry, California, late January 1972: Four teenage boys on their way to Battle Creek to fish on a dark, rainy night saw a brilliant glowing object swoop over their car. Later, as they parked at the

Battle Creek Bridge, they heard a noise, then a scream in the bush.

"We heard a blood-curdling scream," John Yeries, 16, recalled. "I threw the light over in the brush and there was this weird thing."

The beast was about seven feet tall, dark brown or green, had a large teardrop-shaped ear, and was hunched over. It appeared to have lumps all over its body, "like pouches in a flight suit." It turned and ran. So did the witnesses.

"I was wondering what it was," Darrell Rich, 16, said, "and at the same time I was turning to get out of there." James Yeries and Robbie Cross were already hightailing it back to the car. But when they got there, they were horrified to discover that it wouldn't start.* They had to push it before it would.

As they sped away, they all had the feeling they were being watched and followed. Soon thereafter, Darrell saw what looked like "firecrackers" going off on the pavement, only without the accompanying sound. John saw them out the rear-view mirror but soon their collective attention was captured by fiery

* Another creature-related car stoppage supposedly occurred in October 1960 in the Monongahela National Forest near Marlinton, West Virginia. While driving along a road behind a group of friends in a bus, W. C. "Doc" Priestley reportedly encountered an eight-foot hairy apelike "monster with long hair standing straight up." Just moments before he saw the thing, his car engine suddenly had ceased working. "I don't know how long I sat there," Priestley said, "until the boys missed me and backed up the bus to where I was. It seemed the monster was very much afraid of the bus and dropped his hair and to my surprise, as soon as he did this, my car started to run again. I didn't tell the boys what I had seen. The thing took off when the bus started."

Priestley and the bus resumed their journey. Soon, however, the car began to sputter again. "I could see the sparks flying from under the hood of my car as if it had a very bad short. And sure enough, there beside the road stood the monster again. The points were completely burned out of my car." The bus backed up again and the creature fled into the forest.

Priestley's was only one of a number of creature sightings made in West Virginia that year.

objects, blue and white, orange and red, seen moving erratically in the open fields on either side of the road. At one point two of the "glowing balls" came together in the sky while another time one shot straight up and disappeared. One of the glowing objects, weirdly enough, took on the appearance of a human figure beside the road. Strangely and suddenly, at the intersection of Deschutes and Dersch roads, the lights disappeared.

Racing back home, they told Darrell Rich's father, Dean Rich, of the incidents. The elder Rich, though somewhat skeptical, returned with the boys to the Battle Creek Bridge area and walked out into a nearby walnut orchard. All of a sudden they heard an odd "commotion" in the darkness in front of them. As Rich would later describe it, "It sounded like a real deep growl. It was a real weird type of sensation. It was something I've never experienced before." The boys abruptly fled and the father quickly followed suit.

The growling, a long, nerve-wrenching *eeeeaaaaaghhhrrr,* continued as Rich ran backwards to his car. Once there, he and the boys held a brief conference and concluded that the "thing" was warning them to depart from its territory. If it was trying to scare them, Rich said, "it succeeded."

The party went to the Anderson, California, police, who returned to the area but found nothing. However, the lawmen said they doubted the story was a hoax. One officer remarked, "They seemed completely sincere. There was no hint of the funnies or something else. They were really scared."

Summing up the group's feelings, Darrell Rich speculated, "I wonder if we saw something we shouldn't have."

King County, Washington, June 9, 1974: A man named Tony McClennan was driving through the evening darkness when suddenly he slowed to avoid hitting what he thought might be an injured dog. Then the "dog" stood up and McClennan gaped in astonishment at a hairy apelike beast with long, swinging arms and *glowing,* not reflecting, red eyes. It was about eight feet high.

When the police investigated, they came upon a freshly-made path something had made through the thick brush. Strands of dark hair four inches long were found on nearby branches.

Washington State, fall 1975: On October 1 three youths out hunting near Rimrock Lake heard noises in the woods around them. Feeling they were being followed, they began hiking back to camp, which they reached around 9:00 p.m. They built a fire and were sitting in front of it when they heard still more noises. One of the group, Earl Thomas, 18, beamed his flashlight across a small pond nearby and spotted a pair of greenish-yellow eyes staring back at him. Thomas and Tom Gerstmar, 17, returned to camp to talk the matter over.

Finally, all three carefully walked the short distance to the edge of the pond and shone the light again. This time they saw what the eyes were a part of: an eight- or nine-foot hairy creature with humanlike features. The thing shied away from the light. Evidently, despite its size, it was a creature of retiring disposition. This, however, was not enough to keep the badly frightened young men from firing upon it seven times with their rifles. Immediately afterwards they fled back to camp and grabbed their provisions. As they were doing so, the Bigfoot commenced to scream, which only added to their sense of panic. Gerstmar nearly wrecked his jeep in his haste to get away.

When they got to Trout Lodge, they called the Yakima County Sheriff's office. Later Deputy Larry

Gamache interviewed the three youths and their testimony convinced him they had definitely "seen something."

But for Earl Thomas, that was not the end of the episode. Dick Grover, who interviewed all the witnesses and kept in touch with them for a time after their original experience, reports these bizarre developments:

"A two-tone green, four-wheel-drive Bronco with Oregon license plates had for two weeks followed the Thomases to town. The car has been seen driving by their house three to four times a day. The car had also been driven into their driveway. The driver was never seen leaving his car. [He] was described as a middle-aged man in his 50s or 60s, medium build, gray hair, crew cut. He keeps his car clean and appears to be very interested in the Thomases. This investigator had the opportunity to be shown the vehicle and driver when he was interviewing Earl Thomas.

"Earl Thomas also stated that threats have been made on his life. These threats were made via phone on two different occasions. On one occasion the caller, male, told [him], 'Don't step out your door. We'll blow your head off.' "

It is possible that a wealthy lunatic with a great deal of time on his hands decided to frighten Thomas for some reason, but that seems improbable in view of the fact that the harassment continued for several months after Grover made his report. Readers with a background in ufology will recognize this activity as strongly reminiscent of behavior associated with the fabled "men in black" (MIB), who reportedly have threatened some individuals who have had UFO sightings. Curiously, even the observation that the stranger "keeps his car clean" has precedents in MIB reports, for witnesses sometimes remark on the "clean" or "new" appearance of the vehicles these figures are said to drive.

More particularly it reminds the authors of another story we have heard. In November 1974, while Jerome Clark was on a field trip across midwestern America doing research on various Fortean phenomena, he talked at length with a bright, levelheaded man who had conducted an in-depth investigation of reports of an apelike creature in the Sioux City, Iowa, area. The investigator confided to Clark —and his testimony was confirmed by a friend— that in the course of his work he discovered that two very strange men in a red compact car seemed to be keeping him and his apartment under surveillance. On one occasion he discovered that his apartment had been expertly broken into—he could find no evidence of how it could have been done—but nothing had been taken. *The intruders, however, had rifled through his files on the local creature sightings.*

The motif of "burglars" who take nothing takes us back, of course, to the Bowerses' mysterious intruder.

5.

So where does all of this lead us?

Perhaps we can sum it up thus:

1.) There are paranormal overtones to at least some Bigfoot encounters. UFO and psi phenomena figure prominently in certain of the cases.

2.) The best "physical evidence"—the alleged footprints—is ambiguous, inconclusive, and sometimes contradictory. The only unambiguous, conclusive, and noncontradictory physical evidence—bodies or bones—is notoriously nonexistent.

3.) The Bigfoot is more elusive than we could realistically expect a purely flesh-and-blood beast to be. After all, as Napier observes in his excellent book, "Is it really possible that a population of up to 1000 Bigfoot could exist in remote, but by no means untraveled, regions without being formally recognized by zoology? The American puma or mountain lion is widespread from British Columbia to Patagonia in quite large numbers. Yet it is so elusive that few people have seen it in the wild, and fewer still have been able to photograph it. Nevertheless, in spite of its retiring habits, the mountain lion is well known to science."

None of this constitutes conclusive proof that *all* Bigfeet are paraphysical in nature, but it is at least enough to raise some doubts about the popular notion of an unknown hominoid roaming the forests of the Northwest—especially when we discover that seemingly identical creatures are popping up all over the North American landscape in places where their presence is manifestly impossible.

CHAPTER THREE

The Manimals

1.

Our first account is not North American in origin, but it is the earliest one we have. We present it here because of its extraordinary interest.

The story is that one stormy day in the year 1161 English fishermen off the coast of Orford, Suffolk, caught a "wild man" in their nets. As Ralph of Coggeshall, a clerical historian of the early 13th century, has it, "All the parts of his Body resembled those of a Man; he had Hair on his Head, a long peaked Beard, and about ye Brest was exceeding hairy and rough."

The fisherman took the creature to the governor of Orford Castle, one Glanvill, who kept him for some time and allowed his soldiers to torture him in an effort "to make him speak." The wild man was fed on raw meat and fish, which he "pressed with his hands" before eating. Finally, one day he was taken out to the sea "to disport himself therein."

But he broke through a triple barrier of nets and escaped.

Yet not long afterwards he returned to the castle and voluntarily reentered captivity. But at last, "being wearied of living alone," he went back to the sea and was heard of no more.

While—as we shall see presently—our manimals have certain aquatic habits, there is no precise modern parallel to this fascinating old folk tale. The nearest thing we have to it is an August 21, 1955, incident from near Dogtown, Indiana.

Late on the afternoon of the day in question, Mrs. Darwin Johnson and Mrs. Chris Lamble, both of Evansville, were swimming in the Ohio River, about fifteen feet from shore. Suddenly something came up behind Mrs. Johnson and grabbed her left leg. She could see nothing—the attacker was under water—but she could feel large claws and a furry palm gripping her knee. The thing, whatever it was, yanked her under. She kicked and fought and managed to come up once more. Again she went under.

Though she wasn't being attacked, Mrs. Lamble, who was safely in an innertube four feet away, proceeded to kick and scream on the theory that this might scare "it" away. In the meantime, Mrs. Johnson lunged for the innertube and hit it with "a loud, hollow thump." It was then, she said, that "whatever was around my legs loosened its grip."

The two women quickly headed for shore, where they treated Mrs. Johnson's leg, which had begun to sting, with alcohol. But for several days afterwards a green stain with the outline of a palm remained just below the knee. The woman became hysterical from the experience and her husband, who was called from work, had to summon a doctor to give her sedatives.

No one ever saw the creature, but Mrs. Johnson said, "Whatever this thing was, it had a strong grip and it was very furry . . . All I know is that I will never go swimming in the river again."

After the story was published in the *Evansville Press* the next day, several persons came forward to say they had observed a "shiny oval" a few hundred feet above the river at about the time the alleged incident had taken place.

A short time later an Air Force colonel is supposed to have called upon the Johnsons and interviewed them at some length. He urged them not to discuss the matter publicly any further.

Perhaps Mrs. Johnson had encountered the same critter a Saginaw, Michigan, man is reputed to have sighted one day in 1937. He was fishing on the banks of the Saginaw River when a manlike "monster" climbed up the bank, leaned upon a tree, and then returned to the water. The witness allegedly suffered a nervous breakdown from the experience.

Charles Buchanan may not have had a nervous breakdown, but his own experience shook him considerably. On November 7, 1969, Buchanan, camped out on the shore of Lake Worth, Texas, awoke about 2:00 a.m. to find a hairy creature that looked "like a cross between a human being and a gorilla" towering above him. Buchanan had been sleeping in the bed of his pickup truck when the thing suddenly jerked him to the ground, sleeping bag and all. Gagging from the stench of the beast, the camper did the only thing he could think of: He grabbed a bag of leftover chicken and shoved it into the long-armed creature's face. It took the sack in its mouth, made some guttural sounds, then loped off through the trees, splashed in the water, and proceeded to swim with powerful strokes toward Greer Island.

Another creature from the black lagoon—or from

some place—first appeared shortly after midnight on June 25, 1973, and was seen by Randy Needham and Judy Johnson, who were parked on a boat ramp to the Big Muddy River near Murphysboro, a town in southwestern Illinois. The couple, who had been startled by a cry "about three times as loud as a bobcat, only deeper," emanating from the nearby woods, looked up to see a huge biped lumbering toward them, still shrieking but now in altering tones. It was not a human sound.

Randy and Judy agreed the thing was about seven feet tall, white, its short body hair matted with river mud. They were not interested in examining it at close range, and by the time it had got within twenty feet of them, they were roaring away from the scene, bound for the Murphysboro police station.

Officers Meryl Lindsey and Jimmie Nash checked the area and found "impressions in the mud approximately ten to twelve inches long and approximately three inches wide," according to the report they filed later. To Jerome Clark, Needham later described the impressions as "something like a man with a shoe on would make—only the thing wasn't wearing shoes." He suggested that toe prints may not have registered in the mud.

At 2:00 a.m. Nash, Lindsey, Needham and Deputy Sheriff Bob Scott returned to the scene. This time they discovered fresh tracks, similar in general appearance to those they had seen an hour earlier, but deeper and smaller. The police report noted an especially strange detail: "The prints in the mud were very irratic [sic] in that no two were the same distance apart and some were five to six feet apart. Also prints were found very close together."

Officer Lindsey left to get a camera to take pictures of the prints, and while he was gone the other three followed the tracks. While they were bending over to examine some of them, there came "the most incredible shriek I've ever heard," Nash recalled. Apparently the creature was hidden in the trees less than a hundred yards away. The trio didn't stick around to find out. They beat a hasty retreat to the squad car. In the hours that followed, the officers scoured the area in pursuit of an elusive splashing sound but found nothing.

When daylight came, things got quieter, but with darkness the creature returned.

The first to see it this time was four-year-old Christian Baril, who told his parents he had seen "a big white ghost in the yard." They didn't believe him, of course, but ten minutes later, when Randy Creath and Cheryl Ray saw something very much like that in a neighboring yard, parents and police reconsidered the youngster's words.

About 10:30 p.m. Randy and Cheryl were sitting on the back porch of the Ray home when they heard something moving in the trees just beyond the lawn. They saw the creature standing in an opening in the trees, quietly watching them through glowing pink eyes. Cheryl insisted, in an interview with Jerome Clark, that the eyes were glowing, not reflecting, since there was no nearby light source that could have caused the effect.

The creature was either the same one the other young couple had seen the night before or one similar to it. It was white and dirty, weighed close to 350 pounds and stood seven feet tall. It had a large round head. Cheryl thought its arms might be "ape-length," although she wasn't certain because it was standing in waist-high grass.

Randy went down to get a closer look while Cheryl went inside to turn on the yard light. The light did not reveal much more of the creature than they had already seen.

Finally the thing ambled off through the trees,

making considerable noise. Later, investigators found a trail of crushed weeds and broken brush, as well as imprints in the ground too vague and imperfect to be cast in plaster.

Cheryl's mother, Mrs. Harry Ray, called the police. While waiting for them to arrive, they suddenly began to smell a "real strong odor, like a sewer," Cheryl said, but it lasted only a short time.

Soon Officers Nash and Ronald Manwaring pulled up in their car. What happened then is recounted in their report given to Loren Coleman:

> Officers inspected the area where the creature was seen and found weeds broken down and somewhat [sic] of a path where something had walked through. Jerry Nellis was notified to bring his dog to the area to see if the dog would track the creature. Upon arrival of Nellis and dog [a German shepherd trained to attack, search buildings, and track] the dog was led to the area where the creature was last seen. The dog began tracking down the hill where the creature was reported to have gone.
>
> As the dog started down the hill, it kept stopping and sniffing at a slime substance on the weeds; the slime appeared periodically as the dog tracked the creature. Nellis put some of the slime between his fingers [and] rubbed it and it left a black coloring on his fingers. Each time the dog found amounts of it, the dog would hesitate.
>
> The creature was tracked down the hill to a pond, around the pond to a wooded area south of the pond where the dog attempted to pull Nellis down a steep embankment. The area where the dog tracked the creature to was too thick and bushy to walk through, so the dog was pulled off the trail and returned to the car. Officers then searched the area with flashlights.
>
> Officer Nash, Nellis and the dog then pro-

ceeded to the area directly south of where the dog was pulled off the tracks. The area was at the end of the first road to the west past Westwood Hills turnoff. The area is approximately one-half mile south of the area of the pond behind 37 Westwood Lane.

Nellis and the dog again began to search the area to see if the dog could again pick up the scent. Nellis and the dog approached the abandoned barn and Nellis called to Officer Nash to come to the area as the dog would not enter the barn. Nellis pushed the dog inside and the dog immediately ran out. Nash and Nellis searched the barn and found nothing inside. Nellis stated that the dog was trained to search buildings and had never backed down from anything. Nellis could find no explanation as to why the dog became scared and would not go inside the barn. Officers continued to search the area and were unable to locate the creature.

The Murphysboro creature was reported twice more in 1973. During an evening July 4th celebration in a city park near the river, carnival workers said they had seen it watching the Shetland ponies. And on July 7th Mrs. Nedra Green heard a shrill piercing scream from near the shed on her isolated farm. She did not go out to investigate.

The creature supposedly made brief return appearances in July 1974 and July 1975.

So what was it? The authorities frankly admit they have no idea.

"A lot of things in life are unexplained," Police Chief Toby Berger concluded, "and this is another one. We don't know what the creature is. But we do believe what these people saw was real. . . . These are good, honest people. They are seeing something. And who would walk through sewage tanks for a joke?"

2.

Those creatures we shall call "manimals"—the hairy things of varying sizes reported outside the Northwestern Bigfoot/Sasquatch territory—have a long history in this country, if we are to lend some credence to a body of remarkably consistent folklore.

The Indian tribes of what one day would be the eastern states spoke frequently of cannibalistic giants which, except for their reputed taste for human flesh (our modern manimals are actually quite timid, for the most part), sound like the things we are coming to know so well.

Some examples:

The Micmac, a tribe located in New Brunswick and Nova Scotia, refer in their traditional lore to the *Gugwes,* who, Elsie Clews Parsons wrote in a 1925 *Journal of American Folklore,* "have big hands and faces hairy like bears. If one saw a man coming he would lie down and beat his chest, producing a sound like a partridge." The gray partridge of southeastern Canada makes a one-tone whistle; such a whistle is cited among other tribes as the creatures' characteristic cry. The Micmac have three other names for the beasts: *Kookwes, Chenoo* and *Djenu.*

The Penobscot Indians of Maine know of *Kiwakwe,* another cannibalistic giant, which is similar to the Huron and Wyandot *Strendu.* "Half a tree tall" and larger than men, they are covered with flinty scales, which ties them to the Stone Giants of upper New York, about which Hartley B. Alexander writes:

> The Iroquoian Stone Giants, as well as their congeners among the Algonquians (e.g. the *Chenoo* of the Abnaki and Micmac), belong to a widespread group of mythic beings of which the Eskimo Tornit are examples. They are . . .

huge in stature, unacquainted with the bow, and employing stones for weapons. In awesome combats they fight one another, uprooting the tallest trees for weapons and rending the earth in fury ... Commonly they are depicted as cannibals...

The Algonquians call these ogres the *Windigo* (or *Witiko, Wendigo, Wittiko,* and other variants) —creatures known widely in the folklore of eastern and central Canada. "The *witiko* wore no clothes," the Rev. Joseph E. Guinard noted in an article in *Primitive Man.* "Summer and winter he went naked and never suffered cold. His skin was black like that of a negro. He used to rub himself, like the animals, against fir, spruce, and other resinous trees. When he was thus covered with gum or resin, he would go and roll in the sand, so that one would have thought that, after many operations of this kind, he was made of stone."

Among the Passamaquoddy, Cooper wrote in 1933, ". . . a similar habit is ascribed to the . . . *Chenoo* who used to rub themselves all over with fir balsam and then roll themselves on the ground so that everything adhered to the body. This habit is highly suggestive of the Iroquoian Stone Coats, the blood-thirsty cannibal giants, who used to cover their bodies carefully with pitch and then roll and wallow in sand and down sand banks."

Windigos have a frightful, menacing mouth with no lips. Often a sinister hissing is made by them, or a noise described as strident, very reverberating, and drawn out is accompanied by fearful howls. The *Windigo,* a huge individual who goes naked in the woods and eats people, probably is the same creature the Grand Lake Victoria Band of Quebec call the *Misabe,* a long-haired giant.

Among the Ojibwa of northern Minnesota, there were, according to Sister Bernard Coleman, "the

Memegwicio, or men of the wilderness. Some called them a 'kind of monkey' . . . about the size of children of 11 or 12 years of age . . . faces covered with hair." To the Tingami Ojibwa the *Memegwesi* are "a species of creature which lives in high remote ledges," Frank G. Speck recorded in 1915. "They are small and have hair growing all over their bodies. The Indians think they are like monkeys judging from the specimens of the latter they have seen in picture books." The Cree of the James Bay area viewed the *Memegwicio* as diminutive human beings covered with hair and having a very flat nose.

By the 19th century, when white people began to settle the central regions of the continent, the stories got more specific but, interestingly enough, rather less credible.

In 1834 we come upon vague references to hairy "wild men" reportedly seen in St. Francis, Poinsett and Green Counties in Arkansas. Twenty-two years later one such creature supposedly roamed the Arkansas-Louisiana border near Fouke, Arkansas, home of the now well-known "Fouke Monster" which inspired the popular movie *Legend of Boggy Creek.* Tracked by a search party, the "wild man" was finally cornered, but escaped by throwing one of the posse off his horse, severely mangling him in the process, hopping on the animal himself, and galloping off into the sunset. Well . . .

Slightly more believable are the stories of the Giant of the Mountains, allegedly observed "many times in the remote mountains of Saline County during the years after the Civil War," according to Otto Ernest Rayburn's *Ozark Country.* The being in question was a naked white man with long, thick hair, who seemed to reside along the Saline River. Finally, the story goes, he was captured, but escaped not long after, never to be seen again, though local people did find some "enormous tracks."

Assuming these tales to have any factual foundation at all, we still have no business jumping to conclusions, since it is distinctly possible that these were in fact wild *men,* not manimals. After all, the frontier did attract some awfully strange types, some of them individuals of a reclusive nature who may have gone more native than the actual natives (the Indians) themselves. Certainly the curious insistence that the Saline County giant was a "white man," when that sort of identification of a true manimal would be meaningless, suggests this might well be the case.

Further evidence for this possibility comes from another Arkansas "wild man" story. During the fall and winter of 1875, a number of Pulaski County residents asserted, no doubt to the considerable amusement of their contemporaries, that they had seen someone covered with long, bushy, black hair who looked like a "half-wild animal." In early December of that year, he was captured and taken to Little Rock, where an *Arkansas Gazette* reporter, who saw him in the county jail, described him as "the wildest, greasiest, ugliest-looking, half-clad specimen of humanity it was ever our lot to behold." When interviewed—this "wild man" was capable of speech—he proved to be an apparently mentally-deficient railroad worker who four years earlier had wandered into Arkansas from St. Louis.

We are more impressed with the 1869 reports along the Osage River of Missouri and Kansas, where in the latter state's Crawford County residents claimed to have seen a "wild man" or "gorilla." The creature had a stooping gait, very long arms and immense hands. Then, as is often the case in our time as well, local opinion held that the thing was a gorilla or large orangutan which had escaped from a menagerie.

Our favorite story, though, comes by way of our friend and fellow Fortean Brad Steiger, who, in

Mysteries of Time and Space, recounts an 1888 episode which a correspondent claims to have discovered in his grandfather's journal. The grandfather supposedly had accompanied an Indian friend to a cave in the "Big Woods Country" of Tennessee where a "Crazy Bear"—a hairy, apelike creature—was being fed regularly on raw meat. The Indian explained that this was only one of a number of similar beasts which had been left by "skymen," who would land from time to time in "moons." The "skymen," who were basically human in appearance, wearing short hair and shining uniforms, would always wave in friendly fashion to the presumably amazed onlookers. The Indians believed the Crazy Bears had been sent to bring them "powerful medicine."

Readers who wish to accuse us of being unduly skeptical are free to do so, but somehow this story has always struck us as being a little too good to be true. That, of course, is purely a subjective impression on our part. But recently, when we read the following in Slate and Berry's *Bigfoot,* we could not help thinking of the Crazy Bears and their powerful medicine:

> My folks used to tell me of this legend which was passed on to them by their parents about a large man with red eyes who came to live with the tribe [a Yakima Indian fire guard told W. J. Vogel in August 1974]. Whenever any of the Indian people became sick, he would heal them. One day, when he knew he was dying, he asked the Indian people to take him to a particular location so that he might be there when he died. This they did. Shortly after he died, a large flying object came down from the skies, put his body aboard and flew off into the sky.

The first manimal tale with which we are fully satisfied is also our first from the 20th century.

One rainy night in July 1901, three 'coon hunters from Chester County, Pennsylvania, had the displeasure of encountering an "impossible" something that frightened the hell out of them. Milton Brint, his brother Taylor, and Tom Lukens were carefully making their way through Stewart's woods in Pensbury township. The only light they had emanated from a dim bull's-eye lantern. Ahead of them their hunting dogs scurried through the underbrush barking madly.

Suddenly the hounds were silent. The hunters paused, surprised and perplexed. The next thing they knew, the dogs were flying out of the woods with their tails between their legs, whining and growling in terror. They huddled near their masters and would not go back into the trees.

"I never saw dogs so scared in all my life," Milton Brint said later, "and I have been 'coon hunting now for nearly forty years. It appeared to me as if the critters had just escaped from a catamount [cougar or mountain lion]. Presently they led us forward in the direction of a cedar tree. We turned the bull's-eye into the limbs time and again, but it availed us nothing. We were at a loss to discover what had frightened the dogs so badly. While we were yet standing there trying to discover the cause of their fright, a low dismal sound came from the tree top. We were startled. By and by the top of the tree began to shake as if some living, moving object were descending.

"It had not gone far when it let go its hold. Straight as an arrow it came tumbling down to the ground. It all happened so sudden and unexpectedly that it was impossible to tell precisely just what it was, for strange to say, every bull's-eye was instantly extinguished by the impact of the fall. We were left in total darkness. I got a faint glimpse of the thing before it struck the ground, however, and while its head and neck bore every semblance to a man, it had the body and legs of a wild beast. I am not naturally a timid man, but I was scared that night. I looked about me for Taylor and Lukens. They were nowhere to be found. They fled the moment the weird object began its unexpected descent.

"The dogs ran like craven curs and I was shortly seized with the same fear. I struck out as fast as I could, not knowing which way my steps were carrying me. I became so badly bewildered that instead of going toward home I ran in an entirely different direction. I brought up in the neighborhood of Kennett Square so badly exhausted that I could not go any farther.

"I did not see Lukens again for several days and Taylor came to my house on the morrow to make sure that I had turned up. When he found that I was all right, he went away again without mentioning the happening of the night before. It was nearly a week before the dogs put in an appearance in a nearly half-starved condition. We have tried several times to continue hunting in Stewart's woods, but it's of no use. The dogs won't hunt in the woods. The place is haunted and we will give it a wide berth in the future."

Not long after, two other men, Lewis Brooks and Jack Murphy, were riding one night in a wagon along a path through the woods when something with a manlike head and an animal-like body crossed the road directly in front of them. It was walking on four feet. Murphy, who would later call the phenomenon "spectral-like," saw it pass directly *through a fence* and disappear into the forest. Brooks emptied a revolver into the thing but with no apparent effect.

We have here some of the first hints of what will

become familiar motifs of MA lore: their capacity to terrify other animals, such as dogs; their apparent lack of normal physical substance; their immunity to bullets; and the occasional failure of machines and instruments (in this case lanterns) in their presence.

Around 1915 a young man named Crum King, who lived just southeast of Wann, Oklahoma, was returning home from a dance one night when he saw something near the gate of his house. "It was about five or six feet tall and it stood with its arms stretched out," King recalled in 1975. "It was about four feet wide in the chest and hairy all over. It was like a bear or something, but it stood up like a man."

Terrified, King fled. He told no one of the strange encounter.

On January 21, 1932, while passing through an area five miles north of Downingtown, Pennsylvania, John McCandless heard a moaning sound in the brush. There he spotted "a hideous form, half-man, half-beast, on all fours and covered with dirt or hair." After others told of seeing the figure, McCandless and a group of friends armed with rifles and shotguns plowed through the trees and fields every day for a week, but by this time the thing had disappeared.

This letter, signed by Mrs. Beulah Schroat of Decatur, Illinois, was published in the *Decatur Review* on August 2, 1972:

> In reference to the creatures people are seeing, I am 76 years old. My home used to be south of Effingham. My two brothers saw the creatures when they were children. My brothers have since passed away.

They are hairy, stand on their hind legs, have large eyes and are about as large as an average person or shorter, and are harmless as they ran away from the children. They walk, they do not jump.

They were seen on a farm near a branch of water. The boys waded and fished in the creek every day and once in a while they would run to the house scared and tell the story.

Later there was a piece in the Chicago paper stating there were such animals of that description and they were harmless. This occurred about 60 years ago or a little less.

My mother and father thought they were just children's stories until the Chicago paper told the story.

During the summer of 1941, the Rev. Lepton Harpole was hunting squirrels along the Gum Creek bottom near Mt. Vernon, a small city in the southeastern Illinois county of Jefferson, when "a large animal that looked something like a baboon" leaped out of a tree and walked upright toward the startled hunter. Harpole in turn struck the creature with his gun barrel and then frightened it away by firing a couple of shots into the air.

In the months that followed, rural families would report hearing terrifying screams at night in the wooded bottom lands along the creeks. Hunters sometimes found mysterious tracks. By early spring of the next year, after the killing of a farm dog near Bonnie, large parties of volunteers scoured the creek bottoms, some with rifles and shotguns, others with nets and ropes. But the creature easily evaded them (perhaps because of its reputed ability to leap twenty to forty feet in a single bound), and in fact appeared as much as forty or fifty miles from the site of the original sighting, in Jackson and Okaw

Counties. Finally it disappeared and was not seen again—for a time, at any rate.

In its March 1946 issue *Hoosier Folklore* noted:

> About 25 years ago, a 'coon hunter from Hecker one night heard a strange beast screaming up ahead on Prairie duLong Creek. Hunters chased this phantom from time to time all one winter. Their dogs would get the trail, then lose it, and they would hear it screaming down the creek in the opposite direction. It was that kind of creature: you'd hear it up creek, but when you set out in that direction you'd hear it a mile down creek.

3.

From a relatively sparse prehistory we enter the modern period and we discover manimals crawling, and walking, out of the woods in staggering numbers, beginning particularly in the 1960s and proliferating at an incredible rate into the 1970s. There seems little doubt that, while manimals are not exactly a new phenomenon, they are appearing now in larger numbers than ever before, and in the future we expect them to be nearly as frequent as UFOs, in whose company, as we already have observed, they sometimes manifest themselves.

There is not a state in the union which by now has not logged its share of reports. Where once the situation seemed safely confined to the inaccessible Northwest, today it has escaped such confinement and is completely out of hand. A full recounting of all known incidents would prove not only tedious but pointless. For our purposes it should suffice to cite manimal activity in three representative states—

Illinois, Indiana and Oklahoma—and then to take note of parallel events in other places.

Illinois

In Marion County during the last three weeks of May 1970, 24 hogs disappeared. In the three preceding months "hognappings" had occurred frequently at Salem area farms. In the central part of the state near Farmer City three sheep turned up dead in the early spring. Officials assumed—until July 9, anyway—that it was the work of "wild dogs."

On that date Don Ennis, Beecher Lamb, Larry Faircloth and Bob Hardwick, all 18, decided to camp out on a wild ten-acre buffalo grass-covered piece of land a mile south of Farmer City near Salt Creek. Their campsite, often used as a lovers' lane, was very isolated. Before the night was over, they would realize just *how* isolated.

About 10:30 p.m., as they sat around the campfire, they heard something moving in the tall grass. When "it" moved between them and their tent, Lamb decided to turn his car lights on. The thing, with widely-separated eyes gleaming at them, was squatting by the tent. Then it ran off—on two legs. The young men left in such a considerable hurry themselves that one of them ran on one leg—Ennis, who had one foot in a cast because of a broken ankle, left his crutches behind.

Soon word about the Farmer City "monster" spread. On Friday, July 10, more than ten persons said they had seen a pair of glowing eyes near the site of the first sighting. And on the 12th and 14th at least fifteen persons swore they had seen a furry creature in the same area. Witnesses told Loren Coleman that it seemed to be attracted by the sound of loud radio music and by the light of campfires.

Police Officer Robert Hayslip of Farmer City decided to check the stories of the monster. He went out to the campsite/lovers' lane area early in the morning of July 15, between two and three o'clock. Hayslip heard something running through the grass. Then, he said to Coleman soon after the sighting, "out of the corner of my eye I could see these two extremely bright eyes, just like it was standing there watching me." As he turned toward it, it disappeared.

Hayslip returned to the site about 6:00 a.m. He found that the heavy steel grommets in a tent that had been intact at 3:00 a.m. now were ripped out. A quilt lying nearby was torn to shreds.

The Farmer City police chief, who earlier had expressed the curious view that the so-called monster was nothing more than a Shetland pony (evidently one of the bipedal variety), now decided to lock the gate that led to the ten-acre area.

The creature apparently moved on.

A couple driving near the Weldon Springs State Park on the afternoon of July 24 spotted a "bear" near the Willis Bridge on Salt Creek. Stopping at a farmhouse, they asked the residents to notify the Dewitt County Sheriff's office. The Sheriff and State Conservation Officer Warren Wilson found several tracks with definite claw marks around the water's edge, and on a sandbar in the middle of the creek. Wilson said the tracks were more like a large cat's but definitely not a bear's.

This little episode is hopelessly confusing and we place it here in the manimal category for purely arbitrary reasons. It is clear from the evidence of the footprints that the creature in question was *not* a bear, or at least a conventional bear. Imperfectly-seen or briefly-glimpsed manimals are sometimes mistaken for bears (the opposite, of course, occurs occasionally as well). But, to complicate matters further, at the same time (as we shall see in the next chapter), Illinois was undergoing an invasion of mysterious catlike animals whose prints, unlike those of conventional panthers, *Felis concolor,* characteristically contained claw marks. Yet it is unlikely that anyone would mistake a "cat" for a "bear." *However,* in the 1970s we have seen some evidence that a new kind of MA, a "bear" which may leave ambiguous prints in its wake, is beginning to appear on the Fortean scene.

Soon after the Willis Bridge incident, during the first week of August, Vicki Otto sighted something near the Ireland Grove Road three miles southeast of Bloomington. She saw a pair of eyes reflecting her automobile headlights as she approached what she at first thought was a dog. Then, she said, "I saw this ape running in the ditch. The thing I saw was the size of a baboon."

Around 9:30 p.m. on August 16, while driving on Route 136 approaching the Kickapoo Creek bridge north of Waynesville, Dan Lindsey and Mike Anderson encountered a similar creature. "My first thought was a tall man or maybe a bear or a gorilla," Anderson said. The manimal stood six feet five inches tall, was all brown and had stooped shoulders. Walking on two legs and illuminated by the car lights, it more or less trotted across to the west side and along the creek's edge. Then it was gone.

Manimals came back to Illinois during the summer of 1972, though far more dramatic events were going on just across the border, in Louisiana, Missouri, where a smelly, red-eyed creature dubbed "Momo" (for "MO. MOnster") had arrived in the company of UFOs, disembodied voices, religious visions and poltergeist phenomena.*

The *Peoria Journal-Star* for July 26 of that year relates the claim of Randy Emert, 18, who reportedly saw a "monster" two different times over the previous two months. Emert said the thing resembled Momo in most particulars, although its height was between eight and twelve feet and it was "kind of white and moved quick." When it appeared, it brought with it Momo's rancid odor and also seemed to scare the animals living in the woods near Cole Hollow Road. Emert said, "It lets out a long screech —like an old steam-engine whistle, only more human."

Emert asserted that a number of friends had seen either the creature or its footprints. "I'm kind of a spokesman for the group," he said. "The only one who has guts, I guess."

Mrs. Ann Kammerer of Peoria corroborated Emert's story, stating that all of her children, friends of Emert's, had seen the thing. "It sounds kind of weird," she admitted. "At first I didn't believe it, but then my daughter-in-law saw it."

According to Emert, there was an old abandoned house in the woods with large footprints all around it and a hole dug under the basement. Emert thought this might be where the creature was staying. Interestingly enough, Edgar Harrison, the chief personality in the Momo affair, believed his creature might be residing temporarily in an abandoned building. Readers will recall the abandoned barn near Murphysboro and the tracking dog's curious reluctance to enter it. Was it, too, a manimal dwelling?

* Those readers not familiar with this much-written-about episode are referred to our *The Unidentified*, pp. 12-14. A fuller account appears in our article, "Anthropoids, Monsters and UFOs," in England's *Flying Saucer Review*, January/February 1973.

On July 25 a Pekin resident reported seeing "something big" swimming in the Illinois River, which also flows through Peoria. On the night of the 27th "two reliable citizens" told police they had seen a ten-foot something that "looked like a cross between an ape and a caveman." According to a UPI dispatch, it had "a face with long gray U-shaped ears, a red mouth with sharp teeth, [and] thumbs with long second joints . . ." It smelled, said a witness, like a "musky wet-down dog." The East Peoria Police Department said it had received more than 200 calls about the creature the following evening.

Leroy Summers of Cairo saw a ten-foot, white, hairy creature standing erect near the Ohio River levee during the evening hours of July 25. The Cairo police found nothing when they came to investigate and Police Commissioner James Dale warned that henceforth anyone making a monster report would have his breath tested for alcohol content.

The following year, when creatures descended upon White County in southeastern Illinois, Sheriff Roy Poshard, Jr., took an even sterner stance: He threatened to arrest the key witness.

Whatever it was that Henry McDaniel of Enfield saw, it was not a classic manimal—or for that matter classic anything we have ever heard of. Nonetheless, an undoubted manimal was observed during the resulting "monster scare."

McDaniel claimed that late in the evening of April 25, 1973, he heard something scratching on his door. Upon opening the door, he did a double take, for the "something" looked as if it had stepped out of a nightmare.

"It had three legs on it," he said, "a short body,

two little short arms coming out of its breast area, and two pink eyes as big as flashlights. It stood four and a half to five feet tall and was grayish-colored. It was trying to get into the house."

McDaniel, in no mood to entertain the visitor, grabbed a pistol and opened fire.

"When I fired that first shot," he said, "I know I hit it." The creature hissed like a wildcat and bounded away, covering 75 feet in three jumps, and disappeared into the brush along a railroad embankment that runs near the McDaniel home.

State police, summoned to McDaniel's home soon afterwards, found tracks "like a dog's except that [they] had six toe pads." McDaniel told Jerome Clark that two of the prints measured four inches around while the other measured three and one-quarter inches.

Loren Coleman further discovered that ten-year-old Greg Garrett, who lived just behind McDaniel, had been playing in his back yard half an hour before when the creature approached him and stepped on his feet, tearing his tennis shoes to shreds. The boy had run inside, crying hysterically.

On May 6 at 3:00 a.m. McDaniel was awakened by the howling of neighborhood dogs. Looking out his front door, he saw the creature again.

"I seen something moving out on the railroad track and there it stood," he said. "I didn't shoot at it or anything. It started on down the railroad track. It wasn't in a hurry or anything."

Referring to one of the explanations offered for his sightings, McDaniel told Clark, "I've been all around this world. I've been through Africa and I've had a pet kangaroo. This was not a kangaroo. I've never seen this type of creature or track before.

The publicity McDaniel's report received brought hordes of curiosity seekers, newsmen and serious researchers to Enfield. Among them were five young men whom Deputy Sheriff Jim Clark arrested for hunting violations after they said they had seen and shot at a gray hairy creature in some underbrush. Two of the men thought they had hit it but the thing had sped off, running faster than a man. The incident is supposed to have occurred on May 8.

Another witness was Rick Rainbow, news director of radio station WWKI, Kokomo, Indiana. On May 6 he and three other persons saw a strange creature beside—note—an old abandoned house near McDaniel's place. They didn't get a good look at it because its back was to them and it was running in the shadows, but they later described it as apelike, about five and a half feet tall, grayish and stooped. Rainbow taped the cry it made.

Investigators Loren Coleman and Richard Crowe did not see the creature but they did hear a high-pitched screech while they were searching the area around McDaniel's home.

About a month later Edwardsville police received and checked three reports of a musty-smelling, red-eyed, human-sized being said to be lurking in the woods on the eastern edge of town. The creature reportedly was more than five and a half feet tall and broad-shouldered, with eyes that apparently were sensitive to light. It made no sound when it walked. The witnesses said the thing chased them and one man told police the creature had ripped his shirt and clawed his chest.

The summer months of 1973 were taken up, as we have seen, with the events at Murphysboro. The monster season ended on the night of October 16, when four St. Joseph youths—Bill Duncan, Bob Summers, Daryl Mowry and Craig Flenniken, all but Summers high school seniors—supposedly encountered a hairy "gorilla-like" creature on a road south of the town. They had stopped their car to investigate what they thought was a campfire near the bridge on the Salt Fork. One of them lit a match and they all saw the creature, approximately five feet tall, about fifteen feet away. They did not linger to investigate further.

"None of us believe in that outer space stuff," Duncan told the *Champaign-Urbana Courier*. "I wondered if I was nuts or something. I thought it was a bear at first, but I really couldn't say."

This account raises a number of interesting questions which unfortunately we cannot answer, since our efforts to contact the alleged witnesses were unsuccessful. However, there are two obvious questions: What was the nature of the mysterious light the boys at first took to be a campfire? And more to the point, how could a match struck in an outdoor setting generate enough light to reveal a presumably dark object fifteen feet away?

Indiana

On the evening of May 18, 1969, a power blackout blanketed a small rural area outside Rising Sun. For two hours the home of Mr. and Mrs. Lester Kaiser was without electricity. The Kaisers did not connect the blackout with sightings of mysterious lights along a nearby ridge which had been made in previous weeks.

The next evening, around 7:30, the Kaisers' son George was walking through the farmyard on his way to a tractor, when he was startled to see a weird figure standing about 25 feet away.

"I watched it for about two minutes before it saw me," young Kaiser said later. "It stood in a fairly upright position, although it was bent over about in the middle of its back, with arms about the same length as a normal human being's. I'd say it was about five-eight or so and it had a very muscular structure. The head sat directly on the shoulders and the face was black, with hair that stuck out of the back of its head. It had eyes set close together, and a very short forehead. It was covered with hair except for the back of the hands and the face. The hands looked like normal hands, not claws."

When Kaiser, who had been standing transfixed, moved, the creature made "a strange grunting-like sound," turned, leaped over a ditch, and disappeared down the road running at great speed. Subsequently, investigators made plaster casts of footprints found in the dirt by the ditch. These casts show three toes plus a big toe.

The following evening, around 10:15, neighbor Charles Rolfing watched a glowing, greenish-white object for eight minutes as it maneuvered in the sky above him.

For two weeks in August 1970, people in the Winslow area, in the southwestern part of the state, reported seeing a "ten-foot-tall creature covered with hair [which] appears to walk on hind legs, top speed sixty miles per hour." The state police, which investigated, described the witnesses as "reliable."

One night in June 1970 a farmer, whose initials are D. K., was visiting his future wife, who lived in nearby Sharpsville, when suddenly both were struck with a feeling of intense dizziness, coupled with sensations of moodiness and fear. They decided to drive out to the farm in hopes of shaking the "attack."

The night was dark and little patches of fog dotted the road. As they drove down the country road, they came upon an even darker area, which seemed. to extend upward. When they entered it, they were perplexed to find that their headlights did not seem to extend very far ahead and that the air around them was strangely warm.

"We got home and was walking up to the house," D. K. told Don Worley and Fritz Clemm six years later, when "Zipper [the family dog] attacked us twice. I had to almost break his head to keep him off us. The dog felt it. He had known me since he was a pup and had never been hostile to me before. But he did try to attack us twice. Both of us were pretty shaken up."

A year after that, the creature appeared on the scene.

"One night around 10:00 or 10:30 p.m. in June or July, all the dogs started barking," D. K. recalled. "I went outside to investigate and there was my dog [Zipper] lunging at a thing that was standing in a low spot. It was still taller than I was." When the witness stepped out the door, the "thing," about 25 feet away, turned around and looked at him.

It was, he said, "big, real big . . . The head wasn't shaped like an ape's and I don't think that it looked like a man's head either. It looked like a helmet but it was furry. It didn't look natural to anything zoological on earth. It just didn't look right for the ape-looking body that it had. It didn't look like an ape's head or a human's head. It was dark and I couldn't see too well for all the details."

There was, however, no mistaking its "rank and sickening" odor. "The smell of it almost made you want to barf," D. K. said. It was something like a "decaying meat and vegetable combination."

The creature, nine feet tall and covered with stringy, "dirty" hair, was stooped over like an ape, with no neck and long arms. It was growling in a "deep rumbling manner."

"It would swing at the dog," he said. "It was funny the way it swung. Kind of like it was slow motion. Its strokes were coming close to the dog ... It wasn't like a prizefighter throwing a haymaker at an opponent. It was, you know, more like a slow motion type of thing. ... The dog would run up to it and lunge, teeth and paws out, but seemed like before it got there, it would hit the ground and jump back. And before it jumped back, the thing would swing and barely miss it. And this went on for two or three minutes."

D.K. thought the creature acted rather confused and uncertain, "like an animal or a human that was put on a spot and really didn't know what to do."

When he recovered his senses, D. K. dashed inside, searched frantically for shells to put in his shotgun, and ran out again in time to see the creature lumbering off in the direction of the creek. Though he realized the weird intruder was by now too far away for it to do any good, he fired twice in its direction.

Immediately after that, he called the sheriff, who openly laughed at the story, and though the manimal would return five times more over the space of the next year, D. K. never again notified the authorities.

The manimal reappeared around midnight three or four weeks later. The witness, who was inside watching television, was alerted to its presence when he heard the dogs barking wildly. D. K. grabbed his shotgun and followed Zipper, who seemed to be tracking the thing, to the cemetery. Suddenly the dog stopped as if he had lost the scent but he apparently found it again on the other side.

"When I got down to the creek," D. K. said, "the dog started running up alongside the creek, barking and looking down in it. I couldn't keep up. The dog wasn't in the water but along the side of the creek. I heard splashing in the water and again the smell was there. I knew the creature had to be a few yards ahead of him. I proceeded to follow him. I followed him clear back to Beatty's woods and then I turned around and came back. . . . The dogs were restless part of the night, probably an hour or so afterwards."

The third appearance was later that same year. This time D. K. was sleeping—it was around 4:30 a.m.—when the dogs again alerted him to the presence of something unusual. Looking out his bedroom window, he saw the creature moving down by the creek. By this time, D. K. was determined to kill it so that he could prove to skeptical friends, some of whom had sat up with him long nights on his assurances that they might get to see the thing themselves, that it existed. He ran outside, shotgun in hand, and tracked the manimal until it got lost in the thick woods. He did not know until later, when his mother, who had been watching all of this, told him so, that *the thing had doubled back and was now trailing him*. It followed him for a short while before disappearing back into the trees.

That winter D. K. was rabbit-hunting when he discovered that a small pond had mysteriously dried up. Next to it was a thirty- or forty-foot circular area with dead, crushed weeds and grass laid down in a perfect counterclockwise swirl pattern. He had no idea what might have caused it. To ufologists this sounds suspiciously like a "flying saucer nest"—ground traces like these have been noted all over the world and are usually associated with UFO landings. And this is hardly the first time we have heard of dried-up ponds left in the wake of such touchdowns.

One evening in the spring of 1972, D. K. and his brother, both now married and living with their wives at the farmhouse, went out for an evening on the town. When they got back, they found the two women in an hysterical state. The wives said they had heard the thing trying to pry open an aluminum storm window not long before.

The brothers went out with guns and flashlights and examined the window. They could smell the manimal's characteristically foul odor, which lingered at the site. But what puzzled them was the fact that, though one corner of the window had been pulled out, it "wasn't pried out," as D. K. would put it. "There were no marks on it. The screen on the inside wasn't cut or anything. It didn't look like anything had happened using a tool—no marks on the wood around the frame. That's what led me to believe it had to be something super to do it. No marks on the window and it got me shook up again."

A week or two later, at 11:30 p.m., D. K. heard the dogs barking and he knew "it" was back. He looked out his bedroom window and there it was, moving along the creek in the same direction it always went. D. K. decided to let it alone this time.

In the fall it came back for the last time.

"I don't know the month on it," he told Worley and Clemm, "probably September. It was before the first major frost, I know that. The only time it seemed to come around was when it was fair weather. I never saw it after a major frost or before a good summer yet. It didn't appear in cold weather.

"I had taken the gun out again when I heard the dogs raising thunder and went after it, but I never did get a shot at it this time either. Seems like every time I'd try to shoot . . . why, it always got something between me and it. I consider myself good on running shots and I've shot dogs and deer but—it knowed that I was after it. It was cunning. It just knew how far to keep away from me and what to keep in front of me to keep me from firing on it. . . .

"This last time I chased it, it went through the cemetery. I was by myself, no dogs, and I again chased it up toward the woods. Then I doubled back to the cemetery and waited, but it never did come back."

A month before D. K.'s final encounter, and fifty miles directly southwest, a similar creature had caused such a fright that some people in the village of Roachdale thought the Day of Judgment might be at hand. (Before you smile too indulgently at that, wait until we have examined a certain very strange episode from Pennsylvania later in these pages.) Since we have already recounted the Roachdale creature scare in our earlier book,* we will not treat it in detail here.

Briefly, the manimal showed up after a mysterious glowing object had exploded silently over a cornfield. Two hours later the thing was heard just outside the field in a young couple's yard, and for the next two or three weeks made regular nightly appearances. The manimal, which resembled an enormous apelike animal, left no tracks even when it ran, on all fours, over mud, and once the wife thought she could see *through* it. Almost forty persons saw the creature before it disappeared, including a farm family, the Burdines, who lost 170 chickens, which were ripped apart but not eaten. The Burdines fired on the manimal without any apparent effect.

By the last week of August the Roachdale reports had subsided. But just what appeared three weeks later in Parke County (north of Roachdale's Putnam County) no one seems to know.

Shortly before 11:00 a.m. Wednesday, September 20, Parke County Sheriff Gary Cooper broadcast a bizarre warning to authorities in other counties: "Attention all counties surrounding Parke County. Be on the lookout for a ten-foot-tall monster. It is covered with fur and its feet are 21 inches long."

* *The Unidentified*, pp. 14-19.

Cooper explained that he had received several calls from the Lodi, Tangier, Howard and Sylvania area, a sparsely-settled, heavily-wooded region near the Parke-Fountain County line. The creature had been seen on Tuesday night.

"One lady came to my office with the story, and I have had at least three other persons call in sightings," Cooper said. He would not release any of the witnesses' names.

Two 'coon dogs and a pig were killed by something that had slashed them across the stomach. Cooper thought a badger might have done it but he wasn't sure. "I'm not ruling out anything at this point," he said.

"Apparently," the *Crawfordsville Journal and Review* concluded, "this monster, just as the the creature from Roachdale, will be listed as another of West-Central Indiana's UFOs (unidentified furry objects)."

In early October 1973, a manimal appeared near Galveston. The first person to encounter it was Jeff Martin, who was fishing at a lake with two companions. His friends had gone off to another part of the lake when Martin heard something behind him. He turned and saw, about twenty feet away, an apelike figure watching him. At least Martin *thought* it was apelike, since it was dusk and visibility was poor. Frightened, he called to the being, which did not respond. For some reason, though, Martin felt better about the situation, and was almost sorry when the thing slipped away.

A few minutes later something touched his shoulder. Martin, who was sitting, whirled his head around and saw a sandy-colored anthropoidal creature—evidently the one he had just observed. The manimal ran away with amazing swiftness, Martin in hot pursuit. It moved in running leaps, "like a man on a rope being pulled too fast by a car," Martin later would say. As it crossed the road, the witness could hear its feet slapping on the blacktop. It turned around one last time, leaped over a ditch, and disappeared into the woods. Shortly afterwards a glowing bronze object shot out of the trees and into the sky, fading away so quickly that the whole series of events seemed nearly instantaneous.

The next day Martin returned to the scene but saw nothing. The following evening he, his fiancée Nellie Floyd, father-in-law-to-be Gene Floyd, and two friends drove to the spot, trailed all the way by a white, glowing starlike light. The object disappeared near a bridge not far from where Martin had seen the manimal. When they got to that spot, the creature was waiting for them.

The thing, about eight or nine feet tall, was standing in tall weeds. The observers turned their flashlights on it and noticed a very curious detail: The beams seemed somehow "weaker" on the creature, which stood motionless, almost as if in a trance, giving off a "musty" odor. Oddly, its presence did not seem to disturb the crickets, frogs, or other wildlife, which the witnesses thought most unusual. They yelled at the creature but, getting no response, decided to hurl some rocks at it. They could not tell whether the rocks had missed, bounced off or gone through the thing, but, whatever the case, they could not get it to move in any way.

Finally, the appearance of an approaching automobile forced the three remaining witnesses (the other two had fled to the safety of the car) to move their own vehicle from the road. When they returned, the manimal was gone.

Perhaps significantly, Gene Floyd, one of the witnesses, already had an eight-year history of dealings with strange phenomena. Since 1965 he had had a dozen UFO experiences. On one occasion, a peculiar impulse had led him outside, where he saw an orange glow in the sky. An "unspoken command" told him to shine his flashlight up at it, and when he did, flashing the light three times, the glow blinked three times in reply.

Floyd also had a vivid "dream" in which he stood aboard a UFO conversing mentally with a humanoid figure with a large bald head. Since that time, like other contactees (if that is what Floyd is), he seemed to acquire a noticeable degree of psychic ability.

In mid-September 1975 both types of UFOs—a flying one and a furry one—showed up on a farm near Waterloo.

At 3:00 a.m. a farmer on his way to the bathroom happened to look out his upstairs window and noticed a red light the size of an auto headlight in a soybean field about seventy-five yards away. He also saw, at the edge of an area illuminated by a dusk-to-dawn light, a large, bipedal "animal" walking toward the object with a forward swaying motion. Suddenly the red light changed into a brilliant magnesium-like light for five seconds, then vanished. When it did so, the creature disappeared, too.

That morning, when the farmer went out to examine the area where he had seen the mysterious light, he found a thirty-foot circle of browned soybeans. As time went by, he realized that the beans had stopped growing, though the plants outside the circle remained unaffected.

The farmer told Don Worley that in 1966 he and his wife had seen a cupola-shaped UFO hovering over his cornfield. In the nights that followed, he said, he had heard a strange sound like a "baby crying"—a sound often associated with manimals as well as poltergeists.

Oklahoma

One night in November 1968, Roger Boucher of Oakwood was returning home from nearby Canton when a "gorillalike" animal ran across the highway in front of him.

Two months later, in that same general area, Deward Whetstone found tracks measuring 10½ inches long and four inches wide. The plaster casts he made suggested that whoever or whatever made them was primatelike. The tracks showed a deep split between the first two toes, and the weight of the body apparently placed most pressure on the outside edge of the foot. At the time he found the prints, said Whetstone, the ground was soft due to a spell of wet weather.

"There were tracks all the way across the road. I followed them to where whatever made them jumped the fence. There have been a number of sightings of a strange animal in this area."

On Friday, February 26, 1971, C. Edward Green and his wife were driving home along Lake Avenue in Lawton about 11:00 p.m., when they saw a strange figure walking beside the road.

"He was walking bent over like a gorilla," Green recalled not long after in a interview with Jerome Clark, "but not on all fours. He wore black pants that were cut or torn off at the knees and he had a big beard—it began higher up on his face than beards usually do—and long hair, very unkempt."

When the Greens reached their apartment shortly after seeing the strange creature, they called the police. They assumed they had seen a mentally disturbed person.

A few minutes later, at 11:15, the sound of police sirens brought Green to the window of his second-floor apartment. He pulled the curtains aside and found himself staring into the face of the figure he had seen on the road.

"He was crouched down on the walkway," Green reported, "and while I was startled myself, I noticed that the person, or whatever, was either extremely frightened or not oriented to his surroundings. There was a glazed expression in his eyes as if he didn't quite understand where he was.

"His hair and beard were very black, and he himself was darked-complected. He was barefooted—his feet looked normal—and he stood at least six feet tall. Nothing about his body seemed disproportioned.

"When he saw me, he jumped to the gravel below. Now that's about a fifteen-foot jump, but it didn't seem to bother him. He must have been very strong. I didn't stay to watch him run away."

Green was not the only Lawton resident who reported seeing the creature that night. Just before his experience at the window, a group of passersby had seen a "monkeylike" figure running down a street not far away, dodging cars, hiding behind bushes, and then running on. And fifteen minutes after Green's second encounter, several Fort Sill soldiers, leaving a grocery store three blocks away, saw a similar strange creature amble past.

Almost exactly 24 hours later the creature appeared again, and this time it nearly caused a man to have a heart attack.

Donald Childs, a 36-year-old television technician with a history of heart trouble, stepped into his back yard at 11:00 p.m., having heard a noise outside. He thought it might be a prowler. Instead he came upon someone or something "real huge, way over six feet tall. He was trying to get a drink out of the pond," Childs said, "but the pond was empty.

"He had long hair all over his face. Maybe he had a beard, too. I don't know. It was dark and I couldn't tell for sure. He was wearing dark-colored pants that were way too little, and a plaid jacket that was kind of too small. His legs, what I could see of them, seemed hairy, but like I said, it was dark and I couldn't swear to it.

"All of a sudden he saw me, and he was as scared of me as I was of him. He didn't even stand up or get any kind of running start—he just sprung from his squatting position and jumped clear over the pond. The next day I measured it and that pond is twelve feet across!

"He could really run awful fast. He ran kind of hunched over like an ape in a Tarzan movie. He wasn't running on all fours. It was definitely a man. I'm sure he was somebody, you know, mentally off. I've heard that people like that have strength that normal people don't have."

Childs suffered a heart seizure from the excitement and spent the next few days recovering from it.

Later, a police officer told Childs that the department had received about twenty calls from persons who reported seeing a similar person, or animal, between Friday and Monday but the story of the sightings did not appear in the Lawton newspapers until the next Tuesday, March 2. Then the local press gave the reports headline treatment.

After the publicity, Childs heard from a farmer three miles south of Lawton who had an odd problem, one neither the sheriff nor the Cattlemen's Association, to whom he had appealed, could help with.

About once a month for the last year, he said, he had been finding either a calf or a full-grown cow lying dead in his field with one of its legs ripped off. The rest of the carcass was never wounded or marked. It seemed as if someone possessing incredible strength approached the animals, tore off a leg, and left the beasts to die. But no footprints were ever found that might offer a clue to the nature of the attacker.

Maybe the culprit was the same creature which had plagued a farm in the El Reno area. One morning in December 1970, according to an Associated Press story dated February 27, 1971, a farmer found the door to his chicken coop ripped off and lying on the ground. On the surface of the door and inside the coop itself were strange handprints about seven inches long and five inches wide. When he saw that several of his chickens had disappeared without a trace, he called the local state game ranger.

The door was shipped to zoologist Lawrence Curtis, Director of the Oklahoma City Zoo. After a study that included comparisons with the hand- and paw-prints of human beings, apes, monkeys, bears, and other animals, Curtis confessed his bafflement. "I don't know what this is," he said. "It resembles a gorilla but it's more like a man." According to Curtis, the creature's thumb crooked inward as if deformed or injured.

"It appears that whatever made the prints was walking on all fours," he said, judging from prints on the ground outside the coop. Unfortunately these were not preserved.

"We've shown it to several mammalogists and wildlife experts in Oklahoma and some passing through," Curtiss told Jerome Clark. "All agree it is the print of a primate. These were made by some sort of man." The man, if such he was, was barefooted.

Curtis added that he had heard from a man in Stillwater and a woman in McAlester who had discovered similar prints.

Let us return for a moment to the curious events at Lawton and compare them with several unusual reports from elsewhere.

For example, from near the Eel River above Eureka, California, about 1950 or 1951, when a ten-year-old girl, who nine years later would recount the experience to the late Ivan T. Sanderson (who in turn reprinted her letter in his classic *Abominable Snowmen: Legend Come to Life*), allegedly encountered a red-eyed, hairy creature "with the strangest-looking fangs that I have ever seen . . . However . . . the strangest and most frightening thing of all . . . [was that] he had on clothes! . . . They were tattered and torn and barely covered him, but they were still there."

In late September 1973, a family living in a mobile home four miles north of Tabor City, North Carolina, claimed to have had a number of sightings of two "space creatures" which roamed the neighboring woods. Though these creatures were not described as precisely manimal-like, nonetheless, according to witness Rose Williamson, "They are about seven or eight feet tall with big red eyes that glow in the dark. They are dressed in brown shirts *with black pants which are ragged at the bottom.*"

In *Strange Creatures from Time and Space,* John Keel cites a number of instances in which percipients have reported seeing apparitional figures wearing "checkered shirts," perhaps reminiscent of the "plaid shirt" the Lawton witnesses saw.

Just as interesting is Edward Green's observation that the manimal "was either extremely frightened or not oriented to his surroundings"—echoed by Donald Childs' parallel remark that "he was as scared of me as I was of him."

In 1967 Hembree Brandon, editor of *The Winona*

[Mississippi] *Times,* received this letter from an Atlanta man who signed himself "J. H.":

> This letter I am writing will be hard to write. But being it concerns an object and in an area east of Winona on the highway to Europa, I feel like someone in that area should know what me & my brother seen.
>
> The date was about 7th of Nov. [1966], the time one or one thirty appx. A.M.
>
> We were traveling east to Marietta Georgia in Chevrolet pickup when my headlights picked up an object running down a steep hill on my left, on its two legs, as if to run out and stop our truck. Then my headlights was on this creature. It size was liken that of a huge Kodiak Bear. But it was running on two legs not four. Its eyes were bright red appx two inches in diameter. On its body was hair appx 1½" long. Its weight was 5 to 700 lbs. Its height was appx 7 ft tall or more. Its left arm was held up like waving goodbye or giving a stop signal to us. The expression in its eyes was like a human in mortal terror. And my brother & I both agreed it (the expression) was like a person saying "Please help me."
>
> The face of the object was like a person gone wild or crazy. Its shoulders were appx 4 ft wide with narrow waist line.
>
> The object then tried to hide behind the shoulder of the road.
>
> If this object was scared, which no doubt in my mind it was, well I was a hellva lot scardier and I have camped in some of the west's wildest places, seen many bears & mountain lions, which didn't excite me in the least. For I am a prospector, that's my hobby. And I am usually alone in the high Sierra of California or the high country of some other state.
>
> Many a time I have laughed at the stories of

"Big Foot" of northern Calif., a person that picks up 60 gals. of oil & gas & smashes a tractor or catapiller with it. Now after seeing this object I just can't doubt anything anymore. For it was that big. I believe it could've turned over my truck easily. My brother & I was cold sober not even one can of beer all evening or that night.

So I advise all people living in the hill country between Winona & Europa to lock their door at night until some one can explain this. I think it could possible be a huge man gone wild, then I don't know for it looked both human & animal. But no doubt it was pleading for help. But why? ...

Why indeed?

This whole business gets even weirder when we consider that one of the Tabor City witnesses claimed that one of the manimal-like humanoids had scrawled a cryptic message in the dirt: "Help no." She thought the second word might have been incomplete. Whatever the case, during the "Momo" scare in Louisiana, Missouri, the seven-year-old son of a family which had experienced many of the strange phenomena that had converged on the town came home with two pieces of paper with writing on them. He explained to his mother that "something in my head told me" to pick them up and take them with him. The messages, while somewhat incoherent, were written by someone who said he was "lost & forlorn." They seemed to be some kind of plea for help.

Let us return now to complete our survey of Oklahoma manimals.

Nowata County is located in northeastern Oklahoma along the Kansas border. In late July 1974, Mrs. Margie Lee, who lived in the Watova settlement just outside the town of Nowata, saw a six-foot "Bigfoot" (as she would come to call it) from the decidedly uncomfortable distance of only six feet. She admits she was "scared silly."

For the next two weeks, during which she saw the thing repeatedly, her jangled nerves got little chance to rest and she went practically without sleep as she waited for the thing to reappear, which it inevitably did once darkness had set in. Eventually, when she realized the thing meant no harm, she lost some of her fear.

The "Bigfoot" was young, Mrs. Lee believed, and the several other witnesses, including members of her own family and two deputy sheriffs, concurred. It was male, with arms rather longer than a normal man's, and covered with brown hair about an inch long, though on the underside of the arms the hair was considerably shorter. It had five fingers on its hands, whose undersides seemed devoid of hair. "The hair," she told Jerome Clark, "was in those places where it would be on a man, only more so."

She saw it running a number of times. "You wouldn't believe it," she said. "It could go as fast as or even faster than a deer." It ran quietly, making a sound reminiscent of "moccasins over gravel." It exuded an odor so foul that sometimes Mrs. Lee almost got sick from it.

From its eyes, which looked "curious," Mrs. Lee inferred it meant no harm. The eyes were "normal," not self-luminescent.

Its behavior could best be described as timid, but it did exhibit a certain peculiar interest in women, to the extent that it bypassed houses where only men resided. It certainly appeared to be more interested in Mrs. Lee than it did in her husband, John, and from all this the couple concluded the strange visitor was looking for a mate.

Whatever the case, the Lees developed a sort of

affection for their "Bigfoot," and once engaged in a little game with it. They had noticed it kept putting their feed pail in front of the barn door, blocking the entrance; every day they would remove it and every night the creature would put it back. Finally, they took to hiding the pail, but the beast inevitably would sniff it out and put it back in front of the barn door.

"That's how we found out it had a sense of humor," she recalled. She also heard it laugh once, the only sound she ever heard it make.

On the whole, though, it was something of a pest. A neighbor lost a chicken to it, and occasionally it would go into the Lees' barn and thrash around. One evening Mrs. Lee heard it doing just that and ran outside to chase it away. She heard it crash through a window laced with chicken wire and flee into the night.

By this time two sheriff's deputies, Gilbert Gilmore and Buck Field, had been called in, and the two of them saw the thing repeatedly. They were there the last night it appeared, when they blinded it with car headlights and opened fire on it. Weirdly, the creature showed no sign it had been hit as it dashed toward the woods and safety. The next day a thorough search uncovered no tracks, blood, or hair.

It made its last call on Mrs. Lee that morning just as she, by now utterly exhausted from too many nights with too little sleep, was bathing. Suddenly she heard a loud *thump!* against the outside wall. Grabbing a robe, she sped outside, but the creature was already gone—for good this time.

A year later other strange visitors appeared at Noxie, a few miles north of Nowata. The man who had the largest number of sightings, farmer Kenneth Tosh, first encountered one of the things on the evening of September 1, 1975, when he and a friend heard it clawing on the screen door of a dilapidated house twenty feet from the Tosh residence.

"We walked over by that house," Tosh told Clark, "and it was standin' there watchin' us. I don't know how long it had been there. We walked towards it and it started growlin' at us.

"I'd say it was seven or eight feet tall. It had hair all over its body, a dark brown, blackish-brown color, anywhere from an inch and a half to two inches long. It had hair all over everything but around its eyes and its nose. That was the only part where I could see the skin on it.

"The eyes glowed in the dark, reddish-pink eyes. You don't need light or anything to shine on 'em like most other animals. They glow without a light bein' on 'em.

"We was about ten feet away from it. We just ran away and it ran, too.

"About two hours later we seen it again. It was over by the barn, on top of the barn, across the road from me. And then we seen it two nights later after that and it was about every other night we seen it for positive. It was about a week or two and then people got so busy comin' out here that we didn't see it there for a while, and we thought it was gone and then about two weeks later we spotted it again. It was still there."

Another witness was Marion Parret, a friend of Tosh's. Parret saw it for the first time one night when he was sleeping and "it poked its face in the window above the door," he reported. "It looked like someone's face shaved high on the cheekbone."

Parret actually shot at the manimal on three occasions with a .30-.30 hunting rifle. He was sure he had hit it each time, but the creature's only response was once to swat at its arm as if brushing away a mosquito.

"I was in Vietnam thirteen months," Parret said, "and I'm more scared here than I was over there. At least over there I knew what was out there. Here I don't."

Tosh, like Parret and the deputies before him, had the same problem trying to bring down the creature. Once, he claims, he and two companions opened up on it with two shotguns and a .22 rifle. "I didn't see how we could miss," he said, "but it didn't even holler. It just ran off." It left no blood in its path, either.

From all indications the creature had been in the Noxie area some months before it appeared to significant numbers of locals and attracted media attention. Researcher Hayden Hewes, who came to Noxie to investigate reports, maintains that he talked with 24 persons who said they had seen or heard the thing. Gerald Bullock of Noxie realized he had been hearing the creature for about six months after he encountered it one Sunday night near Tosh's place.

"The sound," he said, "is like a kid screamin'. Anyway that's how it sounded to me. It was probably about fifty to seventy-five yards out there and we just seen the eyes of it. They [the eyes] looked like they was kinda reddish, an inch apart, like a couple of little old flashlight bulbs hanging out there in the air. It kinda smelled like dead fish to me.

"We had another gentleman drive in there about fifteen minutes after we seen it. He come in and his lights shined on off the road there and he seen it crossing the road about fifty yards from where about as far as your headlights will reach.

"I still hear that noise, you know, right now. I heard it last night [October 11, 1975] when I came home. But for a long time you know I didn't know what it was. I heard that thing probably a long time before they ever said anything about it, going back probably six months or so. There's people living south of us and I'd thought maybe it might have been one of their little kids. But I guess it wasn't."

Bullock lived half a mile from the Tosh place. A small creek separated their land.

Everyone who saw it remarked on the manimal's awful stench. "It's hard to place just what it smells like," Tosh said. "It smelled like rotten eggs or sulphur. Or it was like somebody left a bunch of dirty diapers, wet, for a while."

The only physical evidence the creature left was a print which Tosh examined before the hordes of gun-toting, beer-guzzling curiosity seekers descended on the scene and destroyed it. Tosh recalls that it "was about eight inches across the toe, about two inches across the heel, and flat-footed. It looked like maybe it had only three toes."

Tosh's final sighting, which took place late in September, was by far the strangest. While it raised all kinds of new questions, it did at least clarify one aspect of the mystery: why the Toshes and other witnesses were hearing different kinds of monster sounds.

"The first time we heard it," he said, "it was growlin'. And then one time we heard it and it sounded like a woman hollerin' or screamin', and then a real strange whistle. Then we heard it and it sounded like a baby bawlin'. And then my sister-in-law and them, they said they was hearin' it last week [week of October 5-11]. They said it hollered and it sounded like it was laughin' real loud. It was such a sound that it was enough to give you a headache if you listened to it and it was close enough to you."

It developed that the reason for all this was that there were at least *two* creatures in the Noxie area.

"My brother-in-law was out and we was lookin' around," Tosh said. "We heard one. Then about that time there was another one out behind us and they was callin' towards each other. That's when we knew that there was two of 'em.

"One of 'em had red eyes and the other had yellow eyes. They was about 300 yards away from each other, just callin' to each other, I guess.

"Their sounds was a little different. One of 'em, the one with red eyes, was more like a woman screamin'. The other one sounded more like a baby bawlin'.

"The one with the yellow eyes was more of a grayish color than the other one. And it was about half a foot shorter. They probably weighed between 300 and 500 pounds."

In an October 12, 1975, interview, Tosh told Clark that his sister-in-law had seen the creature—or one of the creatures—just several days before, but he said she was unwilling to discuss it with outsiders because of all the ridicule the family have been subjected to. Tosh did say, however, that "she was in her bedroom gettin' ready for bed when she got this real weird feelin'. She started lookin' around the room and she looked over to the window. She had the curtains open a little bit and she could see the eyes lookin' in at her, and about a night or two later she seen 'em again.

"Then they started to hear 'em hollerin'. And she and my mother-in-law both could tell there was two of 'em because they could hear 'em hollerin' back and forth at each other."

They did not see anything, probably because of the darkness.

4.

No study of the manimal phenomenon would be complete without a summary of the Uniontown, Pennsylvania, incident, by now a classic—and for good reason, since it is beyond doubt the single most fascinating such report on record.

The episode began at around 9:00 p.m., October 25, 1973, when "Stephen Pulaski"* and at least fifteen other persons observed a red ball of light hovering high above a field just outside Uniontown. Pulaski, 22, grabbed a 30.06 rifle and drove to the scene with two ten-year-old boys, fraternal twins. As they approached, they noticed the UFO slowly descending toward the field. While it did so, the car's headlights dimmed mysteriously.

Pulaski brought the vehicle to a stop, and he and the two boys walked over the crest of a hill. Looking down at the field, they saw the UFO, now bright white in color, resting on or just above the ground. About a hundred feet in diameter, "it was dome-shaped," Pulaski recalled, "just like a big bubble. It was making a sound like a lawn mower." In addition, the three heard "screaming sounds" emanating from somewhere near the object.

Just then one of the boys yelled that there was something walking near the fence. From the light given off by the UFO, they could see two large ape-like creatures with glowing green eyes. A smell like that of "burning rubber" filled the air. Pulaski, who was not wearing his glasses at the time, thought the creatures were bears. To make sure, he fired a tracer slug directly over their heads. This did not seem to affect them in any way, but now Pulaski could see they were something very strange indeed.

Both had long, dark gray hair, and arms that almost reached the ground. The taller one, about eight feet in height, was running its left hand along the fence. The shorter, which stood slightly over seven feet tall, seemed to be hurrying along to keep up

---

* A pseudonym given the percipient by psychiatrist Berthold Eric Schwarz in his article "Berserk: A UFO-Creature Encounter," *Flying Saucer Review*, Vol. 20, No. 1 (1974).

with its companion. Both were making a whining sound, like a baby crying, and apparently were communicating with each other via this strange noise.

By this time one of the twins had fled the scene. But Pulaski stood his ground. He raised his rifle again and fired three times directly into the larger creature, which emitted a whine and reached its right hand toward the other creature. Suddenly the UFO vanished from sight and the noise it had been making ceased.

The manimals turned slowly around and returned to the woods. As they did so, the two remaining witnesses noticed that the area where the UFO had landed was glowing now a brilliant white color, so bright, in fact, that one could easily read a newspaper by it.

Pulaski and the boy noticed that their eyes were troubling them. They made their way to a telephone and called the police.

At 9:45 a state trooper arrived on the scene with Pulaski. The luminous area, about 150 feet in diameter, was still glowing, though less intensely than before. The farm animals, horses and cattle, would not go into the area but would stop just outside it.

When the two men approached the area where the creature had appeared, they heard crashing sounds in the woods, as if something were following them. When they stopped, the sounds stopped. Whatever was making the noise, the two knew it had to be something large—something that could break down trees as it walked.

About this time Pulaski was getting thoroughly hysterical, forcing the officer to abandon his plan to go over to the lighted area to examine it more closely. As they started back to the patrol car, the sounds in the trees started again. Pulaski swore that a "brown object" was moving toward them and fired off his one remaining bullet.

By now Pulaski's manner was beginning to unnerve the officer as much as the weird events going on around them. Suddenly he screamed that something was coming out of the woods toward them, and both jumped into the car and drove about fifty yards before the officer realized he was in the safety of his car. He stopped, turned the vehicle around, and shone the headlights into the trees. He saw nothing, not even the glowing area, which had disappeared.

The officer phoned Stan Gordon, head of the Westmoreland County UFO Study Group, an organization which had worked with the local police forces in the investigation of other creature sightings in the area. At 1:30 a.m. Gordon arrived in the company of four other members of his group. While the twins stayed behind in Pulaski's truck, Gordon's crew, along with Pulaski and his father, searched the area for evidence. The glowing ring was long gone and there were no markings on the hard ground. The radiation level was normal.

At 1:45 the Pulaskis, who were standing by the truck, shouted that the nearby farmhouse area had suddenly lit up with a glow. The group checked out the scene but found nothing unusual.

Dr. Schwarz describes the incredible events that followed:

> The team and the two Pulaskis walked up from the truck towards the area where the creatures were observed. It was about 2:00 a.m. Suddenly the bull (in a nearby field) was scared by something. Stephen's dog also became alarmed and started tracking something. The dog kept looking at a certain spot by the edge of the woods, but the group didn't see anything. George Lutz was asking Stephen some questions when all of a sudden Stephen began rubbing his

head and face. George Lutz asked him if he was OK, and Stephen then began shaking back and forth as if he were going to faint. George Lutz and Mr. Pulaski, Sr., grabbed Stephen. Stephen ... is over 6'2" tall and weighs around 250 pounds. He then began breathing very heavily and started growling like an animal. He flailed his arms and threw his father and George Lutz to the ground. His dog then ran towards him as if to attack, and Stephen went after the dog. The dog started crying. George Lutz and Mr. Pulaski were calling to Stephen to come back, that it was all right, and that they were returning to the car.

Then Dennis Smeltzer suddenly said, "Hey, Stan, I'm starting to feel lightheaded." Dennis became very weak and felt faint. His face was pale.

Dave Baker and Dave Smith went over to help Dennis. Then Dave Baker began to complain about having trouble breathing.

During all this, Stephen was running around, swinging his arms, and loudly growling like an animal. Suddenly he collapsed on his face into a heavily manured area. Shortly afterwards he started to come out of it and said, "Get away from me. It's here. Get back."

Just then Stephen and Stan, as well as the others, smelled a very strong sulphur or chemical-like odor.

George Lutz said, "Let's get out of here." Then he and Mr. Pulaski, Sr., were helping Stephen along when, suddenly on the way down the hill, Stephen pointed and yelled: "Keep away from the corner! It's in the corner!"

Stephen kept mumbling that he would protect the group. He also mumbled that he saw a man "in a black hat and cloak, carrying a sickle." He told Stephen, "If Man doesn't straighten up, the end will come soon." He also said, "There is a man here now, who can save the world." Stephen also said that he could hear his name—"Stephen. Stephen."—being called from inside the woods. When he collapsed, Stephen's glasses fell off.

On the way down, as Stephen was coming out of his confused state, his father handed him the glasses and Stephen asked whose they were. Stan asked if he could see OK and he said, "Just fine."

Subsequently Dr. Schwarz conducted psychiatric interviews with Pulaski, finding that the percipient had no past record of such dissociative, disoriented behavior. Nonetheless there was a history of violence and unhappiness in his life, which Schwarz thought may have caused Pulaski to react as he did. That is certainly possible but it really doesn't explain the dog's reaction (so reminiscent of another dog's at Sharpsville, Indiana), or the foul odor that surrounded him during the period of the trance—unless, of course, all of this was psychokinetically generated.

During the interview Pulaski would drift in and out of trance states. Recalling his vision of the man in black, he said:

Was it a dream? I heard a crying noise. I could see a man in a black robe, carrying a scythe. Behind this man was fire and in front of him was a force, and in this force were the creatures. They were calling, "Stephen! Stephen!" One was laughing. It was a tantalizing laugh, and making me mad. My hands were clenched tight. Behind us was a big light. In this light something was telling me to go forward. "Go forward. Come on!" It was edging me. I could see myself as crazy, as a man so powerful that I wasn't scared of anything. The creatures kept calling me and the light kept saying: "Go, my son, you can't be hurt." I think of a mother sheep calling to her little lambs. As I walked to the edge of the woods, the creatures kept wailing. I looked at them and all I could think of was death and the faceless form in the black robe who was commanding these things to kill me—it was hate ... a hatred for everything. I knew that these things came from this force and if they got to the light they would be destroyed. The tension was so terrific that I passed out. Then I heard, "He is here—He is here." But who is He? Somebody was putting a puzzle in my head. My hands and ankles were hurting. Somebody was telling me that these people are going to destroy themselves. I kept seeing the date 1976—1976. It popped out of my mouth: "If these people don't straighten out, the whole world will burn" . . .

I'm living in hell now. What I'm telling you happened before. This is how the world was destroyed. It will be very soon, and this world will be gone. Somebody better find out before long or the world will end. We're destroying the world. What's the fire? What's going to happen is burning. Is there someone smarter than us that is playing upon us, laying a picture or puzzle out for us? It seems stupid but it seems like I *have* to tell the President of the United States, because somebody else has to know. It seems that somebody else is also being told at the same time, but they're not going to do it. They're scared. I don't know what happened in the field, or what these guys told you, but I felt like an animal. If you could find the one who would believe me—1976 is not far off. I don't believe America is going to live to be 200 years free, because that's been getting to me, too. And the world will go. Man will destroy himself.

Pulaski's "vision" is a strikingly interesting one, and as we already have seen, this is not the first time apocalyptic ideas have been associated with the appearance of a manimal. The fundamentalist population of Roachdale, for example, saw the creature's presence as proof that the Day of Judgment was at hand.

Even more specifically, however, we have the vision of California psychic Joyce Partise, who, handed a sealed envelope containing the photograph of a Bigfoot print, announced (according to B. Ann Slate's "Gods from Inner Space," *UFO Report,* April 1976), "This envelope is like a death certificate! I foresee an impending disaster ... I keep getting the name John ... What could that mean? I see people gathered together, frightened and praying. Some think it's spiritual, those craft in the sky. Some think it's the so-called Second Coming, but God help them!"

Mrs. Partise saw the Bigfoot as subterranean creatures somehow associated with UFOs, and UFOs as associated with the impending doom of the human race.

Her mention of "John" in this context is extraordinarily revealing. In *The Unidentified* we discussed in detail the remarkable contact claims of Paul Solem, an Arizona man who seemed to be able to produce UFOs on command, and the witnesses to these UFOs were not just credulous types but included skeptical newspaper reporters as well. On one of these occasions, as *Prescott (Ariz.) Courier* editor Joe Kraus watched, Solem went into a trance and repeated words allegedly received through mental communication with a being aboard the ship.

"Great sorrow and fear will be coming to this planet very soon," the "Venusian" supposedly said, "and few will escape it. Our leader as spoken of in Hopi prophecy is already here on Earth in mortality and is known as the Apostle John, the same as in the New Testament. The white brother shall be introduced by a huge fire and the earth shall quake at his arrival."

Pulaski's "voices" told him "He is here," and apparently the answer to the percipient's question, "Who is He?" is "John." Pulaski's vision is right out of St. John's Book of Revelation in the New Testament. The man in black is the devil, who traditionally appears from time to time in the company of bizarre creatures. Men in black (MIB), of course, have long been a part of the UFO phenomenon, going back at least as far as 1905 and that year's sighting wave in Wales, which came in the midst of a hysterical religious revival.* According to the *Barmouth Advertiser* of March 30, 1905:

> In the neighborhood dwells an exceptionally intelligent young woman of the peasant stock, whose bedroom has been visited three nights in succession by a man dressed in black. This figure has delivered a message to the girl which she is frightened to relate.

Years later, during the post-1947 Flying Saucer Era, other persons would claim encounters with menacing men in black, some of whom would impart messages "too frightening to relate." These messages usually would involve prophecies of the earth's imminent destruction.

Such visions are also a staple of contactee lore. In these cases, the benevolent space people seem to lament our fate and hold out the hope that we can straighten ourselves out before it's too late. The malevolent MIB, on the other hand, apparently feel that we have it coming to us.

We are not prepared to take these gloomy visions

---

* *The Unidentified*, pp. 116-19.

literally, since human history is littered with failed prophecies about the end of the world. But clearly these mean *something* and Pulaski is certainly right when he says that "someone . . . is laying a picture or puzzle out for us." But what is it?

5.

Any summing up of the data we have examined so far must necessarily be filled with qualifications, since the sole universal feature of these reports is the general description of manimals as hairy, heavy, and hominoid—and even that will come into question shortly. Nonetheless, these points can be made:

1.) In many of the incidents the creature's eyes are self-luminous. The color of this light is most often red, and sometimes green or yellow.

2.) It usually emits a foul odor, often compared to decaying meat, rotting garbage, or sewage.

3.) It is invulnerable to bullets.

4.) It is usually retiring in its behavior, although sometimes destructive to livestock and wildlife.

5.) It makes a variety of sounds, the most frequent of them a low growl or a high-pitched screech which may remind percipients of a baby crying or a woman screaming.

6.) It usually does not leave tracks. When it does, such tracks may be: two-toed, three-toed, four-toed, five-toed, and even six-toed. Even prints which have the same number of toes may have dramatically different shapes in different cases.

This much said, unsatisfactory as it may be, we enter an even denser thicket of uncertainty, and it begins to look as though we are the victims of some cruel cosmic joke. Far from knowing answers, we may not even know the questions. In the case of the Uniontown episode, for example, to whom shall we turn—the ufologist, the biologist, the psychologist, or the demonologist?

The incident at Uniontown was only one of many creature reports being made in western Pennsylvania during 1973 and 1974. Some were of classic manimals, several appearing in the company of UFOs. In one instance, three women driving in a wooded area supposedly came upon a landed rectangular object, from whose door a ramp was lowered and three apelike creatures emerged, disappearing into the trees. In another, two teenage girls reported seeing a manimal with white hair and glowing red eyes; it was, they said, "carrying a luminescent sphere in its hand." In yet another a witness is said to have fired on a creature, which then vanished in a flash of light.

Absurd, all of it, but the observers of these occurrences were so numerous, and so many of sterling character, that the authorities were forced to take them seriously, even if individually or collectively the stories made no sense.

When Allen V. Noe of the Society for the Investigation of the Unexplained probed the mystery, puzzled by the sudden influx of reports of what he thought to be an "eastern Bigfoot," he ended up noting in *Pursuit*, the SITU journal, "We are unnerved, to put it mildly, to think that there might be five types wandering about in western Pennsylvania." Actually, as Noe himself would come to realize, that was an extremely conservative estimate. Some of the creatures resembled nothing so much as—if you will pardon the expression—"werewolves."

Not that werewolf reports are anything particularly new, even in modern-day America. During July and August 1972, a number of people in Toledo and Defiance, Ohio, swore they had seen something which appeared to be "human, with an oversized, wolflike head, and an elongated nose," and between six and eight feet in height. Witnesses said it "had huge hairy feet, fangs, and ran from side to side, like a caveman in the movies." It also possessed glowing red eyes. A trainman working along the tracks near downtown Defiance claimed that the thing had sneaked up behind him in the early morning darkness and clobbered him with a two-by-four board.

"We don't know what to think," Police Chief Donald Breckler said, "but now we're taking it seriously."

In the meantime, during the second week of August, people living near Cleveland's Brookside Park were seeing a more conventional manimal, this one huge, black-haired and apelike. Again the authorities conceded that the witnesses were probably telling the truth. "These people seem very sincere about what they saw," investigating officers said. "It scared the bejabbers out of them." Richard Merrill of the Cleveland Zoo denied that either of the two resident gorillas had escaped.

The final werewolf sighting took place in southwestern Ohio (Defiance is in the northwestern, Toledo in the northeastern parts of the state) one night late in October. Mr. and Mrs. Ed Miller of Carlisle had driven out into the countryside between Carlisle and Germantown to look for a license plate that had fallen off the car earlier. Mrs. Miller happened to look across a field and she noticed a black, partially erect figure running on two legs. "It turned and came at us," she told the *Middletown Journal*, "and then it crouched down and was almost crawling. I screamed for my husband to take me home. I was scared to death."

When the Millers returned home, they told three teenage friends about their experience. Excited, the youths jumped into a car and raced out to the scene, where they observed the same creature and the same behavior. They, too, decided to get out of there.

"Then we went back out," Mrs. Miller said. "But

we still couldn't get a close look at it. It would start to run toward the car, standing up, but then it would crouch down and hide in the weeds. And it howled at us, a loud snarling, hissing sound."

Mr. and Mrs. Gary Moore of Carlisle went separately to the area. Because of the darkness they could not tell how tall the thing was but they could see that it was "wide." They were certain it was not a man. Its eyes, which were huge, "glowed like fluorescence in the light of the car." Its face and body were very hairy.

There is a long tradition of werewolf lore among the Navaho Indians of Arizona and New Mexico, and in modern times the entire question gets hopelessly confused with manimal and UFO phenomena.

In *Flying Saucer Occupants,* for instance, Coral and Jim Lorenzen relate a story told by a friend, who said that around midnight on June 9, 1960, she had seen a little broad-shouldered, long-armed figure in the headlights of her car. It appeared to have no mouth, nose, or ears on its pumpkin-shaped head, but two yellowish orange-glowing eyes were visible.

In the fall of 1965, Roger Heath saw something quite similar. In a letter to Loren Coleman, he wrote:

> I was driving north from Winslow, Arizona, toward the three mesas of the Hopi villages. Nearer the 2nd Mesa end of the road than the Winslow end, and I would guess in the vicinity of Little Jedito Wash, I saw what I first thought was a man charred from an auto wreck crawling from a wash onto the road. I realized almost at once that it would have to be an awfully small man with long arms. I had a gun, an over and under, in the car. I stopped, in short order did the following: rolled down my window, poked the gun out same, turned around and went back. I saw this thing in a kind of hand scramble

headed out the same side, the east, of the road from where I assumed it had come. I did not fire.

Heath described the being as about three feet tall, shiny black (probably fur, he thought), without apparent ears, and having a roundish "harmless-looking face." It departed with a kind of hop, scrambling with its hands. The only detail on the face he clearly recalled was a reddish area over the eyes.

He showed drawings of the thing to the Hopis and Navahos. The Navahos identified it as a "skin-walker"—their name for the werewolf.

A "skin-walker" showed up in the South Valley section of Albuquerque, New Mexico, during October 1966. On the 14th of that month the *Albuquerque Journal* reported that the Clifford McGuire family had complained to the deputy sheriff about "a monster about five feet tall, hairy, and with a small blank face and crying like a baby [that] has roamed through their backyard several times in the past three weeks." The McGuires' eighteen-year-old son went out one night and was struck by something which knocked him unconscious. When he awoke, he found fork-shaped footprints near him. Thereafter, every time the creature reappeared, the McGuires' radio would stop playing, and the young man would feel a pain in the chest. Police officers, taking the stories seriously, said the family was "pretty rational about it—there's something out there." The "monster" was reported fifteen to twenty times in the following week, though apparently a prankster dressed in a costume was responsible for some of the supposed sightings. One informant told the *Albuquerque Tribune* that during the late 1930s and early 1940s residents in the same area had seen the same or a very similar creature.

In January 1970 four Gallup, New Mexico, youths —Clifford Heronemus, Robert Davis, Carl Martinez and David Chiaramonte—claimed to have seen a "werewolf" near Whitewater. They saw a "hairy thing with two legs" pacing their car, which was going about 45 miles per hour.

"It was about five foot seven, and I was surprised it could go so fast," Heronemus said. "At first I thought my friends were playing a joke on me, but when I found out they weren't, I was scared!

"We rolled up the windows real fast and locked the doors of the car. I started driving faster, about sixty, but it was hard because that highway has a lot of sharp turns. Someone finally got a gun out and shot it. I know it got hit and it fell down, but there was no blood. It got up again and ran off. I know it couldn't be a person because people cannot move that fast." *

Tony Zecca passed the same spot earlier in the evening. He also saw something, but he didn't think it was a werewolf, but rather a man from a flying saucer. He did not mention whether or not he had seen the saucer.

6.

One of the creatures observed during the Pennsylvania monster scare was something that looked more like a cross between a human being and a cat than the by now "commonplace" human/ape blending. Another beast resembled the "conventional" manimal in all ways except that its hair was *tan*. We are about to take an even deeper plunge into the abyss of the absurd.

---

* Four decades ago anthropologist William Morgan talked of the human-wolves with a Navaho named Hahago, who said, "They go very fast." "How fast?" Morgan asked. "They can go to A. in an hour and a half," Hahago replied. Morgan noted, "It takes four hours by automobile." ("Human-Wolves Among the Navaho," *Yale Publications in Anthropology*, XI, 1936.)

We can start with an undated clipping (ca. 1964) in our files, citing the testimonies of two young campers on Mt. Tamalpais in Marin County, California, who were disturbed on three occasions during July by a very strange animal—or actually *two* very strange animals, since on one occasion they heard it "chittering" back and forth with another, which apparently was hidden in the bushes.

Speaking of the one they were able to observe, Paul Conant said, "Its head was close to its body and below the shoulders it was very muscular. No ears could be seen." Neither did it possess a tail. It seemed to weigh around 200 pounds *and its tracks indicated that it walked on two feet.*

All unlikely enough, to be sure, but on November 9, 1968, a Mr and Mrs. Cataldo of Lorain, Ohio, reportedly encountered a similar phenomenon.

At about 5:45 a.m. a loud *bump* on the roof of their house awoke the couple. The bump was followed by the sound of something moving near their bedroom window. When they looked up at the window, they saw a huge face staring down at them. The thing's two front paws or hands were resting on the windowsill.

Mr. Cataldo leaped out of bed and frantically searched for his gun, but by the time he located it, the creature was gone from the window. Running on two legs, it dashed around the east side of the house, weaving from side to side like an ape (a detail we have heard before), crossed two streets, and disappeared into the woods.

The Cataldos said the creature stood about six feet tall. Its front side was a light grayish brown, the rest of the body a darker shade of the same color. It resembled, they stated, "a large lion of around 600 pounds." Lions, as we all know, are quadrapedal.

The palm prints found on the windowsill looked humanlike, except that "the prints were reversed and ran in a straight line." Interestingly, the creature seen at Latrobe, Pennsylvania, in September 1973 (the incident alluded to in the first sentence of this section) was described as having hands that were *turned backward.*

That same year—1968—a logging crew in British Columbia had several run-ins with an equally weird creature. They first became aware of the presence of something out of the ordinary when they heard "hooting sounds" unlike anything they were familiar with. They also found footprints that were somewhat "catlike" but still decidedly unusual.

Not long after that, the foreman, a man named Woods, was walking through the Cedar Swamp when he heard the hooting so closeby that it terrified him, and he ran for the safety of his Caterpillar. From that time on, he took to carrying a pistol with him on his rounds.

Finally, Woods got to see the thing. He was driving the Caterpillar one day when he heard something behind him. He turned around to see a creature (which he first thought was a mountain lion because of its tawny color) leap from the trees, land on its back feet, stretch out, and jump across the skid into a tree on the opposite side. It all happened in one quick moment.

Woods was stunned. What he had seen resembled some kind of bizarre cross between a cat and an ape.

Veteran Bigfoot hunter Rene Dahinden went to the scene and spent ten days investigating. Though he himself heard nothing unusual, he did interview buck-bush pickers (buck bush is used in wreaths) who had. They told him they had found an unusual bed which they thought might be connected with the creature in some way.

Dahinden examined the bed, which was situated on an old skid trail overgrown with small (seven- to ten-foot) trees. It was the only sunny spot there.

The ground was covered with snow two and a half feet deep, but there was no snow on the bed, which was three to five feet long, three feet wide and one foot high. Nearby and underneath a dead tree was a hole about a foot and a half in diameter with a nest in it. Around this nest something had carefully placed a number of broken branches with the stems outward and the soft material arranged in the middle.

He found two or three different types of teeth marks on the bark, but the animal or animals responsible did not eat the bark. From these scratch marks Dahinden inferred that a bear could have been the cause, but the other evidence—most notably the fact that all the little twigs from around the bed were cleared away and in little piles—made him question that theory. Two old wolverine trappers, intimately familiar with the area, told him they had never seen anything like it; for that matter, neither had Dahinden, a longtime woodsman himself.

Across the lake from Salmon Run, where the loggers had made their sightings, Dahinden heard stories about monkeylike creatures which apparently were different from the Bigfoot. One woman related that once her daughter had run home frightened, saying she had seen a little hairy man carrying a bundle of moss.

It appears from all this that we are seeing one type of MA (the manimal) shading off into another (the phantom panther). Already we have seen the shading in the "opposite" direction, toward sometimes robotlike "UFO occupants." But for the moment we are adrift in a twilight zone of ambiguity.

Our last series of cases comes out of southwestern Kentucky, where in the fall of 1973 farmers around the town of Albany were confronted with an impossible beast, its mate and its cub.

The "male" reportedly stood over three feet tall

at the shoulders when on all fours; it was also bipedal, and when on two legs it reached six feet. Its hair was dark brown or black, its tail, which it carried like a cat's, was long, bushy, and black. According to one witness, its head was shaped "like an ape/human with a flat face and nose with large nostrils. Its ears are like mule ears and will perk up."

We first heard of the affair when witness Rick Hall wrote the Indianapolis Zoological Society about it. The Society's Education Director, Richard G. France, referred Hall to Loren Coleman. Hall subsequently gave Coleman the following information:

> This animal is very cunning, agile and strong. It can toss a 300-lb. sow around with ease and can leap over fences, with a good distance between foot tracks—10 ft. to 15 ft. It has wiped out two herds of pigs and has been said to have killed a calf and a dog. At night when it is in the area the livestock all start running the pens, while all the wildlife seems to have disappeared from the local area. The grandfather of the girl I'm engaged to owns the mountain, and it's supposed to be loaded with wildlife. But since the sightings the wildlife has moved, and I'm not sure why.*
>
> We tried to track this animal with several dogs, but after they caught its scent, they wouldn't track it, acted scared . . . [The tracks were three-toed and distinctly manimal-like.]
>
> The farmers have seen this animal watch them as they work in the fields as well as engineers who are building a new road in the area. My

---

* "The woods where the cries [of an Ohio manimal] were heard seems to be dying, and many trees have fallen. There appears to be an almost complete absence of birds or animals in this woods, yet across a field there is another wooded area where everything is lush and green, and where animal and bird life abounds."— Allen V. Noe, "And Still the Reports Roll in," *Pursuit*, January 1974.

girl's aunt went home one evening and found it just outside their back door eating old table scraps. She shot at it six times with a pistol & 17 times with a .22 rifle and she says she missed it [?]. But the animal ran about 100 yards and sat at the edge of the woods & cornfield, sat on its haunches and watched her, but disappeared when her husband went after it.

Hall himself claimed to have seen two adults and one "cub"—presumably a "monster family." He and other local folk believed the creatures dwelt in caves and abandoned mines in the area.

In late October eighteen-year-old Gary Pierce allegedly was chased off the mountain by the creature and subsequently had to be placed in the hospital, for hysteria, rather than any physical injury.

Finally, a farmer named Charlie Stern caught it prowling around his barn. He opened fire on it and apparently wounded the creature, which he then tracked to a cave that he chose not to enter. Sightings subsided after this incident.

In many ways this is a classic creature story. We have here the destruction of livestock, the beast's enormous strength, the ability to jump great distances, the capacity to terrify other animals (primarily dogs)—all integral parts of what might be called the Monster Archetype.

And this takes us inevitably to the Phantom Cats and Dogs.

CHAPTER FOUR

Phantom Cats and Dogs

1.

On Friday, April 10, 1970, Mike Busby of Cairo, Illinois, was driving on Route 3 .to Olive Branch, Illinois, to pick up his wife. At about 8:30 p.m., a mile south of Olive Branch, on the dark, mostly deserted road that parallels the edge of the vast Shawnee National Forest, Busby's automobile quit running. He got out of his car and had begun to release the hood latch when he heard a noise on his left. He was startled to see two quarter-sized, almond-shaped, greenish-glowing eyes staring at him.

Before he had a chance to move, the strange form, six feet tall, black and upright, advanced on him. Without warning it hit him hard on the face with two padded front feet, and they rolled over together to the left side of the road. "It" remained on top of Busby as the two tumbled about. Shredding his shirt to pieces, it inflicted wounds on his left arm, chest and abdomen with dull two-inch claws. Busby desperately held its mouth open at arm's length. Certain that it was trying for his throat, he tried to keep clear of its long yellow feline teeth.

While unable to see its features very well (and probably not much interested in the question just at that moment), Busby did feel something "fuzzy" around the mouth which he took to be whiskers. Its general body hair or fur was short and wiry ("like steel wool," he told Loren Coleman) to the touch, and although it was dry it smelled like wet hair. The creature emitted deep, soft growls unlike anything Busby had ever heard before.

Soon a diesel truck passed. Busby now saw clearly that the thing's color was a slick shiny black. He also could see the "shadow of its tail." The truck's headlights apparently scared the creature, and with "heavy footfalls," Busby said, it loped off across the road.

Dizzy, his body aching, Busby crawled back to his car. It started without trouble.

The truck driver, John Hartsworth, was waiting for Busby in Olive Branch. Hartsworth explained that he had been unable to brake his truck and stop for help. From what he had seen in his headlights, however, he said the thing looked like a big cat.

Mike Busby was treated in St. Mary's Hospital in Cairo by a Dr. Robinson, who gave him two inoculations, one for tetanus, another for the relief of pain. Busby's brother Don told Coleman that in the days following the encounter Mike required aid in walking, was often dizzy, and fainted once.

Mike Busby was by no means the first person from extreme southern Illinois to claim an encounter with a "black panther." Four years earlier, in April 1966, the *Cairo Evening Citizen*, recounting the most recent of a long series of reports, asked, "Does the black panther really roam the Shawnee Forest wilderness in Alexander County?" On April 13 Joseph Moad and his wife had gone outside to see what was disturbing the livestock on their farm near Elco. "I turned on a floodlight and could see his eyes shining," Moad told Game Warden Peter Clarke. "He screamed and it was the keen scream of a panther, not the coarse scream of a bobcat or cougar." Moad, who had a deer rifle with him, got off one quick shot before the animal got away.

Commented the *Evening Citizen*:

> One popular version of the black panther in Alexander—still not known to be true or not—is that many years ago a circus train or truck was wrecked in the area and some black panthers escaped into the hills and were never found.
> Thomas Coleman, Cairo IVC service officer and a native of Elco, recalls that in his youth frequent search parties were organized to tramp the hills looking for the black panther after someone had reported seeing one.
> "We would take our guns and go out in large parties looking for them," Coleman said. "We never were able to see one or find a trace of them."
> Deputy Sheriff Gene Rambeau is positive that when he was a child and living in rural Alexander County, he and others saw a black panther that had gone inside a house.
> "It dashed out the door and streaked off fast as greased lightning," Rambeau said.
> There are others in the county who will vow that they have seen the elusive beast.

Conventional zoology, unfortunately, does not allow us to accept stories like these—and there are a great many more just like them. To begin with, there are no panthers, or pumas, or mountain lions—all popular names for the same animal, known scientifically as *Felis concolor,* in Illinois, where they have been extinct since 1850. In fact, except for isolated groups in the Florida Everglades, there are supposed to be no panthers east of the Rocky Mountains, though some zoologists now concede that a small number may have survived in several far eastern states and provinces.

For another thing, New World panthers are not, except in very rare instances, black. In 1843 a melanistic (i.e., black) puma supposedly was killed in the Carandahy River section of Brazil. It is not known what became of the body. There have been several so far undocumented reports of a black subspecies of the Florida panther, but to date no one has photographed, captured, or exhibited a black puma.

The bobcat (*Lynx rufus*), a native of North America, has a range overlapping most of the areas where black panthers have been seen. Bobcats are smaller than pumas, and melanistic bobcats do exist. But they are so rare that only two have ever been caught, at different times in the same place, Martin County, Florida.

Melanism in the *Felidae,* the family of cats, runs the highest, zoology tell us, in the moist tropics and subtropics. The most frequent numbers of black mutations occur in the jaguar (*Panthera onca*) of Latin America and the leopard (*Panthera parus*) of Africa and Asia.

In summary, the likelihood of black panthers in North America, even a tiny handful of them, is slight. Yet reports of them are so persistent and widespread that exasperated zoologists and game wardens have taken to calling them the "flying saucers of the animal world"—an identification whose true significance we shall examine later.

Finally, panthers, whatever their color and whatever their reputation, do not usually attack people. As the late Ivan T. Sanderson observed in *Living Mammals of the World,* "The Puma is the great coward of all the great or not so great cats. Despite voluminous fictional tales and innumerable accounts published as fact, the number of authenticated cases of deliberate attacks upon human beings by these animals is so paltry as to be almost nonexistent and most of these are open to some doubt. The animal is a retiring beast . . ."

Well, then, just what did attack Mike Busby? And just what are the people of Alexander County and other places seeing anyway?

That is not an easy question to answer. We have here the bare hints of an enigma so vast and so impenetrable that, unlike UFOs and Bigfeet, it has remained virtually invisible to society at large. Even Forteans, with a few rare exceptions (Charles Fort being one of them), have failed to recognize its significance or even its occurrence. But what we seem to be dealing with, as will become apparent, are thousands of accounts, spanning at least two centuries and six continents, of unexplained, large, and often dangerous catlike creatures whose appearance and behavior are not really those of any known animal. We are confronted with sightings of "animals" that should not be, doing things they are not supposed to do, in places they should not roam, and doing them in patterns that repeat themselves with discomforting regularity. The sheer volume of these reports leaves us with only two alternatives, neither of them a very happy one: either we reject them all as hoaxes and mistakes, or we forget everything we know about conventional zoology and search for answers elsewhere.

2.

Let us begin our search with an event reported in the August 3, 1823, issue of the Boston-based *New England Farmer*.

The account has it that, not long before, people near Russelville, Kentucky, had begun seeing a "tiger of a brindle color with a most terrific front—his eyes are described as the largest ever seen in any animal." Four men, two of them armed, got a close view of the beast. The two with guns

> fired on him at the distance of 50 yards without forcing him to move from his stand; a furious look and appalling brow frightened the two men without guns who fled to town. Experienced marksmen continued to fire, and on the 12th shot the beast put off at full speed....
>
> When the news reached Russelville about 40 gentlemen repaired to the spot, and had a full view of the ground. The print which the paws of this animal made in the earth corresponds with the account given of his great bulk by those who had an opportunity of viewing him at a short distance for several minutes....
>
> The above Tiger was seen a few days after braving a dozen shots and making its way into the state of Tennessee, and there is still a prospect of its being taken....

But it never was, even though it is difficult to understand how "experienced marksmen" were unable to kill the beast, which was both large and still, at such comparatively close range.

We are reminded of a much more recent tale from Atlanta, Georgia, where in April 1958 two patrolmen emptied their service revolvers into a "black panther" as it charged "like a bullet" from a wooded area they were searching. "Both of us were firing at point-blank range," Officer J. F. Porter said. "I don't see how we could have missed it"—a complaint we have heard before from other Mystery Animal observers. The yellow-eyed creature ran between them and disappeared, uttering not a sound.

One night in December 1877, a badly frightened man appeared at the door of his employer, a wealthy farmer named Hunt, and blurted out an amazing story. At first Hunt did not believe him, but later events were to force him to change his mind.

Earlier in the evening, the young man, a member of one of two tenant families working for Hunt and living on his land, had gone to the village of Rising Sun, Indiana. On his way he had passed through an area midway between the farm and the village called "Halfway Place," a spot where Hunt's fence divided the cleared land from the woods which were locally called the "Black Forest" because of the height and thickness of the trees.

All this had taken place routinely and without incident. But it was on his way back, about 9:00 p.m., that something happened for which he was not prepared. "Some monstrous animal," he said, had come crashing out of the woods and pursued him down the road, clearly, he felt, intent on killing him. He felt that he barely had escaped with his life.

Several evenings later a young woman named Mary Crane was visiting a family on Hunt's farm and someone told her of the young man's experience. She laughed it off, but the story impressed her at least enough to insist someone accompany her when she left. No one was willing to oblige, so she went next door and got another young man to escort her to the village, just a mile away. The two set off in the dark.

As they entered the blackest part of the Black

Forest, Miss Crane and her companion suddenly heard a peculiar shriek from deep among the trees. Mary Crane whirled around to see two glowing eyes descending from the branches of a poplar not more than forty feet away, and to hear the sound of claws scraping against bark.

Deciding to get out of there fast, they sped off down the road and then stopped briefly to look behind them. For a moment they saw nothing—until the animal, "big as a good-sized calf, with a tail as long as a door," leaped onto the fence. Running along the rail of the fence, the creature moved rapidly toward them. The couple started to run again and had begun to outdistance the animal, when it bounded to the ground to follow them down the road, quickly gaining on them.

At this point the young man, who had had about all he could take, let go of Miss Crane's hand and dashed the short remaining distance to the village to sound the alarm—in the meantime leaving his companion to the mercy of the thing that had been stalking them. Soon Mary Crane felt the animal's claws ripping at her dress. She collapsed in a faint, awakening moments later to find herself pinned to the ground, and something licking her face. Knowing she could do nothing else, she lay motionless and prayed.

Shortly afterwards she heard voices. The animal perked up its ears, rose, and growled menacingly, looking for a moment as if it were going to charge the approaching villagers. Instead it let out a piercing shriek, jumped over the fence, and disappeared. The deeply shaken Miss Crane had to be carried to the village where she was treated with stimulants.

The next morning, a large party of men with hunting dogs tracked the creature for half a mile until its footprints, which measured over six inches across, were lost in the high ground. The hunt continued for the next two days to no avail.

As the *New York Times* observed, "The whole affair is wrapped in mystery, which the inhabitants of that region would like to have solved."

So would we. *Felis concolor* supposedly has been extinct in Indiana since 1850. Of course, one might argue, it is possible that one may have wandered back into its old haunts, but that would not explain the creature's ferocious behavior. After all, as puma authority Herbert Ravenel Sass once wrote, "Ninety-nine times out of a hundred a panther, meeting man, woman, or child in the woods, will flee as though from the Evil One himself." We also wonder about those "glowing" eyes. The eyes of a standard panther reflect light but are not luminous in themselves. We already have examined other reports of creatures with glowing eyes (Busby's the most recent example) and the Rising Sun incident may be another of these. Certainly the original account does not mention any light source which the eyes could have been reflecting. But we don't have enough information to arrive at any firm conclusions.

As the reader may have inferred by now, all mystery felines are not black. Some of them even look like conventional giant cats, and some of them undoubtedly are just that. For example, after numerous Minnesotans had reported sighting a mountain lion over a six-year period between 1945 and 1951, two conservation officers conducted an intensive investigation and determined that one or two panthers had meandered down from Canada into the northeastern and southwestern parts of the state.

But what interests us are sightings of catlike creatures that do not behave as large cats are supposed to behave. We are also concerned with reports of things that may resemble known varieties of cats but are woefully out of place—such as the African lion that terrorized central Illinois all through the month of July 1917.

3.

They called her "Nellie the Lion," an oddly affectionate nickname for a creature whose nasty temper made her anything but lovable.

Nellie, or her male companion (there seem to have been two giant cats, not just one), first managed to draw attention to itself by attacking Thomas Gullett, a butler at the Robert Allerton estate southwest of Monticello, while he was in the garden picking flowers. Gullett suffered only scratch marks, but the incident touched off a furor that didn't abate for weeks.

The affair had actually begun around Camargo a few days before, but the Monticello report was the first to receive press attention. It led to the forming of a 300-man posse which spent most of July 15 tramping through the thick woods near the Allerton place. While the hunters were engaged in this fruitless endeavor, the lion nonchalantly reappeared a quarter-mile away from the Allerton house and Mrs. Shaw, the chief housekeeper, got a good look. Unfortunately, she was one of the few persons in the vicinity not carrying a gun at that moment. Like Gullett she referred to the animal as an "African lioness."

On July 17 searchers discovered tracks five inches long and four inches wide near Decatur. Two fourteen-year-old boys, Earl Cavanaugh and Glyan Tulison, claimed to have seen the beast that day walking along Allen's Bend on the Sangamon River, a short distance east of Decatur.

As public hysteria mounted, residents of central and northern Illinois outdid themselves in silly behavior. On a number of occasions they mistook collie dogs for the lion, and one farmer distinguished himself by shooting a hole through the radiator of an approaching car; he had mistaken the headlights for the beast's shining eyes. The papers, of course, had a good time with this, and it must have helped casual readers dismiss the other reports as jokes.

But the families of Earl Hill and Chester Osborn of Decatur were not amused when the lion pounced on their car in an apparent attempt to get at them. The attack took place at 10:30 p.m. on July 29 as the two men and their wives motored west on the Springfield road. Hill and Osborn, sitting in the front seat, first caught sight of the big animal standing in the weeds alongside the road. Suddenly it leaped a distance of twenty feet and crashed into the car, which was traveling twenty miles an hour. The women in the back seat screamed as the creature struck the side of the vehicle and slid off onto the highway.

Osborn, who was driving Hill's car, turned around and headed back to Decatur to tell the police. Two officers and the two male witnesses immediately returned to the scene, to find the creature still there. When it saw them, it disappeared over a bank and the policemen, lacking heavy firearms, elected not to pursue it. At 1:30 a.m. two car loads of police returned with high-powered rifles to search the spot, but after some hours returned to town with nothing to show for their efforts.

On July 31, at about 3:00 p.m., James Rutherford, a farmhand, was driving a hay wagon past a gravel pit when he spotted a "large yellow, longhaired beast." As he gaped in terror, the animal regarded him without interest, then wandered off into a clump of bushes near a small creek. When the inevitable armed posse rushed to the scene, they found only its tracks, which, strangely enough, had claw marks in them. This extremely odd detail should have alerted the searchers to the fact that they were chasing something decidedly out of the ordinary, since virtually all members of the cat family possess retractile claws that do not customarily show in the prints. At any rate, continuing their search into the evening, they came upon the remains of a calf which its owner said had been missing four days.

After that, "Nellie" vanished as mysteriously as she had arrived, leaving behind her innumerable stories of mind-boggling events which the locals chose to forget as quickly as possible. And who can blame them? After all, who would want to try to explain what African lions were doing in Illinois?

Or on Long Island, for that matter? On June 20, 1931, police in Malverne, New York, took a call from Mrs. E. H. Tandy saying that a "lion" was walking around in her back yard. When officers arrived at the scene, the animal was gone; it had jumped over a fence, Mrs. Tandy explained. The lawmen were skeptical, but within the next couple of days two other Malverne residents had called with a similar story.

But that was not to be all. On the afternoon of the 24th, at nearby Albertson Square, Mr. and Mrs. George Ballis and their children saw a "monkey about half the size of a heavy-set man" drop from a tree and dash into bushes alongside the road. About ten persons eventually viewed the creature and agreed it was large, hairy, and had a long gray face.

4.

1948 was the year of the "varmint"—or the "varmints," depending on whose stories you choose to believe. At least four distinctly different animals figured in the reports of the witnesses. Two of the creatures sometimes worked as a pair. Another seems not to have been a member of the cat family at all. One bore enough of a resemblance to a conventional tan-colored puma to convince some individuals, though by no means all, that that in fact was what they were seeing. Most observers, perplexed, confessed they had no idea what it was. One even thought it might be a "wolf with yellow spots"!

The Great Varmint Scare began in the fall of 1947 when weird screeching cries disturbed the sleep of Fountain City people and, as a contemporary news account puts it vaguely, "cattle, sheep, and horses acted in an unusual manner." A group of citizens late one night saw a huge catlike beast in a roadway.

Richmond policeman Louis Danels had the most detailed sighting but did not make it public until months later. "It was so strange," he said, "that I just didn't mention it to anyone at the time. But now that other folks are seeing things and talking, I guess I can talk, too."

He and his family had been out on a casual Sunday afternoon drive along a road southwest of Centerville. "Suddenly," Danels related, "the strangest, most vicious-looking thing walked toward my car down the center of the road. It had long front legs, a large head with small pointed ears, and small glittering eyes."

Its back sloped down in an odd manner, and its body narrowed at the hips, ending in back legs considerably shorter than the front two.

"We got to within ten feet of it and it ran off the road into the weeds," Danels continued. "We all remarked that it was the most ferocious, evil-looking thing we ever had seen."

He thought it might be a hyena. Or anyway, he said, that's what it looked like to him.

It was only when the varmint started killing livestock, though, that the Hoosiers got riled. In mid-

July 1948, farmer Dorten Moore, who lived a mile southeast of Fountain City, complained to Sheriff Carl Sperling that something had slaughtered seven of his small hogs, eating their hearts and livers. Shortly thereafter Sheriff Sperling and three other law officers kept a vigil at Moore's place from dark to 3:00 a.m., but saw nothing.

A night or so later neighbor Harold Erskine heard a "strange caterwauling noise" over in Moore's fields, grabbed a gun, and scooted over to rouse Moore. They set out after whatever made the sound but it already had vanished, leaving in its wake still another butchered hog.

Another neighbor, Lewis Swain, heard a "strange whining call" on several occasions, and found a wide path through his wheatfield as if cut by the animal on the prowl. "Just like the one they found last year in the cornfield," he said. One farmer, unnamed, supposedly got chased out of his barn by an unidentified something.

The night of August 1, Clifford Fath, a game warden, and Charles Cornelius, a county conservation officer, testified they had encountered a varmint on the road between Quakertown and Roseburg. It was sitting in the middle of the road, and Fath had to swerve his car in order to avoid hitting the animal, which looked as though it might weigh close to 350 pounds. Frightened, it lunged at the car and crashed against its side, then fled off into the woods.

Fath and Cornelius hurriedly organized a posse. With the help of dogs they tracked the animal to a tree in whose branches it was hiding. Members of the group opened fire, but all they heard was the sound of something leaping into another tree deeper into the forest.

The next night a farmer near Liberty discovered the carcass of a 1000-pound bull in his pasture, one of many such accounts pouring into Fath's office.

Angry and unnerved farmers gathered in bands and beat through the backwoods, but the varmint eluded them easily.

One thing not hard to find was its tracks, which stretched along the sand at Silver Creek and measured six inches in length. "Such tracks are not those of any of the wildlife living in this section of the country," the *Richmond Palladium-Item* noted.

Three days later, during the evening hours of the fifth, an "African lion" rushed a fishing party at Elkhorn Falls south of Richmond. The party consisted of four adults and two children. According to Ivan Toney, who lived nearby, "About 7:30 p.m. a man came to the house and wanted to use the phone to call the sheriff. He said he and another man, along with their wives and two children, were fishing along the banks of the pool at the foot of the Elkhorn Falls. Their car was parked on the road near the gate to the lane leading to the Falls.

"He said the animal came up the stream from the south. When they sighted it, they started running for the car. They reached it, but the animal lunged at the car, then plowed through the fence into the sandy bar along the stream's edge."

The creature "looked like a lion with a long tail," the witnesses asserted, with bushy hair around the neck. Deputy Sheriff Jack Witherby, who examined the tracks it had left, described them as like "nothing I have ever seen before."

The morning of the 7th two farmboys, Arthur and Howard Turner, sixteen and fourteen, saw a strange shape while walking to the barn at 5:30. It appeared near a plum tree not far from the gate leading into the barnyard. To its right another animal stood on a rise of ground not 200 feet away. Arthur, who like other rural people in the Richmond area had taken to carrying a gun with him on his rounds, raised the rifle to his shoulder and fired away. The creatures wheeled around, jumped a gate, and escaped.

Curiously, the animals, while generally similar, were not identical. The first had the "appearance of a lion": large-headed, "shaggy," and brownish in color. The other, said the boys, "had more the appearance of a panther and was black."

The following afternoon farmers northeast of Abington, in Richmond's Wayne County, watched two varmints similar to the ones the Turners had seen, and the morning after that others sighted identical beasts in the same general locations. At 4:30 in the afternoon a "long black animal" crossed the Robert Martin farm near Middleboro. Police searches proved unproductive except for the usual discovery of five-toed tracks made by animals clearly weighing in excess of 300 pounds. (Ordinary panthers generally weigh no more than 200 pounds and they leave four-toed tracks.) Art Lecamp showed officers a spot in a ravine where apparently some large animal had bedded down for the night.

With panic growing and rumors spreading uncontrollably, many people were ready to shoot at anything that moved. Unfortunately for those trying to stem the rising tide of hysteria, the varmints were moving in closer to houses, even ones in town. One story had it that a giant cat had run a woman into her home. James Leo of Pennville, a little town west of Richmond, nearly fainted when he found a strange animal on his back porch on the morning of the 11th. With nothing to defend himself with but a butcher knife, he was considerably relieved when it sauntered away.

That evening police got a call from Robert Martin, who said he had fired at a varmint through the screen of his bedroom window. "I know I hit him," Martin insisted, "but I'm too scared to go out in the yard to see what I hit." A police check uncovered nothing, though Martin stuck to his story that the animal "reared up" after the second shot and fled in the darkness.

On the 12th a 100-man posse led by Deputy Witherby and H.B. Cottingham, a state conservation official, plowed through a cornfield and the woods near Middleboro. Earlier in the day, Cottingham, after studying the tracks near the Test Bridge south of Richmond, had expressed "an opinion only" that these were from "some type of wildcat." Other tracks, specifically those from Abington and Middleboro, were "different" and much larger.

Suddenly varmints were in other parts of Indiana as well. At Bedford, in the central part of the state, two lions were seen lying in a field near the Crane Naval Ammunition Depot on the 10th. One witness, Andrew Street, said he had hunted mountain lions before and knew one when he saw one. Armed Marine patrols were put on alert and ordered to shoot if they saw the animals. And at Gosport, over forty miles northwest of Bedford, William Sterwalt lost a 400-pound calf to something observer Keith McGinnis described as "long in body, black in color, with short perked-up ears and a long tail." It resembled a panther, he said. The same week Eugene Myers' dogs treed a screeching animal, but in the darkness Myers could not see exactly what it was.

Near Greenville, Ohio, twenty miles northwest of Richmond, Darke County Game Protector Robert Wiegand was investigating large tracks "definitely not made by a dog." After receiving several varmint reports, he interviewed George Royer, who at noon on the 19th watched a strange animal from a distance of twenty feet as it passed by the Slagle gravel pit. "I could not have mistaken it for something else," Royer said. "It was a black panther."

On the 22nd Orris Tate, a farmer in the Sand Creek, Indiana, area, found one of his pigs with claw marks four inches deep and several inches long over its right shoulder and with a hole under each of its front legs; miraculously it was still alive, though it died later in the day. In the ground nearby were mammoth five-inch tracks.

Near Peppertown on the morning of the 28th something jumped Henry Ferguson, Jr., from the rear while he was topping tobacco on a farm. He didn't get a good look at the animal, but it succeeded in tearing his trousers and shirt and cutting his arm before it streaked away. Ferguson's story started a flood of sightings in the area, about thirty miles southwest of Richmond. Most were of a big catlike creature dark yellow in color. There were more posses, now bigger than ever, and some shots got fired, but the prey never had any trouble escaping unscathed.

September 11 marks the last recorded 1948 appearance of the varmint. Harry Rodenberg and Ed Raffe, working on a roof at the Rodenberg farm, observed an animal "about the size of a wolf and having yellow spots." It did not harm any livestock.

For the time being Indiana had shaken itself of its nasty varmints. In January 1951, three persons at a farm near Noblesville in the central part of the state saw a giant panther, "five feet long and pitch black," which left tracks as big as the "palm of a woman's hand." It disappeared into a thicket along Stoney Creek after David Simons took a shot at it.

5.

Certain patterns begin to emerge, even though we have examined only a tiny fraction of the mystery cat reports in our possession. We have seen, first of all, the strange elusiveness of the beasts, shown in the absolute inability of even skilled hunters and trackers to kill or capture them (inevitably recalling Ivan Sanderson's dictum about Fortean phenomena in general: "we'll never catch them"). We have also noted their frightening hostility to human beings, and we have touched on the puzzling matter of clawed footprints.

With the 1948 Indiana varmints something new and extraordinarily significant emerges: a certain element of ambiguity enters the picture and we discover that reports don't quite "add up." Not only do we have sightings of three different kinds of unknown cats, we also have reports of a "hyena" and a "wolf with yellow spots." We will find that, the farther we pursue our Mystery Animals, the more difficult to follow the trail becomes.

Rather than detail the entire history of phantom cats in North America, an effort that would prove pointless and repetitive, let us consider a few representative incidents from the last three decades:

Abesville, Missouri, June 1945: A woman sitting with a baby in a shack near the town heard a scratching at the door. Opening it, she was terrified to see a huge catlike beast standing upright and staring at her. It had a long tail and big teeth, and in general did not look like anything she wanted to let into the house. She slammed the door and spent the next few minutes listening to it trying to break in. The following night it returned and again attempted to enter. When it left, she notified the neighbors, and dozens of them scoured the hollows trying to find it. Several of them got brief glimpses and one even got a shot at it.

For several weeks after, the locals lived in terror, hesitating to go out at night for fear of getting jumped. One person who did, a man named Warren, reported that it sprang at his truck and crashed against it several times trying to get in.*

Santee River, South Carolina, autumn 1948: Sam Lee, manager of the Rice Hope Plantation, and a companion, Troy T. Rogers, out looking for nighttime poachers, stopped at the White Oak Swamp about 10:30, got out of their truck and abruptly heard a "queer sound." Lee switched on his flashlight and saw a huge cat, "like a maneless lion," rear slowly upward and stand erect on its hind legs, staring eye level at the startled Lee, who was armed with only a small .22 rifle. Rogers was already back to the truck by the time it occurred to Lee to follow suit.

Queens County, New Brunswick, Canada, November 22, 1951: In yet another report of an erect panther,** we have this account from Herman Belyea, cited in Bruce S. Wright's *The Ghost of North America:*

> I was returning home about 6:00 p.m. I came to a pole fence and before crossing it hit it with my axe ... within seconds I heard five loud yells off in the woods. ... I walked about 100 yards further ... when I heard four or five more yells. I looked back and saw it coming leaping. I ran a short way when it overtook me, so I had to stop and face it. When I stopped it stopped and stood up on its rear legs with mouth open and

---

*In a 1955 issue of *Missouri Conservationist*, Chief Biologist Dunbar Robb of the Conservation Commission's Mammal Unit, after noting that "reports of 'panthers' have persisted through the years from many parts of the state," conceded "at least a half-dozen sightings were unquestionable. ... The return of the big cats [cougars: extinct in Missouri since 1927 and rare long before that] should not alarm anyone. They are not considered dangerous to humans. ... Unfortunately, many people are obsessed with the idea that a cougar or a panther, as it is often called, has to be black. The truth is quite the contrary. ..."

** Conventional panthers, we might note, do not stand erect.

"sizzling" and with forepaws waving it charged. I swung the axe at it but it jumped back and I missed, so I ran for it and whooped. It leaped off in the woods and I ran for the house but didn't run very far before I saw it coming again and had to stop and swing the axe at it. It jumped to one side so I ran for it and it ran off in the woods again.... It repeated the same thing over and over five or six times until I came to a field where I could see the lights of the houses; then it leaped off and never came back.

The animal was black or dark grey in color. The tail was at least two and one-half feet long, and the animal was at least six feet long.

Decatur, Illinois, September-October 1955: On October 25, Game Warden Paul G. Myers shot at and thought he had wounded a black panther near the central Illinois city. Panther stories had been circulating in the area since September 13, when a woman saw one slinking along the road. The next evening two truck drivers spotted it in the vicinity of Rea's Bridge. Other persons reported hearing its scream in the night. According to the *Decatur Review*, "The animal has been described as long, low-slung and jet black with gleaming eyes."

Monument City, Indiana, June 1962: A large tan-colored animal jumped farmer Ed Moorman and clawed him on the face one day as he was hunting in the woods. Moorman fired a quick round and the thing ran off. Later, after seeing it twice more in the distance, he called Sheriff Harry Walter, who quickly organized a search party. Finding nothing, the group went home.

Several days passed and on the morning of the 25th Moorman discovered ten of his pigs lay dead, the blood sucked from their necks, their sides ripped open so that the attacker could devour their hearts and livers. He called the sheriff again.

In the meantime "blood-curdling howls" in the night were keeping locals on their toes. One man, Everett Widmeyer, a student of wild animals and their habits, theorized that a 400-pound "African lioness," presumably escaped from a circus or zoo, was the culprit. At any rate, that was his impression from Moorman's description and from an examination of claw marks on a wooden fence gate.

When the lion made its last well-publicized appearance near Huntington, several farmers, Moorman among them, were waiting with rifles. Unfortunately two excitable city slickers, employees of an Indianapolis television station, opened up before the animal got in range and it fled out of sight.

Joliet, Illinois, July-August 1964: The Joliet panther actually appeared first one evening in April 1963 at a gravel pit near the DuPage County line. Two nights later, when it returned, it was observed by watchman Emmett McKaney and described as a "huge black leopard."

During July of the next year something hairy resembling a lion, "only larger," began prowling the outskirts of Joliet between the hours of midnight and 1:00 a.m. On one occasion it killed a large dog, and on another, as it passed a cemetery, J.J. Smith shot at it several times.

Suddenly everyone was seeing the creature, and within two days a full-scale panic was on. Joliet police reported taking hundreds of calls from individuals who claimed they had seen the thing. A ripped-open rabbit carcass was found on Joliet's Midland Avenue amid tracks of an animal evidently six feet long which a high school biology teacher asserted had to be a dog. Not long afterwards a "huge black animal, larger than a German shepherd," stepped out of the bushes of Midland Avenue and growled menacingly at two teenage boys. Hal Finkle told police he then threw a piece of pipe at it and the beast screamed and fled into West Park.

The next day City Manager Aaron Marsh, who had been doing everything in his power to stem the mounting public alarm, announced, "The case of the phantom panther is closed. The wild animal expert who was in Joliet identified the tracks as those of a large dog." As if to confirm the unnamed "expert's" claims, that evening Victor Gul was attacked in his barn by what he called a "boxer dog with a long tail."

On the 30th the *Joliet Herald-News* noted, "Although Joliet's case of the black panther was closed officially last week with the identification of tracks left in the vicinity of West Park as those of a dog, reports persist of continued sightings of an unidentified animal." The accounts came from outlying areas of the city, where witnesses saw a "big animal with black, smooth fur."

In mid-August officials dismissed the dog explanation after state police got a look at the animal themselves. They sighted the panther one night on a road near New Lenox (less than ten miles east of Joliet), did a double-take, and called in an airplane on the chase. The panther got away but at least authorities knew what it was—whatever it was.

Lamar County, Texas, 1965: Near the tiny village of Direct there were persistent reports of a Mystery Animal something like a panther. An article in the *Paris News* in July 1965 quotes a woman from Direct:

"We can expect it in the last part of June and again in October just before deer season begins. We figure it migrates through here yearly."

Direct residents called it a "manimal"* and said that it left tracks like a cat's except the claws showed. The prints were so large that a man could put both hands in one track.

The "manimal" made a sound that at first resembled the cry of a wildcat, but soon the voice would begin to deepen and take on the quality of the screams of a man in pain. "Its wail is guaranteed to raise goose pimples," Direct citizens said.

The tracks indicated that the beast weighed about 190 or 200 pounds and ran on all fours in eight-foot leaps. In June it moved westward and in October it reversed direction and came back east.

A Direct woman described her first encounter with the "manimal":

"One evening as I was walking around the house with a flashlight, I turned at the corner of the house and I must have startled the thing as much as it startled me. It made one tremendous jump and left the yard. I hurried back into the house and called my cousin. We stood at the window and watched it as it crossed a fence and then stood on its hind legs staring back at us. It stood about six feet, two inches tall. Finally it walked away on all fours."

Illinois, 1970: Mike Busby's April encounter in Alexander County was only one of several strange phantom cat reports to take place in the state that year.

The first of these occurred in January, when an employee of the Macon Seed Company, west of Decatur, saw a large black animal he described as a "cougar." William F. Beatty told Loren Coleman that he himself had found tracks left by the animal. He also claimed that the thing twice tore down his electric fence. But not until two days after Beatty

* Obviously their use of the expression is different from ours.

had made his report did Game Warden James Atkins bother to investigate. Atkins concluded somewhat imaginatively that the animal was a beaver. A most unusual beaver, to be sure, since the footprints Beatty discovered were "very large" and had claw marks.

A month later and 75 miles away to the southeast, in Jasper County, Mrs. Donald Miller saw what she later described as an all-black cat as large as her German shepherd. Although not as tall as her dog, the cat was longer and had a tail at least as long as its body. The cat came within less than 150 yards of her house and she was surprised that *the dog continued to lie near the house and watch without even barking.*

Late in May, in eastern Winnebago County in the northern part of the state, astounded residents reported what one state trooper described as "a male African lion about eight feet long with hair growth at the end of its tail and a mane." One group of young men said it ran alongside their Volkswagen.

The weirdest incident of all happened on September 19. Six passengers moving along a highway near Pana encountered something they could neither explain nor comprehend. Alongside the road, a small tannish-gray pumalike animal suddenly appeared as if, in the words of A.V. Hamm, who saw it, "it just fell out of the sky." Later Hamm would attempt to convince himself that it had leaped out of a clump of bushes and only *seemed* to have materialized a few inches above the ground. But there was no way to account for the fact that *not everyone in the car could see it* even though it should have been clearly visible to all of them.

Fairfax County, Maryland, February 1971: A black panther prowling through the suburbs of Washington, D.C., killed three dogs and a horse, and avoided an ambush set by two residents, George Correll and Lonnie Dennis, who hung a slab of deer meat on a pole and spent several fruitless nights waiting in hiding with high-powered rifles. The creature left four-and-a-half inch prints with claw marks in them.

Chippewa County, Michigan, November 21, 1972: About 7:30 a.m. Walter Wegner was hunting in the Munuscong Bay region when he heard what sounded like buck deer fighting in the brush. Soon the noises stopped. Three hours later Wegner examined the site and was amazed to discover the body of a 200-pound, ten-point buck, its bones stripped clean. Only the head and rack remained, except for teeth marks on the skeleton.

"There is no animal on the North American continent that can kill and eat a deer that large in such a short time," Conservation Officer Harold Hammond told the *Detroit News*. "A pack of animals might be able to do it, but we found no tracks."

A few days before, Wegner said, he had found panther tracks in the area.

The *News* remarked, "Stories of a mystery killer cat or some other animal have circulated for almost twenty years. . . . The mystery animal . . . has been sighted about a hundred times since 1954 in the area, the last time in 1969 about five miles from Wegner's Chippewa County cabin."

6.

Before we move on to explore the curious question of the "Surrey puma," let us consider briefly one final North American feline MA, this one from Mexico, where an elusive melanistic cat reputedly dwells in the western highlands. Robert Marshall treats the subject fully in his 1961 book, *The Onza*.

The onza, we discover, sounds amazingly like a member of the phantom panther troupe. Said to be about the length of the puma, it is a dark "smutty-gray" with a "dark chocolate streaking" along the spine. As with other mystery cats, the onza "has a foot that is not round, the foot being longer than broad, and . . . the claws are not entirely sheathed; the ends of the claws show in the tracks." It supposedly has been seen over a wide area of Mexico's great Sierra Madre Occidental by modern locals and the Spaniards for over three centuries.

Back in the 1770s Friar Baegert wrote that the onza had invaded his neighbor's mission while he was visiting and had attacked "a fourteen-year-old boy in broad daylight and practically in full view of all the people; and a few years ago another killed the strongest and most respected soldier in California."

Earlier in this century Dr. George Parker found the onza well known to the natives in the districts of the state of Durango. These people, who greatly feared the creature, described it as possessing "yellow eyes that look like balls of fire in the night"—again, the luminous eyes we have noted earlier. Parker called the onza "the most dangerous animal in the mountains."

Although Robert Marshall argues convincingly that another cat besides the jaguar and the puma is being sighted in western Mexico, he is unable to supply us with real physical confirmation to substantiate the claim. Marshall's examples of "slain onzas" seem to be nothing more than pumas. Like others before him, he fails to realize that he is dealing with something other than a conventional animal, and eagerly seizes upon dubious evidence to prove his case. Yet the truth appears to be that our mystery felines cannot be caught or killed, that in fact their elusiveness is basic to their nature.

7.

The history of British MAs is a long one and stretches back into the rich folklore of the Isles. We will deal with these earlier tales, which raise some complex questions, later in this chapter. For now, however, we will borrow from Fort, whose first British account is dated May 1810, when some unseen animal in the Ennerdale area, near the English-Scottish border, went on a rampage and proceeded to slaughter seven or eight sheep a night, biting into the juglar vein and sucking the blood.

Fort also tells us that over a four-month period in 1874 an animal leaving catlike tracks, complete with claw marks, roamed Ireland and killed as many as thirty sheep in a single night.

And during the winter of 1904-05, an incredible season when a hysterical religious revival, a rash of poltergeist infestations, a series of "spontaneous combustions," and a UFO flap all competed for space in the newspapers,* an unknown animal preyed on sheep along the River Tyne. Another appeared in Kent in March. This one was thought to be a jackal, and one was actually shot there about the same time. "There is no findable explanation, nor attempted explanation, of how the animal got there," Fort observed. At any rate, the attacks continued.

A year later, in March 1906, 51 sheep died in one night near Guildford, about seventeen miles from Windsor. Not long afterwards a "panther" grabbed a woman in a field. In October 1925 a creature

* See *The Unidentified*, pp. 116-19.

"black in color and of enormous size" slaughtered sheep in the district of Edale, Derbyshire, "leaving the carcasses strewn about, with legs, shoulders and heads torn off; broken backs, and pieces of flesh ripped off. . . . People in many places are so frightened that they refuse to leave their homes after dark, and keep their children in the house." *(London Daily Express,* October 14, 1925.)

Almost forty years later, we have the sorely-misnamed "Surrey puma," a creature or series of creatures which range far from the area that gave them their name, after a particularly well-publicized wave of sightings in that county in September 1964. As zoologist Maurice Burton, self-appointed debunker of the phenomenon, has written with understandable exasperation, "It was reported from places as far apart as Cornwall and Norfolk, over an area of southern England of approximately 10,000 square miles. It has even been seen in two places many miles apart at the same time on the same day. It seems to have been particularly disturbed during one week when its presence was reported from ten different places in half as many days."

The problem, of course, is that there are no pumas in Britain—a fact numerous witnesses blithely ignore as they continue to report seeing large catlike animals, while the "experts" pull their hair and scream "impossible." The much-beleaguered Burton assures us that the "puma" is actually a feral dog or cat—or otter, badger, fox or deer—as perceived by the hysterical and the imaginative.

Pardon us as we stifle a yawn and note simply that behavior that is unusual for a real feline is normal for our phantom friends. Burton is right, up to a point: We quite agree that *Felis concolor* does not exist in Britain. But it does not therefore follow that all reports of one are mistakes. Burton, like the people in the Illinois Department of Conservation who foolishly try to tell us that "the 'black panther' of Illinois is a black Persian cat, a Labrador retriever or a black Angus calf," is dealing with matters outside his area of expertise.

Perhaps the only real expert on the British mystery felines is our friend R. J. M. Rickard, editor of the excellent *Fortean Times* (formerly *The News*), to whom we are indebted for the information which follows.

The first known written account of what would become known as the Surrey puma appears in the September 1962 issue of the Mid-Wessex Water Board house magazine, where we are told that in August and September something "like a young lion cub—definitely not a fox or a dog" appeared near the Heathy Park Reservoir in Hampshire. Apparently these were not the first sightings in the area. In any case reports persisted through the end of the year.

Then on July 18, 1963, at Oxleas Wood, Shooters Hill, London, a lorry (truck) driver saw a "leopard" leap from the road into the park some time before dawn. Later that day four policemen reported that a "large golden animal" had jumped over the hood of their squad car and into the woods. A huge search involving 126 police officers, 30 soldiers and 21 dogs and covering 850 acres failed to produce anything but large footprints. The *London Evening News* for July 19 noted that this was not the first report of an MA in the area, and that a woman recently had seen a "wandering boxer dog with a curious spotted appearance." (Compare this with Victor Gul's Joliet, Illinois, report of a "boxer dog with a long tail" mentioned earlier. The story also calls to mind the 1948 Indiana animal "about the size of a wolf and having yellow spots.")

A "wild cat" was seen again in Heathy Park in September and October of the same year, and on

February 14, 1964, a "huge" animal with razor sharp two-inch claws left large prints sunk two inches deep into firm ground. The same month people in Norfolk were seeing a creature variously described as a "tiger," a "puma" and a "cheetah."

In September the Surrey flap began, with sightings spilling over into neighboring Sussex, Hampshire and Berkshire of the same or a similar beast, a gold- or ginger-colored giant cat with a long tail. A typical report came from West Sussex in early October, when a woman walking her dogs in the woods encountered a "puma" six feet long and three feet high, "fawn gold" in color. Her dogs chased it into the woods and the witness heard "spitting and screeching sounds." It left prints which showed clear claw impressions.

A stranger, certainly less typical "puma" appeared at Farley Mount, near Winchester, Hampshire, and was shot at by a gamekeeper, who called it a "black slit-eyed animal." A police search failed to uncover anything. At least that much is typical.

In August 1964, according to Burton, "an employee of a dairyman at Crondall . . . reported his minivan had run over 'a strange catlike animal,' which bent the front number plate, rolled under the vehicle, hit the underneath part of the car forcibly, and was then seen to bound over a hedge into a field of uncut barley." Burton, of course, finds this story thoroughly unacceptable; after all, no animal the size of the reported creature could have passed under the minivan, "which is flush, with no space for axles, and only five inches off the ground . . . and survived to leap a hedge."

This tale reminds us somewhat of the car/creature collision at Salem Heights, Ohio, mentioned in Chapter 1.

In the meantime, it is worth noting that throughout the area that fall something was killing and partially eating deer, sheep and cattle, leaving claw marks either on or near the carcasses.

By January 1965 there had been so many "puma" reports in Surrey that the police issued warnings to the public that such an animal might be wintering in the 4000-acre Hurtwood Common. On February 3 a "huge animal" leaped out of the bushes at Ashurst, New Forest, Hampshire, and was seen by a girl on a bicycle. She first thought it was a horse, but after recovering from the initial shock realized that it was "like a leopard" and had "ferocious eyes."

Sightings continued throughout 1966. The most curious of these occurred on September 1, when a woman farmer driving near Chiddingfold, Hampshire, stopped her Land-rover "for some unknown reason," got out and walked through a thistle patch, where she stepped on the tail of a "puma." The animal reared up and hit the woman in the face with both paws. She in turn struck it with a stick, causing it to run up a tree. She went for assistance, but by the time she returned, the thing was gone. A Ministry of Agriculture and Fisheries official found no tracks, just some hair.

On November 23 someone reported seeing a "lion" on a road near Coulsden, Surrey, but a subsequent police search failed to come up with anything.

The number of reported sightings diminished during 1967 and 1968, but by the fall of 1969 Englishmen were seeing panthers, some black, some brown. In December 1970 a "puma," which a number of Kent people claimed to have seen, was held responsible for the killing of four sheep near Dover.

The next year numerous persons, at least two of them police officers, encountered a pumalike animal in various parts of England. Since then sightings have continued unabated and it seems likely that the "Surrey puma" will remain as much a part of British life as UFOs. Rickard tells us that a Godalming police file contains over 350 reports from that area alone. If that is so, there must be thousands of sightings, of which only a comparative few have become public knowledge.

Three different types of cats figure in the reports. Rickard summarizes them thus:

a) Lynxlike: pointed tufted ears; doglike body; short tail; mottled markings.
b) Pumalike: heavy muscular body; small head; large paws; long thick tail; flat catlike face; sandy/mustard color, lighter chest and belly; round ears.
c) Pantherlike: much like above, but black or dark color, face less flat.

All of this, as we shall see presently, is only generally true. Meanwhile we note a couple of problems. Victor Head writes in an article in *Field* (April 18, 1965):

> The puma is a big eater, generally resting up for two or three days between kills. Some authorities in the U. S. believe that it needs to consume one mule deer (300 lbs.) or its equivalent in other foods each week. As this is five times the average weight of a British Roe deer, a fully grown puma would need to kill 250 each year to live comfortably and free in Surrey.

And Burton writes:

> Altogether, from September 1964 to August 1966, the official records show 362 sightings, and there were many more, possibly as many again, claimed but not officially reported. In other words this animal, declared by American experts to be "rarely seen by man," was showing itself on average once a day for a period of two

years. The police . . . reckon that some 47 of the 362 are "solid" sightings. Even this means that this animal belonging to a species characterized by its highly secretive nature was showing itself about once a fortnight throughout a period of two years. In two years it was reported from places as far apart as Cornwall and Norfolk, over an area of southern England of approximately 10,000 sq. miles. It has even been in two places many miles apart at the same time on the same day. It seems to have been particularly disturbed during one week when its presence was reported from 10 different places in half as many days.

8.

On October 25, 1969, the occupants of a car driving down Exeter Road in Okehampton saw a "Great Dane" appear in front of them. Before they could stop, they had driven right *through* the "animal," which then disappeared.

At dawn one day late in April 1972 Coastguard Graham Grant, at watch over the harbor entrance to the beach at Great Yarmouth, noticed something out of the ordinary. "It was," he told the *London Evening News* (April 27, 1972), "a large, black hound-type dog on the beach. It was about a quarter of a mile away from me. What made me watch it was that it was running, then stopping, as if looking for someone. As I watched, it vanished before my eyes. I kept on looking for a time but it did not reappear."

Because bulldozers had recently leveled the beach, there was no place the dog could have disappeared.

Two years later, in April and May 1974, residents of Hampshire and Cheeshire reported a mysterious doglike animal. Some said it was "half cat, half dog."

We have here modern reports of a supernatural MA well known to students of folklore: the black dog, which is apparently a prototype of today's black panther. The black dog, however, is more clearly paranormal and has never been mistaken—for very long, at any rate—for a conventional zoological phenomenon. It figures prominently in the literature of witchcraft, in which Satan takes the form of a dark hell-hound with glowing eyes. To see it is to know that one is damned.

The most frightening of the early accounts is preserved in a report prepared by one Abraham Fleming, who claimed not to be repeating a folk tale but to be recording something he himself had witnessed—an event, he conceded, "which to some will seem absurd."

The incident supposedly occurred on Sunday, August 4, 1577, at Bongay, a town ten miles from Norwich, during a violent storm. Inside the local church the congregation sat in almost total darkness, the only light coming from frequent "fearful flashes of lightning."

> Immediately hereupon, there appeared in a most horrible similitude and likeness to the congregation then and there present, a dog as they might discerne it, of a black colour; at the sight whereof, togither with the fearful flashes of fire which then were seene, moved such admiration in the minds of the assemblie, that they thought doomes day was already come.
>
> This black dog, or the divel in such a likeness (God hee knoweth al who worketh all), runing all along down the body of the church with great swiftnesse, and incredible haste among the people, in a visible fourm and shape, passed between two persons, as they were kneeling uppon their knees, and occupied in prayer as it seemed,

wrung the necks of them bothe at one instant clene backward, insomuch that even at a momet where they kneeled, they straungely dyed.

This is a wonderful example of God's wrath, no doubt to terrifie us, that we might feare him for his justice, or pulling back our footsteps from the pathes of sinne, to love him for his mercy.

To our matter again. There was at ye same time another wonder wrought: for the same black dog, still continuing and remaining in one and the self-same shape, passing by an other man of the congregation of the church, gave him such a gripe on the back, that therewith all he was presently drawen togither and shrunk up, as it were a piece of lether scorched in a hot fire; or as the mouth of a purse or bag drawen togither with a string. The man, albeit hee was in so straunge a taking, dyed not, but as it is thought is yet alive; whiche thing is mervelous in the eyes of men, and offereth much matter of amasing the minde.

Moreouer and beside this, the clark of the said church being occupied in cleansing of the gutter of the church, with a violent clap of thunder was smitten doune, and beside his fall had no further harme: unto whom beeing all amased this straunge shape, whereof we have before spoken, appeared, howbeit he escaped without daunger: which might peradventure seem to sound against trueth, and to be a thing incredable; but let us leave thus and thus to judge, and cry out with the prophet, *O Domine,* etc.—"O Lord, how wonderful art thou in thy woorks."

. . . Now for the verifying of this report (which to soe wil seem absurd, although the sensibleness of the thing it self confirmeth it to be a trueth) as testimonies and witnesses of the force which rested in this straunge shaped thing, there are remaining in the stones of the church, and likewise in the church dore which are mervelously reten and torne, ye marks as it were of his clawes or talans. Beside, that all the wires, the wheeles, and other things belonging to the clock, were wrung in sunder, and broken in peces.

And (which I should haue tolde you in the beginning of this report, if I had regarded the observing of order) at the time that this tempest lasted, and while these storms endured, ye whole church was so darkened, yea with such a palpable darknesse, that one persone could not perceive another, neither yet might discern any light at all though it were lesser then the least, but onely when ye great flashing of fire and lightning appeared . . .

On the self-same day, in like manner, into the parish church of another towne called Blibery, not above seve miles distant from Bongay above said, the like thing Entred, in the same shape and similitude, where placing himself uppon a maine balke or beam, whereon some ye Rood did stand, sodainely he gave a swinge downe through ye church, and there also, as before, slew two men and a lad, and burned the hand of another person that was there among the rest of the company, of whom divers were blasted.

This mischief thus wrought, he flew with wonderful force to no little feare of the assembly, out of the church in a hideous and hellish likenes.

A straunge and terrible Wunder wrought very late in the parish Church of Bongay, a Town of no great distance from the citie of Norwich, namely the fourth of this August in ye yeere of our Lord 1577, in a great tempest of violent raine, lightning, and thunder, the like whereof hath been seldome seene. With the appearance of an horrible shaped thing, sensibly perceiued of the people then and there assembled. Drawen into a plain method, according to the written copye by *Abraham Fleming.*

Black dogs are not solely a British phenomenon. Stories of their appearances can be found in American folklore texts. Often these incidents are reported not as popular yarns, but as actual experiences of the informants. Theodore Ebert of Pottsville, Pennsylvania, gave this fairly typical account to George Korson, who printed it in his *Black Rock: Mining Folklore of the Pennsylvania Dutch:*

> One night when I was a boy walking with friends along Seven Stars Road, a big black dog appeared from nowhere and came between me and one of my pals. And I went to pet the dog but it disappeared right from under me. I couldn't see where it got to. Just like the snap of a finger it disappeared. Well, I'll tell you, I had about two miles to go to get home, and I made it in nothing flat. I never seen anything like that and I never hope to see anything like it again. This happened later to others. No one in the locality had a dog of that type and it was seen by others with practically the same experience. No one could ever explain why or where it came from.

The following story, which Sidney Benton of Horncastle, Lincolnshire, related to British Fortean Nigel Watson, is of particular interest to us, for reasons which will become clear very shortly:

> It was during the winter months of 1922 and 1923, when I was employed at a small local dairy, my job was to fetch up the cows from the fields, help to milk them and then deliver it to local people.
> Part of my deliveries took me to one of the

oldest parts of town. I usually took a short cut by going past an old Iron Foundry, over a small bridge with a water-wheel near it, then by the back of the Vicarage and past the old churchyard. On this particular evening I had made my deliveries and had just climbed over the small wooden palings on my way back to the dairy, when all at once, right in the center of the path, appeared two great bright shining eyes.

I called out thinking the dog from the dairy had followed me, but got no answer. I climbed back over the fence and stood there almost petrified with fear. I don't know how long I stood there but suddenly the eyes were just blotted out. I must have been braver then than I am now, for I took my courage in both hands and got back over the fence and walked back over to the spot where the eyes had been.

My employer and his wife and niece, noting that I looked white and frightened, asked the reason. They informed me that the dog had not left the dairy. After this experience, I was always sent on this particular part of my deliveries in daylight. On mentioning my experience to an old lady neighbor, she said that the spot was reputed to be haunted, as some people had been drowned when the ice gave way on the moat of what used to be an old castle there. A workmate friend tells me that he had seen the same thing years earlier.

It was such a long time ago, but all I can remember of that night are the eyes appearing quite suddenly, only a few yards in front of me, at about two or three feet from the ground. I do remember that everything was still and quiet and that after what seemed quite a few minutes the eyes were just blotted out. I have always been convinced that this was something very strange and the attitude of my employers at the time strengthened my belief. They did not wish to talk about it, and would never let me go that way at night afterwards; and also someone would accompany me when I had to take the pony to the field at nights.

At almost the same time, between 1921 and 1923, D. R. Clark, the father of Jerome Clark, had a remarkably similar experience. It left such a vivid impression on him that when he recalled the incident in May 1976, he said, "I can still see it clearly as I talk now. It was the strangest experience I've ever had."

It began one evening as he was walking home with his parents, Mr. and Mrs. A. L. Clark, from a church function on the north side of LaCrosse, Wisconsin. He was five or six years old at the time. About a block from their house he noticed "something that looked with shining eyes, with the face of a dog." The eyes were yellowish-gold in color, with no detail in the center. The teeth were also luminous but not so bright as the eyes. Behind the eyes and mouth young Clark had the impression of a "dark black body" about the size of a rat terrier.

Frightened, he called his parents' attention to it, but they could not see it. They assured him it was only his imagination at work and they went on their way.

One evening a week or two later, as the three of them passed the same spot, once more returning from church, Clark saw the apparition again. As before, it was on the boulevard side of the sidewalk, halfway through the block where the light from the streetlights was dimmest. Again the child was terrified. Again his parents couldn't see it.

Not long afterwards, the thing appeared for the third and final time, as usual when the family were coming home from church at night. Young Clark was walking on the outside, closest to the creature, and this time when he saw it, he overcame his fear sufficiently to kick at it, only to discover, just as if the thing were anticipating just such an action, his foot landed inside its mouth and it bit down on his shoe. The startled boy could feel its teeth. When he screamed, the black dog vanished and he never saw it again.

The following incident took place during World War II and was reported in a letter to writer Janet Bord:

> The cottage where we lived is still in existence, in Bredon, Worcestershire. My encounter took place one late afternoon in summer, when I had been sent to bed, but was far from sleepy. I was sitting at the end of the big brass bedstead, playing with the ornamental knobs [the witness was a young girl], and looking out of the window, when I was aware of a scratching noise, and an enormous black dog had walked from the direction of the fireplace to my left. It passed round the end of the bed, between me and the window, round the other corner of the bed, towards the door. As the dog passed between me and the window, it swung its head round to stare at me—it had very large, very red eyes, which glowed from inside as if lit up, and as it looked at me I was quite terrified, and very much aware of the creature's breath, which was warm and strong as a gust of wind. The animal must have been very tall, as I was sitting on the old-fashioned bedstead, which was quite high, and our eyes were level. Funnily enough, by the time it reached the door, it had vanished. I assure you that I was wide awake at the time, and sat for quite some long while wondering about what I had seen, and to be truthful, too scared to get into bed, under the covers, and go to sleep. I

clearly remember my mother and our host, sitting in the garden in the late sun, talking, and hearing the ringing of the bell on the weekly fried-fish van from Birmingham, as it went through the village! I am sure I was not dreaming, and have never forgotten the experience, remembering to the last detail how I felt, what the dog looked like, etc.

The years following World War II bring UFOs into the black dog picture. In the first chapter we looked at a Savannah, Georgia, report of ten black dogs running from a landed UFO.

There is also a 1963 story from South Africa. Two men driving at night on the Potchefstroom/Vereeniging road were startled to see a strange, large doglike animal cross the road in front of them. Curious, they stopped, only to have a UFO buzz their car several times, frightening them severely and driving all thoughts of the peculiar animal out of their heads.

The following fascinating account comes to us via letter from Betty Hill, herself a percipient in a famous and much-publicized UFO case:

> In the spring of 1966, Eliot, Maine, was the scene of unusual UFO activity. They came up the river in early evening in groups, night after night. Since this river runs by the flight line at Pease AF Base, they had numerous planes flying, as well as helicopters, and private planes. So it was a spectacular sight—with the sky full of UFOs and flying craft. People came for miles —traffic was bumper to bumper. Police called in police from other areas to direct traffic. People had telescopes, cameras, binoculars. Someone had set up a huge searchlight in a field. Pushcarts sold hot dogs, hamburgers, snacks, cold and hot drinks. In the two to three months

that this activity covered, many strange things happened.

One night a group of prominent people from Portsmouth [New Hampshire] decided to go to Eliot to watch the UFOs. After driving around in a caravan of three or four cars, in all the traffic, they decided to pull over in a gravel pit and watch the skies. They all got out when they saw a huge dark "dog" run through the pit. This dog was larger than any they knew so they decided to try to follow it. They ran through the pit, but unfortunately for the last one in the line, he was stopped by a strange odor. He tried to identify it, and as he was standing there, suddenly a form glided towards him. The form was giving off this odor and he had the feeling he was to follow this gliding form. He broke away and ran back to the car, and told a person who remained behind what had happened. She got out of the car and called for the others to return to the car.

Fortunately they did, for at this moment, the first man jumped out of the car, saying that he had to go back, and started for the woods. The others grabbed him and held him until he quieted down, and then they all left the area, promising not to reveal what had happened. This was told to me in confidence by two who were there, but I do not know the identity of the others involved, although there must have been a large number—possibly 20 or more.

In the previous chapter we have discussed the paranormal manimals which have haunted western Pennsylvania in recent years. Stan Gordon, the leading investigator of the occurrences, has written *(MUFON 1974 UFO Symposium Proceedings):*

Besides the reports of large hairy bipeds being observed . . . there were sightings of animals about as large as a German Shepherd dog. These animals baffled the witnesses because they couldn't figure out just what kind of animal they were looking at. The creature looked like a cross between a monkey and a dog. It had a tail with rings around it and large red eyes. These creatures at times came up on people's porches and were scared away by the occupants of the house. The witnesses normally were attracted to the creature by the sound of a crying baby, which they speculated that someone had dropped off. When they went to the porch, they found the creature making the sound.

9.

On July 8, 1970, the *Topeka Daily Capital* editorialized about some peculiar events in Kansas:

> Even in this practical era when people take scientific marvels for granted, many quickly turn to the supernatural if they can't explain something that has happened.
>
> Nearly everyone has a mysterious episode to relate which apparently defies rational interpretation.
>
> Whole communities can become involved, as witness reaction to several incidents which have taken place near Humboldt Hill, south of Iola [Kansas]. As background, it is explained that the area is reputed to be the location of an Indian burial ground.
>
> Twice recently, motor vehicles traveling nearby have experienced strange losses of power in their electrical systems and conked out.
>
> Add to this a report that cattle stampeded in fright from a pasture at the top of the hill and

there is grist for the superstitious to grind in their mills.

Some even report having seen strange lights and sighting large cat tracks. How the latter ties in with the former isn't explained either.

But people do love mysteries—as shown by the rash of flying saucers reported sighted some time ago.

Then there was the Perry Panther and other such manifestations...

Mike Busby's experience suggests that there may well be a connection between MAs of the phantom cat variety and auto stoppages, which are usually associated with UFO sightings. Ufologists, who believe that UFOs are the products of a superior extraterrestrial technology, theorize that such stoppages are caused by the objects' propulsion system. An interesting idea, but it is by no means clear how it applies to such incidents as one that took place in 1969, along the Choccolocco-Iron, Alabama, road, where all that spring residents had been reporting creatures they called "boogers" and "varmints."

A man is said to have shot at one of the things, causing it to run back into the hills uttering "an almost humanlike cry." "It's darn scary when you hear it," one witness said. "Like something from another world."

Late in May of that year a man driving down the road between Choccolocco and Iron saw a "varmint," described as faintly resembling a humpback combination of bear and panther, appear out of nowhere and force him off the road.

The following night Johnny Ray Teague and three companions were on the same road when their car abruptly stalled. While they were out looking at the motor, they heard something crashing through the leaves and branches. Before they knew what was happening, the "booger" was upon them—so close, in fact, that they could hear it breathing. They jumped back into the car, rolled the windows up, locked the doors and sat petrified with fear as the creature circled the car several times.

It was, they would claim later, "awful looking," the size of a cow, gray to black in color, humped similarly to a camel, with a large head and prominent teeth. It did not try to attack the witnesses.

Soon after the creature had disappeared back into the woods, the car miraculously started right up and the occupants sped away. Half a mile down the road they saw "three or four" more of the creatures, larger than the first.

A Surrey puma story directly links UFOs and a phantom cat. The story was told by Edward Blanks, who farmed near Godalming and who claimed that over a two-year period between 1962 and 1964 the puma had regularly crossed his land and unnerved him with its "yowling" cries. When Charles Bowen, editor of *Flying Saucer Review,* came to the farm to investigate, he discovered the following:

> Part of Mr. Blanks' routine is to make the rounds of his farm before retiring for the night. On two occasions he suddenly became aware of a mysterious light on the roofs of the farm buildings. The light moved from roof to roof, yet he could not see the beam which produced the light. It was certainly *not* produced by car headlights from the Odiham Road: the local topography precluded that possibility. Mr. Blanks could not trace the source of the light, and he was puzzled and worried by the phenomenon, because on each occasion the mystery puma arrived on the scene shortly afterwards!

We are reminded of A. V. Hamm's Pana, Illinois, experience when we read this item from an article by Eileen Buckle in *FSR Case Histories #6:*

> Recently a young man related . . . a remarkable low-level sighting he had at the age of 15 when traveling by car with his family. An apparently solid object kept pace with the car for 20 minutes. All the family saw it clearly, except the father. Strangely, he was unable to see it at all.

10.

There seems little doubt that our mystery felines are not conventional animals but paranormal phenomena of some kind. We base that conclusion upon these considerations:

1.) *Their appearance.* Black pumas are extremely rare and far too many of them show up in the reports we have examined. African lions, for another thing, do not live in the wild in midwestern America. Neither do cats have "glowing" eyes, nor do they leave tracks with claw marks in them.

2.) *Their geographical distribution.* Our MAs appear in areas where conventional large cats either have long been extinct or have never existed.

3.) *Their behavior.* They are extremely hostile to human beings, unlike normal cats. They stand, and even walk, on their hind legs. They are seen frequently, whereas "real" felines, which are very shy, are seldom observed. They sometimes appear in "waves" during which other unknown animals are observed.

4.) *Their elusiveness.* There is no conclusive physical evidence of their existence. No bodies have ever been found and none has ever been killed. Bullets seem not even to affect them particularly. They have managed to elude innumerable large posses over the years.

5.) *Their tie, direct and indirect, with other MA, UFO and psi phenomena.* Car engines may stop in their presence. They may make sounds similar to those heard in other "monster" and poltergeist manifestations. They may materialize suddenly and be selective as to whom they appear. There may also be a certain ambiguity in the descriptions when they are compared to one another.

Before we begin to make sense of all of this, we must go down to south Texas and follow the path of other, even more bizarre Mystery Animals.

CHAPTER FIVE

Things With Wings

1.

By the time we had come to the Rio Grande Valley, in early March 1976, Big Bird was already old hat. When we'd ask about it, people would almost invariably laugh and say, "That was a long time ago," when actually it had been only a couple of months before.

But memories are short there, because life is fast and busy, as fast and busy as the big cars that barrel down Highway 77 on what the promoters proudly call the "longest Main Street in the world," which moves south from Raymondville through a couple of small towns, and down to Harlingen less than twenty miles away. Harlingen fades into San Benito, which soon becomes Olmito, which fades into Brownsville. What little distance separates the cities and towns is bridged by an unending string of farms, barbeque (or, as the signs always have it, "BBQ") stands, Mexican-food joints and roadside bars. "The

Lower Valley towns are so closely linked with rural districts," the tourist guide says, "that the whole area is largely urban. It is the most cosmopolitan district in Texas."

The Rio Grande Valley is not, in short, a wild and primitive place. In fact, the wild and primitive areas in the depressingly overpopulated region are few. One, in eastern Willacy County near Port Mansfield, is on private property owned by the famous King family. It houses an assortment of unlikely animals, including the nilgai, 900-pound antelopes imported from India, and the javelina, piglike mammals which are often dangerous. The birds there include ducks, Canadian geese, storks, cranes, herons and even African cattle egrets, blown over to Texas which keep ticks off grazing cattle. A fairly exotic collection, to be sure, but there is nothing there that is anything like the Big Bird—even though many people insisted, often with a certain unmistakable note of desperation (or at least exasperation) in their tones, that there was, and that it had to be one of the above.

But it wasn't. Not *the* Big Bird anyway.

If you were gullible or indifferent enough, you could believe birdwatcher Gladys Donohue of Mission, who asserted it was nothing more than a large barn owl. Of course, she conceded, barn owls don't look at all like what witnesses were reporting, but then she had an explanation for that, too: "People don't always see what they think they see."

Television stations and private individuals contributed to the nonsense by offering rewards for the Bird's capture, then hastily withdrawing them when zoologists "identified" it as the great blue heron, an endangered species protected by some of the harshest conservation laws in the books. That, however, did not stop gun-toting teenagers from taking to the back roads in search of the thing. And the Bird's presence, real or imagined, gave at least one drunk a story to tell his wife when he staggered home late at night from a barroom brawl—the Bird, he said, had attacked him. And a young Brownsville farmer roared down a country road late one night, terrified that the Big Bird was about to get him, while behind him a pelican sailed in hot pursuit.

There was, it seemed, no end to the silliness. But there was also the Big Bird, and that was quite something else.

2.

Armando Grimaldo says he "wasn't drunk and wasn't smoking marijuana or anything like that" when it happened. What he was doing, he insists, was sitting quietly in his mother-in-law's back yard on the north side of Raymondville and smoking a cigarette. His estranged wife Christina, whom Grimaldo had come to visit, lay sleeping inside. It was 10:30 p.m., January 14, 1976.

"Then all of a sudden," he claims, "I heard a sound like the flapping of batlike wings, and a funny kind of whistling. The dogs in the neighborhood started barking. I looked around but I couldn't see nothing. I don't know why I never looked up. I guess I should have, but as I was turning to go look over on the other side of the house, I felt something grab me, something with big claws. I looked back and saw it and started running. I've never been scared of nothing before but this time I really was. That was the most scared I've ever been in my whole life."

Grimaldo saw it just long enough to determine that it was as big as he was (5'8"), with a wingspan of from ten to twelve feet. Its face was bat- or monkeylike, its eyes two or three inches round and bright red. It did not have a beak and its "blackish-brown" skin looked leathery and was featherless.

Grimaldo could manage no more than a scream at that point—and a face-first sprawl into the dirt when he attempted to propel himself to safety. As he struggled back to his feet, he felt his pants, coat, and shirt being ripped open, his flesh remaining curiously untouched—a feature of the story which would generate as much skepticism as wonderment in the days and weeks to follow. Finally he dashed under a tree and his attacker, now breathing heavily, elected to pursue the matter no further and lumbered off into the night and back into the nether regions.

Christina Grimaldo, who had been awakened by her husband's shouting, came downstairs just as he stumbled through the back door and gasped that something had attacked him from out of the sky. Christina immediately phoned the police, who rushed to the scene and found Grimaldo "in some kind of shock," muttering *"pajaro"* (Spanish for bird) over and over again, still incapable of speaking coherently. He was taken to the Willacy County Hospital and released after half an hour when doctors found there were no physical injuries. Nonetheless, the distraught Grimaldo spent the next two days in bed.

A month and a half later, when we made the rounds in Raymondville inquiring about the supposed incident, the story had become something of an embarrassment to the community, even to Grimaldo's family, who responded to questions about it with either giggles or scowls.

Sheriff Oscar Correa discounted the story entirely. "Oh," he said, "I think he was sincere in what he said. But I firmly think it didn't happen as reported. If this was real, there would have been one or two scratches on his flesh. A bird's going to land on the head if it's going to attack, not on the feet or back. If there were such a thing as this bird, the people we have out on the roads would have spotted it by now."

And in any case, two days after Grimaldo's alleged encounter, Conovia Tijerina had called the sheriff's office to report a huge gray bird with a long beak sitting immobile in the middle of a field three and a half miles northeast of Raymondville. It proved to be a dead pelican. So the mystery of Grimaldo's sighting was "solved"—and never mind that the bird he said he saw was dark brown, not gray, and possessed neither beak nor feathers.

Unfortunately it was still not clear who or what killed Joe Suarez's goat during the early morning hours of December 26. Suarez, a Raymondville resident, had left the animal tied up in a corral behind his barn the night before. The next morning he found it ripped to pieces. Mauled from the right side, the goat lay in a pool of blood, the heart and lungs missing, the snout cut or bitten away. The blood was still wet and warm when police officers examined the carcass. There were no footprints around the body.

Armando Grimaldo was not, by any means, the first Texan to claim an encounter with "Big Bird," as someone dubbed it after the Sesame Street television character. There was, for example, this story which James Rowe, a retired Corpus Christi newsman, recalled hearing many years ago from a man who ran a grocery store along Corpus Christi Beach:

"It was on the Nueces River back before they built the Wesley Seale Dam [in 1958]," Rowe said. "He was fishing up at Swinney Switch with a rod and reel and something grabbed his hook and took off downstream. The thing almost took all of his line before he got it turned around. Then it headed upstream just about as far.

"He fought it and fought it. Then finally the thing just climbed out of the water on a sandbar across the river from where he was standing. It was this creature with fur and feathers and it just took the hook out of its mouth. Then it climbed up a tree.

"The fellow had a pistol in his tackle box, so he took it out and started to shoot at the animal. Then as he took aim, the thing just flew away."

If that sounds suspiciously like a Texas tall tale, the rumors that began in Rio Grande City in November 1975 perhaps deserve more serious consideration, though they are difficult to substantiate. The rumors, which were in circulation before the Big Bird story hit the papers, had it that various citizens, including children, Mexican-Americans and "winter" Texans (northerners who reside in the Valley during the cold months), had observed a "man-bird" skulking about in the darkness. The creature, supposed to be about four feet tall, had a bird's body and a man's head. It was spotted—during nonbusiness hours, we're assured—on the roof of a tavern north of town. Another story had the thing above the Starr County Courthouse, a story which Sheriff Ray Alvarez, who presumably should know if anyone does, discounts as nonsense. Certainly the witnesses seemed as reluctant to step forward and identify themselves as other townsfolk seemed eager to spread wild and unsubstantiated tales.

The first report—that is, an account with which names, places and dates can be connected—is curiously unimpressive, despite the massive media attention and the quality of the witnesses. The witnesses, Patrolmen Arturo Padilla and Homero Galvan, watched a white "stork or pelican type of bird" sailing over San Benito, 75 miles east of Rio Grande City, at 5:15 a.m. on December 28. The two officers, who were in separate squad cars, described the bird as having a foot-long neck "that sort of bent as it glided."

It seems virtually certain that this particular sighting was in fact of a white pelican, a larger than ordinary white pelican, possibly, but still a white pelican. Actually, that is what Padilla and Galvan now believe it to have been, we were told. The bird's estimated wingspan, twelve to fifteen feet, is only slightly larger than the ten-foot span of many pelicans, and it is always possible that the early morning darkness and mist may have caused the bird to appear larger than it really was. Moreover, pelicans retract their necks when they fly.

The San Benito report probably would have received little attention if it had not been for a weird incident that occurred just four days later in neighboring Harlingen. The witnesses were Tracey Lawson, 11, and her cousin Jackie Davies, 14.

The sighting, unlike most of the others, took place in the daylight hours. On January 1, while the children's parents slept off the excesses of New Year's Eve, Tracey and Jackie were playing in the Lawsons' back yard, which faces a plowed field five miles south of Harlingen along Ed Carey Road. Suddenly Tracey noticed something standing a hundred yards away. Dashing inside, she picked up a pair of binoculars and returned to focus on a "horrible-looking" huge black bird. It was over five feet tall and had big, dark red eyes, with wings bunched up at its shoulders, which were three feet wide. Its face was "gorillalike" and gray, and its sharp, thick beak was at least six inches long. The head was bald. On one occasion during their sighting the thing made a loud, shrill *eeeee* sound.

Tracey and Jackie were stunned and frightened. The next thing they knew, the creature, which had been standing near a borrow pit which borders an irrigation canal, had disappeared—apparently, the parents inferred later, running or flying low through the pit—only to reappear on the northeast corner of the property, its head poking above a small clump of trees. That was all Tracey and Jackie cared to see. They went inside the house and stayed there.

When the parents finally awoke, the children told them what they had seen. Perhaps understandably the adults did not take the story seriously.

The next day, however, Jackie's stepfather, Tom Waldon, went out to look for tracks, still skeptical of the tale but concerned at his stepson's insistence that it was true.

The tracks were there. Waldon did a double take before kneeling down to examine them carefully. The first three were close to the fence behind the house. The fourth print was twenty yards out into the field and the fifth twenty yards beyond that. The tracks were three-toed, eight inches across, square at the head, and were pressed an inch and a half into the hard ground.

Waldon called Mrs. Lawson, who was at work. She phoned the Cameron County Sheriff's office and then her husband, who raced home to find that an officer had already beaten him there.

Stan Lawson, who weighs 170 pounds, pressed his own foot down alongside the bird print and found it made practically no impression. "That thing must have been pretty heavy," he said later.

He noticed something strange about his dog's behavior, too. All day it cowered inside the doghouse, leaving it only once, at suppertime, when Lawson went to feed it and it bolted through the door into the main house. It had to be dragged back outside. And that night, around 10:00, Lawson heard something like large wings scraping across his bedroom window screen, but he saw nothing. In the morning he discovered that there was a tear in the screen. He was not sure if it had been there before or not.

Among those who came to talk with the Lawsons after the incident had been publicized on the local television station was Sgt. Sam Esparza of the San Benito police force. Esparza, who lives in the same general area as the Lawsons, told them—and confirmed to us later—that the night of January 1 he had left his house at 10:00 and returned at 11:00. Looking into his back yard, he was startled to see blood on some of the clothing that had been hanging on the line. Two of the four stained items had large, dark stains, rather, he thought, like liver that something had chewed on and disgorged. His wife, who had been inside all the while, had heard nothing. The dog hadn't even barked. As a matter of fact, the Doberman, an animal not known for its timidity, seemed oddly frightened. Apparently, unlikely as it seemed, it had been *too scared* to bark.

Esparza uneasily recalled that the night before something had whammed into his trailerhome. Of course this had happened during a windstorm, but afterwards he hadn't been able to find the cause. He was by no means certain that there was a connection; on the other hand, he was by no means certain that there *wasn't* a connection, either.

On January 7, at 8:30 p.m., Alverico Guajardo of Brownsville heard something hit *his* trailer. Unlike Esparza, Guajardo dashed outside immediately to see what had happened. "It was a little like somebody was shoving something against the trailer, maybe a sack of cement," he recalled.

Guajardo, who did not own a flashlight, got into his station wagon, drove it slowly around the south side of the trailer and shone his headlights on "something from another planet." As the lights hit it, the thing, which had been lying on the ground, suddenly rose up and stared at Guajardo with blazing red eyes the size of silver dollars. For the next two or three minutes it stood gazing at the man, who sat immobilized with fear.

The creature was four feet tall, with black feathers

and a beak whose length Guajardo estimated at between two and four feet. It was making a "horrible-sounding noise" from its throat, which he could see pulsating. Its long, batlike wings were folded around its shoulders.

While Guajardo watched it, the thing backed carefully toward a dirt road three feet away. By the time Guajardo had gathered enough courage to bolt out of the vehicle toward a neighbor's house, it was just vanishing into the darkness.

The next morning, at 9:30, reporter George Cox of the *Brownsville Herald* interviewed Guajardo, who was plainly still terrified. "You could see this was no jive," Cox told us later. "This guy did see something. He's the most convincing Big Bird witness I've met so far. If any of these stories are legitimate, this is the one."

3

By this time Big Bird had become a Valley sensation, but it was being played strictly for laughs, and for ratings. Harlingen's KGBT-TV, which had been first on the scene when the Lawsons reported the Bird and the tracks, led the way with assorted contests to draw or explain the Bird, though privately news director Ray Norton discounted the story. "People have been seeing something, no doubt about it," he said. "They may be seeing a common bird and imagining the rest of it."

Jack Grimm, an Abilene, Texas, geologist who put up a $5000 reward for the Bird's capture, narrowed down the possibilities to three *un*common birds. The first was an Abyssinian ground hornbill, which stands four feet high and sports a four-foot wingspread. Grimm does not explain, however, how the bird made its way from sub-Saharan Africa, its usual abode, to Texas, nor does he tell us why not one witness remarked on its bright red, decidedly unmonkeylike face.

Grimm, an energetic and imaginative man whose enthusiasms include the Loch Ness Monster and the search for Noah's Ark, suggests the jabiru stork as another possible explanation, though the jabiru's dark eyes, red and black neck, white wings, and long black legs again do not match witnesses' descriptions. The marabou stork, Grimm's final candidate, sounds more promising, if only because of its enormous size (four and a half feet) and wingspan (ten feet). Unfortunately, marabous reside in central India and Borneo. In addition, their backs, wings, and tail are slate gray with green iridescence. The wings, moreover, have white edges on the outside and are completely white on the underside.

David Thompson and Don Farst, resident zoologists at the Gladys Porter Zoo in Brownsville, dismissed as "extremely improbable" a theory held, for example, by the Lawson parents, who had not seen the thing themselves, that the Bird was actually a California or Andean condor, neither of which is native to south Texas, nor matches observers' descriptions.

That left those resolutely determined to find a conventional explanation with two alternatives: a pelican and a great blue heron.

The pelican was almost certainly the cause of some reports, as we have seen. The great blue heron undoubtedly generated at least one report (and probably others). This one report led at least one newspaper to bury the mystery a bit prematurely, proclaiming in a headline, "Legend of Bird Is Dead."

In reality, what had happened was that one day in early February farm workers south of Alamo had panicked at the sight of a large bird roosting in a fruit orchard. They quickly spread the word and within the hour a crowd of fifty had gathered, among them a television reporter who shot footage of the fowl as it stood, looking slightly bored, in the orchard's plowed turf. When the film was shown, bird watchers and zoologists had no trouble identifying the subject as a great blue heron.

The great blue heron, an endangered species protected by federal law, is native to south Texas but still not a particularly common sight. The excitement its appearance at Alamo caused says more about the hysteria the Big Bird scare generated than it does about the Big Bird itself, which looked not at all like the heron, a silvery-blue and white creature with a long, winding neck.

Another Big Bird sighting, this one near Laredo, was most likely of a great blue heron. On January 14 Arturo Rodriguez, nineteen, and his nine-year-old nephew were fishing on the banks of the Rio Grande when they heard a rustle of leaves, looked up and saw a large gray bird gliding over the river at a height of approximately fifty feet. They did not stick around to study the sight, choosing instead to scurry home. Two hours later Roberto Gonzalez saw the bird over U.S. Highway 83, which runs parallel to the river.

The bird's appearance and habits—herons forage along river banks and stand silently in or near the water while watching for fish—suggest that this was a big bird (the heron) but not *the* Big Bird.

But apparently the ill-tempered beast which an Eagle Pass man reported was neither.

At 12:45 a.m. on January 21, so the story went, the man had just arrived home and had stepped into his back yard when he spotted a large something stooped over near a clothesline post. Before he knew what was happening, the thing made a hissing sound, jumped him, ripped into his shoulders, and then hopped off. He described it initially, according to the police report, as having "a brown or almost black body, bright red eyes and the wings of a bat . . . short, stubby legs and two arms, each about two and a half feet long. It had pointed ears, the face of a pig, but didn't have a snout." Investigators found mysterious feathers and hair at the scene.

At first these investigators took the story seriously —a UPI account noted, for example, that this was "the first such attack being given credence by officials"—especially after an Eagle Pass physician testified that the wounds, clawlike marks three and a half inches long and half an inch deep, had almost certainly been caused by a large bird or animal. The witness, furthermore, agreed to take a lie detector test, once a Spanish-speaking operator could be found. The man spoke no English.

But unfortunately for those who were trying to find some firm evidence for Big Bird's existence, the story proceeded to collapse in the days that followed, a fact about which the press was oddly silent. Nonetheless an Engle Pass police officer who participated in the investigation, and who has asked not to be identified, passed on the following information to us:

1). Because of the man's past history, local officers regarded the man as unreliable.

2.) The police had interviewed him four times. There were major conflicts between the first account and the second one, and further, less dramatic conflicts in the subsequent versions. The first day, for instance, he said the thing had feathers, the next day that the skin was featherless, leathery and batlike.

3.) The feathers proved to be from a member of the redbird family, while some of the hair was linked to a domestic cat and the rest to a javelina.

4.) The doctor whose testimony had seemed to substantiate the man's report was a close personal friend of the alleged witness. No other physician agreed that a bird or animal had caused the wounds.

The wounds, they said, looked as if they might have been inflicted with cut glass.

5.) None of the man's neighbors had heard anything unusual at the supposed time of the attack. Neither, evidently, did the neighborhood dogs, which did not bark. Across a street a huge mastiff had not made a sound.

6.) Though the Eagle Pass police did locate a Spanish-speaking polygraph operator, the man repeatedly begged off taking the test, giving increasingly unconvincing excuses each time.

Still, the officer hedges his bet slightly by conceding, "There's a possibility it could be true." But not a very great one, apparently.

The report three San Antonio elementary school teachers made on February 24 was something else entirely. Patricia Bryant, Marsha Dahlberg, and David Rendon, driving to work down an isolated road southwest of the city, were startled to see something with a wingspan of "15 or 20 feet, if not more." The enormous bird swooped low over the cars, casting a shadow that covered the entire road.

"I could see the skeleton of this bird through the skin or feathers or whatever," Mrs. Bryant said, "and it stood out black against the background of the gray feathers."

Rendon added, "It just glided. It didn't fly. It was no higher than the telephone line. It had a huge breast. It had different legs and it had huge wings, but the wings were very peculiar like. It had a bony structure, you know, like when you hold a bat by the wing tips, like it has bones at the top and in-between."

Oddly, the same time they were watching the mysterious bird, they saw another unusually large flying object. This one was off in the distance circling like a buzzard over a herd of cattle. It resembled, the teachers thought, an "oversized sea gull."

The first bird, though, was unlike anything they had ever seen. But when they got to school, they rummaged through a set of encyclopedias until at last they found what they had seen: a pteranodon. The only trouble with that was that the pteranodon, a kind of flying dinosaur, has been extinct for about 150 million years.

The teachers were not the first to call the Bird a pteranodon. That achievement went to two sisters, Libby and Deany Ford, who in mid-January spotted a "big black bird" near a pond several miles northeast of Brownsville. "It was as big as me," Libby said, "and it had a face like a bat." Later, paging through a book on paleontology, they came upon a drawing of a pteranodon and concluded that was what they had seen.

Jesse Garcia and Vanacio Rodriguez may have seen the same thing on January 11. Checking out a stock tank on a ranch just north of Poteet, the two sighted a five-foot bird standing in the water. "He started flying," Garcia said, "but I never saw him flap his wings. He made no noise at all." Paleontologists believe that pteranodons and their cousins, the pterodactyls, did not actually fly but used their enormous wings to glide through the air.

The San Antonio sighting was the last Big Bird sighting to make the papers. In fact, it came a month after skeptics, whose numbers included virtually everybody but the witnesses themselves (plus a few reporters who had actually bothered to talk with the witnesses), had declared the Bird a dead issue and press attention had drifted back toward more conventional media pursuits. We did not arrive on the scene until after the scare had run its course. Almost everyone we met was either perplexed, amused, or annoyed when we told them of our interest in gathering material on Big Bird.

But as we probed into the incidents, it became

clear that something, or *somethings,* called Big Bird did exist, that it was not a conventional bird, and that it was more than a delusion born out of the folk imagination. Nearly everyone subscribed to some version of this theory and newspapers gave prominent play to old Mexican folk tales about flying monsters, strongly implying a connection, while failing to note that some of the witnesses were northern-born Anglos.

Furthermore, the armchair theorists did not bother to ascertain whether or not there is a *living* folklore about giant supernatural birds, and whether those who claimed to have seen the Big Bird related the thing to this folklore.

4.

And so it was that we ended up in San Benito hearing stories about the mysterious bird that had haunted the La Palma section of the city for at least thirty years.

We came upon the story purely by accident. We had driven to the San Benito police station in hopes of interviewing Officers Padilla and Galvan, who had seen the pelican the press had transformed into Big Bird, and found ourselves desperately trying to convince a hostile desk officer that we should not be thrown out into the street. Discouraged, we had begun packing up our notebook and tape recorder when Lt. Ernest Flores, who had been listening to the exchange, beckoned us into his office.

"You might be interested in this," he said, searching into a file cabinet. He retrieved several jars of some kind of fecal material and handed them to us. "We've been getting them from a young guy who lives around here. He thinks they're from Big Bird."

The droppings were dried, whitish lumps about one inch thick and two to three inches long.

"We don't have the facilities to analyze this stuff," Flores went on, "and we really don't know where to take it. But I'm sure there's something to it. The guy who brought it to us is honest and intelligent and we know him well. He's telling the truth about it. We've studied this material informally and we've found things like Johnson grass, grain, fragments of hair and even a whole cockroach. In one dropping there's even an inch-long bone, something from a skull, it looks like.

"We've even had some possums in here and had them eliminate. This doesn't look like possum waste. It's not from an owl either. An owl spits out its droppings in pellet form.

"Whatever this thing is, it appears to have a very primitive digestive system."

Flores' informant and supplier proved to be nineteen-year-old Guadalupe Cantu III, a thoughtful, intense young man who had lived in San Benito all his life. Cantu told us that after graduating from the local high school he had worked until recently as a carry-out in a supermarket. Now unemployed, he planned to enter vocational school in the near future. In the meantime he was obsessed with finding out what had caused the droppings.

His father had discovered them on the roof of the house in May 1975. "That was before the sightings of Big Bird, you know," Cantu remarked, "so there was no fuss about it. That was the first droppings but that was what got me interested in climbing up the roof to see if I could find others.

"I live on the city limits near the City Power and Light plant. I first heard it—the Bird—when I was eight years old. I was living in the same house I live in now. I was inside and suddenly I heard a cat sound from up on the roof. The dogs were barking at it. It was real heavy and we heard it for over an hour. Then I heard it fly away and there was no more cat sound.

"Everybody's heard it, my grandparents, uncles, aunts. It makes a cat sound and two other sounds. I've heard just the 'meow' sound and the other, a very rough sound like an eagle or a horse would make, only once. The other sound is a clacking sound, like teeth. Well, of course, I've heard the wings flapping. You can tell the Bird must be pretty big but I've never seen it."

We glanced a bit incredulously at Lt. Flores and another officer, who were sitting by impassively during the interview. Obviously they had heard the story before.

We drove with Cantu down to nearby Brownsville with two jars of feces, which we showed to Curator David Thompson of the Gladys Porter Zoo. Since zoo spokesmen had made it clear some time earlier that they did not care to involve themselves in the Bird controversy, we carefully refrained from using the offending word in Thompson's presence. It did not stop him from asking us, after we'd inquired about "what kind of bird" he thought might have dropped the feces, "You think they might be from Big Bird, right?"

Fortunately he took it all in good humor, explaining that the zoo had no facilities for analyzing feces. "Besides," he said, "it's very difficult to determine what kind of animal made the dropping just from the dropping alone. You can tell what it ate, and that's about all." Thompson theorized that the droppings were from a possum.

At this writing the droppings are being analyzed by scientists connected with the Society for the Investigation of the Unexplained, a New Jersey-based group founded by the late Ivan Sanderson.

As we headed back to San Benito, we asked

Cantu if he would introduce us to some of the other witnesses he had mentioned. "Oh," he said, "they won't talk. They're too shy. They don't want their names in the papers. They know that people will make fun of them."

We said we could understand that. "But how do we know you're not making all of this up out of your head?"

Cantu was silent for a while, then said he would see if he could persuade some of the people to talk with us. When we met the next day in front of the San Benito police station, he had one of the supposed witnesses with him, a man who asked to be identified only by his first name, Chris.

Chris, twenty-six, a bus driver and part-time carpenter, is a life-long resident of San Benito. Shyly, occasionally laughing in embarrassment, he told us, "Yes, I've heard the Bird. I've even been close to it but I've never seen it.

"When I was thirteen or fourteen—about the time I dropped out of school—I used to go out and come back home about 1:00 or 2:00 in the morning. That's when I would hear it. It would make a sound like *tch-tch-tch,* with a whistle, very loud. I told my mother about it. She'd heard those sounds before and she warned me not to be out when it's around because it's a bad bird. She said a lady around here was beaten by the Bird. Another lady, she's dead now, saw it often through her window. Another woman said it has a cat face and no beak. The face is a foot in diameter and it has a thick, foot-long neck. It has big eyes.

"In 1964 or 1965, during the summer, my cousin and I had gone to the drive-in and I came home late through the alley. I could hear the Bird following me. I ran. I was very frightened. I told my mother, 'The Bird's after me!' My mother, dad, and sisters went out. We couldn't see nothing because we didn't have a flashlight. My father hit the tree where the Bird was with a broom until finally it flew to another tree in our neighbor's lot. Three dogs were barking, with their teeth showing. We never did see the Bird. We could just hear it moving among the leaves on the trees.

"Then about three weeks ago [mid-February] something heavy fell on the roof of our house. The TV antenna began shaking. I had a rifle but I didn't want to go out, but not because I'm afraid. I've been living with this for a long time. When I was young, it kind of followed me, you know. That hasn't happened lately, though.

"I used to pick cotton when I was young. Around Santa Rosa. There was a very old lady who would talk about it. That's when I first heard about it. She was scared. She talked about it like it was an evil bird."

"My uncle saw it in 1945," Cantu interjected. "It was an extremely large bird. My father saw it, too, also another uncle. It was a very, very big bird. My father saw it twenty years ago, flying at tree-top level. It had a white breast.

"I could get you twenty people, like that," he added, snapping his fingers. "But they're afraid, too shy. The descriptions are all the same. They say it has a cat face."

First in the company of Cantu and Chris, and later alone, we drove down the streets of the La-Palma Colony, the name given the Mexican-American neighborhood on San Benito's northwest side where the sightings supposedly occurred. The first person we talked with was Chris' mother, Leonor, a small, wrinkled 62-year-old woman who does not speak English. As our two companions did the talking and translating, we watched her as she vividly reenacted the Bird's cries and motions.

She said, according to the translation, that it was

true about the Bird. She had first heard it when Chris was about twelve, one day when she was out feeding the rabbits. It was in a tree, which she pointed to, and making a whistling, clicking sound, which she imitated. She had seen it around 10:00 one evening last year as she was coming from church. It was a big white bird and it flew across the street.

Over ten years ago a lady named Ignacia—she did not know her last name—had been walking to the outhouse when the Bird attacked her from behind. She had heard it flying and was just turning around when it ripped into her with "long, long" claws and tore off some of her clothing. (As Leonor spoke, she enacted the clawing with her own thin, almost birdlike arms.) It had an ugly, catlike face, enormous wings, black feathers, and no bill. The woman, who had been ill long before the attack, was dead now and had left no relatives.

Later, we stopped a young woman on the street and asked her if she knew anything about a strange bird in the neighborhood. Frowning, clearly reluctant to speak, she finally said, "Yes, it is true. We've heard it. It makes a lot of noise and sometimes we can hear it walking on top of the shack back of our house. There was a lady who lived down the street and the Bird attacked her. But she's dead now. That happened a long time ago, over ten years."

She pointed to a house where she said the woman lived. We went over and knocked on the door, but no one was home. Maybe just as well. The young woman had told us that the people living there now were not relatives. The woman had left no relatives, so far as she knew.

A forty-year-old car mechanic related his experience with the Bird three decades earlier, when he was eleven. He and a friend had been lying on top of a trailer filled with cotton, parked between a truck with a small trailer attached and a barn. Suddenly they heard a flapping sound from behind the barn. Soon an enormous bird glided over the barn and passed by about twenty feet above the ground. Its wingspan surpassed the combined length of the truck (twelve feet) and the attached trailer (seven feet), putting the size at well over twenty feet. He did not see its face but saw that it had no feathers.

Tony, twenty-seven, said he and his wife-to-be had seen something very strange in August 1966. "It was about 1:00 a.m.," he recalled. "Maria and I were sitting in the car over by my mother's house and we saw this thing standing on a telephone pole. It was dark so we couldn't see well but I could see enough of it to know I'd never seen anything like it. It was a weird big bird, bigger than a man, a yard wide, with wings folded around it. It was black. We could see it staring at us. We ran over to my mother's house. I haven't seen or heard it since.

"One time in 1967 my mother was sleeping in the living room and she heard something flapping against the house. She was too scared to go outside.

"Once a bird hurt a woman. A little boy was scratched, too. Everybody knew about it."

Maybe everybody did know about it, but we were never able to get direct confirmation of the supposed incident. Nonetheless the story fits so well into the pattern that we are willing to accept it as something other than pure folklore.

There seems little real question that something very weird indeed has been taking place in San Benito for at least the past thirty years, and it is irrelevant to point to old superstitions as the stimulus for the alleged sightings. The hoary legends the newspapers revived did not seem to be part of the living folklore of the LaPalma Colony. The people we talked with, even the old ones, either had never heard the old stories about *Lechuza* (a girl who, having been rejected by her suitor, turned into a bird and attacked evil-doers), or did not connect them with what they had seen. The Bird was not viewed as a supernatural omen. It was "bad" and "evil" for a very simple reason: it attacked people.

That is not to say that a certain folklore had not grown up around it. For example, one informant assured us the Bird was "known" to hide every night in a big tree on Virginia Street, near a certain man's residence. When we called on the fellow in question, our questions were greeted with blank incomprehension. Finally the man said that not only did he not harbor the Bird in his yard, he did not even believe in its existence.

The incidents in San Benito continue. On April 7, 1976, Cantu, whose honesty and common sense we, like the San Benito police, had come to respect, wrote, "My aunt heard it walk on the roof twice since the day you were gone. She said it sounded loud . . . The dogs were barking at it. I got on top of the roof and walked on it. I asked my aunt if she heard me . . . She said no. This kind of gives you the idea of how heavy or strong that bird really is." April 20: "Since the last time I wrote to you, Big Bird stopped on a tree at my aunt's home. The bird stopped at 5:00 a.m."

While Texas' Big Bird was the one that got all the attention, it was not the only one being seen anywhere. On January 1, 1976, Dr. Berthold Eric Schwarz, a Montclair, New Jersey, psychiatrist, author and parapsychologist whom we have already mentioned in another context, was driving down Highway 46 past the quarry near Great Notch when suddenly he spotted an enormous long-necked bird sailing by, hardly flapping its wings as it flew close to the ground.

"I wouldn't have thought anything of it," he said to us, "except that it was so huge and its wings didn't seem to be flapping much at all. But what disturbed me the most was that it was so white, even as dark as it was. *How could it have been so white?* Unless—I know this sounds ridiculous—it was luminous."

But the weirdest one of all appeared on Easter Sunday, April 17, 1976, at Mawnan, Cornwall, England. The witnesses were two girls, June and Vicky Melling, who were there on a holiday outing from their Preston, Lancashire, home when they saw a grotesque-looking "big feathered bird-man" as it hovered over the church tower. The sight so upset them that the family cut their holiday short and returned to Preston three days early.

Fortean investigator Doc Shiels interviewed the girls' father, Don Melling, who gave him a sketch of the thing which June had drawn that same day. The sketch, reprinted in the June 1976 issue of Bob Rickard's *Fortean Times,* shows an unbelievable phenomenon which almost defies description. Firm believers in the old saw that one picture is worth any number of words, we reproduce the drawing here:

The same or a very similar creature was allegedly seen on July 3, 1976, by two fourteen-year-old girls who were camping among the trees near the Mawnan Church, where the first sighting took place. Around 10:00 p.m. they heard a peculiar "hissing" sound, which made them look up and observe a weird figure standing in the trees about twenty yards away.

"It was like a big owl with pointed ears, as big as a man," Sally Chapman told Shiels. "The eyes were red and glowing. At first, I thought it was someone dressed up, playing a joke, trying to scare us. I laughed at it, we both did, then it went up in the air and we both screamed. When it went up, you could see its feet were like pincers."

Barbara Perry added, "It's true. It was horrible, a nasty owl-face with big ears and big red eyes. It was covered in gray feathers. The claws on its feet were black. It just flew straight up and disappeared in the tree-tops."

The sighting lasted only a few seconds.

Shiels separated the two girls and had them draw sketches of what they had seen. The drawings were very similar, though Sally thought Barbara had "done the wings wrong." Sally depicted the wings as being more birdlike, whereas Barbara's illustration showed somewhat humanlike arms with feathers attached. Neither picture precisely matches the one above, but the differences can perhaps be explained as the product of faulty observation caused by poor lighting conditions, the brevity of the sightings, and the extreme fright they evoked in the witnesses.

The next day three women saw the "Owlman" in almost the same spot. This letter from Jane Greenwood of Southport appeared in the *Falmouth Packet* for July 9:

"I am on holiday in Cornwall with my sister and our mother. I too have seen a big bird-thing like that pictured . . . It was Sunday (4th) morning and the place was in the trees near Mawnan Church, above the rocky beach. It was in the trees standing like a full-grown man, but the legs bent backwards like a bird's. It saw us and quickly jumped up and rose straight up through the trees. My sister and I saw it very clearly before it rose up. It has red slanting eyes and a very large mouth. The feathers are silver gray and so are his body and legs. The feet are like big black crab's claws. We were frightened at the time. It was so strange, like something out of a horror film. After the thing went up there were crackling sounds in the tree-tops for ages. Our mother thinks we made it all up just because we read about these things, but that is not true. We really saw the birdman, though it could have been somebody playing a trick in very good costume and make-up. But how could it rise up like that? If we imagined it, then we both imagined the same thing at the same time."

Big Bird (or, at any rate, a big bird) returned to Texas for some final appearances in December 1976. This time, however, it was in east-central Texas, not the Rio Grande Valley. And this time someone shot it and got some physical evidence, which is being analyzed at we write this.

On the afternoon of December 8, John 'S. Carroll, Jr., a Montalba area hog rancher, was walking out of a shed in his back yard when he saw an enormous bird standing in the middle of a pond a hundred feet away. It was trying to fly but seemed to be having a difficult time getting airborne. Stunned, Carroll stared at it for a few moments, observing something about eight feet tall, bluish steel-gray in color, with a golden-hued breast and a twelve-inch bill.

"I was thinking that I didn't want a thing that

big hanging around my place, that I had no idea what it was or what it might do to my pigs," Carroll said later. He dashed to his pickup to retrieve his deer rifle. As he did so, the bird took flight, heading north several hundred feet, then circling briefly before rising above the ravine to the northwest. Finally it alighted in a hardwood tree and stood on a limb about 25 feet above the ground.

"When it settled on that limb," Carroll said, "the whole tree shook and vibrated violently. That bird must weigh 100 pounds."

By this time the rancher was ready to shoot, even though he knew the distance—about a thousand feet—was fairly large. Carroll sighted the target through the scope, squeezed off a single shot and was amazed to see the bird drop from the tree and out of his range of vision.

Neighbor Mike Ellis heard the shot and, thinking Carroll had fired on a deer, came over to help. The two of them raced to the scene but found nothing, at least at first. As they broadened the area of the search, they discovered a blood-stained feather 75 feet from the tree.

Carroll did not exactly hasten to the local newspaper office to tell his story. "I didn't call the newspaper for fear folks would think I was losing my marbles or was drunk," he explained. "What would you do if you saw something almost as big as a horse flying?"

But then he heard of a similar sighting made by a youth from nearby Palestine, Texas. Carroll called the witness, Donnie Simmons, and the two compared notes. Reporter Ernest Jones heard of the incident from a friend of Simmons' and soon after interviewed the reluctant Carroll.

On December 17 Carroll, one of the leading swine breeders in Texas, gave the feather to Palestine biologist Larry Lamely, who in turn sent it on to Steve

Wylie, curator of birds at the St. Louis, Missouri, Zoo. Carroll, who once lived near the Arkansas National Wildlife Refuge, home of the whooping cranes, said he was familiar with many varieties of large birds, but the thing he saw was none of them. Lamely showed Carroll several books which contained numerous pictures of birds, and still the rancher was unable to identify it.

The resulting newspaper publicity caused several other persons to admit they had seen the bird prior to its appearance on Carroll's land. After that, on December 17, a Bethel, Texas, woman named Dolois Moore saw the thing through a window of her home. She described it as "very large, like a big crane seen through a magnifying glass...

"The bird was about 150 yards away from me. Our big Brahman bull was trying to get close to the bird. Every time he did, the bird took wing and flew off a short distance, then resumed feeding in our oats and rye pasture."

Mrs. Moore said it appeared to have an injured wing. Her place is fifteen miles northwest of the Carroll farm.

A further sighting was made by a woman near Catfish Creek, three miles south of the Moore residence, on the morning of December 22.

5.

Winged weirdos are hardly new to the American landscape. The first Americans, the Indians, spoke of giant flying creatures they called "thunderbirds." Sightings, or alleged sightings, are made from time to time even today. In Anglo-American folklore the "Jersey Devil" is often described as a manlike bird with horns.

But if the legends are the stuff of fantasy, there

remain the testimonies of many living persons who attest to the existence of Unidentified Flapping Objects. Undoubtedly the weirdest of all was something called "Mothman," the subject of a 1975 book by John Keel *(The Mothman Prophecies).*

Mothman, named after a character in the once-popular Batman television series, first showed up in the Ohio River Valley before anyone thought to give it a name—as long ago, apparently, as 1960 or 1961, when several unpublicized sightings were made. It was not until the fall of 1966 that the residents of the Valley realized they had a visitor, one which, though distinctly unwelcome, stayed fourteen months and introduced itself to over a hundred persons, none of whom were pleased to make the acquaintance.

Mothman was usually described as being between five and seven feet tall, gray in color, with large glowing red eyes set in or near the top of the shoulders. The wings, which had a spread of ten feet or so, did not flap in flight.

As usual, there were certain variations from the common description. A few witnesses said it looked like an enormous winged man. Two said they thought it might be a machine of some kind, because they had heard a mechanical humming sound as the thing passed overhead. Obviously Mothman, like most monsters, had something for everyone.

It certainly had something for the authors of this book.

In April 1976, after Jerome Clark had returned from his investigatory jaunt through the Rio Grande Valley, he was interviewed by telephone by Vic Wheatman, who hosts a Fortean radio show on Boston's WBUR-FM, and Loren Coleman. The interview, taped for later broadcast (it eventually aired on May 24), went without incident. It was only when Wheatman and Coleman played the tape back that they realized something extremely odd had occurred.

Midway through the conversation Coleman had asked Clark if he saw any similarity between the Big Bird reports and the "Mothman" reports ten years earlier.

"Very definite similarity," Clark replied. "Now, John Keel, of course, is the man who did the research on Mothman. Keel claimed that there is a connection between these sightings and UFOs. If there's any such connection with the Big Bird, I was unable to prove it. . . . All I know is that this thing doesn't have any business existing in the Rio Grande Valley or anywhere. This is really something out of the ordinary. I have no idea where it is coming from."

As he spoke these lines, Clark heard nothing out of the ordinary on his end. Neither did Wheatman and Coleman on theirs. Yet on the tape, immediately after the word "sightings" in the third sentence, there is a loud, unmistakable and very startling EEPPP! sound—precisely the sound Mothman is supposed to have made. ("It squeaked like a big mouse," one of the original Mothman witnesses had commented in 1966.)

When radio station personnel heard the sound, they could offer no explanation, unless it originated with Clark, which it didn't.

And now, our journey through wonderland completed, it is time to make sense of all this nonsense.

CHAPTER SIX

Phantasms

1.

Throughout this book we have had occasion to refer to UFOs, but their role in all of this has never been too clear. In some cases these creatures, especially the manimals, have appeared to be UFO occupants. In other instances UFOs have been sighted in areas where people were encountering creatures, and the link between them has only been implied. Most of the time UFOs have not entered the picture at all.

Whatever the case, we think this much is clear: *UFOs and creatures are generated by a single paranormal mechanism.* The parallels between the phenomena are undeniable:

1.) *Both are far more elusive than they have a right to be—if they are what they appear to be.*

Both have given us what Dr. J. Allen Hynek calls an "embarrassment of riches." We plainly have far too many of them. Extraterrestrial spaceships simply could not be touring the earth in the massive numbers UFO sightings suggest. The mathematical foundations for this statement are ably explained in Chapter 28 of Carl Sagan's *The Cosmic Connection,* to which we refer interested readers. Neither could massive numbers of large unknown animals be roaming countrysides and city streets without long ago having been officially recognized and catalogued (and probably driven into extinction as well).

Moreover, they could not have done all this in such numbers without providing us with more conclusive physical evidence than they have given us so far. The "physical evidence" is always just enough to suggest that the reported manifestation was not purely hallucinatory; it is never enough to prove that it was objectively real. And the "physical evidence," most often ground traces in the form of landing marks (as in UFO cases) or tracks (creature cases), less frequently physical parts in the form of metallic residue or hair, is frustratingly ambiguous and inconclusive. The ground traces differ from incident to incident, and at best some are only very generally similar. The investigator cannot use them to predict the kind of trace a particular kind of UFO or creature will make. The alleged physical parts are invariably agonizingly ambiguous. The most one can expect from them is the suggestion that their cause *could* have been an unknown craft or creature. More often, however, the alleged evidence proves to be something completely mundane.

2.) *They appear in a wide variety of shapes but tend toward certain very general types.*

As we have shown in *The Unidentified,* there are so many different kinds of UFO beings described in the reports that if they are extraterrestrial they must be coming from at least a thousand different planets. Nonetheless most of them do have one head, two arms, and two legs and most are small in size. Many of the dwarfs are said to wear what look like "diving suits."

Beyond that, though, the similarities end for the most part. (There is a small minority of incidents in which precisely similar beings have been observed in different areas.) The humanoids have big heads, little heads and medium-sized heads; bug eyes, slanted eyes, one eye, or no eye; long noses, short noses, or just two holes where a nose should be; a lipless slit for a mouth, a fishlike mouth, or a "normal" human one; any number of fingers or claws on the hand; just about any shade of skin color; and so on and on.

For reasons of space (and maybe sanity, too) we have confined ourselves to several basic creature types, but as we noted in the introduction, that does not mean a virtually endless number are not reported. For instance, a Montana woman recently discovered a huge glob of jellylike substance in her front lawn. An English policeman named Bishop encountered a "walking fir-cone" in a park in Ramsgate, Kent, on April 16, 1954. During the summer of 1969 a number of Texans reported seeing a "half-man, half-goat thing with fur and scales."

Godfrey H. Anderson claimed that while strolling down an Edinburgh, Scotland, street on November 23, 1904, he saw a "vague black shape about four feet long and two and a half feet high" rise out of the gutter. It was shaped, he said, "like an hourglass and moved like a huge caterpillar," and it sprang at the throat of a horse, which abruptly reared up in terror. While it was doing so, the thing vanished.

In 1951 a Calumet, Oklahoma, farm woman spotted a creature that "looked like a cross between a wolf and a deer." Something very similar appeared to two hunters near Canby, Minnesota, on March

27, 1971. That same year a quadrapedal "wolf-woman" terrorized the Delphos, Kansas, area. On July 4, 1974, a father and his two sons observed "a medium-sized dog with a monkey face" and a curved, monkeylike tail leap across a country road near Oakland, Nebraska.

Obviously, we could go on and on* but we hardly need belabor the point. Still, as with UFO occupants, certain creature types predominate, despite their considerable variety. The Texas Big Bird sightings provide the most graphic demonstration of this principle, as we have seen, but even among the relatively "stable" manimals we encounter such variations as:

a). Two-, three-, four-, five- and six-toed tracks, plus varying shapes even among tracks with the same number of toes.

b.) Eyes that glow red, green, orange or yellow, and eyes that do not glow at all.

c.) Long, ape-length arms and shorter, human-length ones.

d.) Machinelike behavior and animal-like behavior.

e.) Enormously huge, broad-shouldered specimens and others that are relatively slender.

f.) Ones that stink and ones that don't.

g.) Some that have large fangs jutting out of their mouths and some that have no visible teeth.

h.) Ones that resemble "apemen" and others that resemble "wolfmen."

3.) *People who see them may experience other types of paranormal phenomena as well.*

Witnesses may find themselves plagued with poltergeists or visited by men in black. They may

* Those who care to pursue the matter should consult *The Books of Charles Fort* and John A. Keel's *Strange Creatures from Time and Space.*

receive odd, sometimes threatening phone calls, or receive psychic "revelations" of an apocalyptic nature. They may find that car engines die mysteriously or electric lights fade when the manifestation is near.

These kinds of things happen to relatively few percipients, and usually only to those who have had some sort of prolonged exposure to a UFO or a creature. The considerable majority of sightings are of short duration and are free of either obvious paranormal content or subsequent paranormal fallout. John Keel has suggested that when a rash of manifestations break out in an area one person or one family is actually the target; it is he, she, or they who are subjected to the whole range of paranormal infestation. Other witnesses are just outsiders whose sightings are of no particular significance, since these people are seeing nothing more than the most obvious surface manifestations. We don't know at this point if that is really the case or not, but it is an extremely interesting idea that researchers should bear in mind during future investigations.

4.) *The phenomena encompass "opposite" qualities at the same time.*

UFOs are at once "technological" and "magical." They look like machines but they behave much like ghosts or fairy-ships. Many of their allegedly extraterrestrial occupants resemble angels (in several instances they have even identified themselves as such!), and so the manifestations are "scientific" and "religious" at the same time; the angels are androgynous beings, with features of both male and female; and so on. The supposed technical powers of the ufonauts (their abilities to vanish instantaneously, to paralyze witnesses, to stop vehicles, and so on) are identical with the supernatural powers long attributed to fairies and other mythical folk.

Creatures may resemble biological animals. Up to a point they may even behave like them, sleeping, eating, defecating, even showing some evidence of a sex drive. There may even be apparent "creature families." Yet at the same time a creature seen eating food on a sandy bank will fail to leave footprints—an apparition, it seems, with purely biological hunger. In other cases the creatures may give every appearance of being zoological while acting mechanical. In the UFO-related episodes, creatures from our evolutionary past manifest in the company of, or even inside, vehicles from our technological future. Werewolves and demon-dogs prowl the countryside while spaceships from other planets zoom overhead.

Most of all, though, UFOs and creatures seem both to exist and not to exist. Neither their existence nor their nonexistence can be proved. They are like fantasies that have come mysteriously, and briefly, to life. Trying to establish their reality is like trying to preserve a revelation one has had in a dream. One of the authors remembers a dream he had several years ago in which he was told how to levitate himself through the air. In the dream it seemed a simple enough matter, and as he felt himself starting to awaken, he thought frantically, "I've got to remember this!" But the instant his eyes opened, the secret was gone.

Likewise, percipients of strange phenomena struggle to prove the things they have encountered are "real." Like D. K. and innumerable others, they seek frantically to hold on to something—a body, a mechanical implement, a new truth—which will survive the encounter and will place it in "this" world. They never succeed. They grasp for the substance and touch only the shadow.

2.

Man is trapped between his past and his future. On one hand he looks beyond the dust speck which has always been his home and gazes out into the unimaginable reaches of infinity, wondering what, and who, waits out there, knowing that one day, inevitably, his curiosity will overcome his qualms and he will go out there to find what he must find.

He is of two minds about it. That future, that prospect, fascinates and frightens. Will he find salvation there? Or beings so superior that all human endeavor seems a futile joke by comparison?

Even more immediately, as his burgeoning technology directs him inexorably toward some distant cosmic perspective, that technology begins to trouble him deeply. Looking about, seeing the terrifying uses to which totalitarian states have put technology, he wonders if it will ultimately enslave him—or already has. Will it also destroy the planet he lives on? He sees the development of weapons of hideous destructive power. He sees the forests disappearing, rivers turning into streams of sewage, whole species of animals disappearing daily, while human beings are packed tightly into little boxes from which they fear to emerge, lest savages who prowl the streets after dark knife them for pocket change.

It is not particularly surprising that the Age of Ecology should follow the Age of Space. It was not so much a rejection of the prospect of space travel as the fear of the technology that sired the Space Age, which caused human beings to think about their role in the terrestrial natural order. The understanding grew that in some way human physical and spiritual survival was tied to the preservation of the natural environment, that if we were surrounded by nothing but machines we might become such ourselves. Nature, once feared and hated, once seen as something from which one must escape, now seemed a more benevolent place, the true home of the soul.

Skeptics have often remarked on what a coincidence it is that, just when we began thinking seriously about space travel and space beings, "spaceships" started showing up in our atmosphere. The implication is that UFOs are nothing but delusions born of the cultural imagination. That is only half true. The skeptics have failed miserably in all their myriad efforts to prove that what are called UFOs are nothing but misinterpreted conventional phenomena and hoaxes. Yet believers in UFOs as spaceships have failed just as fully to make their case. All that we have been able to establish so far is that something unknown, something which has the *appearance* of being extraterrestrial, is being seen and reported with great frequency. Evidently, in some mysterious fashion, our own psychological obsessions created corresponding physical phantasms. As Fort remarked, "If our existence is an organism, in which all phenomena are continuous, dreams cannot be utterly different, in the view of continuity, from occurrences that are said to be real."

The UFO occupants, as we came to "know" them through repeated encounters and contacts, proved to be a curious lot. While they seemed to possess an advanced technology, they were forever warning contactees that technology is dangerously two-edged and that the uses we have made of it are all wrong. Some ufonauts, especially those of the androgynous "Venusian" variety, seemed as much priest/philosophers as scientists. "I would say that their religion and their science are all in one," one contactee observed. They constantly warned percipients that *homo sapiens* is "upsetting the balance of the universe" in its mad obsession with material values over spiritual ones.

No wonder the "scientific ufologists," trapped in a mechanistic view of the universe, despised the contactees.

Other UFO beings were not so benevolent. Though possessed like their kindlier brethren of what seemed to be a "superior technology," they still were the worst kind of savage primitives, grotesque, destructive, stupid. Others, neither friendly nor unfriendly, were machinelike in either appearance or behavior, soul-less and unfeeling, indifferent to the human beings with whom they dealt, betraying no sense but one of overwhelmingly superior authority.

On many levels a message began to emerge. The reports produced wonder and excitement. They also produced bewilderment and fear. On one side, mankind realized that a tremendous adventure—the confrontation with the cosmos—awaited it, and that such a confrontation was made possible by its development of an incredibly sophisticated technology. But it could just as easily lead to the establishment of a frightening order in which men could play out their most violent fantasies on a new and infinitely more dangerous scale. Or it could destroy their every human impulse and reduce them to machines whose sole function was to run other machines, automatons who had lost their capacity for communion with their fellows.

These concerns were not engendered solely by UFO reports, of course. The UFO reports reflected deep concerns of the human psyche, acting out these concerns in what essentially were metaphorical displays. One of the few intellectuals to understand the significance of the UFO phenomenon, the late psychoanalyst C. G. Jung, saw them as symbols of a great crisis in the psychic life of mankind and as portents of an impending profound change in consciousness.

UFOs represented the promise and the peril of

technology, the wonders and dangers of a cosmic consciousness to which technology would ultimately lead. As humanity's doubts about technology grew and as governments curtailed space programs, the back-to-the-earth movement started and societal consciousness shifted to a new awareness of mankind's immediate natural environment. While there were clear logical reasons for doing so (such as the realization that we could not go on polluting the planet indefinitely without serious consequences), there were also decidedly alogical impulses involved. At its core the Ecology Movement was a spiritual movement.

Accompanying the new ecological concern were less attractive manifestations, such as the revival of fundamentalist Christianity, Satanism, and any number of offbeat cults which eschewed the process of reason altogether. As William Irwin Thompson remarked, "The death of materialism will open man up to beasts and demons he has not feared since the Middle Ages." These cults trafficked in unreason and rank superstition.

Just as our obsession with technology and interplanetary visitors brought UFOs to everyone's attention, so did the new concern with nature and intuitive thought bring the creature phenomenon to the forefront. It was as if ghosts from another age in the planet's natural history had returned to haunt us.

Significantly enough, the most prominent were those most like us, or as we probably were in the early days of our evolutionary development: reclusive, hairy, apelike beings living in woods and caves. Actually, the archetype of the beast in the wilderness is an ancient one which has always expressed man's memory of his primordial past, but in recent times it has assumed a new role in what Jung termed "the constellation of psychic dominants." The manimal archetype symbolizes the animal in man, the elemental man freed of the demands of technological order, returned to the forests and caves to live in gentle harmony with nature. In the sense the manimal exists in counterpoint to the flying saucer.

But of course it is not quite that simple. What about those manimals seen in or near UFOs? Such reports are in a minority but that does not mean that we should ignore them or that they have no significance. In fact, we should expect them because, as we have noted several times, *Fortean manifestations tend toward their opposites.* "Everything," Fort wrote, "merges away into everything else." If such events have any meaning that can be expressed intellectually, they may be telling us that "natural man" and "technological man"—the intuitive man and the rational man—can live together in balance. If we can contain technology from being wholly dominated by our natural, arational impulses, with such inevitable consequences as violence, madness and superstition, we will not lose our souls but survive to achieve the cosmic perspective.

There are great dangers in all of this. To maintain what the ufonaut philosophers call "the balance of the universe," we must tread the thin line between conscious rational, technological impulses and unconscious intuitive, natural ones, favoring neither one nor the other, always seeing one as only half of the whole.

The danger we face, as in the current crisis in human affairs we contemplate a return to the wilderness, to the elemental mode, is implied particularly in the phantom cat, dog and bird stories, with their recurring motifs of violence and hostility. They remind us that nature is not quite the benevolent place modern-day sentimentalists would have us believe it is. Perhaps these visions reflect ancestral memories of a time in our dim prehistoric past when men lived in fear of animal adversaries.

Even more fundamentally we confront the prospect of psychic annihilation. Stephen Pulaski was turned into an animal because the archetypal implications of the situation (the appearance of two creatures) were so incredibly powerful that they literally "possessed" him. During his terrifying experience he had a vision which warned him, and all of us, that the stakes are very high indeed. The human race may well be destroyed if it allows itself to be overcome by the contents of the collective unconscious, if it wanders too far into the wilderness.

The man in black who appears in the vision is an archetypal representation of the "shadow" side of the unconscious mind, that part of the psyche in which we repress our darkest impulses. When men in black, in UFO and creature lore go about threatening percipients, they are in effect warning them of the dangers inherent in dealing with paranormal occurrences, whose dreamlike ambience may lure an individual into a shadowy realm of madness and terror from which he may never return. Such a warning is only implicit, of course; often the effect of the MIB visitation is to draw the victim even farther into this other realm. The individual percipient—and by extension the whole human race—stands in danger of losing his hold on the world of conscious reality. When that happens, the individual personality, and all of civilized society, cannot long survive.

3.

If Fortean phenomena do tend toward their opposites, then we can see, at least on one level, why they appear both to exist and not to exist. After all, what is more fundamental than the dichotomy between reality and fantasy? But what are they? Where do they come from? How are they generated? What will happen to us when they force us to alter our perception of the universe?

The answers to these questions await us some time in the unforseeable future. In the meantime, if we keep our bearings, we will learn much from the strange phenomena we have discussed in these pages. Once we understand them, or as much of them as we are capable of understanding—once we come to know that we should neither fear them nor revere them—we will see them for what they are: companions with whom we are walking, in balance, on our way to the next great human adventure.

EPILOGUE

1977—A Year Filled With Monsters

> "I know I saw the creature!"
> —Abby Brabham commenting on her sighting of the
> Dover Demon

The mystery animals discussed in the preceding pages have continued to creep, crawl, fly, and run through the lives of humanity. As this opus quickly approaches publication, we felt it might be interesting to give a cross-section of a few noteworthy cases of 1977: cases which, in fact, further demonstrate the meanderings of the manifestations of the phenomena.

The year was a good one for sightings of the creatures of the outer edge. Bigfoot was allegedly photographed on Mount Baker in Washington State. The "skunk ape" was photographed in Florida, but the photographer and his pictures soon disappeared. The manimals were active in such widely separated locations as Easton, Pennsylvania, and Abilene, Texas. The so-called Bigfoot of Little Eagle, South Dakota, made the Halloween issue of *Newsweek*.

The manimals also returned to the Ohio County, Indiana, "window." As we noted elsewhere in this book (see pages 75 and 123), Rising Sun has been the focus of EM, UFO, and MA activity in the past. In 1977, Tom and Connie Courter saw their hairy, apelike, 12-foot-tall creature on the 12th and 13th of April, outside of Rising Sun. The first night, the couple left Mrs. Courter's parents' home around 11 p.m., and were getting ready to drive home. Tom was reaching into the back seat to get their baby's diaper bag when the creature crashed into the side of the car, denting it. They quickly called the police, but no trace of the thing was found. It was 11:45 p.m. the next night when they saw and heard it. "It was a real funny noise—like an ugh—and then we saw him sitting perched on the hill," Mrs. Courter said. Her husband had come prepared, armed with a sixteen shot .22 caliber rifle, and he emptied all 16 shots into it. Once again, the deputy sheriff found nothing. The creature had simply left.

As for phantom cat activity, we were able to personally check into the reports of a sheep killer in Ohio. Most of the publicity surrounding the Richland Township, Ohio, killings began after Sherwood Burkholder was interviewed by Dayton TV-7, and other local media. On the 25th of April, 1977, Burkholder lost forty sheep to some unknown animal killer. On the 26th, he lost another seventeen.

William Reeder, Dog Warden and Executive Director of the Allen County Humane Society, had been involved with the investigations of the killings for more than a month before Burkholder's sheep were attacked. Reeder was the person most often quoted in the press, and it was with him that Loren Coleman spent the better part of June 29, 1977, discussing the problem. Reeder told us the Burkholder sheep had been grabbed at the rear of their jaws, and then clawed forward. Eight claw marks were visible on the side of the sheep. Although most of the sheep were not dead when Reeder arrived on the scene, he had to destroy all of them. Later he went back and took plaster casts of what he believed were the killer's tracks.

The Burkholder sheep were kept in a large pen located near Tom Fett and Rockport Roads. The killer struck before dawn the first time, then early the next day, and finally on the afternoon of that same day. Carol Benson, who rents the trailer that sits on Burkholder's land (Sherwood Burkholder lives on a farm many miles north), told us she did not hear a thing, and even came home the second time it happened to find Reeder destroying the clawed-up sheep. A month later, Carol Benson, her son Bryan, and Burkholder saw a large black cat walking back and forth among the trees near the creek out back.

While the Burkholder story got most of the media coverage, the killings at the Elmer Nesbaum farm in March are more interesting from an investigative and human point of view. On March 22, 1977, something got into Elmer Nesbaum's sheep. Through interviews with William Reeder and Mr. and Mrs. Elmer Nesbaum, we were able to reconstruct the events as follows.

Elmer Nesbaum, 74, and his wife, a Reformed Mennonite couple, live on a 94-acre farm a couple miles northwest of Burkholder's land. The first time the mystery animal came, it was a windy, snowy March night. Elmer Nesbaum had penned his sheep because most of them were about ready to lamb. He liked sheep; they were easy to keep and these had become his friends; they would all crowd around him when he came out to see them. "When I came in the first morning," Nesbaum said, "only a few were standing. They were all red, and I wondered what happened with these sheep. Something terrible went on in there! It was a bad sight to see." What Nesbaum found was a "bloody mess" of deeply clawed and dying sheep at the end of the pen. He called a veterinarian, and had what sheep could be saved sewed up.

Then Elmer Nesbaum made preparations to protect the survivors. His sheep were housed in a pen at the back part of a U-shaped area, between his barn and his machine and lofting sheds. Nesbaum had heavy farm gates across the front of the pen, regular wire fencing up to the roof of the barn, and then chicken wire on the top. He put six steel muskrat traps in front of the pen.

When the creature came back on the 26th of March, it set off all six traps, and clawed the gate apart. It left chunks of wood strewn about, pockmarked with teeth marks, and apparent claw marks. When we inspected the pen and ground area, pieces of wood, one to two feet long, were still in the same position Nesbaum had found them on the 26th. He had not moved a thing. The wood slats of the fencing showed many signs of teeth and claw. Nesbaum gave us several of these wood chunks. Many semi-circular bites out of the wood and fang-like punctures are quite visible.

At the time, Nesbaum noticed clumps of black and blackish-brown hair sticking to the wood fencing. He did not keep it, not thinking it important at the time. "I didn't realize it was goin' to become such a mystery," Elmer explained.

As Bill Reeder described it, the animal had "literally clawed the Nesbaum sheep; it didn't eat the sheep; didn't hamstring the sheep; didn't gut the sheep. It just put eight perfect claw marks down the side—from the backbone to the stomach. One of the ewes had her udder completely torn off. Also," Reeder continued, "there was fang marks across the neck. Definitely punctures of four in nature, two on each side." That was after the first attack. The second time, Reeder noticed "only clawing, no biting. The only one with fang marks was a lamb which had been born between the first and second attacks. It had the four perfect fang marks. The vet tried to save it, but its ribcage was crushed."

Because the pen was on a concrete slab covered by straw, Reeder and the Nesbaums only found one track. In all, the Nesbaums had lost twenty sheep, most of them pregnant.

To Elmer Nesbaum and his wife, it was a personal tragedy. They had been looking forward to selling their sheep and new lambs, selling the farm, and retiring to a smaller place. Mrs. Nesbaum had been ill over the winter, and Elmer wanted to move closer to the city. The killings ended their hopes, and Nesbaum felt he was "out of the business, but you hate it to go out like that."

Elmer Nesbaum spoke to us of his affection for his sheep and was obviously deeply moved in his retelling of the "bloody mess" he discovered. Bill Reeder told us how the couple had stood there and cried. They finally had had to walk into their farmhouse, for they could not watch Reeder destroy their sheep. Mrs. Nesbaum was philosophical in trying to sum it up: "Well, it's a mystery. The thing'll never be solved."

After the Nesbaum and Burkholder sheep were killed, William Reeder found events occurring rapidly. He took plaster casts of what he felt were the killer's tracks on the 28th of April, at the Burkholders'. On the first of May, five sheep were killed at the

Richard Etter farm on Pandora Road, and two days later Herman Hilty of Lugabill Road lost some tame ducks. At the Hilty farm, Reeder found and took casts of what he was beginning to feel were cat tracks. (The Hilty casts exactly match the Burkholder ones.) Although catlike, the tracks had the by now familiar non-retractable claw marks well known in the historical annals of phantom panthers.

Bill Reeder began getting reports of other sheep kills from Phillips Road. The killer appeared to be moving south down that road towards the town of Lafayette. At about the same time actual sightings of a large cat began to occur. Bill Reeder pulled out a stack of reports for us and started reading through them.

28 April—Maria Henderson was the first person to see the cat. In her statement to the Bluffton Police, she said she was going to work by way of Bentley Road, near the County Line Road, when she saw what she thought was a dog in the road. When she got closer, she saw it was a cat. Finally, out of her car, she walked within four feet of it and definitely saw it was a cat ... a big cat, black and gray in color, and approximately one and a half feet tall. The Bluffton Police checked and found Henderson to be a "good, substantial, solid citizen".

29 April—Bob Cross, an employee at the Lima State Hospital and member of the local news media, watched a large cat, black and gray, with a long tail, for ten minutes.

1 May—Near Lafayette, at 2:30 a.m., the "glassy eyes of a cat" were spotted by a deputy with a spotlight. Reeder later found tracks like the other ones. At the Hardestys' place, this same date, casts of tracks were made by the residents.

6 May—Lou Abial of Napoleon Road went

out to his barn at about 6:45 p.m., and then, returning, found cat tracks in an area that a moment before had been undisturbed. Reeder said it appeared the cat had jumped from a hay loft. They tracked it to the end of Abial's property, but never saw it.

9 May—At 7:30 a.m., Barbara Price reported seeing a 140-pound, black and gray cat with a big head and long tail cross in front of her on Highway 81, near Swaney Road. Two off-duty deputies and Reeder searched the area for two hours. Many tracks were visible, but they failed to locate the cat. On this same day, Mr. Rutherford, 9890 Reservoir Road, found tracks on his property.

12 May—An Allen County veterinarian examined a dead German Shepherd. The dog had fang marks in its neck.

By mid-May, the sheep killer was getting a big play in the local newspapers. The thing was being held responsible for killing five peacocks, some tame ducks, a German Shepherd, and at least 140 head of sheep. William Reeder found a hot political potato had dropped into his lap. The Allen County Sheriff, Charles Harrod, called Reeder into his office and more or less told him they were taking over the investigations. The Sheriff believed the killings were being caused by a pack of dogs, and William Reeder's findings were making them feel a bit uncomfortable.

About the same time Bill Reeder was being confronted by the Sheriff's intrusion and dog-pack theories, the cat "woke up half of Lafayette" at 1:15 a.m. one morning in May. On May 17 two residents (Reeder gave the names to the Sheriff's office, and they never returned his file) of the Lafayette area reported a large dark-colored cat was drinking from their pond.

Despite the Sheriff's Department, Bill Reeder was becoming more and more convinced that what he had on his hands was a large black-and-gray feline. On May 20, Reeder held a news conference and announced his conclusions based upon the mounting body of evidence. Besides the sightings and footprints, Reeder had also found some droppings. He told us these had been found on the farm next to the Burkholder place, and he had given them to Dr. Wayne Kaufman and Dr. R. L. McMahn, veterinarians practicing in Lima, Ohio. The silver-dollar-sized stools had contained balls of hair and hookworms, characteristic of cat scat. ("What color was the hair?" we asked Reeder upon hearing about the hair balls. "I don't know. You're the first people to ask me that question," Bill Reeder responded.) After Dr. McMahn had examined the droppings and sheep kills, he candidly told Reeder: "Bill, this a panther-type animal."

William Reeder was told to not hold any more news conferences.

Then on May 27, the Mayor of Lafayette called Reeder and told him the cat was in Lafayette. Reeder and one other officer joined the Mayor and two Lafayette Police Officers, but failed to locate the animal. Bill Reeder went home and soon got another call. This time it was from the manager of a lake resort and camping area southeast of Lafayette. He said the cat was drinking from a swimming hole near the camping grounds, but asked Reeder not to go down there because it might panic the campers. Reeder "determined" that the cat was not bothering anyone, so he did not go after it.

Home again, the Allen County Dog Warden sat down to a cup of coffee and tried to settle down after the hectic events of the day. His phone rang again. It was the Lafayette Police, and they had the cat in their sights in a plowed field near Lafayette.

Bill Reeder flew out there and quickly located the stakeout. It was 2 a.m. by then and Reeder, an off-duty Sheriff's deputy, and two Lafayette Police Officers were using large flashlights and spotlights. The deputy circled around into the nearby woods. They all had a pretty good view of it in the light of their spotlamps. Reeder slowly began walking toward the cat. They all were within 35 yards of it. Then it began to calmly walk towards them, "like it was going to be a docile animal," Reeder said. It was now only about twenty yards away, and "within tranquilizer gun range." All of a sudden, it broke for the woods and ran "150 yards in two seconds flat." As it came into the woods, it was sighted by the deputy stationed there. And then it was gone.

Bill Reeder's description matched those of the other witnesses in the area. He said it was black, one and a half to two feet tall, and had "the pointed ears of a cat." Because of the animal's position in relationship to Reeder, the tail could not be seen. He strongly felt the "movement was that of a cat, not of a dog". The beam-type flashlights caught the glassy eyes, and they appeared to be gold or yellow. After the cat escaped into the woods, Reeder discovered tracks with claw marks exactly like the Hilty–Burkholder casts.

William Reeder was forbidden to give a news release on the sighting he and the officers had made, and no one in the local media knows about it. We are the first writers with whom he discussed the incidents of May 27. Reeder is a no-nonsense sort of fellow who has taken a good deal of flack because of his "big, black cat" theory, and he was initially cautious as we started examining and cross-examining the Richland Township events. Only after some basic trust was established did Bill Reeder detail his personal experience. He is not looking for publicity and appears to be happily and personally vindicated. Bill

Reeder was very much at peace with himself, finally, after some extremely trying months.

The black cat, the sheep killer, seems to have left Allen County, Ohio. During the first week of June, area newspapers carried articles telling of the sighting of a "large black cat" near the town of Ada which is ten miles due east of Lafayette, in Hardin County. Hancock County Game Protector Brad Lindsey and Hardin County Game Protector Gary Braun were out looking for the cat because of reports from Ada area residents. Braun was quoted as saying he got a good look at the animal and it was definitely a large black animal of the feline family. Braun watched the cat for twelve to twenty seconds through field glasses before it walked into the woods. No livestock has yet been killed in Hardin County.

So what are we to do? Here again, we find a large, black cat in an area where tawny pumas have been extinct for over a hundred years. It is easy to recognize the classic nature of this 1977 Ohio case: the cat's elusiveness, its clawed footprints, its savage attacks on livestock, and the overwhelming number of first-hand sightings. Allen County, Ohio, seems to have been visited by one of our old friends, the phantom panther.

1977 is shaping up as a sychronistically interesting year for the cats. 1877 saw mystery feline reports from Ohio and Indiana. During 1977, besides the Ohio events, there have been sightings in Bay Springs, Mississippi; Edwardsville, Illinois; and California, Kentucky. And as we continued our investigations into the matter of the "Dover Demon" of Dover, Massachusetts, word came of a maned lion's having attacked two dogs near Dover, Arkansas.

Dover, the wealthiest town in Massachusetts, is fifteen miles southwest of Boston. Although it is heavily wooded and its houses are spaced several hundred feet apart, it is hardly a place in which one would expect to encounter a strange creature unknown to science, but that's exactly what four teenagers claim they saw over a 25½-hour period in April 1977.

The bizarre affair began at 10:30 on the evening of April 21 as three seventeen-year-olds, Bill Bartlett, Mike Mazzocca and Andy Brodie, were driving north on Dover's Farm Street.* Bartlett, who was behind the wheel, spotted something creeping along a low wall of loose stones on the left side of the road. At first he thought it was a dog or a cat until his headlights hit the thing directly and Bartlett realized it was nothing he had ever seen before.

The figure slowly turned its head and stared into the light, its two large, round, glassy, lidless eyes shining brightly "like two orange marbles." Its watermelon-shaped head, resting at the top of a thin neck, was fully the size of the rest of the body. Except for its oversized head, the creature was thin, with long spindly arms and legs, and large hands and feet. The skin was hairless and peach-colored and appeared

* Sometime after the end of the Dover Demon flap, we happened to stumble across this passage in Frank Smith's 1914 book, *Dover Farms:*

> Farm Street extends from the Medfield line on the south to Springfield park, on the north, and is the second oldest road in town. This street as present laid out, forms only a part of the original layout, which followed Indian trails. . . . In the early time (i.e. 1600s) this road went around by the picturesque Polka rock which was called for a man by that name, of whom it is remembered, that amid the superstitions of the age he thought he saw his Satanic Majesty as he was riding on horseback by this secluded spot. The location has long been looked upon as one in which treasures are hid, but why anyone should go so far inland to hide treasures has never been told; however, there has been at times unmistakable evidence of considerable digging in the immediate vicinity of the rock. (page 7)

Furthermore, Loren Coleman was able to talk to the Acheson family who saw a barn-sized UFO in this area in June of 1969 with red lights rotating on the bottom and a white triangle underneath. One could begin to wonder if we are dealing with a "window" area.

© 1978 by Loren Coleman

Dover Demon seen by
William Bartlett, 21 April 1977

to have a rough texture ("like wet sandpaper," Bill subsequently told Loren Coleman).

The figure, which stood no more than three and a half to four feet tall, was shaped like "a baby's body with long arms and legs." It had been making its way uncertainly along the wall, its long fingers curling around the rocks, when the car lights surprised it.

Unfortunately neither of Bill's companions saw the creature. Mike was watching his own side of the road, and Andy was sitting in back talking with him. The sighting lasted only a few seconds and before Bill could speak he had passed the scene. Mike and Andy told Coleman, however, that their friend was "pretty scared" and sounded "genuinely frightened." At first they were skeptical but Bill's obvious fear forced them to change their minds.

"I really flew after I saw it," Bill said. "I took that corner at 45, which is pretty fast. I said to my friends, 'Did you see that?' And they said, 'Nah, describe it.' I did and they said, 'Go back. Go back!' And I said, 'No way. No way.' When you see something like that, you don't want to stand around and see what it's going to do.

"They finally got me to go back and Mike was leaning out of the window yelling, 'Come on, creature!' And I was saying, 'Will you cut that out?' Andy was yelling, 'I want to see you!'"

But the creature was gone. Bill dropped his friends off and went home. He was visibly upset as he walked through the door and his father asked him what was wrong. Young Bartlett related the story, then withdrew to sketch what he had seen.

In the meantime another teenager was about to see the creature. Around midnight John Baxter, fifteen, left his girlfriend Cathy Cronin's house at the south end of Millers High Road in Dover and started walking up the street on his way home. Half an hour later, after he had walked about a mile, he observed someone approaching him. Because the figure was quite short, John assumed it was an acquaintance of his, M. G. Bouchard, who lived on the street. John called out, "M. G., is that you?"

There was no response. But John and the figure continued to approach each other until finally the latter stopped. John then halted as well and asked, "Who is that?" The sky was dark and overcast and he could see only a shadowy form.

Trying to get a better look he took one step forward and the figure scurried off to the left, running down a shallow wooded gully and up the opposite bank. As it ran John could hear its footfalls on the dry leaves.

He followed the thing down the slope, then stopped and looked across the gulley. The creature —for now John could see that was what it was— stood in silhouette about thirty feet away, its feet "molded" around the top of a rock several feet from a tree. It was leaning toward the tree and had the long fingers of both hands entwined around the trunk, which was eight inches in diameter, as if for support.

The creature's body reminded John of a monkey's, except for its dark "figure-eight"-shaped head. Its eyes, two lighter spots in the middle of the head, were looking straight at John, who after a few minutes began to feel decidedly uneasy. Realizing that he had never seen or heard of such a creature before and fearing what it might do next, he backed carefully up the slope, his heart pounding, and "walked very fast" down the road to the intersection at Farm Street. There a couple passing in a car picked him up and drove him home.

The next day Bill Bartlett told his close friend Will Taintor, eighteen, of his sighting. And that night —around midnight—Taintor himself would catch a fleeting glimpse of the creature.

He was driving Abby Brabham, fifteen, home when the encounter took place. As they passed along Springdale Avenue, Abby spotted something in the headlights on the left side of the road. The "something" was a creature crouched on all fours and facing the car. Its body was thin and monkeylike but its head was large and oblong, with no nose, ears or mouth. The thing was hairless and its skin was tan or beige in color. The facial area around the eyes was lighter and the eyes glowed *green*. Abby insisted this was the case, even after investigators told her that Bill Bartlett had said the eyes were orange.

Will saw the creature only momentarily and had the impression of something with a large head and tan body, with its front legs in the air. He didn't know what it was but he did know that it was not a dog.

Frightened, Abby urged him to speed up so that they could get away. Will claims that only after they left the scene did he recall Bill's sighting. His own had been so brief and unspectacular that he probably would have thought little of it if Abby had not been with him. He asked her to describe the figure, deliberately phrasing misleading questions about aspects of the creature's appearance he knew not to be true in order to check her story against Bartlett's, which he did not mention to her. But Abby stuck to her story.

On April 28, Loren Coleman, then living in nearby Needham, was visiting the Dover Country Store when a store employee, Melody Fryer, told him about Bill Bartlett's sighting and sketch. She promised to get him a copy and two days later provided him with two drawings. The next day Coleman interviewed Bartlett. On May 3 he questioned Baxter and Brabham and on the 5th talked with Taintor.

Two weeks later Coleman pulled in Walter Webb of the Aerial Phenomena Research Organization, Joseph Nyman of the Mutual UFO Network and Ed

Fogg of the New England UFO Study Group to join the investigation. Although none of the witnesses had reported seeing a UFO in connection with the Dover Demon, the ufologists were struck by the creature's apparent resemblance to humanoid beings sometimes associated with UFOs.*

The investigators interviewed the witnesses' parents, who said they believed the stories. The Bartletts said their son is "very honest and open" and not the kind of person who enjoys playing pranks. Mrs. Baxter remarked that her son "never made up stories"—meaning, apparently, that he never made up stories which he passed off as true; his father told a reporter that his son writes science fiction. But he still didn't question John's honesty. John confirmed that he is a science fiction enthusiast but insisted that had nothing to do with his report.

Will Taintor's father and mother both accepted his story. The father believed Will and Abby had mistaken a conventional animal for the creature; the mother, on the other hand, felt they had seen something genuinely unknown.

Alice Stewart, who owned the land closest to the spot where John Baxter allegedly saw the Demon, said she had not seen or heard anything unusual that night. Her dogs, which were inside at the time of the reported encounter, had not acted up.

Dover Police Chief Carl Sheridan spoke highly of young Bartlett and described him as "a reliable witness." High school principal Richard Wakely told Coleman, "I don't think these kids got together and invented it." They were not troublemakers—just "average students." A police officer said, "At first I was going to ask one of the witnesses to give me whatever it was he was smoking, but I know all four and I know that to all of us they're very reputable people."

* See Ted Bloecher's "Close Encounters of the Third Kind," FATE, January 1978.

On April 25, four days after the first sighting, Robert Linton, science instructor at Dover-Sherborn Regional High School, overheard Bill Bartlett discussing the encounter with classmates. Later Linton asked him about it and the youth provided a full account and drew a picture of the thing. (Bartlett is an accomplished artist and a member of Boston's Copley Art Society.) Linton, who said Bill had told him that the experience "scared the hell out of him," accepted the story because of the young man's good reputation.

The researchers were especially impressed with Bartlett and with Abby Brabham, who declared adamantly, "I know I saw the creature and don't care what happens!"

Is the Dover Demon a hoax? The investigators concluded that was possible, but doubted that this was the explanation. There was nothing in the witnesses' backgrounds to suggest they might be pranksters and much to suggest that they were honest, upright individuals.

As Webb observes, "None of the four was on drugs or drinking at the time of his or her sighting so far as we were able to determine. . . . None of the principals in this affair made any attempt to go to the newspapers or police to publicize their claims. Instead, the sightings gradually leaked out. Finally, the teenagers' own parents, the high school principal, the science instructor and other adults in Dover whose comments were solicited didn't believe the Dover Demon was a fabrication, implying the youths did indeed see 'something' . . .

"As for the idea the witnesses were victims of somebody else's stunt, this seems most unlikely, chiefly due to the virtual impossibility of creating an animated, lifelike 'demon' of the sort described."

But if the Demon is real, what is it? A UFO being? Perhaps—but then nothing precisely similar has ever been reported before, according to Ted Bloecher, who has collected over 1500 UFO-occupant accounts for the Center for UFO Studies.

On the other hand, maybe the Demon is a member of a curious race known to the Cree Indians of eastern Canada as the *Mannegishi*. The *Mannegishi,* Sigurd Olson says in his book *Listening Post,* are supposed to be "little people with round heads and no noses who live with only one purpose: to play jokes on travelers. The little creatures have long spidery legs, arms with six-fingered hands, and live between rocks in the rapids ..."

Indeed, the creatures of 1977 seemed to be playing cosmic jokes on a number of people. The "Big Birds" were at it again during the year. One of these huge things with wings attacked a five-pound beagle puppy belonging to Mrs. Greg Schmitt of Rabbit Hash, Kentucky. The "large bird" snatched the dog from her farm and dropped it in a pond 600 yards away. While local wildlife officials argued over whether or not the dog was attacked by an American Bald Eagle, the dognapping appears to have been a dry run for something more sinister.

On July 25, 1977, a bizarre and dramatic event occurred unlike any in the Big Bird literature to date. At 8:10 p.m., ten-year-old Marlon Lowe was playing hide-and-seek outside his Lawndale, Illinois, home when he was picked up by a huge bird and carried over a distance of thirty feet.

On July 28, Loren Coleman's brother, Jerry Coleman of Decatur, Illinois, traveled to the Lawndale area. He talked with some of the people who were involved in the "big bird" sightings and sent us some notes on his investigations. The following passages are his observations:

> Spoke with Ruth Lowe and Marlon Lowe. Mrs. Lowe is self employed, along with her husband, Jake. They own and operate a Standard Station in Lincoln, Ill. She is a grandmother of

about 45 years of age. She, in my opinion, is a very honest woman, and stated if I didn't believe her she didn't even want to talk about it. People from all over the country have called her. The Logan County Game Warden allegedly sat at her table and called her a liar. All in all, she felt people were laughing at her for what she had seen.

Three officers of the State police went down to Kickapoo Creek, and walked around the open bank of the creek for less than fifteen minutes, and found nothing. There were no feathers or anything to be found in her yard. I also went across the street to an empty lot, and found nothing. This location was where the birds allegedly were starting up.

A Mr. Cox of Lawndale was the first to see the birds, coming out of the southwest. He saw them as they started their descent. That was all he saw.

Marlon states that as he was playing a game of hide-and-go-seek, he was running at the time the bird picked him up. The bird, along with another one, was flying at a height of eight feet from the ground. They were side by side, wingtip to wingtip. Distance of 35 feet. The weight of the boy is around sixty pounds; he is almost four feet tall, red hair. This happened at 8:10 p.m., Monday, July 25, 1977. It was comfortable, warm, with clear skies; sunset at 8:15 p.m.

Ruth Lowe describes the birds as having a white ring around a neck which was one and a half feet long. The rest of the body was all very black. The birds' bills were six inches long, and hooked at the end:

The claws on the feet were arranged with three front, one in back:

Each wing, less the body, was four feet at the very *least*. Although they did not land, the birds on the ground would have stood four and a half feet tall.

When Mrs. Lowe screamed, the boy was released and fell to the ground. At this point, she was within ten feet of the birds. All (there were six witnesses) watched the birds fly off to the northeast. One flap of the wings, and the birds went up. They leveled off at tree-top, and flew toward Kickapoo Creek, which is less than a mile from their house. When they last saw the birds, about nine blocks away, she said they still looked the size of ducks.

Lawndale is a very small town, less than 300 people. The biggest town nearby is Lincoln (17,000), about ten miles to the southwest. North and northwest of Lawndale is Kickapoo Creek—*very heavy* with underbrush and trees for miles. At the point where one might think the birds entered—less than 200 yards from the Lawndale site—Judy (Jerry's wife) and I were able to quickly encounter heavy woods.

By the way, in the front yard where Mrs. Lowe was standing when she screamed, was her Saint Bernard, about twenty feet away. The dog never barked. She said the dog barks at everything, all the time.

More big bird reports are still issuing from Illinois late in 1977. A film has been taken, and the experts have been trotted forth declaring the birds are only turkey vultures. Hmm, must be a big turkey vulture to pick up a sixty-pound boy, but we Forteans are used to such attempts to bury the incredible as quickly as possible.

For us, the circle remains broken

BIBLIOGRAPHY

CHAPTER ONE: Mystery Animals

Bloomington [Illinois] *Pantagraph,* August 11 and 12, 1970.
Champaign-Urbana [Illinois] *News-Gazette,* August 9, 1970.
Clark, Jerome and Coleman, Loren, *The Unidentified,* Warner Books, New York, New York, 1975.
Fodor, Nandor, *The Unaccountable,* Award Books, New York, New York, 1968.
Rimmer, John A., "The UFO Is Alive and Living in Fairyland," in *Merseyside UFO Bulletin,* December 1970.
Stringfield, Leonard H., "The 'Atitseld' Incident," Cincinnati, Ohio, 1973. Privately distributed document.
Swift, Mark, "The Strange Experiences of a Salem

Family," in *Gray Barker's Newsletter,* February 1976.
Webb, David with Hynek, Mimi (ed.), *1973—Year of the Humanoids: An Analysis of the Fall 1973 UFO/Humanoid Wave,* Center for UFO Studies, Evanston, Illinois, 1976.

CHAPTER TWO: The Bigfeet

Beck, Fred and R. A., *"I Fought the Apemen of Mt. St. Helens," Washington, 1967*.
Bowers, Mrs. Wallace, private communication, 1971.
Byrne, Peter, *The Search for Big Foot,* Acropolis, Washington, D. C., 1975.
Centralia-Chehalis [Washington] *Chronicle,* December 16, 1970.
Clark, Jerome, "Saucer Central U.S.A.," in *UFO Report,* April 1976.
Coon, Ken, "Sasquatch Footprint Variations," January 20, 1974. Privately distributed document.
Green, John, *Bigfoot: On the Track of the Sasquatch,* Ballantine Books, New York, New York, 1973.
Green, John, and Sanderson, Sabina W., "Alas, Poor Jacko," in *Pursuit,* January 1975.
Keel, John A., *Strange Creatures from Time and Space,* Fawcett/Gold Medal, Greenwich, Connecticut, 1970.
McClarin, Jim, private files.
Napier, John, *Bigfoot: The Yeti and Sasquatch in Myth and Reality,* E. P. Dutton, New York, New York, 1972, 1973.
Phenomena Research Report, November 1975.
Redding [California] *Record Searchlight,* January 21, 1972.
Slate, B. Ann, "Gods from Inner Space," in *UFO Report,* April 1976.

CHAPTER THREE: The Manimals

Albuquerque [New Mexico] *Journal,* October 15, 16, 17, 19, 20, 23 and 26, 1966.
Alexander, Hartley Burr, *North American Mythology* (vol. X of *Mythology of All Races*), L. H. Gray (ed.), Cooper Square Publishers, New York, New York, 1964.
Arkansas Gazette, June 27, 1971.
Bloomington [Illinois] *Pantagraph,* July 12, 17 and 25, 1970.
Brandon, Hembree, letter to Loren Coleman, August 25, 1968.
Cairo [Illinois] *Evening Citizen,* July 26, 1972.
Carbondale [Illinois] *Southern Illinoisan,* June 26 and 27, 1973.
Carmi [Illinois] *Times,* May 9, 1973.
Champaign-Urbana [Illinois] *Courier,* May 8 and 9; October 17, 1973.
Champaign-Urbana [Illinois] *News-Gazette,* August 9, 1970.
Clark, Jerome, "Indian Prophecy and the Prescott UFOs," in *Fate,* April 1971.
——"On the Track of Unidentified Furry Objects," in *Fate,* August 1973.
——"Oklahoma Monsters Come in Pairs," in *Fate,* December 1976.
Clark, Jerome and Coleman, Loren, "Anthropoids, Monsters and UFOs," in *Flying Saucer Review,* January/February 1973.
——"The Jersey Devil," in *Beyond Reality,* May 1973.
——"Swamp Slobs Invade Illinois," in *Fate,* July 1974.
——*The Unidentified,* Warner Books, New York, New York, 1975.
Coffeyville [Kansas] *Journal,* September 2, 1975.
Coleman, Sister Bernard, "The Religion of the Ojib-

wa of Northern Minnesota," in *Primitive Man* 10 (1937).

Coleman, Loren, "Mystery Animals in Illinois," in *Fate,* March 1971.

Coleman, Loren and Hall, Mark, "Some Bigfoot Traditions of the North American Indians," in *INFO Journal,* Fall/Winter 1970.

Colvin, Terry W., letter to Loren Coleman.

Cooper, John M., "The Cree Witiko Psychosis," in *Primitive Man* 6 (1933).

Crawfordsville [Indiana] *Journal and Review,* September 21, 1972.

Dallas [Texas] *Morning News,* September 6, 1975.

Days, Richard A., letter to Loren Coleman.

El Reno [Oklahoma] *Daily Tribune,* March 9, 1971.

Evansville [Indiana] *Press,* August 22, 1955, and August 15, 1970.

Eyewitness, Vol. 1, No. 7.

France, Richard G., letter to Loren Coleman.

Gordon, Stan, "UFOs, in Relation to Creature Sightings in Pennsylvania," in *MUFON 1974 UFO Symposium Proceedings,* Mutual UFO Network, Seguin, Texas, 1974.

Guinard, Joseph E., "Witiko Among the Tête-de-Boule," in *Primitive Man* 3 (1930).

Gurdon, Lady Eveline Camilla (ed.), *County Folk-Lore: Suffolk,* D. Nutt, Ipswich, England, 1893.

Hall, Rick, letters to Loren Coleman.

Harpole, Marsh, letter to Loren Coleman.

Harris, Jesse, "Strange Beast Stories," in *Hoosier Folklore* 5 (1946).

Heath, Roger, letter to Loren Coleman.

Holtz, Jay, letter to Ted Bloecher.

Idabel [Oklahoma] *McCurtain Gazette,* August 20 and September 5, 1975.

Keel, John A., *Strange Creatures from Time and Space,* Fawcett/Gold Medal, Greenwich, Connecticut, 1970.

Lawton [Oklahoma] *Morning Press,* March 2 and 3, 1971.
Levy, Jerrold E., letter to Loren Coleman.
Lincoln [Illinois] *Courier,* August 20, 1970.
Lorenzen, Coral and Jim, *Flying Saucer Occupants,* Signet, New York, New York, 1967.
Lumberton [North Carolina] *Robesonian,* September 30, 1973.
MacDougall, Curtis D., *Hoaxes,* Dover, New York, New York, 1968.
Middletown [Ohio] *Journal,* October 30, 1972.
Mietus, Kenneth J., letter to Loren Coleman.
Morgan, William, "Human-Wolves Among the Navaho," in *Yale Publications in Anthropology* XI (1936).
Noe, Allen V., "ABSMal Affairs in Pennsylvania and Elsewhere," in *Pursuit,* October 1973.
———"And Still the Reports Roll in," in *Pursuit,* January 1974.
Oklahoma City Daily Oklahoman, February 26, 1971.
Oklahoma City Oklahoma Journal, February 28, 1971.
Parsons, Elsie Clews, "Tales of the Micmac," in *Journal of American Folklore* 38 (1925).
Pekin [Illinois] *Daily Times,* July 26 and 27, 1972.
Peoria [Illinois] *Journal-Star,* July 26, 1972.
Personal interviews with witnesses, authorities, reporters and investigators in British Columbia, Illinois, Indiana and Oklahoma.
Petersburg [Indiana] *Press-Dispatch,* August 13, 1970.
Robinson [Illinois] *Daily News,* May 12 and 15, 1973.
Sanderson, Ivan T., *Abominable Snowmen: Legend Come to Life,* Chilton, New York, New York, 1961.
Schroat, Beulah, letter to *Decatur* [Illinois] *Review,* August 2, 1972.

Schwarz, Berthold Eric, "Berserk: A UFO-Creature Encounter," in *Flying Saucer Review*, Vol. 20, No. 1 (1974).

Slate, B. Ann, "Gods from Inner Space," in *UFO Report*, April 1976.

Slate, B. Ann and Berry, Alan, *Bigfoot*, Bantam, New York, New York, 1976.

Speck, Frank G., *Myths and Folklore of the Timiskaming Alongquin and Timagami Ojibwa*, Anthropological Series, Canada Department of Mines, Geological Survey, No. 9, 1915.

Steiger, Brad, *Mysteries of Time and Space*, Prentice-Hall, Englewood Cliffs, New Jersey, 1974.

Tabor City [North Carolina] *Tribune*, September 26, 1973.

Toledo [Ohio] *Blade*, August 2, 9 and 10, 1972.

Warth, Robert C., "A UFO-ABSM Link?", in *Pursuit*, April 1975.

Whetstone, Deward, letter to Thomas R. Adams.

White Hill [North Carolina] *News-Reporter*, September 27, 1973.

Worley, Don, personal interviews and investigations.

——"The UFO-Related Anthropoids," in *Proceedings of the 1976 CUFOS Conference*, Center for UFO Studies, Evanston, Illinois, 1976.

Young, Robert W., letter to Loren Coleman.

CHAPTER FOUR: Phantom Cats and Dogs

Anniston [Alabama] *Star*, May 30 and June 8, 1969.

Belleville [Illinois] *News-Democrat*, April 16, 1970.

Birmingham [Alabama] *News*, June 5, 1969.

Bord, Janet, "Some Fortean Ramblings," in *The News*, November 1974.

Boston New England Farmer, August 3, 1823.

Bowen, Charles, "Mystery Animals," in *Flying Saucer Review*, November/December 1964.

Bue, Gerald T. and Stenlund, Milton H., "Are There Mountain Lions in Minnesota?", in *The Conservation Volunteer,* September 1952.

Burton, Maurice, "Is This the Surrey Puma?", in *Animals,* December 1966.

Cairo [Illinois] *Evening Citizen,* April 20, 1966, and April 20, 1970.

Chester [Illinois] *Herald-Tribune,* April 16, 1970.

Clark, Jerome and Coleman, Loren, "On the Trail of Pumas, Panthers and ULAs," in *Fate,* June and July 1972.

——*The Unidentified,* Warner Books, New York, New York, 1975.

Coleman, Loren, "Mystery Animals in Illinois," in *Fate,* March 1971.

Decatur [Illinois] *Herald,* July 14, 16 to 20, and 30; August 1, 1917.

Decatur [Illinois] *Review,* September 15, October 27 and November 1, 1955; March 12, 1970.

Detroit News, November 23, 1972.

Fort, Charles, *The Books of Charles Fort,* Henry Holt, New York, New York, 1941.

Gordon, Stan, "UFOs, in Relation to Creature Sightings in Pennsylvania," in *MUFON 1974 UFO Symposium Proceedings,* Mutual UFO Network, Seguin, Texas, 1974.

Gurdon, Lady Eveline Camilla (ed.), *County Folk-Lore: Suffolk,* D. Nutt, Ipswich, England, 1893.

Hill, Betty, letter to Jerome Clark.

Huntington [Indiana] *Herald-Press,* June 27 to 29, 1962.

Jerseyville [Illinois] *Democrat News,* March 12, 1970.

Joliet [Illinois] *Herald-News,* April 24, 1963.

Joliet [Illinois] *Spectator,* August 20, 1964.

Korson, George, *Black Rock: Mining Folklore of the Pennsylvania Dutch,* Johns Hopkins, Baltimore, Maryland, 1960.

London Daily Express, October 14, 1925.
London Evening News, July 19, 1963, and April 27, 1972.
Marshall, Robert E., *The Onza,* Exposition Press, New York, New York, 1961.
Newton [Illinois] *Press,* February 19, 1970.
The New York Times, December 28, 1877, and June 27, 1931.
Paris [Texas] *News,* July 26, 1964.
Personal interviews with witnesses, authorities and reporters in Illinois and Minnesota.
Randolph, Vance, *We Always Lie to Strangers: Tall Tales from the Ozarks,* Columbia University Press, New York, New York, 1952.
Richmond [Indiana] *Palladium-Item,* July 28 and 30; August 3, 5, 6, 8 to 13, 15, 17, 22, 24, 29 to 31; September 1, 5 and 15, 1948; January 8, 1951.
Rickard, R. J. M., "If You Go Down to the Woods Today," in *INFO Journal,* May 1974.
——"The 'Surrey Puma' and Friends: More Mystery Animals," in *The News,* January 1976.
Robb, Dunbar, "Cougar in Missouri," in *Missouri Conservationist,* July 1955.
Rockford [Illinois] *Morning Star/Register-Republic,* May 30, June 2 and August 25, 1970.
St. Louis Post-Dispatch, July 26, 1964.
Sanderson, Ivan T., *Living Mammals of the World,* Doubleday, Garden City, New York, 1955.
Topeka [Kansas] *Daily Capital,* July 8, 1970.
Washington [D.C.] *Daily News,* February 8, 1971.
Watson, Nigel, "Notes on Lincolnshire Ghost Phenomena," in *The News,* September 1974.
Wright, Bruce S., *The Ghost of North America,* Vantage Press, New York, New York, 1959.

CHAPTER FIVE: Things with Wings

Brownsville [Texas] *Herald,* January 18, 1976.
Cantu, Lupe, letter to Jerome Clark.
Clark, Jerome, "Unidentified Flapping Objects," in *Oui,* October 1976.
Corpus Christi [Texas] *Caller,* January 16 and February 8, 1976.
Harlingen [Texas] *Valley Morning Star,* January 13, 1976.
Keel, John A., *The Mothman Prophecies,* Saturday Review/Dutton, New York, New York, 1975.
Palestine [Texas] *Herald-Press,* December 16, 19 and 22, 1976.
Personal interviews with witnesses, authorities and reporters in Texas and New Jersey.
Pretoria [South Africa] *News,* January 15, 1976.
Rickard, R. J. M., "Unidentifieds," in *Fortean Times,* June 1976.
——"Birdmen of the Apocalypse!", in *Fortean Times,* August 1976.
Rio Grande [Texas] *Herald,* January 8, 1976.
San Angelo [Texas] *Standard,* February 17, 1976.
San Antonio [Texas] *Evening News,* January 14, 15, 23 and 29; February 12, 1976.
San Antonio [Texas] *Light,* January 15, 22, 23 and 29; February 26, 1976.

CHAPTER SIX: Phantasms

Bowen, Charles (ed.), *The Humanoids,* Henry Regnery, Chicago, Illinois, 1970.
Clark, Jerome, " 'Manimals' Make Tracks in Oklahoma," in *Fate,* September 1971.
——"Are 'Manimals' Space Beings?", in *UFO Report,* Summer 1975.

———"A Message from Magonia," in *The News*, February 1975.

Clark, Jerome and Coleman, Loren, *The Unidentified*, Warner Books, New York, New York, 1975.

Fort, Charles, *The Books of Charles Fort*, Henry Holt, New York, New York, 1941.

Hynek, J. Allen, *The UFO Experience*, Henry Regnery, Chicago, Illinois, 1972.

Jung, C. G., *Flying Saucers: A Modern Myth of Things Seen in the Skies*, Harcourt, Brace and Company, New York, New York, 1959.

Keel, John A., *Strange Creatures from Time and Space*, Fawcett/Gold Medal, Greenwich, Connecticut, 1970.

———*UFOs: Operation Trojan Horse*, G. P. Putnam's, New York, New York, 1970.

Padrick, Sid, "The Padrick 'Space Contact,'" in *Little Listening Post*, Fall 1965.

Personal interviews with witnesses and authorities in Minnesota, Montana, Nebraska and Oklahoma.

"Psychic Records," in *Occult Review*, October 1905.

Sagan, Carl, *The Cosmic Connection*, Doubleday Anchor, Garden City, New York, 1973.

Thompson, William Irwin, *At the Edge of History*, Harper and Row, New York, New York, 1971.

CPSIA information can be obtained
at www.ICGtesting.com
Printed in the USA
BVHW032147230623
666335BV00004B/8